ACHIEVING SCHOOLING FOR ALL IN AFRICA

T0347645

Achieving Schooling for All in Africa

Costs, Commitment and Gender

CHRISTOPHER COLCLOUGH
SAMER AL-SAMARRAI
PAULINE ROSE
MERCY TEMBON

LONDON AND NEW YORK

First published 2003 by Ashgate Publishing

Reissued 2018 by Routledge
2 Park Square, Milton Park, Abingdon, Oxon, OX14 4RN
711 Third Avenue, New York, NY 10017, USA

Routledge is an imprint of the Taylor & Francis Group, an informa business

Publisher's Note
The publisher has gone to great lengths to ensure the quality of this reprint but points out that some imperfections in the original copies may be apparent.

Disclaimer
The publisher has made every effort to trace copyright holders and welcomes correspondence from those they have been unable to contact.

A Library of Congress record exists under LC control number: 2003056080

ISBN 13: 978-1-138-70942-3 (hbk)
ISBN 13: 978-1-138-70928-7 (pbk)
ISBN 13: 978-1-315-19830-9 (ebk)

Contents

List of Figures and Boxes

Figures

Technical Appendix

Boxes

List of Tables

Preface

Two of the eight Millennium Development Goals adopted by the international community of nations as principal means of tackling poverty by the year 2015, are concerned to achieve universal participation, with gender equality, in primary schooling. This book asks why these objectives remain persistently elusive, and it identifies the constraints which will need to be addressed if they are to be achieved. Educational policies will clearly need to change. But the book demonstrates that powerful sets of economic constraints, and of gender relations in society, have crucial independent roles in affecting children's educational opportunities and performance. It shows that progress towards the goals will require structural changes which extend well beyond the influence of Ministries of Education.

The book has been several years in preparation. It has grown out of an extensive programme of work on gender and primary schooling in Africa, directed by Christopher Colclough, which has combined primary research and policy analysis in nine countries over the period 1995-2000. Chapters Four to Six of this volume draw upon data from these national studies, to provide comparative analysis across the region and to synthesise the most important lessons from the research. These results are set in the context of a more macro approach which utilises both cross-country statistical comparisons and a broader theoretical and empirical analysis of the determinants of school participation.

The research for this book was made possible by a grant from the Rockefeller Foundation, and we wish to acknowledge its generous support. The country studies in Africa were conducted in collaboration with national governments, under the auspices of the Forum for African Women Educationalists (FAWE). They were financed by a donor partnership comprising the Rockefeller Foundation, the Governments of Norway (NORAD) and Ireland (HEDCO), the Association for the Development of Education in Africa (ADEA), the World Bank Institute, and FAWE itself.

In addition to these institutions many individuals have provided particular support. First and foremost we wish to acknowledge the excellent work conducted by the national research teams and the warm professional relationships to which our collaborations have led. The national team members for each country were as follows: Ethiopia – Getachew Yoseph (Principal), Asmaru Berihun, and Tegegn Nuresu; Ghana – Ruby Avotri (Principal), Lucy Owusu-Darko, Hilda Eghan, and Sylvia Ocansey; Guinea – Ibrahima Sory Diallo (Principal), Djenabou Barry,and Alpha Aliou Barry; Mali – Solomani Sangaré (Principal), Alhamdou Tounkara, Diassé Tangara, and N'diaye Assétou Kéïta; Malawi – Esme Kadzamira (Principal), Mike Chibwana; Sénégal – Maréma Dioum Diokhané (Principal), Oumel Khairy Diallo, Alhousseynou Sy and Mafakha Touré; Tanzania – Stella Bendera (Principal), Namsifuel Abrahams, and Maria Kisanga; Uganda – Joseph Tumushabe (Principal), Catherine Barasa, Florence Muhanguzi, and Joyce Otim-

Nape; Zambia – Sophie Kasonde-Ng'andu (Principal), Winnie Namiloli Chilala, and Njekwa Imutowana-Katukula. Pauline Rose, Mercy Tembon and Tessa Peasgood joined the national teams for the first three country studies – in Ethiopia, Guinea and Tanzania – as co-Principals. The remaining six country studies were conducted as a second phase.

Our formal collaboration with national team members ended after completion of the national reports. However, each of the Principal research officers from Ghana, Mali, Malawi, Senegal, Uganda and Zambia provided short additional analyses as material for the boxes which appear in Chapters Four to Six of the book.

Our particular thanks are due to Joyce Moock of the Rockefeller Foundation, for her vision and enthusiastic promotion of the programme since its inception in 1994, and to Paud Murphy of the World Bank, whose commitment to the aims and objectives of the programme was also a source of great strength over a number of years. Our particular thanks are also extended to Katherine Namuddu, of the Rockefeller Foundation, and to Eddah Gachukia and Penina Mlama, successive Executive Directors of FAWE in Nairobi, who provided inspiring leadership in many of the international meetings where the national studies were discussed.

Many friends and colleagues have provided comments and advice at different stages. Henry Lucas and Paul Bennell made helpful contributions to questionnaire and fieldwork design. Kei Kawabata, Frans Lenglet and Trish Tierney from the World Bank, each provided welcome advice and support during preparation of the national studies and in the design of the training programme for national researchers from the six second-phase countries. At a later stage, Naila Kabeer, Adrian Wood, and Howard White provided helpful comments on parts of the book. Many others participated in discussions of our results at seminars in Sussex and elsewhere. Throughout the programme Judi Minost, from IDS, provided the critical administrative support which was necessary for its success. The authors wish to thank all these persons for giving their time and energy so generously.

Chapter 1

Poverty, Schooling and Gender: Some Theoretical Issues

Introduction

Throughout the first decade of the new century, the majority of the world's out-of-school children of primary age will be living in Sub-Saharan Africa (SSA). Although it accounts for only about 10 per cent of the population of developing countries, by 2005, well over one-half of all children not enrolled in school will be from within the region. They will comprise about one-third of Africans of primary-school age, amounting to around 60 million children. Most of them will be girls.

These facts present a major challenge to the prospects for international development. Aid agencies and many national governments in developing countries now emphasise poverty alleviation as the overriding objective of development policy. A set of eight 'Millennium Development Goals' have been promulgated by the international community, the achievement of which would, it is believed, sharply reduce the incidence of poverty by 2015. The objectives of achieving primary schooling for all, with gender equity, comprise two of these goals.

This book investigates how these goals could be met in the region where the risk of failure is greatest. It adopts an empirical approach to identifying the causes of under-enrolment and of gender inequality in schooling in SSA. Using the methods of economics, the main constraints are identified, and conclusions are drawn for their relative importance. Although the challenges and risks are very considerable, the book indicates the educational and economic reforms needed to support the achievement of schooling for all.

Structure of the Book

Over the period 1995-2000 a programme of research and policy analysis on the above questions was conducted by the Institute of Development Studies at the University of Sussex, in collaboration with the Forum for African Women Educationalists. Nine country studies were designed to establish whether the poorest countries of Africa could achieve primary schooling for all children, with gender equity, within a reasonable time-frame and, if so, how this might best be done.[1]

In each of these studies, and throughout this book, a distinction is drawn between the achievement of universal primary education (UPE) and of schooling for all (SFA). The former is defined as the achievement of a gross enrolment ratio (GER) of 100, i.e. the point at which the number of children enrolled in primary schooling is equal to the number of eligible school-age children. It will be clear from the definition that UPE is consistent with some eligible children remaining out of school, to the extent that some primary school pupils are older or younger than the official age group. SFA, we define as the circumstance of having a school system in which all eligible children are enrolled in schools of at least minimally acceptable quality. This would be equivalent to achieving a net (age-adjusted) ratio of 100, in the context of school conditions which are generally better than those which presently exist in SSA. Thus, SFA is a more demanding target than UPE in both quantitative and qualitative dimensions.[2]

Each study used both quantitative and qualitative methods of analysis.[3] The research teams conducted surveys, and less formal group discussions, amongst schools personnel, pupils and parents, as well as those who had dropped out of school or who had never enrolled. These methods, supplemented by reviews and syntheses of earlier national work, were designed to identify the main factors affecting the education of girls and boys in the nine countries. The studies demonstrate that there is a set of constraints which typically conspire to keep girls out of school. Higher levels of opportunity costs, and lower perceived returns to the schooling of girls than of boys, are frequently found. But the importance of these and other explanatory factors differs between countries, as do the sets of policies which appear to be most appropriate to tackle them.

The research teams also collected and analysed a large amount of contextual information on enrolment trends, educational indicators, costs and public expenditures. These analyses show that the choice of selective, or targeted, reforms in favour of girls needs to be set in the context of a broader diagnosis of problems affecting the whole of the education sector. In all the nine countries, public finances are tight, and economic pressures have resulted in substantial variations in real per capita expenditures on education over the last twenty years.

---

[1] The countries, and references for the published reports, are as follows: Rose, P., Yoseph, G., Berihun, A. and Nuresu, T., (1997) (Ethiopia), Avotri, R, Owusu-Darko, L., Eghan, H. and Ocansey, S., (2000) (Ghana), Tembon, M., Diallo, I.S., Barry, D. and Barry, A.A., (1997) (Guinea), Kadzamira, E. and Chibwana, M.P., (2000) (Malawi), Sangaré, S., Tounkara, A., Tangara, D. and Assétou Kéïta, N., (2000) (Mali), Dioum Diokhané, M., Khairy Diallo, O., Sy, A. and Touré, M., (2000) (Senegal), Peasgood, T., Bendera, S., Abrahams, N. and Kisanga, M., (1997) (Tanzania), Tumushabe, J., Barasa, C.A., Muhanguzi, F.K. and Otim-Nape, J.F., (2000) (Uganda) and Kasonde-Ng'andu, S. Namiloli Chilala, W. and Imutowana-Katukula, N., (2000) (Zambia).

[2] More discussion of these differences, and of the ways in which they are operationalised, can be found in Colclough with Lewin (1993).

[3] Methods used are summarised in the Technical Appendix.

Approaches to the expansion of schooling which pay no heed to the need to reduce costs, or to improve quality, are unlikely to succeed either for girls or boys. Each of the national studies quantifies the potential for reducing unit costs and for raising additional resources for primary schooling via budgetary, fiscal and educational reforms. Models of the education system, designed separately for each country so as to reflect their own education and financing structures, are used to demonstrate the different ways in which SFA can be achieved and afforded over a ten-to-fifteen-year planning horizon. The simulated sets of reforms differ from country to country, but the reports show how the resource gaps can, in each case, be closed, and that schooling for all, with gender equity, can be achieved.

The middle section of this book provides a synthesis of the knowledge gained, and the lessons learned from these national studies, whilst the other parts provide a more 'macro' analysis of the problem. The book is primarily an empirical study. However, by way of background, the present chapter discusses some of the main theoretical debates on gender, education and development, and sets out a simple framework which is used in some of the subsequent analysis. Chapter 2 gives an overview of the evolution of primary enrolments, and of gender inequalities in African school systems, and investigates some of the more important potential causes of these outcomes. Chapter 3 examines whether cross-country econometric analysis can provide explanations or insights as to the causes of under-enrolment and of gender inequalities in school enrolments. Chapters 4 to 6, which compare the results of the country studies, deal successively with costs and resources, constraints, and policies. Chapter 7 considers the role of aid, and Chapter 8 concludes.

Broad Theoretical Approaches

Women in Development

Attempts to explain – and thus to theorise about – persistent inequalities in the access of girls and boys to schooling, and in their performance once enrolled, are, of course, informed by (and comprise a subset of) more general analyses of gender relations in society. It will therefore be helpful to begin by briefly considering the main themes and controversies that have influenced the development of this literature over recent decades.

Its roots are found in the 1960s – a period of healthy economic growth, and a time when optimism about development prospects was strong. The end of colonialism ushered in a new age, holding out the possibility of widespread prosperity, under the guidance of development planning, which was widely practised. Nevertheless there was a growing sense that the fruits of development were being unequally distributed, not only between rich and poor, but also between men and women. Early contributions to what became known as the 'women in development' (WID) literature, pointed out the ways in which women were benefiting insufficiently from the development process. Economic growth appeared to be associated with the expansion of urban centres, where men predominated. Particularly in Africa and South Asia, urban growth was driven by rural-urban migration. Males comprised the majority of such migrants, whilst their families typically remained in their home villages. Thus, urban work – and, in societies where female seclusion was practised, much urban outdoor life itself was dominated by men. Accordingly, the opportunities for higher income and for greater choices in both work and leisure, which were facilitated by economic development, appeared to be more directly advantageous to men than to women.

In diagnosing why this was the case, early writers found fault not so much with the process of growth itself, as with its agents – employers and governments – who provided women with insufficient access to the market and its rewards. A paragraph from Ester Boserup (1970), a writer who is generally attributed as being the first and most influential in this tradition, captures the essence of this argument:

> Economic and social development unavoidably entails the disintegration of the division of labour among the two sexes traditionally established in the village. With modernization of agriculture and with migration to the towns, a new sex pattern of productive work must emerge, for better or worse. The obvious danger is, however, that in the course of this transition women will be deprived of their productive functions, and the whole process of growth will thereby be retarded. Whether this danger is more or less grave, depends upon the widely varying customs and other preconditions in different parts of the under-developed world. My object was to identify these patterns and to explain their significance from the point of view of development policies. (op.cit., p.5)

Boserup and others were concerned to emphasise both the crucial role played by women in the rural economy – much of it being neither properly noticed nor valued – and the costs to growth if, on being displaced by industrialisation, they were not re-absorbed into the wage economy. The relative lack of education for women was a frequent theme, and remedies advocated by these writers often included better access to higher levels of education as a central means of reducing their marginalisation and of improving their productivity. The orthodox sex-roles assigned to women in traditional cultures, as well as those assumed in the west, also began to be challenged. Nevertheless, their arguments were delivered rather as though women were missing out on the fruits of development by mistake – an error that was capable of correction, once it had been pointed out to those who had been previously unaware of its implications.

A belief in the equality of men and women is an ancient principle. However, the WID critics of development outcomes based their argument not so much upon some prior principle of equality, as upon the observation that men and women had similar capacities for intellectual development, and were thus equally entitled to participate in, and benefit from, the development process.[4] This amounted to an

---

[4]   It is worth recalling that some of the earliest philosophers had recognised that there was no difference in kind between the native capacities of boys and girls. This had led Plato to argue that both should receive the same kind of instruction and be eligible for the same offices: 'The same education which makes a man a good guardian will

'efficiency' argument for the equal treatment of men and women, derived from their equal productive capacities, and it lay at the heart of the WID case. If women were not being integrated into the development process, potential output was lost, and there was a clear economic case to direct resources towards them. Imperfections in the social and economic system were seen as the main culprits for women's exclusion. They needed to be overcome, in the interests of the general good.[5]

Although the power of these arguments was acknowledged, it took some considerable time for them to become integrated into mainstream academic analysis, and into the policy work of the agency world. Content analysis of academic writings reveals a very delayed recognition of the importance of gender equity issues in attributing development 'success'. This is particularly true of the economics literature, which has been easily the most powerful in influencing development policy priorities. For example, probably the most widely read text in development economics (Meier, 1964), now in its seventh edition, gave no space to topics in gender and development throughout the first 30 years of its successive revisions. This was so, notwithstanding the editor's aim to represent the 'most insightful readings from the diffuse field of development'. It was not, in fact, until the sixth edition, published in 1995, that gender and development was acknowledged as a topic of importance. In that, and the subsequent edition, its treatment covered about twenty pages – a similar allocation as that given to education, and to topics in population, health and nutrition.

As regards policy analysis, a lag was also evident. For example, the influential 'employment' reports published during the 1970s by the International Labour Organisation (ILO), one of the more progressive of the UN agencies, remained unaccountably silent about gender issues in the labour market. The Kenya Mission report (ILO, 1973) comprised almost 600 pages of analysis focussing on the employment 'problem' and its potential remedies (amongst which the redistribution of incomes and assets towards the poor was the major theme), yet, scarcely 5 pages were devoted to the particular problems of women. Four years later, the first national report on 'basic needs' in Africa – for Zambia (ILO, 1977) – allocated two pages (from 350) to the problems faced by Zambian women.

In each of these cases, what was said, notwithstanding its brevity, was clearly informed by WID thinking. But the way it was treated by the authors seemed to imply that, compared with the technical complexity of other types of policy change in favour of the disadvantaged (which were given central and extensive coverage in these reports), gender inequalities, though serious, could be tackled with less difficulty. Since there was no disagreement that women were receiving a raw deal, it was as though to point it out would be sufficient to secure its mitigation.

Thus, the emphasis given to the productive equivalence of the sexes, and the lack of attention given to their differences, became a limitation of WID writing.

---

make a woman a good guardian; for their original nature is the same' (*Republic*, quoted by Russell, 1961, p.128).

[5]   See Boserup (1975) and Nelson (ed.) (1981), in particular the papers by Caplan, Dey, Gordon and Nelson.

Boserup had emphasised the ways in which the preferences of both men and women led to male advantage in the labour market (Boserup, 1970, pp.113-117). It did not lead her to the conclusion that the interests of males and females were, in some important ways, in conflict. Yet, the set of expectations which leads to women having major *de facto* responsibility for reproductive work has implications for the ways in which the similar capacities of men and women are utilised in economic settings. It became increasingly clear that to remain silent about such matters did little to help clarify some of the more fundamental constraints faced by working women.

Gender and Development

A major omission of many of these early writers was the need to understand the position of women in society in relation to that of men. Treating women as the objects of analysis – as poor, disadvantaged, uneducated, unemployed, overworked, etc. – was likely, ultimately, to be misleading. Their plight was heavily determined by the economic and social relationships in which women were placed. Attempting to respond to the material needs of women, in the absence of understanding their context, would be unlikely to succeed. The gender roles allocated to women by society are deeply constraining. Many feminists began to argue that they could not be understood without examining and analysing the nature, basis and reproduction of male power.

A potentially useful framework for these purposes was at hand. Accounting for oppression in society is a strong preoccupation of Marxist analysis. However, for Marx, the main determinant of the incidence of oppression was class. Labour was not subdivided, for analytic purposes, by gender. The site of exploitation was only the work place, and did not include the home. Traditional Marxism is, therefore, largely silent about women.

Nevertheless the analytic tools of Marxist thought, and, in particular, theories about causes and mechanisms of oppression invited obvious extension. Dependency theory, which applied Marxist analysis to the specific conditions of developing countries, had identified class-based mechanisms, working at the international level, which ensured the continuation of poverty and underdevelopment in 'peripheral' states. Feminist scholars working within this tradition argued that the subordination of women was helpful to capitalism – female unpaid labour provided a subsidy to capitalist production, and ensured the reproduction of the labouring class (Saffiotti, 1977). They saw sexual inequality as both a function of, and highly functional to, this process. However, many socialist feminists retained the classical Marxist view that the exploitation of women (as a category within general labour) stemmed from the power of capital rather than, as many later critics insisted, the power of men.

Increasingly, the centrality of relations between women and men became acknowledged in accounting for their unequal roles in development. Some writers (Eisenstein, 1981) posited one system of capitalist patriarchy. Others considered that capitalism and patriarchy operated as dual systems, with different roots in the economy and the unconscious (Mitchell, 1975), or in the exploitation of women's labour (Hartmann, 1979). For other writers (Walby, 1989) these systems are analytically separate, but in conflict, as a result of the demands on women, made by the work place and the home, being competitive from the perspective of men.

Writers have also differed in the importance they assign to the particular sources, or bases, of patriarchy. Such bases include the domestic mode of production, reproduction, the notion of heterosexuality being 'compulsory', and male violence towards women. Some, such as the 'subordination of women' (SOW) group, based in Sussex, pointed to marriage, and the social relations between men and women which flow from it, as the source of men's privileged command over women's labour, as well as exclusive right to their sexuality (Young, 1979). These latter writers focussed their analyses on gender issues in developing countries and, for our purposes, they merit some closer consideration.

They observed that when women enter wage employment, the gender hierarchy of the household remained unbroken, with women obtaining less secure jobs, at lower pay, and with fewer opportunities for advancement than men. 'Thus, their incorporation into waged work is not at all incompatible with the maintenance of forms of the family and of marriage which perpetuate men's domination' (Young, 1979, p.4).

There were three defining tenets of the SOW approach: first, a refusal to accept a focus only on women, as the WID literature had tended to do. Both men and women were included, and the relationship between them was viewed to be central. Second, the relations between the sexes were socially constituted as Oakley (1972) had pointed out – and not derived from, still less determined by, biology. In order to distinguish them from sexual characteristics and differences, which was the province of biology, the term 'gender relations' was used for all matters within the purview of social science. It followed that gender relations, being social constructs, were historically and locationally contingent.

Arguably, the third tenet was the most radical. This was that relations between the genders are not necessarily non-conflictual. 'The belief that what men and women do within their own spheres and domains fits together in a fundamentally co-operative fashion, led to the policy position that the benefits of development can be expected to accrue equitably to both genders, even when programmes are directed specifically to males' (Whitehead, 1979, p.10). Thus, the non-conflictual model of gender relations implicit in the earlier WID literature (and indeed which underlay most development policy prognoses) was rejected in favour of a model which assumed that socially constructed gender relations may be characterised by opposition and conflict.

A shift in focus from 'women' as the key category for analysis towards 'gender' derived from the need to analyse the ways in which inequality between the sexes led systematically to the exclusion, or subordination of women, in the process of development (Young *et al.*, 1981). It was necessary to analyse gender relations in the household, which were seen as being the main source of subsequent inequality. Although men and women are different in physical and biological terms, it is the *socially* differentiated aspects of gender which lead to differences in the ways in which men and women are constrained during the course of their lives.[6]

In this, and much of the subsequent 'gender and development' (GAD) literature, a more eclectic explanation for gender asymmetries is offered than by the more rigid Marxist approach. Rather than being an automatic correlate of capitalism, or of male force or strength, gender inequality is seen as an outcome of a deep-seated set of tendencies which presuppose the range of different activities and outcomes which are 'natural' for men and women, respectively. For example, as Connell (1987) argues, the gendered division of labour derives from long-standing past practice, which ultimately atrophies as a set of informal rules which are continually reinforced in the present. 'In most cultures, women look after children because they have "always" done so. What may have started out as a way of organizing labour takes on a normative significance so that values become embodied in the tasks and in who does them. The recruitment of women and men into different tasks, activities and occupations consequently ends up as a rational response to socially constructed, but nonetheless real, differentials in their skills and aptitudes.' (Kabeer, 1994, p.59).

This is a somewhat looser sense of patriarchy than one which 'defines men as superior and maintains this de facto through a set of institutions, values, laws and norms, including control of women's sexuality'. Nevertheless, the structures within which gender relations are set still imply, for some writers, that the possibilities for achieving fundamental gender reforms are very limited. In this connection, Kabeer (1994, pp.36-7) comments as follows: '... unlike any other form of advocacy aimed at changing institutional norms and practice, advocacy for gender equity impinges directly on the personal beliefs and values, relationships and identities of those who will have to formulate and implement change'. The fact that most men live with women gives them, she argues, confidence that they completely understand women's natures and roles, and a deeply personal stake in anything which threatens their own gender identities, ideas and practices. This suggests that reform is a 'zero-sum' game: since most of the world's elite decision-makers are male, it is to be expected that reforms that affect women's roles positively will prove especially difficult to introduce.

Such arguments may seem to lead to a bleak prognosis of the possibilities for change. On the other hand, advocates of other important strategies for development – such as basic needs, human development, and poverty targeting, for example – espouse approaches which necessarily involve some degree of redistribution of incomes, or in the capacity to earn them, from richer to poorer people. Just as with the advocacy of gender equity, those charged with having to formulate and implement such changes will find their own interests being affected, directly or indirectly, by these policies. It may be true that the types of interest affected are different, but they may be no less powerful for that.

---

[6] The above critique became influential in shifting the household economics literature which, at that time was in its infancy, away from models of 'unitary' households towards the use of more realistic models which took account of the fact that the interests and preferences of household members are different. See below.

Gender Policy Goals

In recent years the goals of development agencies have moved more explicitly towards espousing the elimination of poverty as their major objective. Of course, this has underpinned their stated strategies for many years (at least since the early 1970s – with 'Aid for the Poorest' being a typical unifying slogan). Nevertheless, securing economic growth by the wise use of investment resources provided by the north, was the necessary first objective – with, it was expected, poverty being better addressed, both directly and indirectly, as a result.

Although equity and social justice – including the attainment of gender equity – are now more centrally held objectives than before, programmes which are designed simultaneously to attain both equity and growth targets have an advantage in the competition for funds, in comparison with programmes where only one of these objectives are expected to be secured. Accordingly, agencies have made a particular virtue of research results indicating that the attainment of gender equity also helps achieve other development objectives, because the case for its promotion, using aid resources, is thereby strengthened.

A good example of such a coincidence of goals is provided by the linkages between female schooling, fertility control and child nutrition which are widely documented in the WID literature. More educated women have fewer children than those who are less educated (United Nations, 1987; World Bank, 1993) and, controlling for wealth and the availability of health services, they have longer-living and healthier children (Hobcraft, 1993) who, themselves, are likely to be better educated. These linkages have led many to believe that the education of girls provides a 'silver bullet', capable of hitting a number of important development targets at the same time. It is not surprising, then, to find such associations being reported, so as to provide a ready justification for an emphasis upon girls' schooling, in the aid policy documentation of many northern development agencies.[7]

The strength and importance of these relationships are seldom denied, and they have greatly helped the advocacy of interventions in favour of girls' education in developing countries.[8] However, objections have been made on two sets of grounds. First, some analysts doubt the automaticity of the development payoff, claiming that higher levels of schooling for women are not necessarily associated with increased autonomy, and that changes in fertility behaviour may stem from causes other than education itself (Jeffery and Jeffery, 1998). Second, the instrumentalism of using such associations to strengthen the case is seen by some writers as being profoundly wrong. Seeking to improve women's position as a means to other (more important) ends misses the point that achieving equity via

---

[7]   See, for example, World Bank (1995a, pp.28-31), and UNICEF (1999, pp.51-57).

[8]   Perhaps most notably in the case of Lawrence Summers (1994), then Chief Economist at the World Bank, who declared that providing money to help the schooling of girls was the single most important of all development priorities. These arguments were also used successfully by FAWE, during the 1990s, to gain substantial donor support to assist with girls' schooling initiatives in SSA.

empowerment of women is the major aim. Advocacy by means of association with less 'political' objectives, is seen by some as likely, ultimately, to undermine the strength of the case:

> Tenuous evidence on the relationships between female education and fertility decline, or female education and productivity, can easily be challenged, weakening the justification for addressing gender issues, with a danger that resources will be withdrawn. (Baden and Goetz, 1998, p.10)

Thus, reliance on a WID approach to education policy is insufficient and could be misleading, such that the 'silver bullet' may be misfired. It is not intended to suggest that a focus on female education is incorrect. Rather, an improved understanding of relations in the context of education is required to ensure that female education continues to receive attention, regardless of fads in interpretations of economic returns to education. As Stromquist (1998) notes, attempts to analyse the constraints on schooling by gender in the absence of some theoretical understanding of how women's inferior condition in society emerges, and is maintained, are unreliable. They typically recommend actions which presuppose few, if any, societal constraints to their achievement. While such measures, if implemented, may be helpful, they would not address the fundamental causes of women's inferior status in society and would, therefore, be incomplete. To be effective, the analysis of such constraints and the formulation of interventions needs to be grounded in an understanding of the economic, political and social conditions which shape gender relations in education and society. In this spirit, our own work attempts to use a more complete approach to address the complexities of gender relations in education at the national level.

A related concern about the way development objectives are pursued is that the theory underlying most anti-poverty policy tends to be gender-blind. The concept of poverty cannot serve as a proxy for the subordination of women, nor can anti-poverty policies be expected necessarily to improve their position. Whilst it may be the case that a majority of the poor are female, simply attempting to help them by increasing household incomes, is – as we know from the economic theory of the household (see below) – not guaranteed to succeed. This is because there may exist distributive mechanisms which consistently prevent their becoming better off, which, if ignored, are unlikely to disappear. The point is not merely that a majority of the poor are women, but that poverty is a gendered experience. Anti-poverty policy thus needs to be based upon an understanding of the ways in which women are marginalised, if it is to help them out of poverty. Jackson (1998) points out that patterns of ownership are not gender-neutral. Women in South Asia may own gold, but they seldom own land, bicycles or radios. A woman married to a man who owns the latter commodities may be better off, but this is not necessarily the case. Accordingly, increasing household assets may not be as beneficial for women as for men.

This is also true of income. Movements in household income tell us little about individual access to it. Typically women earn less than men; they have different entitlements to income transfers within and across households, and different expenditure obligations to those of men. Patterns of expenditure also differ. For example, women appear to devote a greater proportion of their expenditures to children and household needs than men. It is also reported that levels of household inequality (measured, for example, by calorific adequacy) rise with household income (Haddad and Kanbur, 1990). If this is true, placing all emphasis upon increasing household incomes may be compatible with making the plight of women worse, rather than better, in the short term.

Jackson (1998) argues that there is a considerable body of evidence that gender relations are more equitable in poor than in richer Indian households. This is because poor Indian women engage in labour markets more than the wealthier women, they contribute more to household income, have greater say in its disposition, and have less physical restrictions on mobility than women from non-poor households. Thus, gender equity seems to be inversely related to household income in India (see also Agarwal, 1986). This does not imply that women are better-off poor – rather that there is sometimes a trade-off for women between material well-being and autonomy, which is not true for men. Their well-being, thus, may not be improved by poverty-reduction policies: much depends upon transactions and transfers within the household.

Where the poor include many female-headed households, improving their incomes should be a fairly unambiguous way of both reducing poverty and empowering women at the same time. In these cases the whole problem of intra-household allocation becomes a generational rather than a gender issue. Poverty alleviation strategies, if successful, will help the cause of women significantly under these circumstances. Nevertheless, the gender question in households which are not female-headed will not necessarily be alleviated by poverty reduction. One cannot elide gender and poverty into the same box. If we do, the former is likely to remain substantially unaddressed.

Theories of Gender and Education

Theoretical explanations for gender inequality in educational access and outcomes include both monodisciplinary and inter-disciplinary approaches. Their implications for policy vary widely, although not always predictably, with their disciplinary perspectives. A brief account of the main issues and arguments follows.

Economic Explanations

In the orthodox economics literature, human capital theory provides the dominant explanation for the economic value of education, and thus for its derived demand.[9] The basic tenet is that education (and other means of skill formation) is economically productive. Its possession brings increased individual productivity,

---

[9]   Of the many expositions and critiques of this theory, one of the best remains Blaug (1976).

which is rewarded by higher individual earnings. Thus, people will undertake education to the extent that the perceived costs they face in its purchase are more than justified by the benefits they expect to receive. In meritocratic systems, however, not everyone is able to succeed in rising to the higher levels of the education system. Differences in educational outcomes between different people are thus a function of the distribution of abilities in the population and of the perceptions of the net benefits that will accrue. According to this model, then, systematic educational inequalities between different groups in the population are likely to stem from differences in one or more of the following: abilities, market rewards, private costs, perceived rewards or costs, and preferences. No supply constraints are envisaged, and necessary household costs will be met either from income, capital or credit.

Although ability differences between small, non-randomly selected groups of men and women may help to explain differences in their average levels of educational attainment, this is not plausible when the groups concerned are male and female national populations. The key question, for our purposes, is how to account for overall differences in educational attainment between men and women of similar intellectual ability. One possibility, as suggested by the second item in the above list, is that the market rewards for similarly qualified groups of men and women differ systematically, and that, thus, the actual and perceived benefits accruing from education for the two groups are not the same. If this is so, how can such biases be explained in economic terms?

That the average wages of similarly qualified women and men do indeed differ, in men's favour, is widely documented for both industrialised and developing countries. Surprisingly, however, the estimated private rates of return to education for men and women appear to be broadly similar for a sizeable group of countries having the necessary data (Schultz, 1995b). The explanation for this apparent contradiction, is that such returns are calculated with respect to education at the next lowest level, for each sex separately. Although the wage increment for each level of schooling is lower for females than males, their estimated opportunity costs (conventionally measured by market wages foregone whilst in school) are also lower, by roughly the same proportionate amount. Under these circumstances, then, the implied private rates of return for the two groups (and thus the economic incentives to undertake schooling) would be closely similar, even where their absolute earnings differed significantly.

Nevertheless, these kinds of calculation, which are intended to provide an explanation for the pattern of private investment decisions in education, can be seriously misleading. Since girls' role in housework is typically greater, parents lose more 'free' labour by sending them to school than is the case with boys. Under such circumstances, social customs governing child labour would result in the opportunity costs of girls' education being systematically higher than boys', even if market wages foregone – as usually calculated – appeared to be equal. Here, then, 'wages foregone' become an inadequate proxy for relative opportunity costs. Moreover, social customs concerning sibling obligations may imply that parents would ultimately benefit materially more from the education of boys than of girls, even were their earnings, in adulthood, to be the same at each level of schooling attained. Both of these factors are capable of resolving the above paradox. They indicate how, judged from the perspective of parents, (the decision-makers in these matters) the perceived costs of schooling may be higher, and the perceived benefits from it may be lower, for girls than for boys, even where 'measured' rates of return appeared to be equal.

It remains the case, of course that where earnings in the labour market for similarly qualified men and women are unequal, the occurrence of sharp schooling imbalances between boys and girls becomes more likely. Why do such differences in market rewards occur? One possible explanation is that they result from market imperfections, the most notable of which is the possibility of discrimination. A relatively large orthodox literature on this topic has developed, initiated, and still closely informed, by the work of Becker (1957). It is based upon the notion that some employers have an aversion to being in close contact with the objects of discrimination, and that they are prepared to pay a premium (or sacrifice profits) in order to avoid such contact in the work place. Similarly, discriminatory employees are prepared to accept lower wages to avoid working with the disliked group, or, alternatively, to demand higher wages where work forces are mixed than where they are segregated in their favour. Becker posits a discrimination coefficient, defined by the relationship between the male/female (white/black) wage differential and the female (black) wage. In a competitive market, however, where a range of values for this coefficient exists, including some zeros, it can be only a matter of time before discrimination disappears, since competition will remove it in the long run. Furthermore, where employers are wage takers, the market's average discrimination will determine the wage differential that can be paid. If the employer's taste for discrimination is different from that of the market as a whole, labour segregation will be the result, with the choice of exclusively male or female employment being a function of whether the employer's coefficient is less (female) or more (male) than the market's. Nevertheless, those firms with low discrimination coefficients, who would thus be prepared to hire more of the cheaper workers, would face the lowest production costs, and would drive out their competitors in the longer run. Becker's theory, therefore, is unable to explain why wage discrimination is able to persist over time.

Various addenda have been proposed to account for this. These include the observation that adjustment costs (e.g. the costs of firing, hiring and induction of new workers) are likely to slow the restructuring process (Arrow, 1972). Others have demonstrated how the efficiency benefits, for employers, of ending discrimination could be counteracted by social and economic censure from other, non-reforming, employers (Akerlof, 1983). A further group of explanations centre upon persistent discrimination being a function of imperfect information. Since employers do not know the full skills, commitment and productive potential of recruits, proxies have to be used to indicate their extent. These include educational background, age and experience. The sex of candidates is, it is argued, also used in this context, because women as a group carry a disproportionate share of family responsibilities, which, *ceteris paribus* involves firms in higher costs (Aigner and Cain, 1977). Although this may be part of the story, such arguments cannot explain why employers still cannot discern the productive capacities of individual women once they have been employed for some time, so as to deliver consequent adjustment in their salaries towards those of their (male) peers.

Circumstances such as these are likely to affect people's decisions about education. If girls (or their parents) anticipate entry barriers to some jobs, or that they will face discrimination in pay, it is rational for them to choose to invest less in education than is the case for boys. On the other hand, for the reasons indicated earlier, there may well be additional social and cultural constraints, not originating from the labour market, which act to depress the demand for female schooling relative to that for males.

For example, the question as to whether peasants – the majority rural population in most of Africa – are rational in the allocation of household resources for production has been the focus of an extended debate over the past four decades. Schultz (1964) argued the pure neo-classical case for individual profit maximising behaviour on the part of peasant producers. Production systems were judged reasonably efficient (based upon highly selective, and often dubious evidence),[10] and prospects for increased output were dependent upon new inputs and better crop prices. The peasant was expected to allocate resources rationally in response to favourable prices and to opportunities to innovate. However, this schema left no space for considerations of individual differences – personality, motivation, skills – of inadequate information and its impact upon perceptions of risk, and, indeed, of different social histories, and their implications for culturally-constrained action. The model did not account for peasant-farmer behaviour in a literal sense. As others have pointed out, maximising behaviour is influenced not only by present prices, but also by uncertainty about the future, by starting resources, and by traditional mores (Bliss and Stern, 1982).

These debates about the status which should be given to economic rationality in explaining peasant behaviour are directly relevant to the interpretation of gender inequality in African schooling. Under-investment in girls' education, relative to that of boys', persists throughout the region, notwithstanding the balance of well-documented social and private advantages that should lead to this hierarchy being removed. Does this imply that African parents are responding irrationally to the incentives they face? Or is it that many economists continue to count only some of the benefits and costs which are relevant to African household decision-makers? The latter seems, often, to be true. One example – that rates-of-return studies typically ignore the greater non-market opportunity costs of girls' schooling (hours of work lost to the household, rather than wages foregone) – has already been mentioned. Furthermore, where the calculated returns are weighted for expected rates of unemployment, the greater incidence of hidden unemployment amongst women than men is not acknowledged. Equally, since far fewer women than men work in the formal economy, their qualities and capabilities are likely, on average, to be greater than the men with whom they are compared. Selection bias may, under these circumstances, tend to inflate their expected returns to schooling, as estimated by these methods. For each of these reasons, it is likely that the 'true'

---

[10]   See Adams, (1986), for a critique.

rates of return to the schooling of girls, which would be relevant for parental decision-making, are lower than those suggested by typical calculations. Where the main factors considered by these studies are limited to current prices, rather than prices as modified by factors such as uncertainty, poverty and custom, it is highly unlikely that sensible results will be obtained. Irrationality, here, lies with the tools used to reveal it, rather than with the objects of study themselves.

There has been much debate, also, about the interaction between individual rationality and collective action. Scott (1976) argues that the primary aim of a peasant farmer and of a peasant community is survival in the face of uncertainty about food. Stability, rather than quantity, of output is valued, as is a system of social relations which is redistributive enough to provide security even in the worst of times. Accordingly, Scott believes that 'the study of the moral economy of the peasantry, while it begins in the domain of economics, must end in the study of peasant culture and religion.' (Scott, 1976, p.vii). His point is that the undoubted rationality of peasants has to be understood in the context of their economic, political and social circumstances. Such circumstances imply, for some analysts, that individual and collective actions are in harmony – since safeguarding the interests of one is dependent upon retaining the support of all. Others have pointed to the ways in which individuals' interests set them against the best interests of the community. Problems of free-riding, and prisoner's dilemma have occupied an important part of the development literature in recent years, which variously imply sources of conflict between individual and collective interests, leading to challenges to village-level security mechanisms and procedures.

The optimal strategy for individuals, in the face of the risks of cooperative breakdown, provides an opportunity for endless theorising. However, individual economic gain operates in a complex context, far removed from the perfect world of neoclassical theory.

> What has probably not been stressed enough in the discussions of rationality, and the relative roles of individual action and culture, is the extent to which cultural practices – rules, customs, habits – are a substitute for practical decisions, including those having to do with farm production. (Adams, 1986, p.279)

Such cultural practices also affect many other time-allocation decisions by household members, including the relative priorities of work, leisure and school attendance. For example, if the traditional relationships between elderly parents and children differ for sons and daughters – such that, say, the responsibility for providing support is stronger for sons – it will not be surprising to find that parents attribute greater priority to securing their earning power, compared with that of daughters. Giving greater priority to the education of sons would, in these circumstances, be rational for parents, even if the actual distribution of private returns to schooling between the sexes were roughly equal.

Thus, widely shared values and attitudes, carefully transferred from one generation to the next, provide a substitute for decision-making under uncertainty. If the expected, conventional thing is done, household security and well-being will probably be promoted. The culture, which leads to such actions being taken, is the inheritance, or synthesis, of past decisions made by people facing rather similar circumstances to those that presently hold. Decisions are often determined by, and, usually, are strongly informed by this inheritance. Expectations of economic rationality need to be mediated by this tendency.

Socio-Economic Explanations

There is little emphasis, in the orthodox human capital and discrimination literatures, upon the forces which lead to different social and educational outcomes prior to individuals joining the labour market. Although it is recognised that feedback effects are bound to exist, these are not the central terrain for enquiry. Human capital theory tends to see the different investments made in education by men and women (and by blacks and whites in USA), as reflecting the different labour-market outcomes expected for such groups, as determined by required family roles or social and cultural traditions. The ways in which these contextual variables interact are generally not theorised.[11]

Empirical studies which attempt to measure the impact of different socio-economic conditions upon educational outcomes, however, are growing in number. We review the econometric evidence, and present our own cross-country analyses in Chapter 3. Generally, they confirm that household income, direct costs, parental education and school quality each have a role in explaining differential demand for the schooling of boys and girls. But there are problems with finding adequate statistical proxies for some of these variables. Furthermore, as suggested above, it may be that opportunity costs, benefits to parents, and household preferences differ systematically for the schooling of girls and boys. Although statistical measurement of these latter variables is possible, their importance is sometimes better revealed by more micro, qualitative enquiries, many of which have been conducted by WID/GAD analysts.

A number of such studies have documented the ways in which girls are systematically excluded, or marginalised within schooling systems. Attention has been placed not just upon access, which is clearly less easy for girls in a majority of African, Middle-Eastern and South-Asian countries, but also upon the school and family characteristics that influence what happens to children once they are enrolled. Important factors identified by this work include the presence of male bias in curricula, gender-blind teacher-training practices, unhelpful streaming policies, teacher attitudes, school facilities, school locations, parental attitudes and demands, patterns of house/farm work, and a range of others. A convincing picture of systematic preference towards the needs and interests of boys relative to girls emerges. Our own evidence for nine African countries (Chapters 4-6) adds to this body of knowledge.

Explanations for the persistence of these phenomena vary according to the theoretical framework adopted. Writers in the WID tradition argue that deviations

---

[11]   Useful discussions of the relevant literature on discrimination, and on human capital theory, can be found in Fallon and Verry (1988), Sapsford and Tzannatos (1993), Siebert (1985) and Sloane (1985).

from equality of educational opportunity arise mainly from inadequate knowledge of the benefits of schooling, from faulty socialisation, or prejudice. Social attitudes about women being wives, mothers and home-makers, and the fact that job rationing gives women access to work in a more restricted range of occupations than men, are cited as examples of 'bias' or 'imperfection', which lead to schooling being less beneficial for women than men. Boserup (1970, p.122) pointed to a deep-seated fear of marriages where the wife was more educated than the husband. This encouraged parents to suspend their daughters' education at a point where potential husbands with similar or higher levels of education might still be found.

More recently, many writers have documented the detailed sources of male educational bias in Africa, and have indicated implied strategies for reform. Writings in this liberal tradition include studies financed by, or associated with, NGOs promoting women's rights, and with the aid agencies, where a practical policy agenda has often been strong. In general this work sees the state as being tractable, if not benevolent. Governments are judged able to design and implement reforms to ensure women's rights to education and other social goods, equally with men. They may need to be persuaded to do so – often by being shown how such reforms would support the achievement of their other stated goals – and sometimes, owing to knowledge gaps about what works, or about reform sequencing, agenda for action may need to be suggested. Ultimately, however, the forces of reason, which indicate that the promotion of women's education is in the interests of all, will, it is assumed, prevail.

Radical feminists, on the other hand, differ from WID analysts primarily in the power they attribute to patriarchy. These writers usually hold that the state is a coalition of (mainly) male forces, committed to preserving a patriarchal order and society. This reproduces a system of social structures and practices in which men dominate, oppress and exploit women (Walby, 1989, p.214). The state perpetuates subordination via a strong defence of family, the latter being a major locus for the sexual division of labour. This creates a clearly defined private world for women, compared with a public world for men. 'To the extent that the state needs the family to fulfil a specific mission, and given that women have a particular role in it, it would be very unlikely for the state to initiate a process of change in which women's conditions could change substantially' (Stromquist, 1989, p.171).

Within this framework, the school is seen as an important agent in the maintenance of patriarchy. Inequality in educational access and attainment become a means of legitimating and reproducing the different roles which men and women will have in society. Patriarchy thus governs parental decisions in educating their sons and daughters, teachers attitudes in preparing children for adult life, and girls' subject choices, which prepare them to opt for 'female' jobs, judged consistent with their forthcoming family responsibilities. On this interpretation, then, schools are an important instrument for ensuring that gender inequality remains in place from generation to generation.[12]

---

[12]   In this context, it is worth recalling the work of an earlier group of socialist economists, who saw schools as providing the primary means whereby existing class

Those who deny the possibility of reform, however, have some difficult facts to account for in view of what has actually been achieved in the field of women's education. Only 50 years ago, in Africa, the education of women was very limited indeed, with enrolments being often only one-fifth to one-third those of men. Furthermore, where girls were in school, they were often taught subjects, and subject-content, which were significantly different from those taught to boys. In the Belgian colonies, for example, girls followed a completely separate syllabus, which emphasised practical domestic studies, sewing, cooking and child-care. Such separation in curriculum content for the schooling of girls and boys was typical of mission schools throughout Africa. This meant that it was not possible for girls to progress up the formal school system in the same way as boys – even if their abilities, and the wishes of their parents, supported it (Hailey, 1957, pp.1209-10; Hunter, 1962, pp.239-47).

Things have, of course, changed substantially since then. Gender ratios are more equal, curricula are usually common and a far greater proportion of girls progress up the educational ladder than before. Is this because women's interests are now more strongly espoused by policy-makers? Or have the needs of the economy changed, such that present forms of subordination require women to have more (and different) education than before, but still not quite as much as the men?

Socialist feminists, who, it will be recalled, retain a more specifically neo-Marxist framework than the radical feminists alluded to above, would argue that it is the interaction between patriarchy and economic interest that governs the particular forms of subordination, and their evolution over time. For capitalism to prosper, class relations must be reproduced, and the required characteristics of wage labour will continually evolve. On this interpretation schooling is an important site for the reproduction of the sexual division of labour – both domestic and industrial. As the characteristics of market production change, so must the school system. Accordingly, it would be argued, the recent apparent benefits for women have been determined by the evolving needs of the economy, mediated by the continuing patriarchal ideology which underlies its institutions. Stromquist (1995, p.445) comments as follows:

---

relations in society are reproduced (e.g. Bowles and Gintis, 1976). These 'correspondence' theorists argued that the values and traits encouraged by each level of education were those required by workers at the corresponding level of the occupational hierarchy. Thus, the lowest levels of schooling – which tend to lead to employment in manual occupations – encourage obedience, memory work and little, if any, questioning of authority by pupils. At higher levels of education, on the other hand, independence of mind, innovation, creativity and autonomy are increasingly valued. These theorists were concerned to explain the role of schools in the reproduction of social and economic inequality, expressed in terms of class. Oddly, gender featured hardly at all in their analyses (Bowles and Gintis, for example, had only two or three brief references in over 300 pages of text). It was left to later feminist analysts to use this approach to explain the role of the school system in reproducing gender inequality.

From the state's perspective, if women get an education that does not address the nature of gender ... in society, then women become capable of making more and better contributions to the economy and to the family as presently constituted, while their increased schooling does not threaten the status quo, and so the basic structures of ideological and material domination are retained and sustained.

On this view, reform is not possible without going outside this framework: progress, expressed in terms of increased participation and performance of girls in school, is simply exploitation by another name.

Whether one chooses to call it 'reform', or change driven by the requirements of capitalist development, the fact of change cannot itself be denied. As documented in the next chapter, girls and women are now gaining much greater access to schooling in Africa than in the past, they are staying in school longer, and more of them are proceeding to higher levels of the system, than in earlier decades. There is, however, much further to go, and the question arises as to how it might be encouraged further, and accelerated. Need it simply await the process of growth and development, or are there means of changing policies faster, and further than has happened in the past, so as to give girls greater, and earlier, access to schooling, in parity with boys?

We have seen that there are considerable differences of opinion, in the literature, on this matter. Socialist feminists tend to be negative about the prospects for more rapid change. Radical feminists are also pessimistic about such possibilities: for them, only those changes which are consistent with, or supportive of, the prevailing patriarchy will prove viable. This might include some degree of increased access for girls, but changes in curriculum content, in ways which aim to target and undermine patriarchy, are less likely (Stromquist, 1995). Those in the WID tradition, on the other hand, take a more optimistic view. States are here judged to be potentially supportive of the interests of poorer people. They are open to reform in favour of women, although they often need both technical and political encouragement to move in this direction. Some economists (e.g. Knodel and Jones, 1996; Knodel, 1997) take a sanguine view of the connection between poverty alleviation (through development) and growing access to schooling. They argue that, as development occurs, rising enrolment and school quality will be achieved *pari passu*. They conclude that there is no need for special measures to help women's education, since these benefits will be achieved, provided resources are used sensibly in support of general economic development.

Each of these sets of perspectives adds something to our appreciation of the reality facing women and girls. At present, however, we do not know enough about the real constraints which prevent African girls attending schools, or which cause them to under-perform when there, to be able to arbitrate between them. To what extent are the supply constraints binding? Can we speak of girls' exclusion being particularly heavily influenced by state actions, or are they more the result of household, demand-side behaviour and values? What leads to such systematic outcomes? Can one generalise across countries and regions about causes, or is each example spatially and temporally unique?

Any explanations for the occurrence of gender inequalities in schooling need to be broad enough to encompass the wide range of schooling outcomes which exist, at given levels of economic development. Even quite detailed description of a society's 'level' of development provides only moderate predictive ability as regards the extent and content of girls' schooling available. A pronounced tendency to favour boys is evident in most, though not in all countries, but its detail differs profoundly from place to place. An aim of the present study is to clarify the causes of such differences, and to investigate strategies for their mitigation.

Household Economics and Policy Targeting

We have seen that decisions about school attendance do not necessarily reflect the best long-term interests of each individual child. This raises the question as to whose best interests *are* served by such decisions. Are they the interests of the household as a whole, in some sense, or of one or more individual members of it? This question is one upon which economists have dwelt in recent years. The early work on household economics was, again, dominated by Becker (1965). He argued that households were best represented as a unit, the resource allocation decisions of which maximised the utility of its members. It is obvious that the characteristics of the single set of preferences, acted upon by such unitary households, will be an important determinant of welfare outcomes. For example, if household decision-makers accord all members equal importance, the welfare impact of increased household income is likely to be evenly spread. However, members of unitary households are not required to demonstrate selfless behaviour. Thus, if the consumption of some household members is accorded greater importance than that of others, the welfare impact of increased income will be unequally distributed amongst the household. A considerable amount of attention has been given in the literature to modelling the outcomes of intra-household resource allocation, under different assumptions for the preferences of household decision-makers in this unitary model. The implications for welfare – and for policy – are different in circumstances where parents privilege boys (owing to customary or efficiency reasons) in resource allocation, than where they privilege girls, or where they treat both of the sexes equally.

Some authors have increasingly questioned whether the unitary model satisfactorily accounts for all aspects of intra-household distribution. In response, a whole set of 'collective' approaches to theorising the problem have been developed. These accept the notion that individual household members have different preferences, and confront the problem as to how these can be aggregated for the purpose of arriving at a household welfare function (Sen, 1990). Some of these approaches investigate cooperative solutions to bargaining among individuals, whilst others rely on non-cooperative game theory (Haddad *et al.*, 1997, Chapter 1).

The view that income is not pooled, implying that the assumptions of the unitary model are incorrect, has long featured in the sociological and anthropological literature. There is also a growing body of econometric evidence that the income-pooling assumptions of the unitary approach are inappropriate. It seems that marginal income accruing to different household members has different implications for household expenditure patterns – except in cases where both adult men and women in the household are occupied in the labour market. In particular, women seem to spend more on education, health and household services than do men. Hoddinott *et al.*, (1997) find that the evidence against income and labour pooling, and against family altruism is strong, and that some form of collective approach better captures the reality. But further empirical work is required.

What are the policy implications of this? We should recall that, were we to take a welfarist approach to poverty alleviation, the most efficient type of intervention, if household decision-making were unitary, would be lump-sum transfers, rather than wage or price policy. The reason is that this would maximise the choices for households, to spend net income in ways supportive of their own welfare. If planners had views about how best to improve well-being, lump-sum transfers would remain best only if there were no conflict between planners' and households' preferences for the disposition of increments to income. On the other hand, if household allocation is collective there is no general implication for preferred policy instruments. Here, it is unclear as to how best to affect behaviour at the level of the individual, where the outcome of household bargaining strategies over household resources are unknown.

Nevertheless, the major difference between the unitary and collective models of the household, is that the identity of the recipient of income transfers does not affect outcomes at the household level in the former case, whereas in the case of the latter it does. Equally, the assumption that information is shared and that production is joint, is vulnerable as soon as one allows the possibility of there being different sets of household interests which are in competition with each other. Under these circumstances, the chances of targeting being successful are improved if it is aimed below the household, to the individual level.

Accordingly, income transfers to individuals in the household who are not the heads can have superior impact upon their welfare, than if their share of a household transfer were allocated to heads. If women are the intended beneficiaries, targeting below the level of the household is likely to be a more efficient strategy. Furthermore, in circumstances where we know that girls are given more restricted access to schooling than boys, planners seeking to change those outcomes must aim their resources at the individual children themselves. This is so, whether the appropriate household model is unitary or collective. Resources transferred need to be non-fungible. Thus, subsidies for school attendance, meals, uniforms, books or transport, are superior to income transfers. The latter, under a unitary model, would end up being spent on general improvements to household welfare, which may, or may not, include girls' schooling.[13]

---

[13]   In cases where income transfers are made conditional on demonstrated school attendance, however, some of these dangers can be avoided (see ILO/UNCTAD, 2001).

Interactions between Poverty, Schooling and Gender – A Theoretical Framework

We have argued (and the next chapter will demonstrate) that securing growth in average household incomes is neither a necessary, nor a sufficient condition for improvements in the gender gap in African school enrolments to be gained. On the other hand, we also know that children who do not attend primary school are overwhelmingly from poor households in poor countries, and that the majority of such non-attendees are girls. How can we explain this apparent paradox? Figure 1.1 sketches a simple model which connects poverty and gendered outcomes of schooling.   Its main constituents are as follows.   The main loci for poverty/schooling interactions are at the levels of the household and of the State.[14] As regards households, in cases where the ease of access to schools of reasonable quality is similar for all, there are two main reasons why poorer households may choose not to send their children to them. The first is that the direct costs which parents have to meet may be too great. Such costs exist even where school fees are not charged. In most cases, parents incur some expenditures for school uniforms, text and exercise books, and many also have to contribute to the construction or upkeep of school buildings, and provide other inputs in cash or kind.   Poor households may judge such costs to be beyond their means.[15] The second reason is that poorer households may depend, more so than richer households, upon the labour of their children in order to supplement household income – either directly, on the farm or in the market place, or indirectly, by children undertaking household tasks which liberate adult labour for other remunerated work. For each, or both, of these sets of reasons, poor households may decide not to enrol some or all of their children in school.

Quite separately, however, this outcome may arise from there not being schools sufficiently close at hand, or from those which are accessible being of such poor quality that parents do not wish to use them.   Although there may be no compelling set of reasons why even the poorest States cannot provide their populations with sufficient primary schools of reasonable quality, it remains the case that shortages of school places, of materials and of trained teachers, are much more prevalent in poorer than in richer countries, and that they tend particularly to affect the poorer households and communities within them.

The above are the four main factors which link poverty, at the level of the State and at the level of the household, to a circumstance where not all children in the eligible age group attend primary school. The gendered characteristics of this under-enrolment are, however, determined by a further, more diverse, set of

---

[14]   In some cases, the community is also an important locus, and grows in importance as more States devolve responsibility for school provision to communities.   But such circumstances are as yet a minority, and their addition to the framework shown in Figure 1.1 would provide little additional analytic insight for present purposes.

[15]   It is assumed here that, under the conditions specified, the incidence of benefits from primary schooling would be independent of the income level of the parental household.

factors, which are broadly grouped together in Figure 1.1 under the heading 'gender relations'.   These include phenomena which cause rationed enrolment opportunities to be unequally allocated between boys and girls.   They operate in the domains of the household, the school, the labour market and the society as a whole.

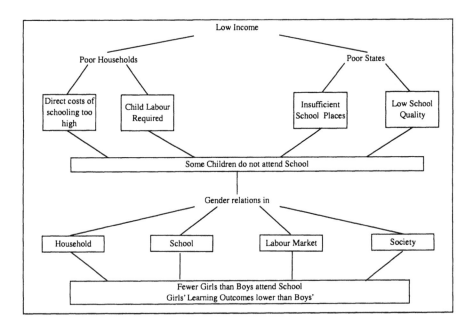

Figure 1.1 Relationships between poverty, gender relations and schooling

As regards the latter, gendered roles in society change the balance of incentives for girls and boys to attend school.   In societies where the main local and national leadership roles are occupied by males, where girls marry at a much younger age than boys, where religious or customary beliefs discourage social interaction between the sexes, or where women are discouraged from seeking a future outside the home and the family, the incentives for girls to attend and to perform well in school are less than those for boys.

The labour market also has a critical influence upon the perceived benefits of schooling.   Where many jobs are reserved – whether formally or informally – for males, where unemployment is high and the gender balance of formal employment is strongly male, and where gender discrimination in the labour market reduces the average earnings of women relative to men with similar abilities and qualifications, the perceived benefits of schooling will be greater for boys than for girls.

The environment of the school may also be more conducive to the attendance and performance of boys than of girls. Male teachers may not provide girls sufficient support, and they may even be sexually threatening. Toilet facilities for girls may be inadequate, and other facilities (such as a shortage or absence of chairs) may be unfriendly to girls. Harassment from boys may occur, and the journey to school may have greater attendant risks for the safety of girls than of boys.

Finally, much household behaviour is responsive to the broader contextual conditions of the society and the labour market. However, the gendered division of labour within the household can also sharply affect the relative chances of girls and boys attending school. Where girls are expected to perform household chores, and to look after younger siblings, the demands on their time may be greater than upon the boys, and their school attendance may be more affected. Furthermore, where a girl's allegiance after marriage is mainly to her future husband's family, the balance of perceived benefits to parents are likely to favour the education of sons over daughters. Where schooling decisions in families are mainly taken by men, the education of boys may again find greater favour.

In each of the above ways, custom and circumstance lead to a range of gender relations which cause the outcomes of schooling to be less favourable for girls than for boys. Subsequent chapters provide evidence for their diversity and strength, and there is much other evidence available from the wider research literature. The next three chapters use standard economic methods to analyse the determinants of under-enrolment and gender inequality in schooling. We return to the above framework in Chapter 5, which synthesises some of the results from our national surveys.

Chapter 2

Causes of Enrolment Outcomes:
Costs versus Commitment

Introduction

It is an extraordinary fact that, at the turn of the century, the probability of an African child attending primary school was no higher than it had been in 1980. It was also lower than in any other world region – particularly so in the case of girls. For generations, the expansion of schooling has been associated with economic progress. In the minds of most people, schooling is wanted for their children to enable them to live useful, fulfilling and profitable lives. The popular demands for more schooling have almost everywhere led to inexorable expansion of facilities, and steady – sometimes extremely rapid – growth of enrolments amongst both boys and girls. Yet in SSA this seemed to be halted, even reversed, during the final two decades of the twentieth century. As far as we can tell, there has never been a time when the proportion of children enrolled in school has fallen to the same extent as it did in SSA, over as many years and affecting such a large regional population.

This chapter asks why this happened. It goes beyond the obvious circumstance of economic decline, to investigate whether the costs of African schooling made expansion unaffordable, whether governments or households were unable to allocate the necessary resources to primary schooling, or whether they became, in some sense, unwilling to do so.

The Growth of Primary Systems: Africa and Elsewhere

Between 1960 and 1980, education systems in developing countries expanded rapidly. These years, with some interruptions during the 1970s, were generally marked by healthy economic growth, and so it was with education. At primary level, enrolments in Africa tripled, whilst in Asia and Latin America they more than doubled over the two decades. At secondary and tertiary levels of education, enrolments increased even more rapidly, with ten-fold increases being not uncommon – albeit often from a very small beginning. This pattern of expansion, however, changed after 1980. In every major developing region, the rate of growth of school and college enrolments slowed, as compared with the previous two decades. This was particularly so for primary schooling, and especially in Africa, where primary enrolment growth fell below the rate of growth of population, and where, in a number of countries, enrolments actually declined in absolute terms.

Figure 2.1 shows the impact of these expansion patterns upon primary gross enrolment ratios (which express primary enrolments as a proportion of the school-age group) in developing regions.[1] During the period 1960-80, when the growth rates of enrolments greatly exceeded rates of population growth, GERs increased substantially in most countries, with the fastest growth occurring in Africa. However, the subsequent slowdown, which involved actual retrogression for Africa, can be clearly seen. There, the combination of economic decline and continued rapid population growth caused the GER to fall by more than 5 per cent over the 1980s, even though the number of children attending school actually increased from approximately 48 million in 1980 to 58 million in 1990. Thus, the educational gap between Africa and other developing areas widened over these years, confirming, by a considerable margin, its position as the most under-educated region in the world.

Some reduction of earlier rates of enrolment growth might be thought to have been inevitable after 1980, since, by then, developing countries, as a whole, had reached average GERs of around 95 – not far from 'universal' enrolment levels. However, widespread over-age enrolment implied that many school-aged children remained out of school. Net (age-adjusted) enrolments were reported by UNESCO to comprise 75 per cent of gross enrolments in 1980.[2] Thus, GERs large enough to include all the school-aged population in these regions would have to have risen to levels greater than 100, and plenty of scope for further growth remained.

After 1990, the regional statistics provide some evidence that the decline in Africa was arrested, with some recovery of enrolment ratios being achieved by 1995, taking the region as a whole. However, progress remained slight, with significant gains being registered in only a few countries. Of the 33 countries having data on enrolments for the 1990-95 period, only 16 achieved increases in their GERs; 14 experienced falls, with no change being reported for the remaining three countries (UNESCO, 1995a and 1998a). By consequence, in 1995 the sub-continent still had the lowest GER of any of the world's major regions, with

---

[1]   The gross enrolment ratio (GER) is the most widely used indicator of schooling availability. It expresses total enrolment at a given level of schooling – irrespective of the age of the students – as a percentage of the population which, according to national regulations, is of an age to attend at that level. The net enrolment ratio (NER) takes account of the age structure of those enrolled by excluding all those children who are older or younger than the officially eligible age group from the numerator of the ratio. That statistic provides a better indication of the availability of schooling than does the GER, but it is less frequently used owing to the required age-adjusted enrolment data being less available and less accurate on an internationally comparable basis than the unadjusted data.

[2]   See UNESCO, (1989, Tables 2.10 and 2.11). Later evidence suggests that this has changed little over the intervening years. Although UNESCO no longer publishes regional averages for NERs, data are available for 26 countries in SSA for various dates in the 1990s. The unweighted average ratio between NERs and GERs for this sample of countries and years is 0.77 (calculated from UNESCO, 1998a, Table 3.2).

primary enrolments which were equivalent only to about three-quarters of its school-age population. Moreover, uniquely amongst developing regions, a majority of countries in SSA had a smaller proportion of their children in school, in the late 1990s, than had been the case in 1980.

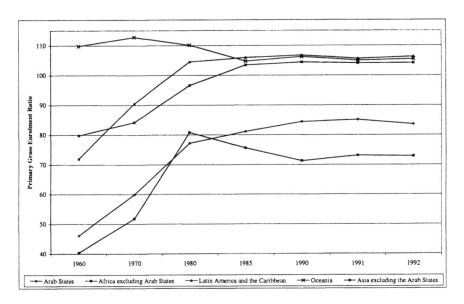

Figure 2.1 Regional gross enrolment ratios over time

School quality, too, in much of SSA is low. Children are typically taught in much larger classes than is compatible with effective learning, and the average number of pupils per teacher in SSA is higher than in any other world region except South Asia. Teachers are often unqualified; teaching aids are few, and textbook provision is desperately poor in many countries. In some countries it is not uncommon for pupils to be taught in schools without desks, chairs or windows, nor is it unusual for classes to be held outdoors. Where quality is low, learning is slow and children are unable to meet the demands of the curriculum. Consequently, repetition tends to be higher in systems of low quality, which in turn tends to raise the average age of the student population. It is significant that only about three-quarters of pupils in primary schools in SSA are within the official school-age group, compared with over four-fifths in each of the other developing regions. This is partly because the average age of first enrolment is higher in Africa than elsewhere, and it is not uncommon for less than half of the new Grade 1 entrants to be of the right age. But it is also because rates of repetition are higher (typically two or three times greater than other developing regions) with the result that one in every five pupils is repeating a grade, causing a greater proportion of children to complete primary schooling at ages beyond the top of the official age range.[3]

Low quality leads to reduced effectiveness of schooling and thus to lower actual and expected benefits from the schooling process. By consequence, for any given level of first enrolment, more pupils will tend to drop out, where school quality remains low or declines. High rates of drop-out are a major problem in SSA primary schools. In about half the countries in the region, less than three-quarters of first-grade entrants will reach Grade 5, and thus will, almost certainly, leave school prior to attaining durable standards of literacy and numeracy. In some countries, such as Chad, Madagascar, Mozambique and Ethiopia, things are much worse, with no more than half of enrolees staying in school until Grade 5 (UNESCO, 1998a, Table 2.5). Here then, the problem of low Grade 1 enrolments is compounded by subsequent high rates of drop-out, so as to reduce to tiny proportions the number of children able to gain lasting benefits from primary schooling.

Table 2.1 Trends in primary GER by region and gender, 1965-1997

		1965	1980	1990	1997
SSA	male	52	87	79	84
	female	31	68	66	69
	total	41	77	73	77
Arab States	male	n.a.	92	93	92
	female	n.a.	67	75	77
	total	n.a.	80	84	85
LAC	male	99	106	109	117
	female	96	103	105	110
	total	98	105	107	114
East Asia and	male	n.a.	117	122	118
Oceania	female	n.a.	103	115	118
	total	n.a.	110	118	118
South Asia	male	83	92	103	107
	female	52	61	77	83
	total	68	77	91	95
Developing Countries	male	84	104	106	108
	female	62	85	92	95
	total	78	95	99	102

Source: UNESCO (1998a) and(2000b).

---

[3]   See UNESCO (1996b, p.8).

The Gender Balance of Enrolments

The problems of restricted availability of schooling and low school quality, together with their associated phenomena of high rates of repetition and drop-out, are widely believed to affect the enrolment, persistence and performance of girls particularly sharply. The dynamics of both total and gender-disaggregated primary enrolments, in the main developing regions of the world, are summarised in Table 2.1. Although the long-term enrolment growth, alluded to above, has involved both girls and boys, it shows that a gender gap in enrolments persists in all regions. As indicated in Table 2.2, the enrolment of girls at primary level in developing countries as a whole is estimated at about 84 per cent of that of boys. Girls' enrolments, relative to those of boys, in Sub-Saharan Africa are slightly less than this average, whilst in the Arab nations and South Asia the gap remains even wider. Nevertheless, because overall enrolment ratios are lower, girls in SSA are less likely to be attending school than those in any other major world region.

Table 2.2 Female enrolments at primary level in developing countries, relative to male enrolments (percentage), 1980 and 1997

	1980	1997
Sub-Saharan Africa	78	82
Arab States	73	80
Latin America and Caribbean	97	91
East Asia and Oceania	83	92
South Asia	66	73
All Developing Countries	79	84

Source: UNESCO (1998a) and (2000b).

Somewhat surprisingly, the gender balance of enrolments in SSA improved over the years 1980-97, notwithstanding the region's unfortunate record on total enrolments. However, closer inspection of Table 2.1 reveals that the reason for this improvement was that, relative to the size of the school-age group, boys' enrolments fell, whilst those of girls were largely maintained.

This is shown in more detail in Table 2.3. In 28 of the 39 countries in SSA for which we have time-series data, the ratio of girls to boys enrolled at primary school increased over the years 1980-95. However, in almost half (13) of the cases, the reduction of the gender gap occurred in countries in which the overall primary GER declined, implying that total enrolments in those countries increased less quickly than the school-age group. Thus, moves towards gender equity occurred here because the proportion of boys enrolled at school fell faster than did the proportion of girls – hardly a circumstance which can be welcomed unreservedly.[4]   In the remaining 11 SSA countries (almost one-third of the total), gender ratios were either unchanged over the period, or they deteriorated further in favour of males. Consequently, the apparent progress made, as regards the gender balance of school enrolments in SSA, turns out to be both a more ambiguous, and a less generalised phenomenon than the aggregate regional data might otherwise suggest.

**Table 2.3 A comparison of total and gendered enrolment changes in sub-
            Saharan African countries, 1980-1995**

No. of Countries in which:	F/M Increased	F/M Unchanged	F/M Fell	Total
GER Increased	15	2	2	19
GER Fell	13	5	2	20
Total	28	7	4	39

Notes: GER = primary gross enrolment ratio.
         F/M = female primary enrolment ratio as a percentage of male primary enrolment
         ratio.
         Lesotho and Botswana are excluded. There, F/M fell over the period, but female
         enrolments exceed those of boys.

Source: UNESCO World Education Reports, (various years).

Causes of Enrolment Outcomes in SSA

Past causal processes may well conspire again to prevent the attainment of enrolment targets for boys and girls. How, then, may we explain SSA's poor enrolment record, including its gendered characteristics? Many of the key determinants can be expected to be country-specific. However, we know that, at the macro level, there are a number of economic variables that jointly determine both the number and proportion of children attending school. These comprise the amount of expenditures on schooling made by governments and households, the average cost per student and the size of the school-age population. The greater are the first two of these variables, and the smaller are the last two, the greater the

---

[4]   It would, of course, still have been possible for the absolute enrolments of both boys
       and girls to have risen, provided the growth of each had been less than that of their
       respective age groups.

proportion of children who will be enrolled in school.[5] Changes in any of them are capable of affecting the achievement of a given level of enrolments. Accordingly, a review of recent changes in their magnitudes, in SSA, is a productive way of beginning our answer to the question posed above. In what follows, each of them is briefly investigated.

Public Spending on Primary Schooling

The enrolment capacity of school systems is strongly influenced by the amount of money governments and households are prepared to spend upon them. Where additional children are enrolled without a *pro rata* increase in financial and/or human resources becoming available, class sizes grow larger and the per-pupil availability of learning materials deteriorates. A limit to this process is imposed by the availability of space in classrooms, and by the extent to which both the bureaucracy and pupils' families will tolerate larger pupil/teacher ratios. Ultimately, for given ways of organising the school system, more expenditure becomes necessary if higher enrolments are to be achieved.

As regards public spending, it is not easy to make valid international comparisons of absolute expenditures. This is partly because national incomes differ strongly, thereby making high absolute per pupil expenditures easier for richer than for poorer states, and partly because the purchasing power of national currencies also varies widely. For example, the absolute cost of employing teachers of a given quality is much lower in India than in the USA. Accordingly, the fact that, in 1995, the public cost per child of primary schooling in India was $US37, compared with $US4,856 in the USA, does tell us something, but it may not be as informative as, at first, it seems.[6]

A different and, for some purposes, more useful way of comparing spending patterns is to express national expenditures on education (and on each level of the system) as a percentage of GNP. This provides one measure of the national priority assigned to such expenditures: arguably, similar proportionate allocations

---

[5] More formally, this can be seen by considering the following identity:

$$GER = x_g + x_p / a(c_g + c_p)$$

where:
a = primary school-aged population as a proportion of the total population.
c_g = publicly funded primary unit costs as a percentage of GNP per capita.
c_p = privately funded primary unit costs as a percentage of GNP per capita.
x_g = public recurrent spending on primary schooling as a percentage of GNP.
x_p = private spending on primary schooling as a percentage of GNP.

Further discussion of this identity is given in Colclough with Lewin, (1993, pp.80-81) and Colclough and Al-Samarrai (2000).

[6] For these reasons, comparisons of costs in dollars, after having adjusted for differences in national purchasing power, provides a more reliable measure. This approach is used for the comparisons afforded by our case-studies in Chapter 5 below.

by different national governments would suggest that they each had a similar level
of commitment to providing the service. Some of these data are shown, at a
regional level, in Table 2.4.

Table 2.4 Public expenditure on education in \$US, and as a percentage of GNP

	Percentage of GNP				US$ (billions)		
	1980	1985	1990	1995	1980	1990	1995
Sub-Saharan Africa	5.1	4.8	5.1	5.6	15.8	14.8	18.8
Arab States	4.1	5.8	5.2	5.2	18.0	24.4	27.5
Latin America and the Caribbean	3.8	3.9	4.1	4.5	33.5	44.6	72.8
Eastern Asia and Oceania	2.8	3.1	3.0	3.0	16.0	32.0	59.9
Southern Asia	4.1	3.3	3.9	4.3	12.8	35.8	62.6
All Developing Countries	3.8	3.9	3.9	4.1	97.4	155.6	247.7
Least Developed Countries	2.9	3.0	2.7	2.5	3.5	4.3	5.3
Developed Countries	5.2	5.0	5.0	5.1	407.8	816.4	1109.9

Source: UNESCO (1998b).

The table shows that Sub-Saharan African countries maintained – and,
indeed, somewhat increased – their public expenditures on education, expressed as
a proportion of national incomes, over the period 1980-95. This is perhaps
surprising, in the light of the declining enrolment ratios and low quality of
schooling in SSA discussed earlier. Furthermore, the table shows that the region's
educational malaise seems not to have been caused by any general neglect of
education in comparison with practice elsewhere. In SSA, a higher proportion of
GNP is allocated to education, via public expenditures, than typically occurs in
other regions, including the developed market economies. A similar trend
characterised public spending on primary schooling. This had risen to around 2.0
per cent of GNP, in SSA, by the early 1990s, compared to an estimated 1.5 per cent
in Latin America and 1.3 per cent in Asian countries.[7]
Table 2.5 shows the ten countries, from Sub-Saharan Africa, for which there
are data on primary schooling expenditures for each of the years 1980, 1990 and
1995. For the intra-period years (1980-90 and 1990-95) the total number of rises
and falls were not very different. However, a comparison of 1980 with 1995
reveals that public expenditures on primary schooling increased, as a proportion of
GNP, in eight of the countries, whilst in one (Burundi) it remained unchanged, and
in one (Zambia) it fell sharply. Taking these ten countries as a group, public
expenditures on the primary system increased, on average, from 2.0 to 2.7 per cent
of GNP, over the years 1980-95. The table also provides some support for the

---

[7]   These data are calculated from UNESCO (1995a).

view that 1990 marked the start of some acceleration in the growth of public spending on primary schooling. Its average annual growth over 1990-95, measured as a proportion of GNP, was running at more than twice the level of the previous decade.[8] Thus, the governments of SSA have been placing more emphasis, via their spending priorities, upon education in general, and also upon primary schooling, than have those in other regions. It also seems that the intensity of that effort increased during the 1990s, as compared with earlier years.[9]

Table 2.5 SSA public spending on primary schooling as a percentage of GNP, 1980-1995

Country	1980	1990	1995
Burundi	1.2	1.6	1.2
Ethiopia	0.8	2.6	2.5
Gambia	1.5	1.6	2.5
Kenya	3.9	3.9	4.6
Lesotho	2.0	1.6	3.0
Malawi	1.2	1.4	3.4
Swaziland	2.3	2.1	3.0
Togo	1.8	1.7	2.0
Zambia	2.7	0.9	0.7
Zimbabwe	2.7	5.7	4.4
Average	2.0	2.3	2.7
Average annual change to year shown (%)		1.4	3.4

Source: UNESCO World Education Reports (various years) and World Bank World Tables.

Nevertheless, the economic decline suffered by SSA during the 1980s, when real GNP per capita fell, for the region as a whole, by about 12 per cent, meant that

---

[8] This result may, of course, be sensitive to the particular selection of countries included in the comparison.

[9] In 1990, the World Conference on Education for All, held in Jomtien, Thailand, gave very strong international backing for a renewed policy emphasis on primary and basic education, throughout the world. The declaration to this effect was signed by education and/or finance ministers from 168 countries. Accordingly, the somewhat increased priority which appears to have been given, after 1990, to public spending on primary schooling in SSA, may provide mildly heartening news for those who seek evidence for some positive impact of UN resolutions and conferences on development policy.

these increased efforts to support primary schooling were greatly outweighed by the effects of the region's declining incomes.[10]   The resources available for education (and other services) were not keeping pace with population growth, and it was, therefore, difficult to provide the number of school places necessary to maintain enrolment rates at past levels, let alone to raise them. Table 2.4 shows that total public spending on education in SSA actually fell from $US15.8 billions to around $US14.8 billions over the 1980s, and that it managed to increase only to $US18.8 billions by 1995. This amounted to scarcely a 20 per cent increase, in current dollar terms, over the fifteen years, and, of course, it represented a very sharp real reduction in the public resources available for education. Accordingly, Africa's increased relative commitment to expenditures on primary schooling was not enough to avoid a precipitous decline in the real resources available per pupil enrolled. By consequence, school quality was badly affected. As one symptom of this, class size – already much too high in many places – increased in almost two-thirds of SSA countries over the period 1990-95.[11]   Teacher salaries were decimated, and non-salary expenditures were squeezed to insignificant levels.

In contrast to SSA, Latin American spending almost doubled in current dollar terms, whilst that of South Asia increased five-fold, over the same period (Table 2.4). Thus, reduced *relative* commitment in South Asia still allowed substantial increases in the value of real public spending per pupil. Whilst school quality in SSA declined sharply and perilously, elsewhere in the developing world it gradually improved. These financial privations, in the public sector, undoubtedly provide an important part of the explanation for the dismal enrolment progress made by SSA over the past two decades.

Although, as we have seen, the countries of SSA can be said to have made greater efforts, in recent years, to achieve schooling for all children, this is by no means true of all of them, taken individually. Some of the countries with low primary enrolments have been spending far less than is both desirable, and affordable, on the primary sector. Which are they?

Tables 2.6 and 2.7 bring together information on the constituent elements of the financing identity, presented earlier in this chapter, for those countries which had, and had not, achieved GERs of 100 by the years shown. All of the estimates presented in these tables have been derived from the same source, to ensure, as far as is possible, consistency of the population and enrolment parameters used in their

---

[10]   The change in GNP per capita is calculated from World Bank (1998).

[11]   The data showing an increase in pupil/teacher ratios are given in UNESCO (1996b, p.16). Such trends need not necessarily imply increases in average class size, depending upon whether or not other reforms, such as shift systems, changes in the frequency of class teaching, etc., are introduced. However, in most cases these have generally not been used so as to prevent changes in pupil/teacher ratios affecting average class size.

Table 2.6 SSA countries with GERs less than 100: public expenditures on primary schooling and related characteristics

	year of data (1)	ger (2)	female ger as % of male ger (3)	GNP per capita 1995 (US$) (4)	x_g (5)	c_g (6)	a (7)	x_g required for GER=100 (8)
Low Commitment – Low cost								
Eritrea	1996	54	83	180	0.6	8.5	13.6	1.2
Guinea	1995	48	54	540	0.7	8.9	16.6	1.5
Madagascar	1990	84	98	240	0.7	5.9	14.8	0.9
Ghana	1990	77	83	370	0.8	6.3	16.8	1.1
Chad	1996	65	52	210	0.9	8.3	16.1	1.3
Zambia	1995	89	99	350	0.9	4.7	20.9	1.0
Central African Republic	1990	66	64	350	1.2	11.0	16.0	1.8
Senegal	1996	69	82	550	1.2	10.4	16.2	1.7
Comoros	1995	74		440	1.4	11.1	17.3	1.9
Mauritania	1996	83	90	450	1.5	10.9	16.1	1.8
Low Commitment – High Cost								
Burkina Faso	1985	27	59	220	0.7	16.2	16.5	2.7
Mali	1995	34	66	250	1.0	16.9	16.5	2.8
Ethiopia	1996	37	57	110	1.2	20.8	16.2	3.4
Gambia	1990	64	68	350	1.3	14.2	14.6	2.1
Burundi	1990	73	84	150	1.5	13.4	15.8	2.1
Moderate Commitment – High Cost								
Mozambique	1990	67	75	140	1.9	21.3	13.3	2.8
Djibouti	1990	38	71		2.0	32.2	16.1	5.2
Cote d'Ivoire	1996	71	74	670	2.1	17.7	16.7	3.0
Tanzania	1985	75	97	160	2.1	14.6	19.4	2.8
Benin	1995	72	57	350	2.5	19.5	18.0	3.5
Lesotho	1994	99	114	670	2.6	14.2	18.7	2.7
Kenya	1990	95	97	260	3.2	14.0	24.2	3.4
Average		66	77	334	1.5	13.7	16.8	2.3
Francophone Average		62	71	368	1.3	14.0	16.4	2.3
Anglophone Average		83	93	360	1.7	11.3	15.9	1.8
SSA Average		83	83	777	1.9	13.6	17.0	

Notes: Low Commitment = public spending on primary < 1.9 per cent GNP.

xg = public spending on primary as a percentage of GNP.

cg = publicly funded costs per primary child as a percentage of GNP per capita.

a = percentage of population of primary school-going age.

Source: GNP per capita 1995, Atlas method World Development Indicators (2000). All other data UNESCO Statistical Yearbooks (1998, 1997, 1996, 1994).

calculation.[12] All SSA countries with the requisite data are included, and they amount to two-thirds (32) of the countries in the region. The years shown are the latest for which data are available for each country. It can be seen that they are mainly from the early-to-mid 1990s, although in four cases data from the mid-1980s are shown.

It will be recalled that, according to regional data, by the early 1990s SSA countries were allocating, on average, about 2.0 per cent of GNP to public expenditures on primary schooling. The (unweighted) average value for this variable (x_g), for the sub-set of countries and years shown in Tables 2.6 and 2.7, was 1.9 per cent, indicating that they are not atypical of the region as a whole. Considering, first, the low-GER group shown in Table 2.6, each of the first fifteen countries in the table were allocating, in the early to mid-1990s, substantially less public spending to the primary-school system than this SSA average (column 5). Thus, as a group, they can be considered to have been demonstrating only a low commitment to its provision.

It is not surprising to find that many of these 'low commitment' countries had extremely low primary enrolments, with nine of them having GERs less than 70 (column 2). Furthermore, many of them were also spending only modest sums per pupil (column 6). In seven of them this was equivalent to less than one-tenth of per capita income (compared to an unweighted average value of 13.6 per cent for SSA as a whole). Such low average per-pupil expenditures imply that, for the first 'low-commitment, low-cost' group of ten countries shown in Table 2.6, universal provision of schooling (as proxied by GERs of 100) would have been easily affordable. Column 8 of the table indicates the amount of public spending on primary schooling, expressed as a proportion of GNP, which would have been required so as to achieve GERs of 100 in each country (assuming the maintenance of the schooling costs and population sizes prevailing in the base year, and no demand constraints). It can be seen that the 'required' x_g value for UPE in this first group, under these assumptions, would in no case have exceeded 1.9 per cent of GNP – the amount that the SSA countries were then, on average, spending on primary schooling. Furthermore, in many cases the required financial allocation would have been considerably less than that: the governments of Eritrea, Madagascar, Ghana, Chad and Zambia needed to allocate little more than one per cent of GNP for universal provision to have been achieved.

Unit Costs

The above comparisons remind us that the level of primary enrolments attainable with a given aggregate expenditure, depends upon the costs per student at primary

---

[12]   The source used was the UNESCO Statistical Yearbook (various years). Earlier published estimates, in Colclough and Al-Samarrai (2000), were calculated from a mix of UNESCO and World Bank sources. This approach was less satisfactory, and accounts for differences, for some countries, between the earlier estimates and those shown in Tables 2.6 and 2.7, above.

level. The middle group of five countries shown in Table 2.6 would have been unable to reach GERs of 100, even if public spending had increased to its regional average value, because all of them had relatively high unit costs. These 'low commitment, high cost' countries mainly spent considerably more, per primary pupil, than the average across SSA. Although UPE was still financially practicable for them, a higher proportion of GNP would need to have been allocated for this purpose than the average for SSA. Burkina Faso, Mali and Ethiopia were particularly affected by high costs – if per-pupil expenditures were to have remained unchanged, between 2.7 and 3.4 per cent of GNP would have been needed to secure universal provision of primary schooling. Accordingly, for these countries, some combination of increased public spending on primary schooling and reduced unit costs would probably be necessary, if schooling for all were to be achieved in the near future.

A further group of low-GER countries, shown in Table 2.6, were spending more on primary schooling than the others, yet high costs of school provision remained a significant constraint. Enrolments in these seven 'moderate commitment, high cost' countries have not mainly been limited by an unwillingness to commit public resources to primary schooling: each of them was allocating 2-3 per cent of GNP for these purposes in the years shown. Rather, enrolment growth was constrained by their primary systems being relatively expensive, in comparison with their levels of economic development. In a majority of these countries – Kenya, Benin, Côte d'Ivoire and Djibouti – between three and five per cent of GNP would have been needed, in order to achieve universal provision of the system (column 8). Here, too, strategies to reduce unit costs would be critically important if affordable expansion were to be secured.

Table 2.7 shows the cost, expenditure and enrolment data for 10 countries which had already achieved GERs of at least 100. They each had school capacity sufficient to educate all the primary age-group, even though high rates of repetition meant that that goal, for many of them, still remained elusive. It can be seen that many of the richer SSA countries are included in this group. Their average 1995 GNP per capita, at $US1709, was more than five times that of the countries included in Table 2.6. Clearly, these countries could afford to spend much more on primary schooling, in absolute – and perhaps in relative – terms, than their poorer counterparts.

Nevertheless, it can be seen that the governments of two of the richest SSA countries – Mauritius and Botswana – in fact allocated expenditures of only between 1 and 1.5 per cent of GNP to primary schooling in the years shown. Their relative unit costs, being less than 10 per cent of per capita income, were also amongst the lowest in SSA in the years shown.[13]

---

[13]   We should note that the data for Botswana are for 1985. However, per capita income in that year (in 1995 prices) was still high, and, at around $US2000, higher than most of the 1995 values for other countries included in Table 2.7.

Achieving Schooling for All in Africa

Table 2.7 SSA countries with GERs greater than 100: public expenditures on primary schooling and related characteristics

	Year of data	GER	Female GER as % of male GER	GNP per capita 1995 (US$)	x_g	c_g	a
	(1)	(2)	(3)	(4)	(5)	(6)	(7)
Low Commitment – Low Cost							
Mauritius	1996	107	99	3420	1.1	9.7	10.3
Botswana	1985	105	111	3360	1.5	7.3	19.8
Moderate Commitment – Low Cost							
Togo	1996	119	74	310	2.0	9.6	17.2
Cape Verde	1985	117	95	1210	2.2	11.5	16.0
Swaziland	1996	129	95	1380	2.3	10.1	17.8
Malawi	1995	135	90	180	2.6	8.9	22.1
High Commitment – High Cost							
South Africa	1996	116	98	3740	3.2	16.4	16.6
Namibia	1995	133	102	2220	3.7	15.4	18.0
Congo	1995	114	92	640	3.7	19.3	16.8
Zimbabwe	1990	116	98	630	5.6	25.9	18.5
Average		119	95	1709	2.8	13.4	17.3
Francophone Average		117	83	475	2.9	14.5	17.0
Anglophone Average		118	99	2118	2.7	13.1	17.5
SSA Average		83	83	777	1.9	13.6	17.0

Notes: Low Commitment = public spending on primary < 1.9 per cent GNP.
x_g = public spending on primary as a percentage of GNP.
c_g = publicly funded costs per primary child as a percentage of GNP per capita
a = percentage of population of primary school-going age.
Source: GNP per capita 1995, Atlas method World Development Indicators (2000). All other data UNESCO Statistical Yearbooks (1998, 1997, 1996, 1994).

Thus, notwithstanding their relative wealth and their having achieved high GERs, these countries demonstrated a relatively low commitment to primary provision, both with respect to their economic strength, and in comparison with other states. The quality of primary schooling in both of these countries remained highly variable in the years shown, with schools in the poorer and rural areas being much less well resourced than those serving the richer communities.

The remaining eight countries with GERs greater than 100 have each allocated relatively high proportions of GNP to public expenditures on primary schooling. There is a middle group of four countries which achieved high GERs with the advantage of relatively low unit costs of provision. These comprise Togo, Cape Verde, Swaziland and, most notably, Malawi, a very low income country which moved rapidly to UPE during the 1990s following the introduction of fee-free schooling. The remaining four countries – South Africa, Namibia, Congo and Zimbabwe – achieved UPE despite having high unit costs. This is particularly so in Zimbabwe, where unit costs, relative to per capita income, were twice the regional average. There, the achievement of high enrolments required the annual allocation of 5.6 per cent of the country's GNP to public spending on primary schooling – almost three times the average for SSA.

Anglophone/Francophone Contrasts

Tables 2.6 and 2.7 show that the range of values across countries, for both public spending and relative unit costs, is large. For example, the proportion of GNP allocated to primary schooling by the Zimbabwe government was nine times as much as that spent by Eritrea. Equally, publicly-funded costs-per-pupil amounted to less than five per cent of per capita income in Zambia, whereas in Djibouti, they represented about one-third – almost seven times Zambia's relative unit costs. We have suggested that the variation of public spending on primary schooling provides some indication of the extent of public commitment to its provision. The large variation in unit costs across countries, however, is more problematic to interpret, and the question arises as to how they are determined.

In one sense, costs, too, are a matter of government choice. For example, they may rise by consequence of increasing the per capita resourcing of schools – by supplying better books, equipment and other materials, or by increasing the skills and quality of the teachers. On the other hand, costs may be high not so much through choice, but as a result of inappropriate teaching and salary structures which may prove difficult to influence.

One of the ways in which school costs in Africa appear to differ systematically can be illustrated by comparing Anglophone with Francophone countries. It is well known that Francophone countries have tended, in the past, to have high schooling costs, the cause of which has often been attributed to the salaries of teachers being higher than elsewhere. Eicher (1984), for example, reporting on a survey of 59 developing countries, found that the average salary of primary-school teachers in Francophone Africa was 1.8 times the average for other developing countries. The World Bank (1988, p.147) reported the mean ratio, around 1983, between primary teachers' salaries and per capita income as 8.8 in Francophone countries, compared with only 3.6 in Anglophone states. The same source indicated that public expenditures per primary student were, on average, 23 per cent of GNP per capita in Francophone, and only 12 per cent in Anglophone states (op.cit., p.141). Again the data were for 1983 (or close to it), but information reported for earlier years suggested that these ratios had been stable throughout the previous decade. Such sharp differences in teachers' salaries were one obvious source of the large differentials in unit costs between the two country groupings, and led to the teacher-cost problem being identified as an important cause of under-provision of schooling, and, thus, of under-enrolment, particularly in Francophone Africa.

The data in the penultimate two rows of Tables 2.6 and 2.7 allow more recent comparison of the average cost, expenditure and enrolment characteristics of Anglophone and Francophone country groups.[14] Amongst the countries with GERs less than 100 (Table 2.6), six Anglophone and thirteen Francophone states are included. It can be seen that the Anglophone countries typically have much higher primary enrolments. Their average GER (at 83) is 21 percentage points higher than that of the Francophone group, notwithstanding the fact that the 1995 average income per head of the two groups of countries was almost exactly equal.

The evidence in the later columns of the table indicates that unit cost differentials between Anglophone and Francophone countries have narrowed substantially. In the Francophone countries, public expenditures per primary student had fallen from 23 per cent of per capita income – reported by the World Bank for the early 1980s – to around 14 per cent ten years later. The Anglophone group, on the other hand, had remained roughly unchanged, at 11.3 per cent (column 6). Thus, whilst relative unit costs remained 24 per cent higher in Francophone than in Anglophone SSA, this was only around one quarter of the differential reported for the earlier period.

Nevertheless, even a cost differential of this magnitude can have a significant effect upon enrolment outcomes. We know that public spending on primary schooling has been higher in the Anglophone countries: column 5 of the table shows that their recurrent spending on primary schooling, as a proportion of GNP, was about 30 per cent more than in the Francophone group. With lower unit costs, and larger budgetary allocations, it is not surprising to discover the strong enrolment advantage being held by the Anglophone states. What, then, accounts for these cost differences?

Although non-salary expenditures are believed to have an important impact on the quality of schooling, African governments spend only small amounts on such provisioning. Books, materials, teacher aids, etc., typically account for less than one tenth, and often less than 5 per cent, of recurrent expenditures on primary

---

[14]   Tables 2.6 and 2.7 include 12 Anglophone and 15 Francophone states. The Anglophone group comprises Ghana, Zambia, Gambia, Tanzania, Lesotho, Kenya, Mauritius, Botswana, Swaziland, Malawi, South Africa and Zimbabwe. The Francophone group comprises Guinea, Madagascar, Chad, CAR, Senegal, Comoros, Mauritania, Burkina Faso, Mali, Burundi, Djibouti, Côte d'Ivoire, Benin, Togo and Congo. The countries of Eritrea, Ethiopia, Mozambique, Cape Verde and Namibia, which also appear in the tables, are excluded from both of these categories. The data shown are, in each case, unweighted means, calculated from the entries in the rest of the table.

schooling. Easily the greatest part of such expenditures is allocated to teachers' salaries. Hence the two major determinants of the unit costs of African primary schooling are the average salary of primary teachers, and the pupil-teacher ratio. Thus, examination of how these two elements vary will allow us to explain most of the observed variation in unit costs.

Table 2.8 provides this information, for 1992, for those countries with available data. The table confirms that, at that time, Francophone African countries still paid much higher teacher salaries (relative to GNP per capita), at both primary and secondary levels, than their Anglophone counterparts. The differential was particularly large for primary teachers, where average salaries in Francophone countries were 2.7 times their levels in the English-speaking nations.

Table 2.8 Teachers' salaries and pupil-teacher ratios in Francophone and Anglophone countries

	Pupil-teacher ratios		Average teachers salaries as a proportion of GNP per capita	
	1st Level	2nd Level	1st Level	2nd Level
Anglophone Africa				
Botswana	29	20	1.13	4.50
Gambia	30	29	1.16	2.79
Ghana	29	18	0.91	1.81
Malawi	68	27	3.95	14.40
Mauritius	21	21	1.31	2.36
Swaziland	33	18	1.42	2.88
Anglophone Average	**35**	**23**	**1.65**	**4.79**
Francophone Africa				
Burkina Faso	60	39	6.80	14.11
Burundi	63	25	4.95	14.73
Central African Republic	90	38	6.13	5.18
Chad	64	35	3.75	7.38
Comoros	39	24	2.96	9.64
Guinea	49	29	3.45	6.98
Mauritania	51	20	3.19	7.50
Morocco	28	15	2.96	7.14
Rwanda	58	14	7.49	5.99
Senegal	59	23	7.48	6.80
Seychelles	18	13	0.94	4.00
Togo	53	43	3.66	12.63
Francophone Average	**53**	**27**	**4.48**	**8.51**

Source: UNESCO (1995b).

These potentially enormous cost-differences were reduced, to some extent, by pupil-teacher ratios at primary level being 51 per cent higher in the Francophone countries. It will be recalled that their primary systems had considerably lower coverage than those in Anglophone SSA. But even so, the high salary costs could only be met by the Francophone nations tolerating pupil-teacher ratios, at primary level, which were much higher than is compatible with effective student learning.

These data confirm, therefore, that teachers' salary costs have remained the most important source of unit cost differences between Francophone and Anglophone African countries.[15] The differential has been much reduced, over the past two decades, as salaries in the former countries have fallen particularly sharply. Moreover, unit cost differentials are lower than those of average-salary/per-capita-GNP ratios, owing to the compensating effects of the excessively large numbers of pupils per teacher which exist in the Francophone systems. Nevertheless they pose a significant constraint to the achievement of schooling for all.

This is demonstrated by Table 2.6, which shows that, to achieve GERs of 100, the low-GER Francophone-African countries would have needed to allocate 2.3 per cent of GNP to public expenditures on primary schooling (column 8). This was some 28 per cent more than the Anglophone countries, where only 1.8 per cent of GNP was required. Comparing these estimates with the budgetary allocations actually made (column 5) shows that Francophone governments would have had to increase their expenditures by 77 per cent, whereas only an additional 6 per cent would have been required in the Anglophone countries. The cost, expenditure and enrolment challenges in Francophone Africa are, therefore, considerably greater than in the Anglophone group.

The practical importance of making a strong public expenditure commitment is further demonstrated by comparing the high and low-GER cases. All of the Francophone and Anglophone countries shown in Table 2.7 had achieved GERs greater than 100. Unit costs remained highest in the former countries, and were similar in magnitude to those in the low-GER cases. There was a major difference, however, in the extent of public spending on primary schooling. In this case the Francophone high-GER group allocated a higher, rather than a lower, proportion of GNP to public expenditures on primary schooling than the Anglophone high-GER group. Furthermore, the governments in both language groups spent considerably more – close to three per cent of GNP – on their primary systems than their counterparts in the low GER countries. The increase was particularly marked in the case of the Francophone allocations, which were more than twice as great as in their low-GER counterparts, compared with a 50 per cent difference for the two Anglophone groups.

---

[15]   Mingat (1998) produces similar results, using different data.

Population Size

We have, so far, been silent about the fact that, amongst countries at given levels of income and of unit costs of schooling, those with higher rates of population growth (and, thus, proportionately larger school-age populations) face greater costs of achieving schooling for all.   In the case of the Francophone/Anglophone comparisons, such differences were not important, since the proportion of the population of primary-school age differed by only about three per cent, as between the two country groups (see Tables 2.6 and 2.7, columns 7).   However, more generally, demographic variation between countries can make an enormous difference to the cost-burden of achieving universal enrolment.

For example, in the developed market economies, with zero, or even negative rates of population growth, children aged 6-11 years typically comprise 5-8 per cent of the population as a whole.   In Africa, by contrast, the school-age group is a much larger segment of the population.   The data in Tables 2.6 and 2.7 indicate that the range, in the SSA countries shown, is from 14 per cent in the Gambia to 20 per cent and more in Tanzania, Rwanda, Zambia and Kenya.[16] The figures imply that the costs of achieving a given GER in Kenya would be more than 70 per cent higher than in the Gambia, and about three times as high as in typical developed countries, assuming all other cost parameters were the same. This underlines the importance of population policy as a means of achieving and maintaining schooling for all. It is easy to forget that the cost-impact of reductions in fertility can, over the medium term, have a more powerful impact upon providing all children with access to schools, than many of the direct measures of educational reform.

Expenditures by Households

Data on private education expenditures in Africa are not systematically collected by governments, so evidence as to their magnitude is rather patchy. Since almost all children attending school incur at least some associated private costs – for books, uniforms, transport and other items – it is likely that, were these summed, the magnitude of private expenditures would turn out to be considerable.   In addition, the opportunity costs of children's time are significant for poorer households – indeed, for older pupils, they can often exceed other costs by a considerable margin. On the other hand, it is not clear how the balance of these direct and indirect costs have been changing in recent years.

Some countries charge fees for school attendance, even at primary level, which were often introduced, during the 1980s, in response to economic adversity. However, the enrolment declines that frequently followed, forced governments to

---

[16]   These differences are also influenced by the length of primary schooling, which is eight years in Kenya, seven years in Tanzania, Zambia and Rwanda and six years in the Gambia. Thus, roughly half of the difference in eligible population size as between the Gambia and Kenya is attributable to the longer duration of primary schooling in Kenya.

reassess the rationale for cost-recovery policies (Colclough, 1997, ch.1). They had initially been advocated as a form of hypothecated taxation, which held out the possibility of raising revenues with which to finance school expansion. Cost-recovery policies aim to substitute private for public expenditures.[17] Such policies are obviously regressive for poorer households, and experience has shown that demand elasticities are high for these groups. In cases where demand for primary schooling was already under threat from declining school quality and low household incomes, cost recovery policies were shown to be inimical to the goals of SFA, and the demand for schooling fell. As a result, there has been a recent trend to switch back to fee-free primary schooling, which has often delivered large enrolment increases – as in Malawi and Uganda, where such policies have been part of national campaigns to achieve universal primary education.[18]

Enrolments in private schools are reported by some observers to have been growing rapidly in Africa (Heyneman, 1999). However, UNESCO data suggest that, at primary level, there was little change over the decade 1985-95: private enrolments increased from an average of 10 to only 11 per cent of total primary enrolments in the 23 SSA countries having data for that period (UNESCO, 1998a, Table 2.10). There were some large increases in the Congo, Madagascar and Malawi, but these were compensated by strong falls in Cameroon, Gabon and Ghana. Elsewhere, the general picture was one of small increases in the proportion of private enrolments, by one or two percentage points.

This result is consistent with what has been happening in the public education sector. As indicated earlier, enrolments have been stagnant in SSA, relative to the age group, and falls in enrolment ratios have been common. This was associated not only with real reductions in public spending per pupil, but also with much reduced household incomes, which have made the direct and indirect costs of school attendance more difficult to meet – particularly amongst the poorest households. Under circumstances of downward demand pressures on public school enrolments, it is unlikely that the relatively more expensive private sector would be facing the opposite pressures. That may have been happening where richer families have found the services offered by increasingly under-resourced public schools to be unsatisfactory, and where the private sector offers better, if more expensive alternatives. But this is likely to have been so for only a minority of households.

---

[17]   In terms of the identity equation given earlier, cost-recovery implies attempts, on the part of government, to reduce the value of c_g and to secure an equivalent increase in the value of c_p.

[18]   Malawi was, in fact, one of the first countries to raise fees at primary level, with encouragement from the World Bank, as part of an explicit strategy to enhance revenues for the further expansion of primary schooling (see Thobani, 1984). The impact of fees was, however, to constrain enrolments, as witnessed by the fact that the primary GER, having remained roughly constant throughout the 1980s, doubled within 18 months of fee-free schooling being introduced, by the new government, in 1994. This is discussed further in Chapter 5, below.

It seems likely then, that both public and private expenditures upon schooling in Africa have been falling in real terms in recent years. Efforts by beleaguered governments to pass some of the costs of schooling on to households have not, generally, been successful. The poor majority in SSA has been unwilling or unable to pay more for the schooling of their children, and demand has fallen in response to changes in their incomes and in schooling costs. A critical aspect of these demand changes concerns the question of gender.

Gender and Household Demand for Schooling

We have seen that, internationally, the enrolment gap between the sexes is narrowing: the female/male enrolment ratio increased by about seven percentage points in South Asia and in the Arab States over the period 1980-1995, and, in SSA, by about five points – from 78 to 83 per cent – over those years. Do these international trends suggest, as some have argued, that gender inequalities are disappearing, and that we can expect the normal process of development to deliver gender equity in schooling? Unfortunately, even when confining our attention to the macro level, there are reasons to be sceptical about this suggestion.

First, the rate at which the gender gaps are closing is slow. In SSA, for example, if the rate at which the female/male enrolment ratio narrowed over the 14 years 1980-1994 were maintained, it would take fully 42 years for it to reach unity, the value at which equal enrolments between the sexes would be achieved. In the cases of South Asia and the Arab States, the interval would be 24 years in each case. These time periods are much greater than those adopted by national governments in these regions, as target dates for the achievement of schooling for all.[19]

Second, we should recall that the overall enrolment situation in SSA actually deteriorated over 1980-1995, and that the improvement of the female/male enrolment ratio since 1980 has been caused, in almost half of the countries concerned, by male enrolment ratios falling more quickly than those of females.[20] Just as boys are often first to be enrolled in schools, so they are often withdrawn

---

[19]   The most recently reaffirmed goals are those for the attainment of universal primary education by 2015 and for gender equality in primary school enrolment and completion by 2005. The former was adopted by the World Summit for Social Development in 1995 (UN, 1995a) and the latter by the Fourth World Conference on Women (UN, 1995b). These targets continue to reflect the stated goals for educational development of UNICEF, UNDP, UNESCO and the World Bank. They are advocated by the Development Assistance Committee of the OECD (OECD, 1996), and by the policy papers of a number of its members, including DFID, the Netherlands and Sweden. More generally, they were re-confirmed in the 'Framework for Action' agreed at the Dakar World Education Forum, in 2000, and represent two of the eight 'Millennium Development Goals' which have become the focus for aid efforts by the international community.

[20]   The average male gross enrolment ratio (GER) for countries in Sub-Saharan Africa fell by about 6 percentage points over the decade 1980-90, whilst girls' enrolment ratios were hardly changed (Table 2.2).

first, when economic adversity sets in, and as more cash incomes are needed to supplement those of adults.[21]   It cannot be assumed, therefore, that further improvements in the gender gap will follow as total enrolments begin to rise. The first response may well be a growth mainly of male enrolments, causing the gender gap again to deteriorate. As shown later in this book, this has been happening in Guinea, Ethiopia and a number of other African countries.[22]

Third, if under-enrolment in the least-schooled countries is particularly concentrated amongst girls, some of its causes may be gender-specific, and policies which do not recognize this may not succeed. The relationship between the total GER and the ratio of the female and male primary enrolment ratios (henceforth F/M ratio) is shown in Figure 2.2. The axes cross at the point where the GER is equal to 100 per cent and where there is no gender gap in enrolments (i.e. where the male and female GERs are the same). Countries in the left half of the graph have GERs of less than 100. Those in the lower left quadrant have gender gaps that favour boys, whilst those in the top left quadrant have gender gaps favouring girls. It is clear that most countries with GERs of less than 100 per cent appear in the lower quadrant and have considerably more boys enrolled in school than girls. Nepal is one of the more extreme cases, having a primary GER of 82 per cent and yet a F/M ratio of only 50 per cent. If the populations of school-age boys and girls were equal, this would imply that for every ten boys in school there were only five girls. Although this difference is exceptional, in about one quarter of the countries shown, the F/M ratio is less than 80 per cent. Most of these are countries with low GERs.

In general, as GERs rise, so too will both male and female enrolment ratios, and the gender gaps will decline.   This is because, even with extreme discrimination against girls, the minimum possible value for the female GER becomes non-zero for values of GER greater than 50 (assuming no over-age enrolment), and rises with GER thereafter. But, as Figure 2.2 shows, the actual relationship across countries is loose.   Whilst the extent of gender bias in enrolments does reduce as GERs rise, it can be seen that even amongst countries where GERs are close to 100, there is great variation in the gender gap. Togo, for example has 40 per cent fewer girls enrolled than boys, whereas Lesotho has about 20 per cent more girls than boys, notwithstanding that the GERs for both of these countries well exceeds 100 in each case. The reason for this is that enrolments outside the 'official' age range permit continued gender inequalities. We can conclude, then, that gender discrimination in school enrolments is greatest where overall enrolments are low, but that it may not completely disappear even as GERs approach 100.

---

[21]   Rose (1995) shows that the sharper fall in male, relative to female, enrolments was particularly concentrated in adjusting countries, where both real incomes and public expenditures were in decline.

[22]   This is also suggested by data collected for the World Education Forum in Dakar. For a sample of SSA countries, the net female/male enrolment ratio deteriorated further in favour of boys over the years 1990-98. See UNESCO (2000a, p.34, Table 3.2).

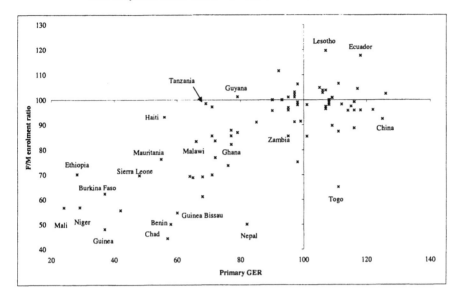

Figure 2.2 Scatter plot of the female/male enrolment ratio against the total gross enrolment ratio

Similar conclusions can be drawn about the influence of income differences on enrolments. The scatter plot of primary GERs vs. GNP per capita (Figure 2.3) shows that, whilst enrolment ratios rise with income, there is considerable variability around the line. Hence the ability of per capita income to predict levels of GER is quite limited ($r^2 = 0.29$). This is particularly true for countries in the $US300–$US500 per capita income range, where most SSA countries are grouped. Niger and Rwanda, for example, at similar levels of per capita income in 1990, had primary GERs of 29 and 71, respectively. Thus, the level of per capita income is only one of many factors which influence the ability of both states and households to send children to school.

As Figure 2.4 demonstrates, national income per capita appears to have even less influence upon the gendered inequality of enrolments than it does upon their absolute levels. Most African countries have F/M ratios of between 50 and 100, in a distribution which appears unrelated to the incomes of the countries concerned. Thus, in terms of the framework set out in Chapter 1, the relative poverty of states seems to be only loosely associated with levels of primary enrolments, and hardly at all with the extent of gender inequality within them. The bivariate relationships are weak and, as will be demonstrated in the next chapter, there are other important influences on enrolment outcomes and their gendered characteristics.

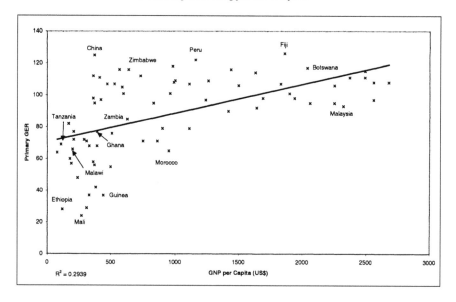

Figure 2.3   Scatter plot of primary gross enrolment ratio against GNP per capita: low and middle income countries

Finally, it should be recognised that even if equal female and male enrolment ratios, where GER = 100, were achieved, this would not necessarily mean that the balance of disadvantage against the schooling of girls at primary level would be removed. A problem hitherto obvious in only quantitative terms may now be detected as a qualitative problem – or one that is perhaps more easily identified by analysing female/male progress at secondary or tertiary levels. Even if all children attend primary school, examination success for girls may be less, and continuation rates to secondary or higher levels may be lower than is the case for boys. Thus it is ironic that the achievement of equal male and female enrolment ratios at, say, an overall GER of 80, is likely to indicate a higher level of gender equality in schooling than where it is achieved at a GER of 100.

This is because for the former, but not for the latter, to occur, there is *prima facie* evidence that at least one aspect of discriminatory practice has been assuaged.[23] By the same token, where discriminatory forces are entrenched, we

---

[23]   An example of such a case is Tanzania, where male and female enrolments remained closely similar, even during many years of economic adversity and enrolment decline. The equal importance of schooling for girls and boys has been a strong theme of the ruling party since the 1970s, and is well espoused by both rural and urban society. Not all discriminatory practices have been removed – but the country is closer to this goal than most in Africa (see Peasgood *et al.*, 1997).

cannot assume they have disappeared merely because universal enrolment has been achieved. The latter is too blunt a criterion to be able to reveal what is happening.

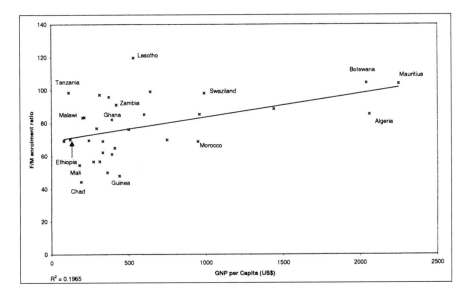

Figure 2.4   The relationship between GNP per capita and the ratio of female/male GER, Africa

Conclusions

Taken together, the governments of SSA substantially increased their allocation of GNP to primary schooling over the 1980-1995 period. They spent proportionately more, over those years, than the governments of any other world region. However, the value of these resources was affected strongly by Africa's economic decline: although relative expenditures increased, their absolute value fell very sharply. This is undoubtedly an important part of the explanation for the declining primary enrolment ratios which have characterised much of the last two decades, and which have confirmed SSA's status as the most undereducated of the world's major regions.

Moreover, this high relative commitment to spending on primary schooling was not shared universally within the region. Many of the low-GER countries in SSA allocated much less to public spending on their primary systems, during the 1990s, than was both possible and desirable. In about half of the low-GER countries for which we have data, universal enrolment could have been achieved with a level of public spending on primary schooling no higher than the 1995 expenditure/GNP average for SSA as a whole. Thus, the variance of the public effort was wide, and the countries in the tail of the distribution have exhibited low commitment to the objectives which they espoused at Jomtien in 1990, and reaffirmed subsequently.

In the remaining low-GER countries costs were an important constraint to wider schooling provision. Five of them spent insufficiently on their primary systems, and, like the first group, demonstrated low commitment to achieving schooling for all. Nevertheless, even if their spending had been adequate, high unit costs would have severely hampered their progress. In a further seven countries, commitment was moderately good, but high costs were the critical constraint. A willingness to allocate greater priority to primary schooling was necessary in the former countries, but both groups were cost and resource constrained. Reforms to tackle both these problems will be a necessary precursor of successful expansion strategies.

High unit costs are a particular problem in the Francophone countries of Africa. Although costs have fallen substantially in recent years, they remain significantly above those in Anglophone states. With no change in the present cost structure, the Francophone governments would almost have had to double their expenditures on primary schooling to achieve universal provision, whereas the Anglophone group required less than a 10 per cent expenditure increase. We have shown that high teachers' salaries remain the main source of the cost differential between Francophone and Anglophone countries, the effects of which are only partly countered by pupil-teacher ratios being much higher – often to the detriment of school quality – in the former group. The Anglophone countries allocate a larger proportion of their national incomes to primary expenditures, which, together with their lower unit costs, ensures that primary enrolments exceed those in the Francophone states by a considerable margin.

In most SSA countries the difficulty of achieving universal schooling is increased by high rates of population growth. Within Africa, the difference in the cost-burden from this source alone is more than 30 per cent, and, in comparison with more developed countries, Africa's task is two-to-three times as great.

Efforts by governments to pass on schooling costs to households have not, by and large, been successful. Poor households have been unwilling or unable to pay more for the schooling of their children, and demand has fallen in many countries. A related phenomenon is that most countries still face significant gender gaps in school enrolments. For SSA as a whole, the proportion of girls enrolled, relative to boys, had improved somewhat by the mid-1990s, to around the developing country average. However, there are two major concerns about this apparent progress. First, the improvement was secured not via growth, but by girls' enrolments declining less quickly than those of boys. Second, there are reasons to believe that the gender gap will widen again, when more 'normal' conditions for enrolment growth return. Just as boys are first to be withdrawn in conditions of economic adversity, so they may be first to be enrolled when prosperity returns.

Gender gaps can be reduced effectively and quickly, as some African States have shown, and the extent of gender inequality in primary schooling varies substantially amongst African countries at similar levels of per capita income. Its reduction is not simply contingent upon income growth. Other variables have an important influence, some of which are explored in the next, and subsequent, chapters.

Chapter 3

The Gender Gap in Primary Enrolments: A Cross-Country Analysis

Introduction

This chapter presents the results of a cross-country empirical analysis of the correlates of low and high female enrolment ratios at primary level, in comparison with those of males. The aim is to explore some of the causes of low primary enrolments in general, and of low female enrolments in particular, on the basis of international statistical comparisons. The chapter also draws lessons from the large country-level empirical literature which explores the determinants of household demand for primary schooling.

There have been few earlier analyses of the determinants of primary-school enrolments across countries. However, Schultz (1985 and 1995c) examined the effects of per capita income, educational costs and population growth on enrolments and school expenditure patterns across a range of countries. Similar empirical work has been conducted for American States (McMahon, 1970) and across countries (McMahon, 1999). These authors used simple demand and supply models to analyse the determinants of school enrolments. Log-linear demand functions are specified and equated with production functions representing the supply-side. The work reported in this chapter follows a similar methodology, although a formal model is not presented. It enhances earlier results in two particular ways: first, it uses a richer set of variables to explore the demand for primary education, and second it sheds further light on differences in the determinants of school enrolments for boys and girls.

Four dependent variables are used in our analysis. These are the primary gross enrolment ratio, the female primary gross enrolment ratio, the male primary gross enrolment ratio and the ratio between the female and male primary gross enrolment ratios (the relative gender gap). Each of these dependent variables are regressed on a set of demand and supply side factors suggested by the framework presented in the first chapter. The next section explains the proxies used in these analyses.

Determinants of School Enrolments

Supply Side

The supply of schooling is determined by the availability of teachers and other
staff, and of material inputs, including buildings, books and equipment. The
number of school places is given, in practice, by the particular ways in which these
inputs are combined, and by their costs, to employers, and/or to the State. There is
a range of variables which affect the ability to finance and provide schooling.
Costs are strongly influenced by the size of the school-age population relative to
the total population, and by the pupil-teacher ratio, both of which are open to
policy influence, and which are included as variables in our analysis. Direct
information on average teacher wages is lacking, but we include, as a proxy,
reported public recurrent expenditure on primary education per pupil, expressed as
a proportion of GNP per capita (unit costs being largely determined by the
interaction of average teacher salaries and the pupil-teacher ratio as discussed in
Chapter 2). Accordingly, the expected signs on these variables are, with respect to
the enrolment ratios, positive for the pupil-teacher ratio, and negative for both the
population of primary-school age and for relative unit costs. These variables are
not expected to influence the gender gap from the supply side in any consistent
way, although they may have gendered effects upon the pattern of demand.

Demand Side

The demand for schooling is influenced by incomes, costs and by a range of other
socio-cultural conditions which may have a differential impact for boys and girls.
As regards incomes, where these are low, the direct and indirect costs of schooling
can be difficult to meet for many households. Equally, poorer nations find the
budgetary costs of universal primary provision to be a greater burden than richer
States (Colclough with Lewin, 1993, Chapter 2). In the last chapter it was shown
that the simple relationship between per capita income and the primary GER is
only weakly positive across countries (see Figure 2.3, Chapter 2), which implies
that the level of per capita income is by no means the only factor affecting the
ability of both States and households to send children to school. Nevertheless, its
importance may change, when other factors are allowed for, and income per capita
is, therefore, included as a proxy for household incomes. To the extent that the
level of national income affects the ability of States to provide schooling, the
variable may also capture some supply-side effects (although it is a somewhat
blunt measure, for these purposes, in the absence of information about the
distribution of incomes and about the size of government). Since both the demand
and the supply of primary schooling appear likely to increase with income, the
expected signs for this variable are positive with respect to both total and gender-
disaggregated primary school enrolment.

The direct costs of schooling can be significant for families, even where fees
are not charged by schools. They often include the costs of providing school
uniforms and equipment, such as texts or exercise books and writing materials, and

the costs (in time or money) of getting children to school. Data on these items are not available on a cross-country basis. However, as proxies for transport costs we include estimates of national population density, and of the proportion of the population living in urban areas. Our hypothesis is that transport costs are likely to be an inverse function of both of these variables since, for a given number of schools and teachers, average commuting distances for pupils will be less, the closer together people live.

The division of labour between men and women in society provides a context for economic life which can be resilient to market pressures. The nature and strength of this division of labour varies internationally, but it is present to some degree in every society. In many countries, there remain substantial differences in the wages and salaries earned by men and women with equal human capital characteristics and work time-inputs. Typically, these stem from what might be termed 'gendered job-reservation', whereby some low (or high) – paying jobs are traditionally perceived to be a female (or male) preserve, or from other forms of gender discrimination in the labour market. If such role differences are prominent, they may result in the returns to investments in human capital for girls lagging behind those of boys, which is likely to affect schooling decisions, particularly in poor communities.

Outcomes in the labour market are also influenced by the division of labour within the household. For example, where the responsibility for reproductive tasks falls predominantly on female members, the requirements of parents for help with household tasks will involve very different burdens for girls and boys, and different opportunity costs will be associated with their attending school. Equally, where the allegiance and responsibilities to parents differs sharply for boys and girls after marriage, the perceived benefits to parents of educating their sons and daughters are also likely to differ. Further, where marriage occurs earlier for girls, and where formal economic activity is much lower for women than for men, the returns to schooling will be lower, and the direct incentives to attend school will be less for girls than for boys. In these, and other, ways, the gender division of labour leads to different sets of costs and returns being associated with the education of girls and boys, which, in turn, lead to gendered patterns of enrolment and school performance.

It is difficult to find cross-country proxies which can be used to measure the influence of the gender division of labour on enrolment. We include in our regressions the average age of first marriage. Early marriage, which occurs in more traditional societies, is likely to indicate low participation in the formal economy, and low wage returns to schooling for women. In addition, we include the proportion of primary-school teachers that are female, as a proxy both for female participation in the labour force, and for a variety of other factors that influence enrolment more directly. For example, traditional attitudes towards female seclusion/privacy, and fears about the physical and sexual safety of girls may tend to be allayed when more teachers are female, and girls' schooling is often believed by parents to be less effective where the classroom culture is heavily male-dominated.

As indicated above, the gendered division of labour within households is likely to lead to differences in the opportunity costs of school attendance for boys and girls. However, the measurement of such differences across countries is difficult, since no direct measures are published internationally. We include as a proxy for opportunity costs the proportion of value added in agriculture.[1] It is well known that economic development is associated with a change in economic structure, away from a dependence upon agricultural production towards a more diversified set of activities. This is also associated with changed labour patterns at the household level where, particularly for women, the incidence of agricultural work declines, in favour, initially, of work in the home, and subsequently of employment in other, more highly remunerated activities. It follows that we might expect a negative relationship between the proportion of value added contributed by agriculture and enrolment, particularly of girls, as household labour demands on girls decrease.

Some cultures require the privacy or seclusion of girls; in others there are cultural biases which directly affect the roles which are judged appropriate for women to play in society. These traditions reduce the participation of women in the economy outside the home, and lead to female education being assigned a lower value than that of males. One of the proxies for the role of women in society, which, in earlier work, had proved to be a useful determining variable for the gender composition of school enrolments, is religion, measured as the proportion of the population being attributed to the Hindu or Islamic faiths. The relationships between this variable and both the primary GER and the proportion of girls enrolled at primary level were negative and significant, in a multivariate context (Colclough with Lewin, 1993, pp.67-70).

A further important set of questions concerns the ways in which school-related variables may also influence both male and female enrolment outcomes. If improvements in school conditions are associated with an improvement in learning, such changes could – at least in principle – influence the returns to schooling and the perceptions of their magnitude on the part of parents. Two school-related proxies are included in our regressions to capture the impact of quality on the demand for education. The pupil-teacher ratio is included on the demand side because parents may associate large pupil-teacher ratios with low school quality, and lower returns to schooling, bringing negative enrolment implications, particularly for girls. A second potentially important variable is the rate of repetition. This appears to be quite strong and negatively associated with the female primary gross enrolment ratio. This suggests that parents may be prepared to bear the costs of repetition for boys more than for girls, and that in inefficient systems, boys survive to the higher levels of the school system more frequently than the girls.

In summary, the demand for schooling is determined by both economic and socio-cultural conditions. Four sets of factors would appear to be important: the income and other characteristics of households; the direct costs to households of

---

[1]   Many different proxies for opportunity costs were tried, including the child economic activity rate. However, none of them were fully satisfactory.

sending children to school; the opportunity costs of so doing; and a set of other contextual factors including both cultural and in-school circumstances. Some of these factors are expected to have different effects upon the demand for the schooling of boys and girls.

Empirical Analysis

Our approach is to estimate a reduced-form equation as follows:

$$\ln X = \alpha + \beta Z_d + \gamma Z_s \qquad (1)$$

where X is the enrolment ratio, Z_d is a matrix of demand factors and Z_s is a matrix of supply factors. Equation (1) is estimated in log-linear form, using the demand and supply-side proxy variables identified above. Data for these proxy variables have been assembled for 56 low and middle income countries.[2] The data series of the World Bank and other UN agencies have provided the main sources, with more specialised publications providing information on some of the variables. Table 3.1 shows the regional distribution of the countries included. All countries where all the required data were available are included in our analysis. Table 3.2 reports definitions, sources and some descriptive statistics for the proxy variables used. The first four variables in the table – the male, female and combined enrolment ratios, and the gender gap in enrolments – are used as the dependent variables in the regression analysis.

Table 3.1 Number of countries included, by region

Region	No.
Europe	5
Oceania	2
Sub-Saharan Africa	21
Asia	7
Arab States	7
Latin America and the Caribbean	14
Total	56

---

[2] Low and middle income countries are defined as those countries having a per capita GNP less than $US3,000 in 1990 (measured in purchasing-power-parity terms).

Table 3.2 List of variables used in the analysis

Variable	Definition and Source	Mean	Std. Dev	Min	Max
GER	Primary gross enrolment ratio. UNESCO Statistical Yearbook 1993	4.44 (89.8)	0.38 (25.6)	3.18 (24.0)	4.84 (126.0)
Female GER	Primary female gross enrolment ratio. UNESCO Statistical Yearbook 1993	4.36 (85.2)	0.48 (29.0)	2.83 (17.0)	4.84 (127.0)
Male GER	Primary male gross enrolment ratio UNESCO Statistical Yearbook 1993	4.50 (94.2)	0.32 (23.9)	3.40 (30.0)	4.90 (134.0)
Gender Gap (Female GER/ Male GER)	Female GER divided by Male GER expressed as a percentage	4.46 (88.8)	0.22 (17.4)	3.79 (44.3)	4.78 (119.6)
Urban	Urban population as a percentage of total population Human Development Report 1992 (UNDP)	3.57 (41.2)	0.62 (19.5)	1.79 (6.0)	4.51 (91.0)
GNP per capita	GNP per capita in 1990 US$ World Bank 1994a, World Tables	6.60 (1028.4)	0.88 (783.7)	4.70 (110.0)	7.93 (2780.0)
Age at marriage	Average female age at first marriage 1980-1990 Human Development Report 1994 and 1995 (UNDP)	3.03 (20.8)	0.13 (2.8)	2.76 (15.8)	3.39 (29.7)
Religion[1]	Muslim and Hindu population as a percentage of total population R.V. Weekes 1978 and Economist 1990	2.16 (29.8)	1.77 (38.6)	0.00 (0.0)	4.60 (98.0)

Table 3.2 (Cont'd) List of variables used in the analysis

Variable	Definition and Source	Mean	Std. Dev	Min	Max
Female Teachers	Primary female teachers as a percentage of total teachers. UNESCO Statistical yearbook 1993	3.82 (52.1)	0.58 (23.6)	1.79 (6.0)	4.55 (95.0)
Repetition	Primary school repeaters as a proportion of total primary enrolment. UNESCO Statistical yearbook 1993	2.26 (11.6)	0.80 (9.0)	0.00 (0.0)	3.61 (36.0)
School-age population	Primary school age population as a percentage of total population 1990. STARS World Bank Database	2.76 (16.1)	0.22 (3.7)	2.16 (8.6)	3.41 (30.3)
Pupil-teacher ratio	Primary pupil teacher ratio. UNESCO Statistical yearbook 1993	3.50 (36.1)	0.41 (15.4)	2.48 (12.0)	4.50 (90.0)
Unit cost	Public current expenditure per primary and pre-primary student as a proportion of GNP per capita 1990. UNESCO World Education Report 1993	2.36 (12.4)	0.57 (8.1)	0.92 (2.5)	3.83 (46.1)
Population density	Population density per thousand hectares 1990. Human Development Report 1992	6.07 (942.8)	1.33 (1454.4)	3.00 (20.0)	9.06 (8632.0)
Agricultural value added	Agricultural value added as a percentage of GDP 1990. STARS World Bank Database	2.99 (23.5)	0.61 (12.7)	1.62 (5.0)	3.95 (51.9)
Africa	Dummy variable. Equals 1 if country is African, 0 otherwise	0.46	0.50	0	1

Notes:
* Statistics for each variable in their non logged form are reported in brackets.
[1] To avoid logging zero values one unit is added to each observation and then the variable is logged (i.e. ln(x+1)). Statistics in brackets are for the original variable.

The results of the regression analyses are summarised in Table 3.3[3] and discussed in what follows. The regression analysis allows us to examine the effect of a single explanatory variable on the enrolment rate whilst controlling for (i.e. keeping constant) all of the other explanatory variables. Scatter plots of the regression results are also presented in this section so as to provide a more visual representation of the results.

Supply Side

It will be recalled that the costs of providing schooling are strongly influenced by the size of the school-age population relative to the total population, and by the pupil-teacher ratio. As regards the former, it can be seen from Table 3.2 that the range of values for the size of the school-age population is very large – ranging from around nine per cent of the population (in China) to more than 30 per cent (in Jordan). Since the size of the school age population relative to the total population is negatively related to per capita income (Appendix Table 3A.1) this means that the cost burden of achieving universal enrolment in poor countries is often two or three times greater (relative to per capita income) than in richer ones. Surprisingly, however, school enrolments appear not to be related particularly strongly to the size of the school-age population, after the effects of per capita income (and other variables) are allowed for: the results in Table 3.3 show that a 10 per cent increase in the school-age population as a proportion of the total population is associated with falls in the male GER of less than two per cent, and in the female GER of only around one-tenth of one per cent, neither of which results achieve statistical significance.

For countries at similar levels of per capita income, where the school-age population relative to the total population is higher, it follows that output per worker would also be higher. It may be, then, that these results reflect there being stronger past and present educational policies in countries with higher levels of labour productivity, which could more than compensate for the burden imposed by a proportionately larger school age group. In the countries in the present sample, girls have been advantaged, as a result of these policies, more than boys – as indicated by the positive relationship between the gender gap and the school-age population shown in Table 3.3.[4]

Values for the pupil-teacher ratio also vary markedly – from under 20 in some of the developed market economies to over 60 in parts of Africa and Asia – as indicated by the range for those countries included in our sample (Table 3.2).

---

[3]   The reported standard errors are corrected for heteroscedasticity. The use of the log of the gender gap, in the final regression, implies that the coefficients in this regression are the difference between the male and female regression coefficients. Significance in this regression implies that the male and female coefficients are significantly different from each other, in a statistical sense.

[4]   The result here is similar to that in Schultz (1995c) for his within-country estimates. The between-country estimates show a positive and statistically significant effect of the size of the school-age population on the enrolment rate.

Table 3.3 Regression results

Variable	Model 1 GER	Model 2 Female GER	Model 3 Male GER	Model 4 Gender Gap
Urban	0.15*	0.17*	0.14*	0.04
	(0.09)	*(0.10)*	*(0.08)*	*(0.04)*
GNP per capita	0.11*	0.12	0.11*	0.004
	(0.07)	*(0.08)*	*(0.06)*	*(0.03)*
Religion	0.02	0.02	0.02	0.004
	(0.02)	*(0.03)*	*(0.02)*	*(0.01)*
Female age at marriage	1.56***	1.73***	1.48***	0.25
	(0.50)	*(0.62)*	*(0.41)*	*(0.26)*
Female teachers	-0.003	0.14	-0.11	0.26***
	(0.11)	*(0.13)*	*(0.10)*	*(0.06)*
Repetition	-0.08	-0.11*	-0.05	-0.06***
	(0.06)	*(0.07)*	*(0.06)*	*(0.02)*
School age population	-0.12	-0.06	-0.16	0.09
	(0.13)	*(0.15)*	*(0.12)*	*(0.06)*
Pupil teacher ratio	0.29**	0.36**	0.26**	0.10
	(0.13)	*(0.16)*	*(0.12)*	*(0.07)*
Unit cost	-0.22***	-0.23***	-0.22***	-0.01
	(0.07)	*(0.08)*	*(0.07)*	*(0.03)*
Population density	0.03	0.05*	0.02	0.03*
	(0.03)	*(0.03)*	*(0.02)*	*(0.01)*
Africa	-0.09	-0.09	-0.09	0.00
	(0.08)	*(0.09)*	*(0.08)*	*(0.04)*
Agricultural value added	0.09	0.09	0.10	-0.01
	(0.10)	*(0.12)*	*(0.09)*	*(0.04)*
Constant	-2.01	-3.69*	-1.08	1.99**
	(1.76)	*(2.19)*	*(1.50)*	*(0.99)*
R squared	0.73	0.76	0.69	0.80

Notes: * significant at the ten per cent level.
         ** significant at the five per cent level.
         *** significant at the one per cent level.
         Standard errors reported below each coefficient in italics.

Since the unit costs of schooling are strongly determined by teacher earnings, the average number of pupils per teacher is capable of affecting the relative costs of universalising primary schooling dramatically. It should be expected, then, that increased values for this ratio will, *ceteris paribus*, be associated with higher enrolments. It is worth noting, however, that the simple bivariate relationships between the pupil-teacher ratio and the male and female enrolment ratios suggest quite the opposite (correlation coefficients are –0.29 and –0.44 respectively, see Appendix Table 3A.1). Here then, higher values for the pupil-teacher ratio appear to be associated with lower enrolments – and particularly strongly so in the case of females. The explanation for this lies in the fact that the pupil-teacher ratio is a variable which not only influences the costs, but also the perceived quality of schooling. Thus, large pupil-teacher ratios are judged by parents to be associated with low school quality, and, in richer countries, there is usually strong pressure upon governments to resource schools generously enough to bring class sizes at primary level down to 20-25 children.[5] By consequence, where countries with high levels of overall enrolments can afford low pupil-teacher ratios, they choose to do so because they believe that the quality of schooling will be better served. This is the reason why the pupil-teacher ratio falls as per capita incomes (and school enrolments) rise.

On the other hand, when investigated in a multivariate context, the pupil-teacher ratio emerges as a very significant facilitator of high enrolments – both for all children, and for each of the sexes taken separately. For example, Figure 3.1 shows the relationship between the gross enrolment ratio and the pupil-teacher ratio. The variable on the vertical axis is the gross enrolment ratio having controlled for the other explanatory variables in our model (i.e. urbanisation, GNP per capita, age at marriage, religion, proportion of female teachers, repetition, school age population, unit cost, population density and agricultural value added) and the variable on the horizontal axis is the pupil-teacher ratio, having controlled for the same set of other explanatory variables.[6] The figure shows that the relationship between the gross enrolment ratio and the pupil-teacher ratio is positive and reflects the result shown for the pupil-teacher ratio in Table 3.3. The scatter plot also shows the regression line and reports the magnitude of its slope (coefficient).[7] The latter indicates the percentage increase in the enrolment ratio

---

[5]   In fact, most studies suggest that class size has little impact upon cognitive achievement (for a review, see Hanushek, 1986). But the range of values for class-size which is said to be innocent of qualitative implications lies well below those found in many of the countries included here.

[6]   The variables are actually residuals from regressions of the variable on all other explanatory variables, which explains why the variables take on positive and negative values. The value taken by any observation shows the difference between that part explained by other variables in the model and the actual value of the variable for that observation. This difference, and hence the unexplained part of the variable, can be either positive or negative. For example, Ethiopia has a value for the unexplained part of the pupil-teacher ratio in Figure 3.2 of –0.44. This implies that, based on the other variables in the model, the pupil-teacher ratio in Ethiopia is predicted to be higher than it actually is. Thus, the residual for Ethiopia, from the regression of the pupil-teacher ratio on the other variables in the model is negative.

[7]   It should be noted that the coefficient of the straight line in each of the partial scatter plots corresponds to the regression coefficient, for the same relationship, in Table 3.3. The square root of the R-squared from this regression is the partial correlation

which is associated with a one percentage rise in the pupil-teacher ratio. Keeping GNP per capita and other variables constant, a ten percentage increase in the pupil-teacher ratio – i.e. from its mean level of 35.5 to around 39 pupils per teacher – is associated with an increase in the gross enrolment ratio of around three per cent (slightly more for girls and slightly less for boys). This confirms the fact that the pupil-teacher ratio is a powerful policy tool. The cross-national analysis indicates that the perceived qualitative problems associated with large classes are not so great as to undermine the demand for schooling where they exist, in comparison with better-resourced systems. This appears to be true even when – as in the analysis reported here – some of the systems included have much larger values for the pupil teacher ratio than could be compatible with maintaining a conducive environment for good teaching and learning.

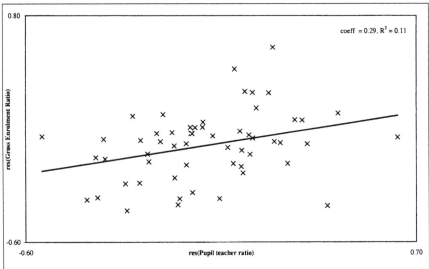

Notes: The variable on the vertical axis is the unexplained part of the gross enrolment ratio once the other variables in our model (see Table 3.2) have been controlled for. The variable on the horizontal axis is the variation in the pupil teacher ratio not explained by the other independent variables in our model.

Figure 3.1 Partial scatter plot of GER against the pupil-teacher ratio

A final important supply-side variable is the average teacher wage, proxied here by recurrent expenditure on primary education per pupil, expressed as a proportion of GNP per capita. A negative relationship is expected between unit costs and each of the enrolment ratios, with no influence expected on the gender

coefficient between these two variables. This measures the independent (i.e. having controlled for the other variables in the model) association between the two variables.

gap from the supply side. However, there may be gendered effects upon demand, via the implications of variations in unit costs for levels of school quality, and thus for the willingness of families to send their children to school.

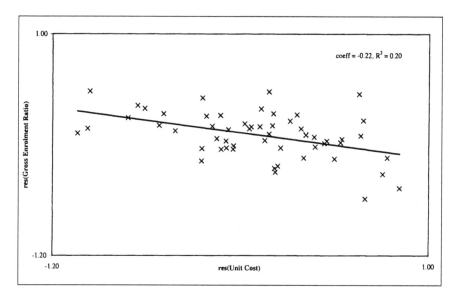

Notes: The variable on the vertical axis is the unexplained part of the gross enrolment ratio once the other variables in our model (see Table 3.2) have been controlled for. The variable on the horizontal axis is the variation in the unit cost not explained by the other independent variables in our model.

Figure 3.2   Partial scatter plot of GER against the unit cost

It can be seen from Figure 3.2 that increases in the unit cost do indeed bring negative implications for enrolments. A 10 per cent increase in the unit cost of primary schooling is associated with a 2.2 per cent decline in the gross enrolment ratio.[8] For given school-aged population sizes and pupil-teacher ratios, higher unit costs, relative to per capita income, are associated with lower enrolments – both overall, and for each of the sexes taken separately. This implies that, across all countries, higher real wages (relative to per capita income) are typically afforded in the context of lower enrolments: no other variables, apart from pupil-teacher ratios, appear to have been generally used to secure maintenance of enrolments in countries with higher relative unit-costs. Enhanced levels of budgetary provision,

---

8   McMahon (1999) uses the same unit cost variable and in his unlogged regressions also finds it to be negative and statistically significant. Schultz (1995c) uses teachers' salaries in his enrolment regressions. He, too, finds a negative and statistically significant effect.

for example, appear not to have significantly prevented lower enrolment outcomes in such circumstances.

Demand Side

Table 3.3 confirms our earlier judgement that income per head appears to have little direct influence upon enrolment outcomes.[9] Figure 3.3 illustrates the very loose relationship between the gross enrolment ratio and GNP per capita in our regression analysis. Having controlled for the other variables in our analysis a regression of the gross enrolment ratio and GNP per capita results in an R-squared

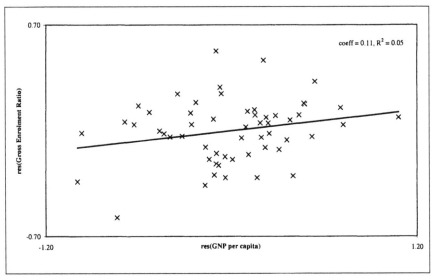

Notes: The variable on the vertical axis is the unexplained part of the gross enrolment ratio once the other variables in our model (see Table 3.2) have been controlled for. The variable on the horizontal axis is the variation in GNP per capita not explained by the other independent variables in our model.

Figure 3.3   Partial scatter plot of GER against GNP per capita

of only 0.05. Furthermore, in both the combined and gender-disaggregated regressions, the size of each of the estimated coefficients, in an economic sense, is small: a 10 per cent increase in GNP per capita, from the mean level of approximately $US1,200, is associated with an increase of GER of only about one

---

[9]   This is found also by Schultz (1995c). The coefficient on income per adult in his between country model is 0.132 when the dependent variable is the log of the gross enrolment ratio. Thus, the size of the coefficient is similar to the coefficient of GNP per capita shown in Table 3.3.

per cent, with little difference being apparent between the results for girls and for boys.

Urbanisation, on the other hand, emerges as an economically (and statistically) significant factor in explaining school enrolments. Across the countries included in our analysis, a 10 per cent increase in the urban population (i.e. from a mean level of 41 per cent to around 45 per cent) is associated with a two per cent rise in the proportion of children enrolled (see Figure 3.4). Both boys and girls appear equally affected by urbanisation, and the effect of urbanisation on the gender gap is, therefore, insignificant.

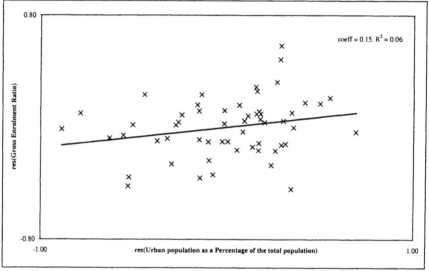

Notes: The variable on the vertical axis is the unexplained part of the gross enrolment ratio once the other variables in our model (see Table 3.2) have been controlled for. The variable on the horizontal axis is the variation in the degree of urbanisation not explained by the other independent variables in our model.

Figure 3.4 Partial scatter plot of GER against the degree of urbanisation

Population density, however, both influences girls' enrolments and helps to explain the gender gap: in cases where population density is higher, female enrolments tend to be slightly higher, relative to males, than elsewhere. These results imply that densely populated, urbanised countries have higher enrolments than similarly crowded, less urbanised ones: urbanisation is associated with higher income, whereas high population density is as much associated with poverty (the simple correlation between these two variables is –0.21). Urbanisation, with or without high density, increases the enrolments of both sexes, but it is high density (and thus greater relative ease of getting to school) which tends to give girls an enrolment advantage relative to boys.

As indicated above, the gender division of labour within households is likely to lead to differences in the opportunity costs of school attendance for boys and girls. Girls of primary-school age are often reported to spend more time on household chores than boys – in particular, looking after younger children – thereby liberating the time of adults for other household, or income-earning, tasks. The contribution of agriculture to GDP does not appear to play a significant role in determining enrolment outcomes across countries. On the other hand, our micro evidence discussed in Chapter 5 strongly shows the importance of opportunity cost, which suggests that the contribution of agriculture to GDP is not a successful proxy for this variable.

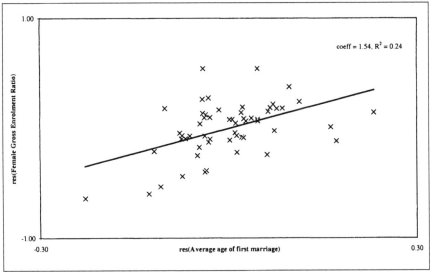

Notes: The variable on the vertical axis is the unexplained part of the female gross enrolment ratio once the other variables in our model (see Table 3.2) have been controlled for. The variable on the horizontal axis is the average age of first marriage not explained by the other independent variables in our model.

Figure 3.5   Partial scatter plot of the female GER against the average age at first marriage

As argued earlier, a low average age of first marriage is a feature of more traditional societies, where there is often both low female participation in the formal economy, and low economic returns to schooling for women. Figure 3.5, shows the partial scatter for the relationship between age at first marriage and the proportion of girls enrolled at primary school. It can be seen that the relationship is strongly positive, with a 10 per cent increase in the age at which girls marry being associated with a 15 per cent increase in the female enrolment rate. The relationship between girls' marriage age and the male GER is also positive – since, in more traditional societies, enrolments of both boys and girls tend to be lower than elsewhere – but weaker. However, the differential impact of the average age of girls' first marriage on the gender gap is not statistically significant.

In the present sample of countries, the religion variable appears to have no impact upon any of the dependent variables: the coefficients shown in each of the models in Table 3.3 are in each case small and not statistically significant. Here then, the proportion of the population espousing the Islamic and Hindu faiths does not appear to affect enrolment.

We proxy school-related effects on demand by using the primary repetition rate and the proportion of female teachers as explanatory variables. The repetition rate impacts negatively on the female enrolment ratio but appears to have no significant effect on male enrolment ratios. Therefore, higher rates of repetition appear to widen the gender gap in primary enrolments. Figure 3.6 below shows that a ten per cent increase in repetition rates is associated with a decrease in the ratio of female to male enrolments of about half of one per cent.

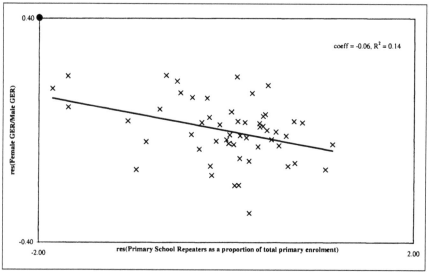

Notes: The variable on the vertical axis is the unexplained part of the gender gap once the other variables in our model (see Table 3.2) have been controlled for. The variable on the horizontal axis is the part of the repetition rate not explained by the other independent variables in our model.

Figure 3.6   Partial scatter plot of gender gap against the proportion of primary school repeaters

What is happening here? Is it that some parents of girls are put off by inefficient education systems, leading them to doubt the value of the schooling process for their offspring? A more likely explanation is that parents are more prepared to meet the costs of repeating for boys than for girls, and that where systems are very inefficient it is the boys who survive to the higher levels of the school system more frequently than the girls.[10] In addition, high repetition rates for boys may crowd out female enrolments, thereby exacerbating rates of drop-out amongst girls. Whatever the cause, it seems that school systems with higher levels of repetition also have higher gender gaps in enrolments. Thus, attempts to secure increases in school efficiency are also likely to be promotive of greater gender equality in school enrolments.

The second important school-related variable which emerges from our cross-section data is the proportion of teachers who are female. Figure 3.7 shows that the differential impact of female teachers on the enrolment of boys and girls results in a strong relationship between it and the gender gap. Table 3.3 suggests that a 10 per cent increase in female teachers – from their mean value of 52 per cent – is associated with a 2.6 per cent increase in the ratio between female and male enrolments.

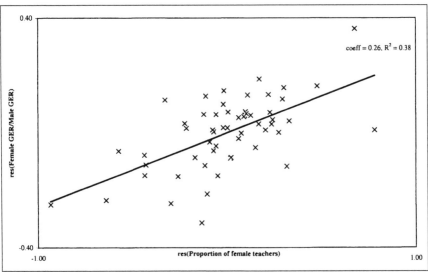

Notes: The variable on the vertical axis is the unexplained part of the gender gap once the other variables in our model (see Table 3.2) have been controlled for. The variable on the horizontal axis is the part of the proportion of female teachers not explained by the other independent variables in our model.

Figure 3.7 Partial scatter plot of gender gap against the proportion of female teachers

---

[10] See other evidence on this for West Africa in Brock and Cammish (1991).

This is a moderately strong result in an economic sense, with some implications for policy. Other things being equal, a teacher-supply strategy which aims to place women teachers in the majority, is likely to achieve a better gender balance amongst the pupils in the system, than one which does not do so. It should be recalled that our models incorporate both per capita income and urbanisation as determining variables. This is important, because it is clear that the primary school teaching profession becomes increasingly female as per capita income rises ($r = 0.55$). Thus, the estimated influence of the presence of female teachers on the gender gap in enrolments, reported above, is net of these effects. Our results suggest that, other things being equal, there is a reluctance on the part of some parents, to send girls to school when male teachers predominate. The reasons for this differ from place to place. But, as shown in Chapter 5, they include the influence of traditional attitudes towards female seclusion/privacy, fears about the physical and sexual safety of girls which tend to be allayed when more teachers are female, and beliefs that the schooling of girls may be less effective where the classroom culture is heavily male-dominated.

It should be noted from Table 3.3 that the coefficients for the regional dummy variable for Africa are substantially negative in the regressions for each of the enrolment ratios. Although these results are not significant in a statistical sense, amongst those in the sample, the African countries were not affording the same priority to primary schooling (at national or household levels, or both) as countries outside the region at similar levels of development.

In conclusion, we have shown that under-enrolment at primary level is particularly concentrated amongst girls: in general, the lower is a country's primary gross enrolment ratio, the greater is the proportionate inequality between female and male enrolments. The proportion of children enrolled in primary school tends to be higher in the richer countries, but the relationship is weak, and we have shown that, once a range of other contextual factors is controlled for, per capita income differences have limited impact upon both the level of school enrolments and their gender composition.

We have also shown that the supply of schooling is strongly influenced by both pupil-teacher ratios and by teachers' wages. Both of these variables have a strong impact upon the costs, per pupil, of providing schooling. As expected, our results indicate that higher pupil-teacher ratios and lower teachers' wages are associated with higher enrolments, internationally. Thus, the cost effectiveness of school provision differs widely between countries, and is associated with substantially different enrolment outcomes.

The direct costs to households of school attendance – proxied, in our analysis, by population density and urbanisation – have an impact upon enrolment, and upon the gender gap: the enrolment of girls, in particular, improves when people live closer together, and, therefore, when schools are nearer homes. Other demand side factors also appeared to be important in our analysis. The age of girls' first marriage has a significant impact upon the enrolment particularly of girls, but also of boys. On the other hand, religious beliefs were found not to be strongly associated with schooling behaviour: the proportion of the population being Islamic or Hindu has no significant impact upon enrolment outcomes for either sex. Finally, we have shown that some in-school variables critically influence the gender composition of enrolments. In particular, increases in the proportion of female teachers and higher levels of school efficiency – as indicated by lower average rates of grade repetition – are strongly associated with a better balance of girls being enrolled relative to boys.

Evidence from National Studies of Household Demand for Schooling

Our cross-country evidence, discussed above, suggests that the demand for schooling is an important factor in overall enrolment outcomes. It has identified a potentially important set of 'stylised facts' that are worthy of closer investigation. However the proxy variables we have used are not able to fully identify the causal relationships underlying household demand for education. Some of the variables turned out to be rather weak. For example, proxies for direct and opportunity costs proved very difficult to construct for international comparative purposes. A more accurate analysis of the demand for schooling requires more detailed information on the characteristics of individual households, which is best conducted within, rather than across, countries.

Many econometric studies of the determinants of educational participation have been carried out in SSA. Some of them have focussed on educational attainment measured by the number of years of schooling attended or levels completed, whilst others have explored school performance (e.g. Glewwe and Jacoby, 1993). Many have analysed household demand and the determinants of children's access to primary school. In the remainder of this chapter we review 18 such studies, which provide econometric analyses of household demand for schooling and the determinants of current access to primary school in Sub-Saharan Africa.[11]

Models of the demand for education have generally taken the household to be the decision-making unit and have explored the relationship between household characteristics and enrolment. Household production function (or unitary) models have generally provided the theoretical underpinnings of this empirical work, although collective models, which model household resource decisions as a process of bargaining between different members of the household, have also been used (Handa, 1996). As indicated in Chapter 1, unlike the household production function approach these models neither assume common preferences amongst household members, nor pooling of income within the household. This allows the characteristics of household members, in addition to those of the household head, to influence schooling decisions. Whilst the differences between these theoretical models are important, the empirical literature on the demand for schooling has usually included intra-household characteristics (e.g. mothers' and fathers'

---

[11]   This review represents an exhaustive search of all published sources on SSA, together with some unpublished material collected in the nine countries of the Gender and Primary Schooling Programme. Appendix Table 3A.2 lists the studies included in this review.

education) to allow for different preferences for education within the household. Beyond this, however, data constraints have implied that variables capable of distinguishing between the two household models could not be used.[12] Accordingly, the reduced form equations estimated in most of the studies (irrespective of the model used to arrive at the reduced form) have been very similar, and both theoretical models inform the insights from, and interpretation of the results of these studies.

Most studies of the demand for schooling have used 'qualitative response' models to look at the probability that a child is currently in school.[13] This type of model is useful because, after some manipulation, the coefficients can be interpreted as indicating the change in the probability of attendance associated with variations in the independent variable. This allows for easy interpretation and comparison. A small number of studies (Mingat and Tan, 1986; Birdsall and Orivel, 1996) have examined the probability of school attendance by exploring the determinants of the proportion of children within households that are currently enrolled in school (i.e. the household enrolment ratio). The following sections review this econometric literature. Where attendance is examined by age, rather than educational level, only those studies which cover the primary-school age-group have been included. We highlight the important variables identified by these studies and explore, where possible, how their effects vary by gender.

Gender

The studies reviewed here have used one of three approaches to exploring gender differences in household schooling outcomes. The most common approach has been to include a dummy variable for sex in a single regression examining the probability of enrolment. This approach assumes that the relationship between all the other characteristics included in the regression and the demand for schooling do not differ by gender. For example, the approach assumes that the level of education of mothers and fathers affects equally the probability of a boy or girl being in school. This restricts the coefficients on the determinants of attendance to be the same for boys and girls. The impact on the probability of enrolment by gender can be very large. For example, in urban areas of Côte d'Ivoire girls are 30 per cent less likely to be in school than boys (Grootaert, 1999). Whilst the majority of studies including a gender dummy report a negative coefficient for girls there are some studies in Tanzania and Botswana where the reverse is true (for Tanzania see Mason and Khandker, 1997, and Al-Samarrai and Reilly, 2000; for Botswana see Chernichovsky, 1985). In these countries the gender gap in enrolments from national statistics is very small and in some cases girls' enrolment

---

[12]   Haddad *et al.* (1994) provide a useful discussion of differences between the two theoretical models and review some of the literature. For a useful discussion of differences in the two approaches with specific reference to education see Glick and Sahn (2000).

[13]   'Qualitative response models' are those using non-continuous dependent variables in the analysis.

rates are higher than boys'. Thus, the measured negative impact of gender reflects the countries chosen for study and is silent about the reasons for differences in attendance between boys and girls.

The second approach has involved separate regressions for boys and girls, which allows the coefficients for all characteristics to vary by gender (Glick and Sahn, 2000, Mason and Khandker, 1997, Tansel, 1997). The final approach has been a mix of the others, and allows some of the coefficients in the demand for schooling regressions to vary by gender (e.g. Chao and Alper, 1998; Al-Samarrai and Peasgood, 1998; Rose and Al-Samarrai, 2001). The results of using these different approaches are reported below.

Income Effects

Household income affects whether or not a child attends school in a number of different ways. When the decision to send a child to school is seen purely as investment, household income should not, in principle, affect this decision directly. In practice, things are more complicated. For example, richer households may be less risk averse, they may have better information on the benefits of education, and they may discount future benefits at a lower rate than poorer households. Furthermore, due to credit constraints, household resources play an important direct role in the investment decision. Richer households are more able to afford the direct and indirect costs of schooling from current income, and they are less likely to be credit-constrained than poorer households. As regards the consumption aspect of expenditure on schooling, where education is seen as a 'normal' consumption good household demand for it could be expected to rise with income.

There are also a number of other linkages between household resources and education – highlighted in the literature – where income proxies for other unobserved factors. Due to their power or political leverage, richer households may be able to secure greater access to better-quality schools and better post-primary opportunities for their children than poor households, thereby improving their relative returns to education (Behrman and Knowles, 1999).

In the SSA studies of the determinants of school enrolments, measures of household income are generally significant and suggest that increases in income improve the chances of a child attending school.[14] This positive impact of household income on access to education tends to remain, even when some of the factors correlated with income are included. For example, studies in SSA have controlled for household location (region and urbanisation), community characteristics and quality of local schools and found that income remains a

---

[14]   A common measure of household income, in these studies, has been income proxied by household expenditure per capita. An expenditure-based measure of income may be subject to less measurement error than an income-based measure since it smoothes transitory income fluctuations, and more adequately reflects the long-run resource constraint facing the household.

Table 3.4 Income elasticities of schooling

Study (1)	Country and year (2)	Sample Size (3)	Income measure (4)	Regression specification/Sample (5)	Marginal effect/(coeff est.) (6)	Sig. (7)	Elasticity (8)
Qualitative response models							
Al-Samarrai and Reilly (2000)	Tanzania, 1993/94	2378	Household per capita expenditure, instrumented	Rural	v. small	1%	0.48
Lavy (1996)	Rural Ghana, 1987	2289	Log of household per capita expenditure, instrumented	Urban	v.small	1%	0.51
		1733		w/o middle school quality	(0.25)	5%	0.09[1]
Appleton et al. (1990)	Côte d'Ivoire, 1986	2433	Household income per capita	with middle school quality	(0.12)	n.s.	0.04[1]
				Total	n.a.	1%	0.24[1]
Glick and Sahn (2000)	Conakry, Guinea, 1990	1265	Log of household expenditure per adult	Boys	n.a.	n.s.	0.27[1]
		1168		Girls	n.a.	5%	0.21[1]
		899		Boys	0.03	n.s.	0.42[1]
Chao and Alper (1998)	Ghana, 1991/92	766	Log of household per capita expenditure	Girls	0.26	1%	0.04[1]
		2222			0.03	5%	0.03[1]
Montgomery et al. (1995)	Côte d'Ivoire, 1985/87	8175	Log of non-exceptional expenditure per adult	Total	(0.29)	1%	0.34
		5067		Rural	(0.28)	1%	0.38
		3108		Urban	(0.35)	1%	0.30
Household enrolment ratio models							
Birdsall and Orivel (1996)	Rural Mali, 1981-82	123	Log of household income		(0.03)	n.s.	0.06[1]
Mingat and Tan (1986)	Malawi, 1983	1455	Father's income		(0.001)	n.s.	n.a.

Notes:

a) Further descriptive details, including the age-range covered and the definitions of the dependent variables in each of these studies is given in Appendix Table 3A2; (b) Column 6 reports marginal effects (where reported) or coefficient estimates (in brackets); (c) Column 7 reports the level of statistical significance. n.s. not significant; (d) Column 8 reports income elasticities. [1] denotes income elasticities. Column 7 reports the study; (d) n.a. – denotes not available.

positive and significant determinant of enrolment (see Lavy, 1996). Studies that have included measures of household income show that current enrolment tends to be fairly income-inelastic (see Table 3.4).[15] Where information on household income or expenditure has not been available measures of assets, such as land and livestock ownership, have been used as proxies for household resources.[16] In many of these studies household assets have been positively associated with enrolment (see, for example, Lloyd and Blanc, 1996).[17]

Some authors have suggested that the elasticity of income with respect to girls' enrolment is likely to be higher than that of boys. Glick and Sahn (2000) argue that richer households' demand for child labour is lower because they can afford to pay for domestic labour-saving devices and for processed foods. This reduces the opportunity cost of girls' schooling more than boys'. Thus, the demand for girls' schooling is expected to increase by a greater amount as income increases. Furthermore, since limited income constrains the number of children that the household can send to school, the choice between them will be based on the costs and benefits associated with each individual child. If the costs of sending a girl to school are higher and the benefits lower than those for boys, the latter will tend to be favoured in the schooling decision when income is constrained. However, as income rises more children can go to school which disproportionately affects girls' schooling chances.

Nevertheless, the evidence on the gendered impact of income is too scarce to draw any firm conclusions. Glick and Sahn (2000), using a sample of urban households in Conakry, Guinea, show a very large difference in the income elasticity between boys and girls favouring the latter (see Table 3.4). However, studies in other SSA countries exploring this relationship have been far less conclusive (for Côte d'Ivoire see Appleton *et al.,* 1990, and Tansel, 1997; for Ghana see Chao and Alper, 1998 and Tansel, 1997; for Tanzania see Mason and Khandker, 1997).[18]

Direct Costs

The direct costs of schooling are made up of fees, the cost of books and supplies, uniforms and transport costs. Household education expenditure can be divided

---

[15] Not all the studies reviewed in this section are included in Table 3.4 because either it was not possible to estimate income elasticities from the information available in the studies or income was not included as an explanatory variable.

[16] It is argued that income measures are endogenous to the household schooling decision (see Behrman and Knowles, 1999) and some studies have excluded household income for that reason (Grootaert, 1999). Others have instrumented the income variable using amongst other things household asset variables (see for example, Tansel, 1997).

[17] Where household income/expenditure and asset variables have been together included in the same regression, their coefficients are less likely to be significant (compared to when only one household resource measure is used) owing partly to mulicollinearity.

[18] These studies either show the opposite relationship – no difference between the impact of income on girls and boys schooling – or that the impact of income on girls and boys schooling is not significant.

between non-discretionary and discretionary elements. Non-discretionary expenditures are those expenditures which are absolutely required for the child to attend school (e.g. the payment of school fees, where they exist). Discretionary expenditures on the other hand, may be desirable, but not strictly necessary for a child to attend school (e.g. additional textbooks).[19] Particular items of schooling expenditure may have both discretionary and non-discretionary elements. For example, expenditure on the minimum required number of exercise books might represent non-discretionary purchases, whilst any expenditure over and above this minimum might be judged to be discretionary. An ideal measure for the direct costs of schooling would be the minimum (non-discretionary) expenditure required to enrol one child in school for each household. However, this information is generally not available from the cross-sectional data used in the studies under review. Furthermore, information on the direct costs of schooling is available only for those sampled children who are attending school. Instead, information on household expenditure per primary child is typically used to indicate marginal private costs for those remaining out-of-school. The most common measure of direct costs included in these studies has been a cluster-level fee[20] (which would cover some, but not usually all, of the non-discretionary direct costs of schooling). Birdsall and Orivel (1996) used fees charged by the school nearest to the household. Lavy (1996) used cluster-level average fees as the measure of direct costs. Others have used an average of total household education expenditure for each school-cluster (Grootaert, 1999; Chao and Alper, 1998). A more sophisticated approach was used by Montgomery *et al.* (1995) who predicted the costs of schooling for those out of school by using costs faced by enrolled children, corrected for the selectivity of the sample.[21]

Table 3.5 summarises price elasticity estimates for schooling in SSA.[22] It can be seen that the estimates of elasticity vary markedly from study to study. However, it appears that those studies using a simple cluster average to measure the fee produce very similar (usually small, and insignificant) coefficients. In the two cases where it is significant the probability of school enrolment appears to increase with increasing fees. Two studies using a household enrolment ratio as the dependent variable (Mingat and Tan, 1986; Birdsall and Orivel, 1996) report negative price elasticities. The direct cost measure, in the Malawi study, is the overall cost to the household of enrolling all eligible children in school. The fee elasticity, derived from the larger overall cost elasticity, is estimated to be only

---

[19]   Household expenditure on education is positively correlated with income in most countries (see Weir and Knight, 1996, and Tan *et al.*, 1984, for examples of the determinants of household expenditures on schooling).

[20]   'Clusters' are the enumeration areas used in household surveys.

[21]   Heckman's two-stage procedure was used for this. See Montgomery *et al.* (1995) for details.

[22]   Not all of the studies reviewed in this section are included in Table 3.5, either because it was not possible to compute fee elasticities from the information in the study, or because the study did not include fees as an explanatory variable.

-0.03 (Tan *et al.*, 1984).[23] This result supports the results shown for those studies in Table 3.5, using cluster-level fee effects.

Where a measure of overall household education expenditure has been used as the direct cost measure the impact of this variable on enrolment tends to be positive (Grootaert, 1999; Chao and Alper, 1998). This may indicate that in locations with high discretionary education expenditures by households, education is highly valued and enrolment rates are high. This suggests that average household expenditure may not be a satisfactory proxy for overall non-discretionary education expenditure. Montgomery *et al.* (1995) report the highest price elasticities and use the most complicated estimation procedure for the cost variable. However, the results from this study should be treated with caution because the cost variable was estimated using very restrictive assumptions.[24]

It seems clear that the overall direct cost of schooling has been difficult to include and measure in the studies reviewed here. The available econometric evidence suggests that fees are relatively unimportant in determining enrolments. However, in all the available studies, fees have been proxied, rather than being measured directly. Variations in the fee across households (or clusters) in cross sectional data may be too small for the elasticity estimates to indicate the likely impact of a large changes in fees. Nevertheless, many studies have shown that fees usually represent only a small part of the overall costs of sending a child to school. For example, Mason and Khandker (1996) find that in Tanzania fees represented approximately 25 per cent of direct primary school costs whilst in Malawi they amounted to approximately 6 per cent of total primary and secondary costs (Tan *et al.*, 1984).[25] In these circumstances, increases in school fees – at the levels normally set in SSA – may have relatively little impact on the overall cost of sending a child to school.

---

[23] The cost variable in this study is the total estimated cost of educating all the children in the household. It appears that the primary and secondary costs used to construct this variable only differ across rural and urban areas. This implies that the cost variable will be positively associated with the number of eligible children in the household and hence the relationship between the household enrolment ratio and cost may just be reflecting this. Responding to this criticism the authors use a uniform cost for both primary and secondary in the construction of the total cost variable to see what happens (this removes any variability of this variable due to cost and leaves only the household structure varying). The authors argue that because the R-square of the regression falls, this shows the importance of costs. However, they do not report whether the constant cost variable is significant and negative, which would suggest that the result is driven by the number of eligible children.

[24] This paper uses the two-stage Heckman procedure to produce the predicted education expenditure variable. The 'cost-of-schooling' function is estimated on the basis of cluster-level characteristics and the child's age. It is unclear what is included in the first stage probit of attendance and, more importantly, what the identifying variables are.

[25] Fees become an even lower share of total education expenditure once opportunity costs of schooling are also included (Mason and Khandker, 1996).

Table 3.5 Fee effects and elasticities of demand for education in SSA

Study	Country and year	Sample Size	Cost of Schooling Measure	Notes	Quality?	Marginal effect/(coeff est).	Sig.	Elast-icity
(1)	(2)	(3)	(4)	(5)	(6)	(7)	(8)	(9)
Qualitative response models								
Al-Samarrai & Reilly (2000)	Tanzania, 1993/94	2378	Cluster level average primary enrolment fee	Urban	no			
		2289		Rural				
Lavy (1996)	Rural Ghana, 1987	1733	Cluster average primary enrolment fee	w/o middle school quality	no	(0.003)	n.s.	0.64[1]
		1733		with middle school quality	yes	(-0.002)	n.s.	-0.43[1]
Weir (2000)	Rural Ethiopia, 1995	387	Average school fee as a percentage of consumption per adult equivalent.	with aggregate attitudinal index	yes	-0.08	n.s.	n.a.
		387	Average school fee as a percentage of consumption per adult equivalent.	with disaggregated attitudinal index	yes	-0.13	10%	n.a.
Grootaert (1999)	Côte d'Ivoire, 1988	1177	Cluster average household education expenditure	Urban	no	0.11	n.s.	n.a.
Chao and Alper (1998)	Ghana, 1991/92	1650	Community average annual school related real expenditures	Rural	no	-0.17	n.s.	n.a.
		2222		Junior secondary costs included but n.s.	yes	0.021	1%	0.02[1]
Montgomery et al. (1995)	Rural Ghana		Community average third year school fee		no	(0.002)	5%	n.a.
Montgomery et al. (1995)	Côte d'Ivoire, 1985-87	3108	Predicted values of cost of schooling.	Urban	no	Negative v.small	1%	-0.76
		5067	Predicted values of cost of schooling.	Rural	no	Negative v.small	1%	-1.41

Table 3.5 (Cont'd) Fee effects and elasticities of demand for education in SSA

Study	Country and year	Sample Size	Cost of Schooling Measure	Notes	Quality?	Marginal effect/(coeff est).	Sig.	Elast-icity
(1)	(2)	(3)	(4)	(5)	(6)	(7)	(8)	(9)
Household enrolment ratio models								
Birdsall and Orivel (1996)	Mali, 1981-82	123	Fees to parents' association for school nearest household		yes	-0.03	n.s.	-0.02
Mingat and Tan (1986)	Malawi, 1983	1455	Total cost of enrolling all eligible children (primary and secondary)		no	-0.28	1%	-0.48

Notes:

a) Further descriptive details, including the age-range covered and the definitions of the dependent variables in each of these studies is given in Appendix Table 3A.2.

b) Column 7 reports marginal effects (where reported) or coefficient estimates (in brackets).

c) Column 8 reports the level of statistical significance. n.s. – not significant.

d) Column 9 reports price elasticities.

e) [1] denotes authors' calculations from information in the study.

f) n.a. denotes not available.

School Quality

An additional problem with measuring fees in the above ways is that apparent differences in the computed fee may in fact reflect differences in quality across clusters. If school quality is correlated positively with education fees,[26] the omission of controls for school quality is likely to bias upwards the estimated effect of fees on demand and may explain why, in some studies, higher fees appear to be associated with higher enrolments. It is important to note, therefore, that more of the studies which control for school quality report negative fee elasticities. Nevertheless, the majority of such elasticities remain insignificant (see Table 3.5).

A common indicator of the quality of schooling used in these studies, is the pupil-teacher ratio (Weir and Knight, 1996; Birdsall and Orivel, 1996; Chao and Alper, 2000). Higher pupil-teacher ratios (at least above a certain range) are associated with lower quality teaching. The results from the studies in SSA show that demand for education is sometimes related positively and sometimes negatively to the pupil-teacher ratio.[27] Of course, the pupil-teacher ratio can be interpreted as an indicator of both quality and capacity. High pupil-teacher ratios can be associated with high levels of enrolment (e.g. in urban areas) and low ratios may imply low population density. Thus, it is not surprising that the measured relationship between the pupil-teacher ratio and the demand for schooling is uncertain. Other proxies for school quality have been used (average education of teachers, dummy variables for textbooks, quality of classrooms etc.). Although statistically significant relationships are found, their interpretation is ambiguous and the true impact of school quality on demand remains uncertain. Given the frequent aggregation of school quality indicators to regional or cluster-level averages this is, perhaps, not surprising.[28]

Opportunity Costs

Conceptual complexity and data constraints have meant that only two SSA studies attempted to include direct measures of the opportunity costs of schooling (Tansel, 1997; Mason and Khandker, 1997). A common proxy for the opportunity costs of schooling has been to use the prevailing child wage-rate.[29] It is argued that higher child wage-rates result in higher opportunity costs. Tansel (1997) shows that, in Côte d'Ivoire, the relationship between the child wage-rate and demand for

---

[26]   Such correlation may be even more likely where fees are proxied by the average education expenditures of households.

[27]   The Chao and Alper study (1998) uses regional pupil teacher ratios whereas the other two studies use lower level pupil teacher ratios.

[28]   For a more detailed look examination of link between the quality and the demand for education see Bergmann (1996).

[29]   Gertler and Glewwe (1992) provide a more satisfactory measure of the opportunity cost of going to school. Their measure is the opportunity wage (measured as the prevailing wage rate for children) multiplied by the child's lost hours due to school attendance.

primary schooling was positive and significant. The author explains this counter-intuitive result by suggesting that the lack of a strict distinction between work and school implies that children who command higher wages more easily earn money to cover the costs of their own schooling.[30] In Ghana, on the other hand, the child wage-rate had a negative, although not statistically significant impact on schooling demand (Tansel, 1997).

Tansel (1997) also includes the adult male and female community wage-rates as measures of the opportunity costs of parents' time. Here, the impact of high wages on the demand for primary schooling will be the result of an income and a substitution effect. The income effect is likely to raise demand for schooling whilst the substitution effect (between the household labour time of parents and children) is likely to reduce demand. The overall impact is not predictable. Community wages may also, of course, influence expectations of the benefits of schooling, resulting in a positive relationship between the two variables. In fact, however, no consistent picture emerges. Tansel (1997) finds, in Côte d'Ivoire, that higher male wages are associated with lower demand for girls and boys schooling, whilst the impact of the female wage is positive for boys and negative for girls. In Ghana the demand for both girls' and boys' schooling increases with the male wage, whilst the female wage coefficient is positive for girls and negative for boys. Thus, little can be learnt about the impact of opportunity costs on the demand for schooling from these measures.

Distance to School

The demand for schooling is likely to be influenced by the distance between households and their schools. Households living further away from schools face higher costs and are less likely, *ceteris paribus*, to send their children to school. Most studies find that distance to the nearest primary school has a negative and significant impact on the demand for schooling (Table 3.6).[31] This result is stronger, generally, for younger children and for those in rural areas (World Bank, 1996; Chao and Alper, 1998; Al-Samarrai and Reilly, 2000).[32]

---

[30]   As discussed in Chapter 5, the survey work undertaken in Ethiopia, Guinea and Tanzania found that a significant number of pupils work in order to earn money to cover their school expenses.

[31]   Table 3.6 includes qualitative response studies which report either distance elasticities or marginal effects.

[32]   Lavy (1996) shows primary school distance to be negative in rural Ghana for children aged between five and 12. When the sample is reduced to those aged between seven and 12 the primary school distance variable is no longer significant. Tansel (1997), using the same data, also shows that for his sample of 16 to 36 year olds, primary school distance is not significant. In Tanzania, rural distance elasticities are significant irrespective of the age group but fall from –0.1 (7-15 age group) to –0.06 (10-15 age group). Distances to the nearest primary school in urban Tanzania are very small and insignificant (Al-Samarrai and Reilly, 2000).

Table 3.6 Impact of distance on the demand for primary schooling

Study (1)	Country and year (2)	Sample Size (3)	Distance measure (4)	Regression Specification/Sample (5)	Marginal effect/ (coeff est). (6)	Sig. (7)	Elasticity (8)
Qualitative response models							
Al-Samarrai & Reilly (2000)	Tanzania, 1993/94	2289	Primary (km)	Urban	0.009	n.s.	0.01
Lavy (1996)	Rural Ghana, 1987	2378	Primary (km)	Rural	-0.039	1%	-0.10
		1733	Primary (km)	w/o middle school quality	(-0.12)	10%	-0.07
		1733	Middle (km)		(-0.100)	1%	-0.30
		1733	Secondary (km)		(-0.02)	1%	n.a.
		1733	Primary (km)	with middle school quality	(-0.17)	n.s.	-0.10
		1733	Middle (km)		(-0.10)	1%	-0.30
		1733	Secondary (km)		(-0.01)	5%	n.a.
Tansel (1997)	Ghana, 1987/89	3366	Primary (km)	Boys	-0.5	n.s.	n.a.
			Middle (km)		-1.0	5%	n.a.
			Secondary (km)		-0.1	5%	n.a.
		4015	Primary (km)	Girls	-0.1	n.s.	n.a.
			Middle (km)		-3.0	1%	n.a.
			Secondary (km)		-0.4	1%	n.a.
	Côte d'Ivoire, 1985/87	2983	Primary (km)	Boys	-4.0	1%	n.a.
			Secondary (km)		-0.2	1%	n.a.
		3628	Primary (km)	Girls	-2.0	1%	n.a.
			Secondary (km)		-0.2	1%	n.a.

Table 3.6 (Cont'd) Impact of distance on the demand for primary schooling

Study (1)	Country and year (2)	Sample Size (3)	Distance measure (4)	Regression Specification/Sample (5)	Marginal effect/ (coeff est). (6)	Sig.[1] (7)	Elasticity (8)
Chao and Alper (1998)	Ghana, 1991/92	2222	Primary (miles)		-1.4	1%	-0.003[1]
			Middle (miles)		-1.0	n.s.	0.01[1]
			Secondary (miles)		0.0	n.s.	0.0[1]
Birdsall and Orivel (1996)	Rural Mali, 1981-82	123	Primary (km)		(-0.04)	1%	-0.18

Notes:

a) Further descriptive details, including the age-range covered and the definitions of the dependent variables in each of these studies is given in Appendix Table 3A.2.

b) Column 6 reports marginal effects (where reported) or coefficient estimates (in brackets).

c) Column 7 reports the level of statistical significance. n.s. – not significant

d) Column 8 reports distance elasticities.

e) [1] denotes authors' calculations from information in the study.

f) Dependent variable in the Birdsall and Orivel study is defined as the number of people enrolled in primary school divided by people aged 6-14.

g) n.a. denotes not available.

Some studies have argued that girls face additional issues of security on their way to school and that the negative impact of distance is greater for them. However, Tansel (1997), finds that in Côte d'Ivoire an additional kilometre between home and primary school implies a two per cent decline in the probability of enrolment for girls, compared to a four per cent decline for boys. In this sample at least, distance appeared to be a larger constraint for boys rather than girls (Tansel, 1997).[33]

Some studies have explored the effect on the demand for primary education, of the distance to both primary and higher levels of schooling. This assumes that the demand for primary schooling is partly determined by opportunities for post-primary education. From Table 3.3 it can be seen that Lavy (1996) included variables measuring the distance from home to middle and secondary schools in rural Ghana. These distances were found to have a significant negative effect on the demand for primary schooling, whilst the elasticities for the higher levels of schooling were larger than at primary level.[34]

Household Structure

The size and structure of the household have been shown to be important determinants of the demand for schooling. The number of children within a household may affect the level of resources available to each – either negatively, because of the need to share, or positively, because older children can provide support for younger ones. Children may also share household workloads, so that those with larger numbers of children potentially have a reduced average workload.

A number of different model specifications have been used in the literature to explore these relationships. In some studies the number of children in the household has been used as an independent variable, showing, in general, a positive impact upon their probability of enrolment. Al-Samarrai and Reilly (2000) find that controlling for household size, more children in the household increases their probability of enrolment in rural but not in urban areas. These results appear to support the view that in larger families, particularly in rural areas, household chores are spread across more children, thereby reducing the opportunity cost of schooling.[35] Other studies have examined whether or not the

---

[33]   Along similar lines, Chao and Alper (1998) actually show a positive relationship between distance and enrolment for girls and a negative relationship for boys.

[34]   This seems to be contradicted by the Chao and Alper (1998) study from Ghana in 1991/92. However, apart from this study being undertaken five years after that of Lavy, it pools urban and rural areas together. Given the apparent sensitivity of the impact of distance on rural and urban location these two results are, therefore, not necessarily contradictory. Similar results to those of Lavy (1996) have been found for Ghana and Côte d'Ivoire (Tansel, 1997) and for rural Ethiopia (Weir and Knight, 1996).

[35]   It should be noted, however, that the number of children appears to have no differential impact on the probability of enrolment for boys and girls (see Al-Samarrai and Peasgood, 1998; Tembon and Al-Samarrai, 1999).

age distribution of the children matters. It appears that the presence of young children (aged less than seven) in the household reduces the probability of enrolment of those of school-going age. However, where this has been explored by gender, the negative impact appears to be significant only for girls (Glick and Sahn, 2000). In this case, it is plausible that larger numbers of young children in the household increase, particularly, the opportunity costs of girls' schooling.

Birth order within the family is also likely to be important, as well as the relative age of other siblings. Where children, mainly girls, take on the responsibility for caring for younger siblings, the opportunity cost of educating the older girls will be higher. Where education is treated as an investment good, once some children in the family have been to school, thereby assuring some future income for the parents, household preferences for more educated children may alter. In the SSA studies, children with siblings have greater probability of enrolment at a given age if they are earlier in the birth order (Al-Samarrai and Peasgood, 1998; Weir, 2000; Al-Samarrai and Reilly, 2000).[36]

Thus, it appears that the size and age-structure of households affect their pattern of demand for schooling. These household characteristics are probably, to some extent, reflecting the opportunity costs of sending individual children to school. Whilst the number of young children in the household tends to impact negatively on the chances of enrolling, the overall number of children has a positive effect. This seems to go against the conventional quantity-quality trade-off argument used to explain the fall in fertility and rise in education experienced in Southeast Asia and Latin America.[37]

Parents' Education

Parental education levels are also an important determinant of a child's chances of attending school. Educated parents are more able to assist their children's learning and to recognise its benefits. From a consumption point of view, educated parents may derive more satisfaction from educated children than uneducated parents and hence 'tastes' for educated children may also differ by parental education level.

Mothers' and fathers' education levels are generally entered into the analysis separately to allow for their different potential impacts on enrolment. Recent models of household decision-making assume that members with stronger bargaining positions will have greater influence upon the allocation of household resources. Some have argued that mothers may have greater preference for

---

[36]   Al-Samarrai and Peasgood (1998) show that the effect of birth order is different for males and females in rural Tanzania. Birth order does not play a significant role in the chances of boys' attendance whereas older girls are more likely to be enrolled compared to younger girls. This suggests either that younger girls come low in the priority for allocating resources, or that household preferences towards education change.

[37]   This paper suggests that there is a positive association between family size and child schooling in rural areas of Côte d'Ivoire but a conventional quantity-quality trade-off in urban areas.

Table 3.7 Percentage changes in the probability of male and female enrolment associated with mother's and father's education

Study	Country and year	Sample size	Measure of schooling	Notes	Girls		Boys	
					Mother	Father	Mother	Father
Al-Samarrai & Peasgood (1998)	Rural Tanzania, 1992	2617	Dummy for primary education	Rural	11.1	4.9	3.8	11.4
Tembon & Al-Samarrai (1998)	Guinea, 1995	380	Formal education dummy		18.0	-3.0	11.0	7.0
Tansel (1997)	Côte d'Ivoire, 1985-1987	Boys - 2983 Girls - 3628	Years		3.9	7.4	3.5	5.7
	Ghana, 1987-1989	Boys - 3366 Girls - 4015	Years		2.1	3.0	1.6	1.3
Appleton et al. (1990)	Côte d'Ivoire, 1986	Boys - 1265 Girls - 1168	Some primary dummy		21.0	23.0	2.0	4.0
Grootaert (1999)	Côte d'Ivoire, 1988	1177	Years	Urban	0.0	1.0	-1.0	1.0
	Côte d'Ivoire, 1988	1650	Years	Rural	-3.0	2.0	1.2	1.0
Glick & Sahn (2000)	Conakry, Guinea, 1990	Boys - 899 Girls - 766	Years		2.8	2.3	0.4	1.1

Notes:

a) Further descriptive details, including the age-range covered and the definitions of the dependent variables in each of these studies is given in Appendix Table 3A.2.

b) If boys' and girls' sample size reported separately then two separate regressions were reported in the study.

c) If the measure of schooling is a dummy variable then the percentage changes reported in the last four columns of the table show the change in probability of attendance associated with a particular level of education compared to know education.

d) If the measure of schooling is years of formal education then the percentage changes reported in the last four columns of the table show the change in probability of attendance associated with an additional year of parental education.

educating their children and that their own education increases their bargaining power within the household. Here, mothers' education would play an independent role in the decision to send children to school (Al-Samarrai and Peasgood, 1998). In almost all the SSA studies both mothers' and fathers' education appear to be very important determinants of access to school. Table 3.7 summarizes the results.[38] The data in the final four columns of the table show either the change in probability associated with parents having an additional year of schooling or, in the case of the dummy variable specifications, with either parent having had a particular level of education.[39]   It can be seen that the possession of primary education by mothers or fathers increases the probability of enrolment of their children by between 2 and 23 per cent (Appleton *et al.*, 1990). There does not appear to be any consistent difference in the size of the mothers' and fathers' education effects in the studies reviewed.

As regards the specifications using education (in years) as a continuous variable, an additional year of mother's or father's schooling (evaluated at the means of the data) generally increases the chances of enrolment.

Some studies have explored the hypotheses that mothers' schooling has a larger impact on the enrolment chances of girls than boys, and vice versa for fathers (see Glick and Sahn, 2000). From the figures presented in Table 3.7, it appears that mothers' education generally has a larger impact on girls' schooling chances than on boys'. However, a similar relationship between fathers' education and sons' schooling does not appear to hold. In fact in many of the studies shown in the table the impact of fathers' education appears to be stronger for girls than boys.

It could be argued that education is proxying in these models, for other characteristics of the household, which are not observed or controlled. However, many of them do include controls for the income and occupational status of parents and other variables associated with socio-economic differentiation. In view of the many different specifications and variables that have been included in the SSA studies we can be confident that parental education plays an important, independent role in household schooling decisions.

Religion

Finally, some studies have included religious groupings as an independent variable in demand equations, in order to examine the differing practices of different faiths (Al-Samarrai and Peasgood, 1998; Al-Samarrai and Reilly, 2000; Chao and Alper,

---

[38]   There are other studies that have looked at this issue. However, it was not possible to include them in the table as they either did not report the coefficients for the variables in question or it was not possible with the information given to calculate the impact/marginal effects (for example Mason and Khandker, 1996).

[39]   The dummy variable specifications tend to have larger impacts on enrolment chances. This is because the dummy variable in effect represents a number of years of schooling.

1998; Weir, 2000; Weir and Knight, 1996).[40] However, no consistent relationship between religious groupings and the demand for schooling has been identified. Religious variables are difficult to interpret as they may be proxying for a number of different factors, including cultural attitudes towards education, differences in household production systems or supply side effects. The most common religious group to be included is Islam, it being argued that Muslim households have lower demand for schooling, particularly of girls. The evidence on this from the SSA studies is mixed, but, in general, Muslim girls do not appear to be more disadvantaged than the boys, with respect to schooling (Al-Samarrai and Peasgood, 1998; Chao and Alper, 1998).

Conclusions

The cross-country evidence in this paper indicates the importance of influencing a range of social, cultural and school-related policy variables if moves towards schooling for all, with gender equity, are to be widely achieved. Comparisons with other regions indicate that the potential for making progress in African enrolments is strong – particularly for girls. Improving the resources available to school systems is important, but our results strongly indicate that the efficiency with which resources are used is as important as their absolute levels. After controlling for broad differences in the gender division of labour, societies having school systems with lower unit costs, higher average pupil-teacher ratios and lower levels of repetition secure the highest and most equitable primary-school enrolment profiles. However, our work also demonstrates that there are a set of contextual factors, including some fundamental aspects of gender relations in society at large, which have a major impact upon both the overall level of school enrolments and their gender composition.

　　While the cross-country evidence points to the importance of demand-side factors in determining overall enrolment outcomes, the proxy variables used in the analysis generally do not identify well the causal relationships underlying household schooling decisions. To gain a better understanding of these relationships, country-level empirical studies of the demand for primary education in Sub-Saharan Africa were reviewed. Some – but not all – of these studies examined gender differences in schooling outcomes in detail, either by looking separately at the demand for boys' and girls' schooling, or by allowing specific coefficients to vary by gender.

　　These studies show that higher household incomes improve the chances of children attending school. Although some analysts have argued that income elasticities might be higher for girls than boys, this is not supported by the available African evidence. As regards costs, the total direct costs of schooling to households are hard to measure, owing to data constraints. As a result, many studies have explored the particular impact of school fees on demand. Their

---

[40]　Ethnic dummies are included in some studies but these are country-specific and are not reported here.

evidence suggests that fees are relatively unimportant in determining enrolment. These results should be interpreted with great caution, however, because fees may represent only a small proportion of the total direct costs and their range of variation, nationally, may also be quite small. The distance from home to the nearest school influences household demand for schooling by proxying both for a direct cost (if transportation to school is used) and an opportunity cost. The evidence from SSA shows that living further away from schools reduces the enrolment chances of younger children and rural children more strongly than for other groups of children. Although no difference between the impact of distance on girls' enrolment, as compared with boys', is apparent, too few studies have explored this relationship to be confident of its generality.

Although few studies have successfully included measures of opportunity costs, household structure emerges as an important determinant of demand. Although the potential direct costs of schooling to households increase with the number of their children, it appears that the opportunity costs, per child, may fall. The probability of enrolment is influenced more by a child's gender and age relative to other siblings, than by simple measures of household size.

The evidence shows that parental education plays an important, and independent, role in household schooling decisions. Mothers' education appears to have a larger impact on the schooling chances of girls than of boys. Many studies find a similar relationship between fathers' education and girls' schooling. The impact of school quality on the demand for schooling has also been addressed in African studies, but the aggregation of school quality indicators makes it difficult to interpret these effects adequately.

The country-level empirical studies reviewed in this chapter contribute a great deal to our understanding of the nature of household schooling decisions, and in particular their gendered character. Widespread data inadequacies, however, have compounded the intrinsic difficulties of measuring some of the key concepts. Conventional demand theory indicates that both the direct and the opportunity costs of education will play an important role in schooling decisions. Strong empirical evidence on this is still lacking, however, primarily because adequate statistical proxies, which are suited to the available data for SSA, are yet to be identified. More qualitative research methods are required to shed further light on these issues. This is demonstrated in Chapter 5, which discusses the findings of our in-depth school-based survey work in a range of African countries.

Chapter 4

Costs versus Commitment
in Nine Countries

Introduction

We now turn from analysis at global and regional levels to a more detailed examination of the problems facing primary schooling in nine African countries. This endeavour will occupy the next three chapters of the book, before returning later to more macro questions. We begin, in this chapter, by investigating aspects of the costs and financing of education in the nine countries, in so far as they are relevant to problems in the primary sector. The evidence from the demand studies examined in the last chapter indicated that household income and cost constraints interact with gendered attitudes towards schooling amongst parents, and others to cause under-enrolment, and particularly the exclusion of girls from school. The cross-country evidence also suggested that under-provision (manifest in large distances from home to school and poor school quality) provides additional disincentives for school attendance which, again, act on girls more strongly than on boys. Some, but not all, of these constraints can be addressed by public spending on schooling. Increased expenditures can help to improve school availability and quality; they can, by substituting for fees and other charges, reduce the level and incidence of direct private costs; and, under some circumstances, they can more directly alleviate the income constraint for poorer households. Thus, although achieving the right balance for public expenditures is only part of the challenge of achieving SFA in Africa, it is nevertheless a critically important aspect of any national strategy so to do.

This chapter examines the extent to which problems in primary schooling in the nine countries are caused by a lack of public resources being allocated to the system, and, in turn, whether resource constraints, where they occur, are unavoidable, or are more a matter of policy priority. We have shown (Chapter 2) that SSA as a whole devotes a greater proportion of GNP to public expenditure on education than most other developing regions. Nevertheless, there is considerable variation between individual countries. Whilst some spend a large part of their discretionary resources upon education – and upon primary education within it – others could clearly afford to increase further their spending on the sub-sector. In these cases, a lack of public commitment to primary schooling is an important part of the explanation for its present demise. These issues are examined for the nine countries included in our research. Each of the cost and resource determinants of the GER identified in Chapter 2 – levels of public and household spending on the primary system, its unit costs, and the size of the school-aged population – are investigated, using data collected from national sources.

Primary Enrolments in the Nine Countries

It can be seen from Figure 4.1 that there is a wide variation in primary enrolments amongst the nine countries: the GERs in the mid to late 1990s range from a mere 24 per cent in Ethiopia to well over 100 per cent in Malawi and Uganda. The West African Francophone countries, together with Ethiopia, have the lowest primary enrolment rates. They also have the largest gender gaps in enrolments, with, in Guinea, only half as many girls as boys being enrolled and only around two-thirds in Ethiopia and Mali. Thus, as was suggested by the cross-country analysis in Chapter 3, low enrolment countries in SSA, which require a considerable effort to achieve schooling for all, simultaneously face a challenge to overcome more acute gender constraints than exist in other countries. Although we shall see that many of these constraints require demand-side interventions, a move to SFA will often also require an increased commitment by governments to the financing of primary education, at the same time as improving the efficiency of the system.

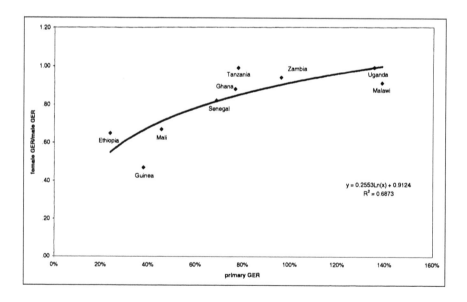

Figure 4.1 Primary GER and gender gap

Public Spending on Education

Previous chapters noted that levels of national wealth do not appear to be strongly related to primary enrolment ratios. This is also true of the nine countries studied here. Figure 4.2 shows that the three richest countries in per capita income terms – Ghana, Guinea and Senegal – have lower primary enrolment ratios than the three poorer countries of Malawi, Uganda and Zambia. Moreover, Ethiopia has the lowest primary enrolment ratio of the eight countries. Yet, its GDP per capita is similar to Malawi which has achieved UPE. Furthermore, the richest of the nine countries – Guinea – has the second lowest GER, with enrolments equal to less than 40 per cent of the school-age group. The scatter of the observations shown in the graph is very wide, and the lack of association indicates that the level of economic development of this group of SSA countries does not help to explain the diversity they manifest in primary enrolments.

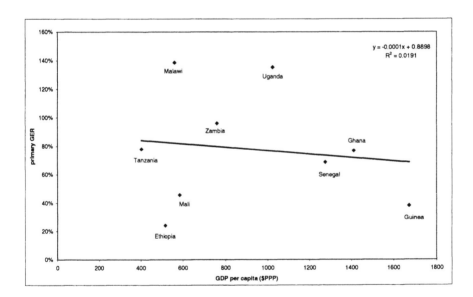

Figure 4.2 GDP per capita and primary GER

The size of government (measured by total public expenditure expressed as a proportion of GDP) varies substantially between countries, and is influenced both by national economic policy as well as by the ability of a particular government to mobilise resources through taxation. Public expenditure, as a proportion of GDP, is low in Guinea (only 10 per cent), compared with 26 per cent in Ghana (Table 4.1). So, although both of them allocate about 22 per cent of total spending to education, this amounts to a considerably greater per capita allocation of resources

Table 4.1 Recurrent expenditure on education, 1993/1994

	Eth	Gha	Gui	Malw	Mali	Sen	Tanz	Ugan	Zam
Government expenditure as a percentage of GDP	21	26	10	20	14	13	18	13	18
Recurrent education spending:									
As a percentage of government recurrent (excl. debt repayments)	19.7	21.6	21.8	20.9	19.2	33.0	21.6	21.9	16.5
As a percentage of government recurrent (incl. Debt repayments)	15.3	20.9	18.1	19.5	n.a.	17.7	15.6	n.a.	n.a.
As a percentage of GDP	2.7	4.3	1.7	3.6	2.4	3.3	3.5	2.5	2.5

Notes: n.a. – not available.
Sources: authors' calculations from unpublished national data sources; SSA for 1995 from Chapter 2.

in Ghana than in Guinea (since, as shown in Figure 4.2, per capita incomes in the two countries are not too far apart). Accordingly, given the diversity in the amount of resources available to governments, a focus on the proportion of the budget available to education can be misleading as an indicator of resource availability. It is nevertheless worth noting that, in general, the countries included in our study do allocate to education a significant proportion of their discretionary government recurrent expenditure (i.e. excluding debt repayment): in all countries except Zambia, at least one-fifth is spent on education.[1] Of course, SSA countries' ability

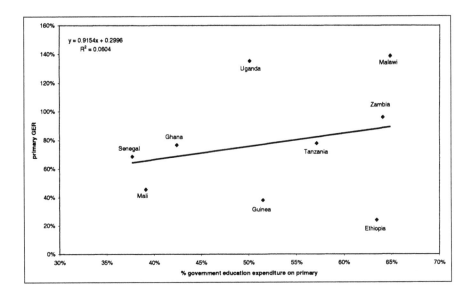

Figure 4.3 Public education spending on primary and GER

to spend on education (and on anything else) is generally constrained by their obligations to repay international debt. After such repayments in government expenditure, it can be seen from Table 4.1 that the proportion of total spending available for education is reduced – sometimes by a considerable amount. Thus, in the early 1990s, a significant proportion of public resources in these countries,

---

[1]   The focus of this chapter is recurrent expenditure. Capital spending tends to be very volatile, reflecting general fiscal constraints, changing conditions and dynamics in the education system. Furthermore, recurrent spending typically accounts for over 90 per cent of government expenditure on education in these (and most other) countries (see UNESCO, 2000c, Table 10).

which might otherwise be spent on the social sectors, was being allocated for debt repayment.[2]

The priority assigned by government to different levels of education can be illustrated by the proportion of recurrent education expenditure allocated to each level of the system. Figure 4.3 shows that these countries allocated between 38 per cent and 65 per cent of education budgets to primary education in the mid-1990s. In general, however, the graph confirms that there is no simple relationship between these proportionate allocations and the level of enrolments at primary level. This is mainly because total expenditures on education vary widely relative to GDP per capita. These differences generate odd comparisons between extremes.

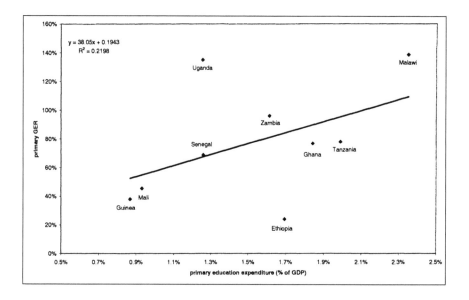

Figure 4.4 Public commitment to primary education and GER

For example, we can see that Malawi, having a GER of around 140, was allocating a similar proportion of its government education expenditure to the primary level as Ethiopia, which had a GER of only about 25. One explanation for this is that Malawi's unit costs of primary schooling were very low, whilst Ethiopia's were extremely high – for reasons we investigate later.

---

2   In practice, governments might not spend any more on education even if debt repayments were removed. However, HIPC programmes in each of the countries attempt to alleviate some of the burden of debt repayment with the intention of channelling resources that are freed to social sectors, including education. See Chapter 7 for a discussion of the implications of this.

As argued in Chapter 2, public spending on primary education, expressed as a proportion of GDP, provides a better measure of national commitment to primary education. It can be seen from Figure 4.4 that a fairly strong positive relationship between public spending – measured in this way – and primary enrolments, is apparent. Those countries with GERs lower than 75 are spending 1.7 per cent of GDP, or less, on primary education. Spending is particularly low in the Francophone West African countries, each of which have had very low enrolment ratios. On the other hand, it can be seen that Malawi and Uganda have achieved UPE with very different proportions of GDP being allocated to primary education. This partly reflects the fact that Uganda's GDP per capita, expressed in PPP terms, is almost double that of Malawi which means that a smaller proportionate allocation of GDP in Uganda provided a greater absolute level of resources per child than in Malawi. Ethiopia, on the other hand, contributed a relatively high proportion of GDP to primary education expenditure, whilst realising an extremely low primary GER. These variations can be explained by differences in public unit costs, as shown below.

Unit Costs

Table 4.2 compares the enrolment, cost and expenditure characteristics of the nine primary systems.[3] Countries are grouped according to their levels of spending on primary education and their levels of unit costs (shown in columns 7 and 8 of the table, respectively).[4] 'Moderate commitment' and 'moderate costs' are those

---

[3]   Costs in this chapter are shown both as a percentage of GDP per capita as well as in $US using purchasing power parity (PPP) exchange rates. Expressing costs as a percentage of GDP per capita avoids problems associated with currency conversion. This measure illustrates the extent to which expansion is constrained by the income level of a particular country. Costs are also converted into $PPP (calculated from World Bank, 2000a) to control for differences in the price of education inputs between countries. This enables a comparison of the absolute amount spent on education across the countries. It is useful to include both measures since, while a country might spend a small amount in $PPP terms compared with other countries, the amount it is able to spend might be constrained by a relatively low level of GDP per capita. See the Technical Appendix for more details of the calculation of $PPP.

[4]   Publicly financed unit costs are influenced by the proportion of students enrolled in private schools, taking the system as a whole. The unit costs presented in this chapter have been adjusted to indicate the average cost to the government of educating a child, including the subsidies paid by the government to private schools. For example, in Ethiopia a relatively sizeable proportion of children are enrolled in private schools (10 per cent). This reduces the average cost to the government per child in school, even though the government pays the wages of some teachers in private schools. The unit costs presented here are, therefore, influenced by the relative size of enrolment in private primary schools, which is separately reported in Table 4.2. These weighted unit costs have been calculated as:

Table 4.2   Public expenditures on primary education and related characteristics

	year of data	GER (%)	F/m GER (%)	% priv.	GDP pc ($)	GDP pc (PPP$)	x_g (%)	c_g (%)	a (%)	X_g for GER=100
GER less than 100%	(1)	(2)	(3)	(4)	(5)	(6)	(7)	(8)	(9)	(10)
Low commitment – low cost										
Guinea	1993/94	38	47	4	548	1673	0.9	11.7	17.7	2.1
Senegal	1997/98	69	82	12	498	1276	1.3	11.1	16.6	1.8
Zambia	1996/97	96	94	2	380	760	1.6	8.5	19.1	1.6
Low commitment – moderate cost										
Mali	1997/98	46	67	14	212	585	0.9	13.6	15.0	2.0
Moderate commitment – high cost										
Ethiopia	1993/94	24	65	10	102	517	1.7	38.7	17.9	6.9
Moderate commitment – moderate cost										
Ghana	1996/97	77	88	13	316	1411	1.8	14.1	17.1	2.4
Tanzania	1993/94	78	99	1	133	403	2.0	13.7	18.6	2.6
GER greater than 100%										
Low commitment – low cost										
Uganda	1997/98	135	82	8	303	1024	1.3	4.4	20.9	-
High commitment – low cost										
Malawi	1997	139	91	1	278	643	2.4	7.4	23.0	-
Mean		78	79		308	921	1.5	13.7	16.3	
Median		77	82		303	760	1.6	11.7	17.8	
SSA mean		83	83		777		1.9	13.6	17.0	
SSA median		76	84		350		1.5	11.5	16.6	

Sources: national data; SSA – Ch 2

Column Notes:

F/m GER = female GER as a percentage of male GER

a = primary school-aged population as a proportion of the total population

c_g = publicly funded primary unit costs as a percentage of GDP per capita

x_g = public recurrent spending on primary schooling as a percentage of GDP.

% priv. = private enrolment as a percentage of total.

(public recurrent unit costs × *proportion of enrolment in public schools)* + *(subsidy per private pupil* × *proportion of enrolment in private schools)* (see Al-Samarrai, 1997).

falling within a 10 per cent band around the SSA means for expenditures and costs, respectively. 'Low' and 'high' categories refer to countries with primary systems operating outside those margins.

We find that of the seven countries with GERs of less than 100, four of them – Guinea, Senegal, Zambia and Mali – were allocating, as public expenditures, a significantly smaller proportion of GDP to primary schooling than the average for SSA as a whole. The same countries, moreover, were not particularly constrained by having high unit costs of provision. Only Mali was at a cost-level equal to the mean for SSA, and the others were well below it. As shown in the final column of the table each of these countries would be able to achieve GERs of 100, at then present levels of unit costs, by increasing their resource allocations for primary schooling to around two per cent of GDP or less.[5] These countries, therefore, need to allocate no more than was spent on primary schooling by the average SSA country, in order to achieve UPE.[6] In these 'low commitment' cases, it is clear that the governments needed to increase their spending on primary education: UPE, at least in expenditure terms, appears to have been within relatively easy reach.

Two other countries – Ghana and Tanzania – were also within reach of UPE. In both of them, however, expenditures were already at around the average level for SSA countries. It can be seen from Table 4.2 (Column 10) that UPE expenditures would have required increased allocations by their governments of around one half of one per cent of GDP. This would have brought public spending on primary schooling to a similar level as that in Malawi. Only a modest increase

---

[5] Recalling the identity expressed in Chapter 2, the required amount of public recurrent spending, on primary schooling, as a percentage of GDP, (Req. x_g) to achieve a GER of 100 per cent, (with no change in unit costs, no real per capita growth in the economy, a constant proportion of primary school-aged population to the total population, and no demand constraints) is calculated as follows:

Req. $x_g = 100(a \times c_g)$

where

a = primary school-aged population as a proportion of the total population

c_g = publicly funded primary unit costs as a percentage of GDP per capita

x_g = public recurrent spending on primary schooling as a percentage of GDP.

[6] Strictly, this assumes both that there would be no significant difference between average and marginal unit costs as expansion proceeded, and that any demand constraints would be alleviated by the increased public expenditures. Neither of these conditions may hold. As regards the former, the cost of educating an additional student might initially be less than the average if it is possible to achieve economies of scale. On the other hand, as the country approaches universal primary education, the marginal cost may well exceed the average, where it proves more difficult, or expensive, to enrol those remaining out of school.

in commitment was required, and we know from Chapter 2 that similar allocations have been commonplace elsewhere in Africa.

Ethiopia, however, was in a different category. There was limited space for public expenditures on primary schooling to increase – accounting as they already did for 1.7 per cent of GDP. However, unit costs were three times the SSA average, and would have required an allocation of around seven per cent of GDP annually for UPE to be achieved. Thus, the high unit cost in Ethiopia represents a major constraint on the expansion of primary schooling in the country. Here, UPE would require both an increase in spending and sustained reforms to reduce unit costs.

As regards Uganda and Malawi, the two countries that had already achieved UPE (though not the more demanding SFA), it is notable that each of them are countries with very low unit costs of primary provision. Such costs in Malawi were around half the SSA average, and, in Uganda, they were less than one-third the average SSA value. In both cases, although they facilitated the rapid expansion to universal provision, these costs were too low to promote a viable quality of schooling. Uganda, furthermore, was spending, in the late 1990s, considerably less than two per cent of GDP on primary schooling. An early priority in that country was to increase such spending, so as to allow unit expenditures, and the quality of educational provision, to rise.

Unit Costs and Enrolment[7]

The strong negative relationship between unit costs and primary enrolments in the nine countries is shown more clearly in Figure 4.5. As was found in the cross-country data analysed in Chapter 3, those countries with low unit costs tend to have a higher proportion of children in school. It can be seen that in Uganda, Malawi and Zambia – the three countries with the highest enrolment ratios – recurrent government spending per pupil amounted to less than 10 per cent of per capita income. The West African group, with unit costs reaching up to twice as high as those in the Anglophone East African countries, have much lower levels of primary enrolments. Ethiopia is the extreme case, spending the equivalent of almost 40 per cent of per capita income on each pupil, yet having less than one quarter of its children enrolled in school. Unit costs in Ethiopia were, relative to per capita income, more than four times their levels in Uganda, Malawi and Zambia. In the light of such large cost differences Ethiopia's much lower level of enrolments should be no surprise.

The absolute differences in unit costs measured in $PPP terms, are also substantial. Figure 4.6 shows that the Anglophone East African countries spend around $50 per pupil, whereas Ghana, Guinea and Ethiopia spend about $200. It remains the case that those countries with the higher unit costs tend to have lower enrolments, Uganda and Malawi still being at one extreme and Ethiopia at the

---

[7]   As indicated earlier, we define unit costs as average recurrent costs per student. We should note, however, that marginal costs may be different.

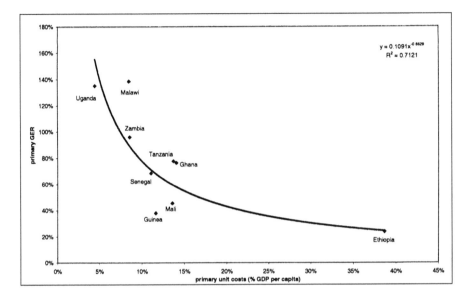

Figure 4.5 Primary unit costs and GER

other. But the countries are less closely bunched: Ethiopia is now less of an outlier, with its costs per pupil being equalled by those of Ghana and Guinea. Why, then, are there such differences in the costs of educating primary school pupils in these countries? To what extent are the lower costs, in some of the countries, a sign of greater efficiency or low school quality? Further analysis of these costs will help to suggest answers to these questions.

Costs per Primary Graduate

We should first note that limiting ourselves to a consideration of annual costs per pupil risks underestimating the magnitude of the economic challenge faced by governments seeking to achieve SFA. The total costs per primary completer have a separate and important influence upon this. Such costs are strongly affected by changes in efficiency at the school level even though, if children repeat classes, or leave school before completing the primary cycle, unit costs are also affected to some extent. For example, high rates of drop-out reduce the size of the age-cohort in the higher grades of primary school. Particularly in rural schools, this can cause average class-size and, in turn, the pupil-teacher ratio to fall below intended levels, with a concomitant increase in unit costs across the system. Repetition can sometimes have similar effects, where its incidence differs substantially between grades. However these two phenomena have a more substantial impact upon total, than upon average annual costs.

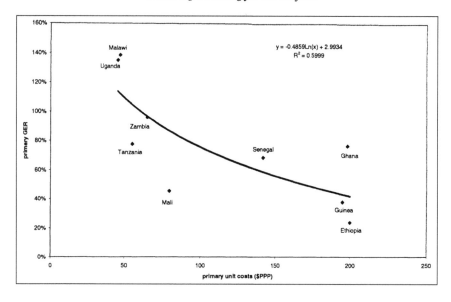

Figure 4.6 Primary unit costs ($PPP) and GER

   This is demonstrated by Table 4.3. It can be seen that repetition rates are particularly high in Malawi and in the Francophone countries, where up to one-fifth of pupils are repeating their previous year of study at any one time. Elsewhere, rates are below 10 per cent, but only in Tanzania and Ghana are repetition rates down to levels – at around three per cent – which would be considered acceptable in European countries.[8] Differences in rates of drop-out between the nine countries are, however, much more dramatic. The table shows that, although in Ghana, Mali and Zambia the great majority of entrants do stay in primary school for its duration, this is not so elsewhere. Only around three-quarters of the pupils in Senegal and Tanzania, about half in Ethiopia and Guinea, and less than one-fifth in Malawi and Uganda, stay the course. By consequence the average number of pupil years taken to produce a primary-school graduate (including both the years spent in repeating grades and those spent prior to dropping out) is considerably higher than the official length of the primary cycle in

---

8   It could be argued, however that these higher levels of 'efficiency' are sometimes achieved at the expense of quality. For example, of those who complete in Tanzania, only one-half of students perform sufficiently well to gain a primary-school-leaving certificate. Whilst this is partly a consequence of limitations placed on access to secondary schools, it significantly increases the costs of educating a 'successful' primary student (Peasgood *et al.*, 1997).

Table 4.3 Average annual costs per pupil and per completer

	Uganda	Malawi	Zambia	Senegal	Guinea	Ghana	Tanzania	Mali	Ethiopia
% repeaters (1)	7.3	15.1	6.4	13.3	21.9	3.6	3.1	17.9	8.9
% cohort completing primary cycle (2)	16.3	18.9	95.6	79.5	48.1	95.0	76.6	95.0	55.3
Official length of primary cycle (years) (3)	7.0	8.0	7.0	6.0	6.0	6.0	7.0	6.0	6.0
Average total years of study per graduate (4)	20.8	22.1	8.4	7.8	12.8	6.5	8.2	9.1	8.2
Average annual cost per pupil as % GDP per capita (5)	4.0	8.0	9.0	11.0	12.0	14.0	14.0	14.0	39.0
Average annual cost per completer as % GDP per capita (5 × 4/3)	12.0	22.0	11.0	14.0	26.0	15.0	16.0	21.0	53.0

Source: National data

most of the countries. To take the extreme cases, in Malawi, where the official duration of the primary cycle is eight years, the average number of pupil-years taken to produce a primary-school completer is 22, whilst in Uganda, with a cycle-length of seven years, it is 21 years. This three-fold difference arises mainly because, in both cases, a large proportion of children do not make it beyond Standard 3. Here, then, the cost of educating a child who completes the primary cycle is, on average, almost three times as high as it would be if there were no repetition and dropout.

It can be seen from the table that the cost-ranking of countries changes when the focus shifts from a consideration of annual costs per pupil to annual costs per primary completer. Zambia displaces Uganda as the lowest cost case, and Malawi's costs become similar to the high-cost cases of Mali and Guinea. Ethiopia's costs per completer, however, continue to mark it as easily the highest cost country, owing to its highly inefficient school system. These facts serve to emphasise the importance of improving internal efficiency, so as to ensure that much higher proportions of children complete their primary schooling, and to reduce the overall levels of costs. Both of these conditions are necessary if SFA in Africa is to be achieved.

Teacher Costs

In all nine countries, spending on teachers' earnings has constituted the largest part of government recurrent spending on the primary system, ranging from around 80 per cent in Mali and Uganda to close to 100 per cent in Ethiopia and Senegal (Table 4.4).[9] Accordingly, with so little margin left for other expenditures, the main determinants of expenditures per pupil in these countries, are the average salaries (and allowances) of teachers and the average pupil-teacher ratio. These items will now be discussed in turn.

Figure 4.7 compares primary teachers' wages for each country, with their primary unit costs. In each case the variables are shown relative to GDP per capita. It can be seen that the distribution of teachers' wages was large – from around twice the level of per capita income in Uganda and Zambia, to about six-fold in Mali and Senegal, and as high as 13-fold in Ethiopia. The very strong relationship between unit costs and teachers' remuneration is evident from the graph. Clearly, in cases where cost-control is at the top of the reform agenda, policies on teacher earnings would need to represent an early priority for review.

Ethiopia again stands out as an exceptional case, with well over 80 per cent of the working population engaged in agricultural activities, and only 54 per cent of the population of working age, those engaged in formal employment are a small

---

[9]   Accounting systems in most of these countries do not separately identify teachers' wages, those of administrators and other workers in schools. Nevertheless, very few primary schools in the nine countries employ administrators or other workers, and, where they do, the salaries are often paid by the community rather than by the government.

Table 4.4 Average teacher costs

	Ethiopia	Ghana	Guinea	Malawi	Mali	Senegal	Tanz	Ugand	Zambia	SSA
Percentage of school-level expenditure on wages	99	95	89	93	78	99	92	81	92	n.a.
Average teacher salaries (% GDP pc)	12.8	4.3	4.3	3.7	5.5	6.5	4.1	2.2	2.4	3.5
Average teacher salaries ($PPP)	6592	6070	7264	2406	3192	8248	1666	2247	1786	n.a.
Pupil teacher ratio	30	32	46	61	73	56	36	55	38	48

Notes: Teacher salaries are calculated by dividing the primary teacher wage bill by the number of primary teachers employed by the government.
n.a. – not available

Sources: National data; Chapter 2 for SSA data.
$PPP data from WDI 2000 CD Rom

minority of the population. Given its under-expanded school system, it is to be expected that teachers in Ethiopia will be well paid in comparison with per capita incomes, and indeed with many other waged employees. The extent to which it is out of line with other countries, however, indicates that there will be strong pressures on teacher wages in Ethiopia to fall – not necessarily absolutely, but in relation to per capita incomes – as expansion proceeds.

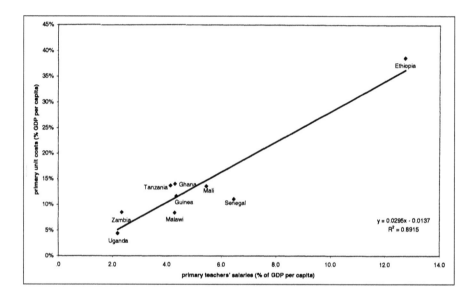

Figure 4.7 Primary teacher salaries and unit costs

Amongst the other countries, the Francophone group – Senegal, Mali and Guinea – emerged with the highest salary costs, as Chapter 2 led us to expect. There had been a longstanding acknowledgement that teacher costs in these countries needed to be reduced. Senegal initiated a number of policies to secure reductions in the real average earnings of teachers (see Box 4.1), and all three countries adopted a strategy of recruiting contract teachers in order to reduce costs. But even the earnings of the latter remained high in relation to teacher earnings in many of the Anglophone countries. For example, the annual salary of a contract teacher in Senegal was equivalent to three times its GDP per capita in the late 1990s. This was higher than average teacher costs for the whole primary teaching service in Zambia and Uganda, as shown in Figure 4.7.

More generally, the average primary teacher costs in Malawi, Uganda and Zambia were, as a proportion of GDP per capita, the lowest of all nine countries. It should be noted that part of the reason for these differences is that wages in East and Southern Africa have been particularly sharply eroded by inflationary pressures in recent years (see Box 4.1). In addition, the rapid expansion of the education systems in Malawi and Uganda required the recruitment of a large number of new teachers. In Malawi, 18,000 untrained teachers were recruited in

Box 4.1   Different approaches to reducing teacher costs in Zambia and Senegal

After dramatic falls in the international copper price in the mid-1970s, the Zambian economy, being dependent upon copper for more than 90 per cent of its export earnings, was plunged into recession, and a long period of economic adjustment began. During the last two decades of the century, national and household incomes, and the value of public spending, fell sharply. Real wages and salaries began a period of secular decline, instrumented by a series of major devaluations of the Zambian Kwacha.

Not all workers were equally affected. In the public sector, the government aimed to narrow the gaps between the highest and least well-paid employees. Thus, by 1997 senior managers in the public service were receiving only one-tenth of the real value of their 1975 salaries, whereas junior clerical and unskilled workers faced somewhat lower declines of 50-60 per cent of 1975 earnings. Teachers, however, were not amongst the most favoured groups: their salaries, by 1997, had declined to about 18 per cent of their 1975 real values. Further, their differential treatment meant that starting salaries for trained primary school teachers were scarcely 20 per cent higher than unskilled rates, and only 8 per cent more than the earnings of telephonists and junior clerks. Living standards were even more adversely affected, because housing and other allowances, which had been additional to cash earnings until 1992, were incorporated in basic salaries thereafter.

Facilitated by these reductions in teacher costs, government spending on education fell from around 5 per cent of GDP in the early 1980s to only about 2.5 per cent in the late 1990s. However, primary teachers earned less than was necessary to provide food for an average family, and their morale was very low, even compared with other public sector workers. Our surveys revealed high rates of absenteeism and moonlighting amongst teachers – necessitated by their need for supplementary earnings. Clearly, this approach to cost reduction was counterproductive for the quality of Zambian schooling.

In Senegal, too, the real salaries of civil servants fell by almost 50 per cent between 1980 and 1998, although, unlike Zambia, teachers were not more disadvantaged than other groups. Moreover, at the end of the period, their earnings in $PPP terms remained amongst the highest in Africa. Recognising the need to reduce costs, the government followed a number of strategies. First, teacher assistants (with lower qualifications and salaries) rose from around one-third to two-thirds of new recruits to the profession. Second, a new category of 'volunteer teacher' – secondary school leavers with three months of teacher training – was introduced. For a period of four years, volunteers received an allowance equivalent to about one-third of a fully qualified teacher's salary. Third, a category of 'contract teachers' was formed, into which volunteers could be promoted after their four-year term, subject to merit. Earnings were equivalent to those of fully qualified teachers, although, not being civil servants, they did not qualify for housing or education allowances. In these ways the teaching force, and school enrolments, were expanded at lower cost than before, without imposing further reductions in standards of living on those teachers who were already employed.

Sources: Colclough (1997b); Kasonde-Ng'andu (2000a); Dioum Diokhane (2000a).

1994/95 in response to the massive increase in primary enrolments, thereby doubling the number of teachers available. Accordingly, by 1997, 51 per cent of the primary teaching force were untrained (Kadzamira and Chibwana, 2000). Similarly, in Uganda, one-third of primary-school teachers were untrained in 1997 (Tumushabe *et al.*, 2000). Given the age profile, level of qualifications and years of experience of these recently recruited teachers, the average teacher salary was, therefore, considerably closer to the start of the salary scale in these countries than would otherwise have been the case.

We should note, however, that comparisons of the relationship between average teacher salaries and GDP per capita can be misleading. Teachers' salaries, measured in this way, tend to fall as GDP per capita rises, mainly because the education (and, thus, the earnings) of an average income-earner rises relative to the education level of a teacher, but also because the proportion of the population of working age also tends to increase as countries become wealthier (see for example Cox Edwards, 1993, cited in Mehrotra and Buckland, 1998). Expressing teacher salaries in $PPP terms, provides a different way of comparing costs, and an indication of the relative purchasing power of teacher salaries in the different countries. In Figure 4.8, the strong relationship between average primary teachers'

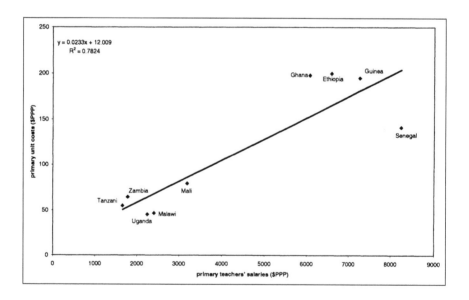

Figure 4.8 Primary teacher salaries and unit costs ($PPP)

salaries and primary unit costs, measured in this way, is again evident. It can be seen that teachers in East and Southern African countries receive, on average, extremely low salaries in $PPP terms (less than $PPP2,500 per annum), whereas their counterparts in Ethiopia, Guinea and Senegal receive three times that amount.

In countries where salaries are particularly low, including Tanzania and Zambia, teachers are often found to be engaged, during school hours, in other casual employment, so as to supplement their income (Peasgood *et al.*, 1977; Kasonde Ng'andu *et al.*, 2000). It can be argued, therefore that in some of these countries, average salaries of teachers have been too low and need to be increased. Implications of this for government education expenditure are investigated in Chapter 6.

Pupil-teacher Ratios

The second major determinant of unit costs is the pupil-teacher ratio. For given levels of average teacher salaries, lower pupil-teacher ratios, generate higher unit costs of provision, because a larger number of teachers are thereby required to teach the same number of pupils. Although Figure 4.9 provides some evidence that primary unit costs tend to fall with higher pupil-teacher ratios, this relationship is not very strong across the nine countries. The main reason for this is that, as indicated in Chapter 2, the cost difference in average teacher salaries between the Anglophone and Francophone countries is, to some extent, compensated by the latter having higher pupil-teacher ratios than the former. The evidence from our case-study countries provides some support for this. As Figure 4.10 shows, Ethiopia is, again, an exception. But otherwise, relatively high average teacher

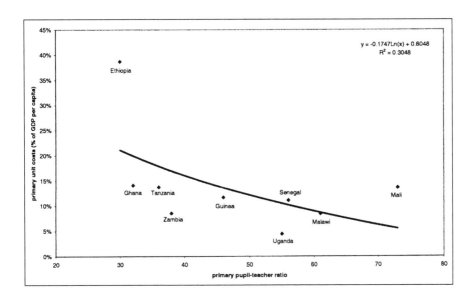

Figure 4.9 Pupil-teacher ratio and unit costs

salaries as a proportion of GDP per capita in Mali, Senegal and – to a lesser extent – in Guinea, were offset by relatively high pupil-teacher ratios. Ghana, Tanzania and Zambia, on the other hand, achieved an acceptable average pupil-teacher ratio whilst having moderate average teacher salaries.

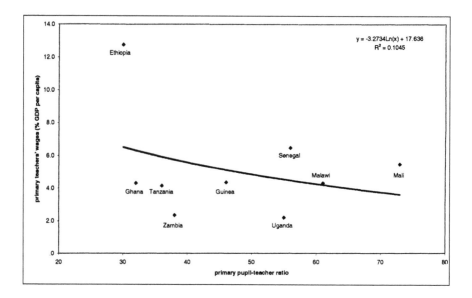

Figure 4.10 Pupil-teacher ratio and teacher salaries

One interesting pattern revealed by both Figures 4.9 and 4.10 is that the group of countries with very high pupil-teacher ratios (in excess of 55:1) includes not only two Francophone countries, but also Malawi and Uganda from the Anglophone group. In all these cases, however, the high pupil-teacher ratios can be seen as a response to high costs. In the former Francophone pair, the high average teacher wages prompted large class sizes, so as to bring unit costs within an affordable range. In the latter, the high pupil-teacher ratios were a function of the high total costs of running the primary system given its then recent quantitative expansion, notwithstanding the low-to-average levels of teacher costs that held in both these cases.

In sharp contrast, the average pupil-teacher ratio was relatively low in Ethiopia, despite its having extremely high average teacher salaries and thus unit costs, relative to other countries. As will become clear from the next chapter, the main reason for the low pupil-teacher ratio in Ethiopia is the low rural demand for education. Thus, many rural schools operated below capacity, while the pupil-teacher ratio in urban areas was considerably higher. Furthermore, the size of the teaching force was maintained during the enrolment decline of the late 1980s, resulting in a sharply lower pupil-teacher ratio (Rose *et al.*, 1997). This, combined with high average teacher salaries, is, therefore, an extremely important explanation for Ethiopia's unit costs being much higher than those in other countries. We should note, however, that unit costs would be likely to decline in response to an increase in demand for education, since that should allow an increase in the pupil-teacher ratio in areas where schools were operating below capacity.

Learning Materials

The availability of adequate learning materials is an extremely important condition for the achievement of good-quality education, although the effectiveness of their use is strongly influenced, *inter alia*, by the quality of the teaching force and by class size. Evidence from the nine countries shows, however, that the availability of learning materials is usually grossly inadequate. In most of the countries, textbooks were provided by international agencies whose expenditure was generally included in the capital budget. Expenditure on learning materials by the governments was mainly limited to office supplies, teaching aids, exercise books, pens and pencils. Classroom observations in the countries showed that these supplies were frequently insufficient, and sometimes not available at all. Table 4.5 shows that learning materials usually accounted for a very small percentage of unit expenditures in each of the countries, and that they were tiny in absolute terms. Thus, they had little impact upon total unit costs, and no particular patterns are evident across low and high cost countries, or between Francophone and Anglophone groups. In all cases, expenditures amounted to less than $PPP20 per pupil, and in seven of the nine countries they were only $PPP10 or less. Ethiopia and Malawi, having the lowest and highest GERs, respectively, each spent amongst the lowest amounts on learning materials per pupil ($PPP3). In Ethiopia, the high teacher costs discussed earlier squeezed resources which might otherwise have been available for learning materials, whilst in Malawi, such spending was eroded following the introduction of free primary education (Kadzamira and Chibwana, 2000). Uganda, by contrast, sustained a somewhat higher per capita expenditure on learning materials ($PPP9), at the same time as achieving much higher enrolments. This was facilitated by the introduction of a 'UPE capitation grant' to schools to compensate for their loss in income following the abolition of school fees in 1997 (Tumushabe *et al.*, 2000). The governments of Mali and Uganda both allocated around one-fifth of their unit expenditures to learning materials – the highest in the group. However, as Chapter 6 shows, even where spending on learning materials was high relative to the other countries, resources in schools were still often insufficient to ensure that minimum basic learning requirements were met. Senegal, by contrast, spent least on these provisions,

Table 4.5 Expenditure on learning materials and operating expenses

	Ethiopia	Ghana	Guinea	Malawi	Mali	Senegal	Tanzania	Uganda	Zambia
Learning materials and operating expenses									
Percenatge of primary unit costs	1.0	5.0	11.0	7.0	22.0	0.4	8.0	19.0	5.0
Per pupil cost (as a percentage of GDP per capita)	0.6	0.7	1.1	0.5	2.4	0.1	1.5	0.9	0.3
Per pupil cost ($PPP)	3.0	10.0	18.0	3.0	14.0	1.0	6.0	9.0	2.5

Sources:　National data

relying on parents to buy textbooks and other materials for their children.[10] It is clear that increased commitment by governments to expenditures on learning materials, whilst ensuring a higher quality of teachers and appropriate class size, is required in all the countries to secure schooling of acceptable quality over the long term.

The Influence of Population Size

As indicated in Chapter 2, the relative size of the school-age population can make an important difference to the cost burden of achieving SFA. For countries with similar levels of income and unit costs of schooling, a higher population growth rate and, therefore, larger proportion of school-age population, implies that the cost of achieving SFA will be greater. Table 4.2 (Column 9) shows that, in all of the case-study countries, the proportion of the primary school-aged population was high, varying between approximately 15 per cent in Mali and 23 per cent in Malawi. Differences in the relative sizes of eligible populations between these countries arose partly because of differences in the length of the primary cycle. They were higher in the Anglophone countries which had a longer primary-school cycle (eight years in Malawi and seven years in Tanzania, Uganda and Zambia, compared with six years in the other countries).[11] Thus, the school-age population would be reduced from 23 per cent to approximately 17.3 per cent in Malawi, if it had the same length of primary cycle as Mali. This means that Malawi's total cost-burden (in population terms) was almost one-third higher than that of Mali owing to differences in the length of the primary cycle. On the other hand, however, even if the length of the cycle were the same in both countries, Malawi's SFA costs would remain 15 per cent higher than Mali, because of differences in the age-structure of the population. This indicates that, given population growth rates of between 2.5 per cent and three per cent in each of the nine countries, demographic pressure and trends will strongly influence the cost trajectory of achieving SFA.[12]

---

[10]   More recently, education sector development programmes, financed by the World Bank in Senegal and Mali, made available sufficient quantities of textbooks, free of charge, for all primary-school pupils. Laudable though this is, it does not provide a sustainable long-term solution.

[11]   From 1994/95, the primary school cycle in Ethiopia was extended to eight years. Data for the previous year are shown in Table 4.2.

[12]   Population growth rates in some East and South African countries, in particular, are being negatively affected by HIV/AIDS. While some account in taken of this in national estimates of the school-age population, its precise effect is not known.

Private Spending on Education

Government expenditure on education in each of the countries was supplemented by non-government sources of educational finance, including from households, communities and the private sector. Households contributed to education through the payment of fees, and by buying books, stationery and school clothing.

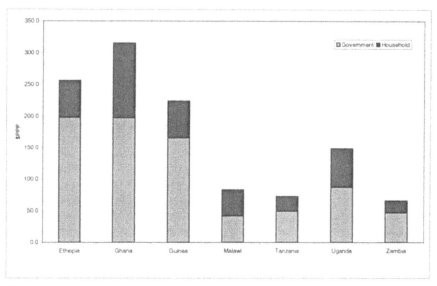

Sources:
Ethiopia – Weir and Knight (1996) – education sub-sample of the Ethiopia Rural Household Survey (data include fees, stationery and clothing)
Ghana – Penrose (1998) – 1995 survey (data include tuition, PTA fund, uniform, stationery, textbooks and food)
Guinea – Tembon *et al.* (1997)
Malawi – Rose (2002) – 1998 household survey (data include school contributions, stationery, clothes and pocket money)
Tanzania - Mason and Khandker (1996) from HRDS (data include fees and contributions, uniforms, textbooks and stationery, and other expenditure)
Uganda – Opolot (1994) – 1992 survey (NB pre-UPE) (data include uniforms, PTA fund, building fund, textbooks and stationery, extra tuition and other expenditure)
Zambia – World Bank (1996) from 1996 survey data (data includes uniform, stationery, PTA-fund and general purpose fund)

Figure 4.11 Private/public expenditure per primary pupil ($PPP)

Estimates from household survey data show that households typically contribute substantially towards the costs of primary schooling, and provide a sizeable proportion of its total costs (Figure 4.11).[13] While part of these costs is fees, a large proportion of household expenditure is spent on non-fee items, with the highest spending often being on clothing. Tanzania is a typical example, where approximately one-quarter of household school expenditures is spent on fees, one-half on uniforms, one-fifth on books and supplies and the remainder on miscellaneous costs (Mason and Khandker, 1996). For the countries shown in Figure 4.11, Ethiopia, Ghana and Guinea have the highest levels of publicly financed unit costs. Even in these cases between 23 per cent (Ethiopia) and 37 per cent (Ghana) of total costs are met by households. Higher proportionate contributions by households are made in the lower-cost countries, with half or more of schooling costs being met in Malawi and Zambia. In the case of Malawi, despite the abolition of fees, households more-or-less match the government's expenditures, partly because the latter are so low. The greatest part of this expenditure is on school clothing, although households continue to supply exercise books and pens and pencils despite the government having promised that these would be provided under the free primary education programme (Rose, 2002). The absolute contributions to costs are surprisingly similar across the countries. In five of the seven cases, these varied between $40 and $60 per child per year. Outliers are Ghana, where parents provide around $120, and Tanzania where the PPP average contribution was around $24.

Although household contributions can help to improve the supply and quality of schooling by complementing the resources provided by the government, the next chapter will show that high costs are an important deterrent to children attending school, particularly for poorer households. Policy in the 1980s and early 1990s focussed on shifting costs from the public to private domains, resulting in a negative impact upon enrolments, or their rate of growth. In Senegal during the 1990s, the proportion of public spending allocated to education fell, whilst that from households increased from nine per cent of national education spending in 1992, to 20 per cent in 1997. During those years enrolment ratios throughout the school system declined. More dramatic was the impact of fee-abolition in Malawi and Uganda, which resulted in a doubling of enrolments in each country within a few years. There is ample evidence then, from our studies, that high direct costs of schooling provide strong disincentives for enrolment – particularly for girls. Progress towards SFA with gender equality will require reductions in these direct costs in most of the nine countries – particularly in those, such as Ethiopia and Guinea, which are characterised by both low enrolments and large gender gaps.

Communities often provide labour and materials for school construction and maintenance. However, household and community contributions are often diverse and difficult to estimate (Bray, 1996). Although information may exist at the local

---

[13]   The types of costs collected by household surveys often vary (for example, some include non-discretionary costs such as clothing, whereas others may not), making comparisons between countries problematic. Data shown in Figure 4.11 are estimated from surveys which include all direct costs (clothing/uniform, fees and other contributions, stationery and textbooks, food, travel etc) incurred by households.

levels of administration, the availability of nationally aggregated data is uncommon. For example, although in Guinea the government required village communities to contribute 10 per cent of the total cost of building new schools, there were no records kept of total contributions made, either at local or national level. In Malawi and Uganda, despite the abolition of officially-set fees, communities were still expected to contribute to school development in cash or kind. Similar community contributions were raised in the other six countries and in all cases they were accounted for and spent at the school level. Finance may also be generated from income-earning schemes operated by the schools. In Ethiopia, for example, the main source of non-salary income at the school level was often from renting or sharecropping arrangements on school farm-land (particularly in areas where fees were no longer charged) (Rose *et al.*, 1997). In Tanzania, pupils undertook self-reliance activities – such as collecting thatching grass, working as hired labour on surrounding farms, clearing, cultivating and harvesting for villagers – in order to earn income for the school (Peasgood *et al.*, 1997). These contributions were, as reported in Chapter 5, found to be an important reason for absenteeism and drop-out. They were often not monetised and usually accounted for at the school level, such that national data on their magnitude are not available.

Finally, the private sector (including voluntary organisations, NGOs, religious bodies, individual and corporate businesses), in each of the countries, supplements government expenditure by financing, or directly providing, private schooling. Private schools are also, of course, supported by households through the payment of fees, and by government subsidies (for example, in the training of teachers, or, in some cases, the payment of teachers' salaries, or the purchase of textbooks). The quality of these private schools varies substantially, and in some countries not all private schools are registered, making regulation of the private sector difficult. This was particularly evident after the achievement of UPE in Malawi and Uganda, where private schooling mushroomed following the massive increase in enrolment and subsequent deterioration in quality of government schools.[14] Of the other countries, Ethiopia, Ghana, Mali and Senegal have a sizeable private sector in education (with 10-14 per cent of children enrolled in private schools), whereas Guinea, Tanzania and Zambia have fewer than five per cent of their children similarly enrolled. Thus, the encouragement of the private sector in education, with due care being given to its regulation, can sometimes help to alleviate part of the cost burden in education which otherwise faces the government, thereby allowing public spending to be targeted towards the needy groups.

---

[14]   In Malawi, national statistics on private primary schools are not collected. It is not, therefore, known how many such schools exist, nor how many children are enrolled in these schools. Data from Ministry of Education statistics in Uganda indicate that eight per cent of children in school are typically enrolled in private schools. However, given that many new schools remain unregistered, it is likely that the figure is higher than this. This also suggests that enrolment rates in Malawi and Uganda could be even higher than those presented above.

Conclusions

This chapter has highlighted considerable differences in the amount spent by governments in the nine countries on primary schooling, which has had a fundamental influence upon their ability to achieve SFA. Teacher costs have dominated government spending in each of the countries, whilst expenditure on learning materials has been minimal in most cases, bringing adverse implications for the quality of education.

In Ethiopia, where enrolment remains amongst the lowest in the world and the gender gap is wide, spending per pupil was considerably higher than in the other countries owing to the high cost of teacher provision. This was found, in turn, to be caused by Ethiopia's high average teacher salaries relative to GDP per capita, and to its maintenance of a relatively low average pupil-teacher ratio. Its move towards SFA will require the realisation of some strong efficiency gains. By contrast, Malawi and Uganda achieved UPE at relatively low spending levels per pupil, although both internal efficiency and the quality of education need to be improved in these countries, in order for SFA to be achieved.

Guinea, Senegal and Zambia all have had relatively low levels of public spending per pupil, and allocated a smaller proportion of GDP than the SSA average to primary education. Senegal afforded its relatively high teacher salaries by maintaining high pupil-teacher ratios and low expenditure on learning materials, bringing costs for school quality. Guinea's low commitment to spending on primary education was witnessed by its low GER of just 38 per cent, with less than one-third of those in school being girls. In Zambia, low spending per pupil primarily reflected its very low teachers' salaries. Notwithstanding its risks for teacher morale, the country had achieved relatively low pupil-teacher ratios, and a higher enrolment rate than most in the group. Public spending per primary pupil in Ghana, Mali and Tanzania was close to the SSA average, although there were again important differences in cost structures between these countries. Ghana and Tanzania showed moderate commitment to the provision of primary education, with levels of public spending, as a proportion of GDP, being similar to the SSA average. These two countries had reasonably low (less than 40:1) pupil-teacher ratios and teacher salaries, relative to GDP per capita, in the middle range. These attributes have helped to deliver GERs greater than 75 per cent. Mali, by contrast, showed a low commitment to primary schooling on the expenditures criterion. It followed a pattern similar to other Francophone countries, with a high pupil-teacher ratio and relatively high teacher salaries relative to its per capita income. This cost structure translated into a low GER and a wide gender gap.

Although the governments in each of the countries maintained primary responsibility for the provision and financing of education, public expenditure was supplemented by households who often bearing a substantial proportion of schooling costs. We have seen (and the next chapter confirms) how this can affect household demand for education, particularly for girls. Pressure on government resources was also commonly relieved to some extent by the private sector, although its role was usually small, yet bringing attendant problems of equity and regulation. External support to education by international agencies also played an important role in the financing of primary education during the 1990s. Each of these different cost features requires targeted reforms, discussed later in the book. Meanwhile, the next chapter examines the specific constraints influencing the demand for girls' and boys' education that our studies identified. These, too, will need to be anticipated and assuaged, if programmes to achieve SFA are to stand much chance of success.

Chapter 5

Gender Disparities in Schooling: Causes and Constraints

Introduction

Statistical analysis can identify trends in, and associations between, socio-economic characteristics which can be quantified. However, in order to establish the reasons why such associations exist, supplementary methods are often required. For example, if we wish to understand why there appears to be a link between the proportion of teachers who are female and the enrolment of girls in primary school, it may be helpful to ask parents whether, and in what ways, the presence of female teachers affects their decisions about the schooling of their children. Similarly, just as we have shown that both household surveys and cross-country comparisons have not succeeded satisfactorily in demonstrating the role of opportunity costs in schooling decisions, so more detailed, qualitative survey work may be needed, if real insights about these matters are to be gained.

In each of our nine SSA country studies, school-based surveys were conducted using questionnaires, supplemented by focus-group discussions. These discussions involved a wide range of people in the community, including teachers, parents, pupils and others. This approach allowed the collection of qualitative case-study information which greatly enhanced our interpretation and understanding of the quantitative results.

In presenting and discussing these results, a more selective approach is adopted than that used in the preceding chapter. Discussion of the constraints bearing on school enrolment, and of the causes of gender disparities, requires at least some consideration of the historical, social and political context for the state of education in these countries. Since this cannot easily be provided for all nine cases, the chapter focuses upon the detailed results for Ethiopia, Guinea and Tanzania. The studies in these countries were conducted during the first phase of fieldwork on the project. The six second-phase studies – for Ghana, Mali, Malawi, Senegal, Uganda and Zambia – were somewhat larger in scale, but followed the same methodology as those in the first phase. Thus, our discussion of the results from the first group of countries is supplemented, where relevant, by information from the second group, to provide confirmation, comparison or contrast. In this way, we indicate the extent to which the causes and constraints revealed in the first set of countries have more general validity throughout the region. Accordingly, the chapter begins with brief accounts of the historical evolution of educational policy, and of the policy environment for girls' education, in Ethiopia, Guinea and Tanzania, before discussing the main findings from the schools surveys.

Educational Development in Ethiopia, Guinea and Tanzania

The economic and social circumstances of Ethiopia, Guinea and Tanzania differ in important ways. Whilst Ethiopia has the second largest population in sub-Saharan Africa (54 million in 1995), those of Tanzania and Guinea are smaller (28.8 million and 6.2 million, respectively). Partly as a result of Guinea's mineral wealth (bauxite, diamonds, gold and iron), its GNP per capita ($US540 in 1998) is slightly higher than the SSA mean, and substantially higher than that for Ethiopia and Tanzania (US$100 and $210, respectively) (Table 5.1). However, notwithstanding Guinea's greater wealth, it has only achieved relatively low levels of social and human development. This is so, not only in comparison to the average for SSA, but also to Tanzania which, amongst the three countries, has had a much better record on mortality and literacy rates, and on access to services.

Table 5.1 Socio-economic indicators, 1997-1998

	GNP pc (US$) 1988	Life Expectancy at Birth	IMR (per 1,000 live births)	Adult literacy rate (%)		Without Access to Services (%)		
				M	F	Drinking water	Health facilities	Sanitation facilities
Ethiopia	100	43	111	42	29	75	45	81
Guinea	540	47	126	52	24	54	55	69
Tanzania	210	48	92	82	62	34	7	14
SSA	480	49	105	50	48	50	NA	56

Source: United Nations (1999), World Bank (2000b).

The current status of the education systems in each of the three countries is inextricably linked to their historical past. In each case, traditional education provided by the elders, the church or the mosque pre-dates the establishment of formal education. Formal schooling was first introduced by Christian missionaries whose aims were furthered by educating the local population to read the Bible. Secular schools were introduced in the late nineteenth/early twentieth centuries. Whereas the education systems in Guinea and Tanzania developed from their colonial heritages, Ethiopia, which was only briefly colonised, chose to develop its system along European lines, partly to facilitate easier communication with the outside world (Tekeste, 1990). These different histories will now be briefly discussed.

Although the Germans introduced secular schools to Tanzania in the 1890s, the British who took over the colony after the First World War had the major impact on its educational development. The British administration laid new emphasis on the political and economic goals of education. A policy of 'Education for Adaptation' was introduced in 1925 which sought to combine Western values with the development needs of local people. The government believed education to be the key to political and socio-economic development, and expanded its provision. Nevertheless, African education was mainly provided by missionaries in village or bush schools which, by 1931, still accounted for approximately 82 per cent of total primary enrolments (Buchert, 1994). After the Second World War, greater emphasis was laid on 'Education for Modernisation'. This aimed to develop post-primary education, to provide knowledge and skills for political and economic development. However, there was a dual system: 'Education for Adaptation' for the African masses and 'Education for Modernisation' for Asians and Europeans and a few selected Africans. The curriculum and costs of the two systems differed substantially. The medium of instruction for primary education in African schools was Kiswahili and the curriculum was based on vocational agricultural education (Brock-Utne, 1993). By contrast, the language of instruction in European and Asian schools was English, and the purely academic curriculum prepared children for post-primary education. Unit costs in European schools were five times those in Asian schools, and 60 times those in African schools (Temu, 1995). Although the size of the African system was large compared with the European and Asian systems, very few Africans had access to secondary education. This, therefore, severely restricted their access to formal employment, where the language of administration was English, and for which they were not appropriately trained.

In Guinea, the colonial administration's educational aims and policies were rather different from those of Tanzania. Unlike the expanded system for Africans in Tanzania, access to primary education in Guinea was limited to the few who were needed to assist in local administration. Education policy aimed to eradicate local cultural values and to achieve complete acculturation of the educated elite. Consequently, schools provided education based on the French curriculum and eliminated traditional education, which was believed to be a barrier to development. The language of instruction at the primary level was French, and the curriculum was purely academic. It did not include agriculture, which was the main occupation of the majority of the population, nor any vocational subjects to prepare students for work outside the colonial administration. Missionaries were actively involved in educational provision and they were supported financially by the French government. Although parallel systems (Koranic schools and *medersas*) existed, these were neither funded nor encouraged by the colonial administration. Tension existed between the population and the French administration regarding these discriminative educational policies, which favoured the few Christians rather than Muslims, who were in the majority.

Although Ethiopia was not colonised (other than briefly by the Italians from 1936 to 1941), its education system was also heavily influenced by Europe, because the monarchy sought to administer the country along European lines.

Textbooks were mainly from UK and USA, and were not adapted to suit local culture (Abraham, 1994; Teshome, 1979). Languages of instruction were either English or French, depending on the school. The Italian occupation brought major setbacks to the development of education, with many schools being destroyed or converted into hospitals or barracks. Furthermore, many educated Ethiopians were killed. After independence, expansion of the system resumed with greater vigour. The language of instruction, initially English, became Amharic from 1955. The change partly derived from nationalism, and partly from the practical impossibility of continuing to use expensive expatriate teachers in the expanding system (McNab, 1989). Expansion was increasingly constrained, however, by a lack of funds (Tekeste, 1990). Unlike in Guinea and Tanzania, where the colonial administrations used both national and external resources to finance education, the Ethiopian system relied mainly on national resources. Over the decade ending in 1961/62, for example, the number of schools remained at around 500 despite a nine per cent average annual increase in enrolments over the period (Teshome, 1979). Given the traditionally strong link between the Church and the monarchy, a Christian bias in education was evident in the early stages, while Muslims (approximately one-third of the population) were discriminated against. This was exacerbated by Arabic not being taught in schools, by all children being required to attend school on Friday, and by the predominance of Christian teachers and administrators. Furthermore, Muslims had difficulties in gaining access to government employment, which was traditionally reserved for the politically dominant Christian population. All these factors reduced the incentives for Muslims to gain education (Markakis, 1974).

In each of the countries, formal education was initially available only for boys. Although girls' schools did become established, places for girls continuously lagged behind those for boys. In Guinea, less than 10 per cent of the school-aged population were enrolled in 1956, only about one-quarter of whom were female. In Ethiopia, enrolment rates were even lower such that by 1961/62, only five per cent of the school-aged population were in school, one-quarter of whom were female (Fassil, 1990; Teshome, 1979; Seyoum, 1986). In Tanzania, because of the British policy of education for adaptation, schools were more widespread, and the native authorities had some control over educational provision. But in spite of this, only about one-quarter of the school-aged population was enrolled in school by 1960, of whom about one-third were female (Cameron and Dodd, 1970; World Bank, 1988, pp.131).

Independence for Guinea and Tanzania (in 1958 and 1961, respectively) brought new socialist governments, which saw education as an important vehicle for renewing African identity and values. Policy changed towards providing a more relevant and practical education, accessible to the masses (Buchert, 1994; Adamolekun, 1976). Ethiopia's transition to socialism began a decade later, following the downfall of the monarchy in 1974. Here, too, major policy reforms were introduced. However, the effects of these changes had different consequences for the expansion of education in each of the countries.

In Ethiopia, although enrolments in the entire education system had increased approximately six-fold between 1960/61 and 1974/75, when the monarchy fell, the primary GER was still only about 12 per cent (one-third of whom were girls) (Tekeste, 1990; Fassil, 1990). However, an important outcome of the expansion of educational opportunities was to raise the consciousness of the youth and, from the early 1960s, university students became increasingly involved in political activity. Student unrest escalated, challenging the social, economic and political foundations of the monarchy (Halliday and Molyneux, 1981). In 1971 a committee of professionals was established, to provide a comprehensive evaluation of the education system. The resulting 'Education Sector Review' published in 1972 criticised the imported curriculum, and identified problems of elitism, wastage at all levels, inequitable distribution of facilities between regions and rural/urban areas, and an over-centralisation of education administration (Fassil, 1990; Tekeste, 1990). The Review recommended restructuring, to provide a massive expansion of primary and non-formal education, with the aim of providing 'Minimum Formation Education' (MFE) of four years to all school-aged children by 2000, whilst reducing the possibility of promotion to the next level (McNab, 1989; Teshome, 1979; Tekeste, 1990). These recommendations were not, however, popular with the politically conscious educated elite, and students and teachers protested against the Review's proposals. Meanwhile, 1972/73 was a year of severe drought, inflation accelerated following the oil price increase in 1973, and the army, teachers, workers, and civil servants demanded salary increases. These and other factors led to a group of military officers (known as the *Derg* or 'Committee') seizing power in 1974. Unlike in most other African countries, the revolution in Ethiopia was directed against an indigenous ruling class, rather than a colonial power.

The aims of the *Derg's* education policy were to reach the rural population, provide free education at all levels, and disseminate socialist ideology – political education being taught even at the primary level (Fassil, 1990; Halliday and Molyneux, 1981). During the first decade under the *Derg*, enrolments expanded at all levels, and by an average of 10 per cent per annum in primary schools. As a result of increased demand for education, schools were often built by the community who requested the government to supply teachers and textbooks (Tekeste, 1996). However, private schools, (other than those owned by missionaries and foreign communities), were nationalised, and education and health taxes on rural land were abolished. Thus, resources available to the sector fell, and became an important constraint on further expansion (Tekeste, 1990). Earlier problems – including high pupil/teacher ratios, a large proportion of unqualified teachers, overcrowding, high drop-out in grades one and two, shortage of learning materials and poor management – were further aggravated (Fassil, 1990). Moreover, continued repression of opponents of the *Derg* diverted public resources away from social sectors to defence, with the proportion spent on education falling from 20 per cent at the end of the monarchy to just 14 per cent a decade later (World Bank, 1994b). The constraints on further expansion then became severe.

In Guinea, the government committed itself to the provision of mass education, and 28 per cent of public spending went on education by 1970 (or 6.4 per cent of GDP). Initially, enrolments grew rapidly – at an average annual rate of

10 per cent at the primary level over the first 16 years after independence – but slowed dramatically, to a mere three per cent per year between 1974 and 1984. Four main factors explain this change. First, weak economic growth in the 1970s constrained the resources available to the government, and the priority accorded to education in government spending halved, to around 13 per cent by 1983 – or 3.8 per cent of GDP). Here, too, private schooling was banned (including missionary schools), so the system suffered further from lack of resources. Second, a breakdown in political and economic ties with France meant that external resources dried up, and the government had to rely mainly on internal revenue sources. Third, education spending was focussed increasingly upon post-primary levels during the 1970s. Fourth, the demand for schooling in rural areas appeared to decrease as the country's economic difficulties intensified, and increased preference for alternative schooling provided by Koranic schools and *medersas* was felt, especially in rural areas.

Tanzania's ideology of *Ujamaa* (socialism and self-reliance) was more successful in ensuring a strong political and community commitment to education. Education was given highest priority. Between 1962/63 and 1975/76, the proportion of GDP allocated to the education sector increased from 2.7 to 5.7 per cent. In addition, local authorities and regional administrations raised funds for education. Parents, churches and communities, as well as non-governmental organisations, also raised funds on a voluntary basis (Buchert, 1994). Major education reforms were introduced to harmonise the three racially segregated education systems, giving the same structure, organisation, curriculum and criteria for access to higher levels for everyone. The government also made special efforts to reduce social inequalities by giving every village the opportunity of having a primary school. Adult literacy programmes ran concurrently with access to primary education. By 1981, the primary GER had reached 97 per cent, and the proportion of illiterates had declined from 90 per cent in 1962 to 20 per cent of the adult population. These policies helped to reduce gender and other inequalities. The post-independence ban on private schools was subsequently lifted so that the government's supply of school places could be supplemented, thus helping further to raise enrolment rates (Buchert, 1994).

At the UNESCO Conference on African Education in 1961, the three countries, along with the rest of SSA, had committed themselves to achieving, by 1980, universal primary education. However, despite rapid expansion of their education systems over two decades, Ethiopia, with 36 per cent of children in school by 1980, and Guinea, with only 32 per cent, fell far short of achieving this target (Ministry of Education, 1994, MEPU-FP, 1996). Girls continued to be significantly disadvantaged, comprising only one-third of those enrolled. Despite the presence of similar economic constraints, Tanzania was more successful in reaching this target, although a gender gap in enrolments was also apparent (Komba, 1995). It would appear that weak government commitment to the provision of educational opportunities and low demand for education in Ethiopia and Guinea, relative to Tanzania, were two important constraining factors.

In each of the countries, economic decline during the 1980s resulted in falling enrolment rates, and a deterioration in the quality of education. In Ethiopia, public resources were drained by drought and famine, exacerbated by the intensification of civil war. Thus, the gains that were made during the initial period of the *Derg* were soon eroded. As a result, primary enrolments in the country fell from their peak of 39 per cent in 1982/83 to scarcely 20 per cent of the age group a decade later. Although the enrolment of girls continued to lag behind those of boys, during the war years, the gender gap in enrolments narrowed substantially (Figure 5.1). This was because the enrolment of boys fell faster than girls: many boys wished to avoid conscription, the risks of which were greater for school attendees. With the end of the war and the installation of a new government, enrolments rose from 1993 onwards. It can be seen, however, that enrolment growth was particularly strong for boys, causing the gender gap to widen again.

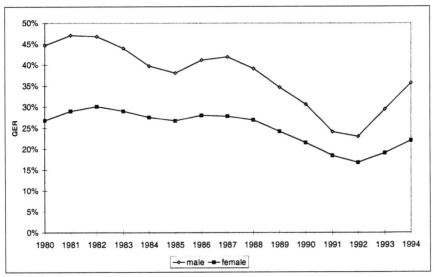

Source: Ministry of Education (1995, 1996)

Figure 5.1 Ethiopia, primary GER, 1980-1994

In Guinea, enrolment trends have shown a different pattern. In 1984, the new government introduced a structural adjustment programme, shifting the country towards a market economy. Initially, enrolment rates remained unchanged at around 30 per cent. However, implementation of the 'Programme d'Adjustment Sectoriel de l'Education' (PASE) from 1990, which addressed both the demand and supply constraints and reaffirmed government and donor commitment to education, played an important role in raising enrolments. Here, too, however, the gender gap widened as growth resumed (Figure 5.2). Furthermore, girls' enrolments comprised only 34 per cent of the total in 1994/95, compared with

37 per cent in Ethiopia, notwithstanding Guinea's substantially higher income and overall enrolment ratio.

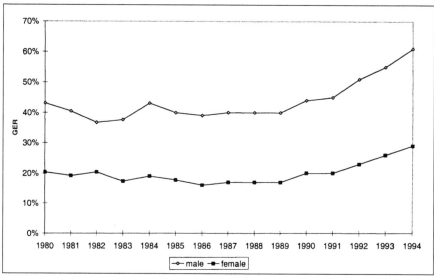

Source: MEPU-FP (various years)

Figure 5.2 Guinea, primary GER, 1980-1994

Tanzania, by contrast, was one of the first countries in the region to achieve universal primary education – although there remained considerable regional variations in the proportion of girls enrolled (Swainson *et al.*, 1998). However, with the onset of severe economic problems during the 1980s, this record was not sustained. Following a change in government in 1985, a strong economic reform programme was introduced. Cuts in government expenditure led to increased emphasis on cost-sharing, shifting the burden of schooling costs from the government to communities and households. This, together with a deterioration in the quality of education, led to a fall in demand for education, and declining enrolment rates. As had happened in Ethiopia, falling enrolments were accompanied by a narrowing of the gender gap owing to boys' enrolments falling more sharply than girls'. More recent policy reforms have reversed the downward trend. Furthermore, in contrast to Ethiopia and Guinea, a relatively narrow gender gap has been maintained whilst enrolments have risen, partly thanks to a longstanding commitment to addressing gender differentials, and to the implementation of gender-focused education policies.

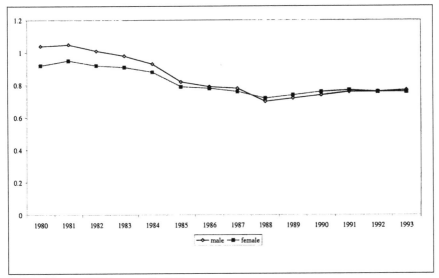

Source: Komba (1995, Appendix 2.1).

Figure 5.3 Tanzania, primary GER, 1980-1994

In the mid-1990s gross enrolment ratios in Ethiopia and Guinea remained amongst the lowest in SSA – at 24 per cent and 38 per cent respectively (Table 5.2) – and both compared poorly with the overall average for the region (74 per cent in 1995). The gender gap in enrolment was also extremely wide. By contrast, the GER for Tanzania was slightly higher than the SSA average, and the gender gap was very narrow. Net (age-adjusted) enrolment ratios were considerably lower than GERs in each of the countries because of high rates of over-age enrolment, repetition, and drop-out with later re-entry into the system. The disparity between gross and net enrolment ratios were, however, larger for boys than for girls, because the latter were less likely to be in school when they reached the age of puberty.

Thus, as shown in Table 5.2, the education systems in Ethiopia and Guinea suffer from very severe internal inefficiency. In Guinea, over one-fifth of both girls and boys in primary school were repeaters in 1993/94, compared with 11 per cent and eight per cent, respectively, in Ethiopia. In the same year, more than one-quarter of girls and boys dropped out before completing the first grade of school in Ethiopia. In both countries, repetition and drop out rates are highest for girls in most primary grades. In Tanzania, on the other hand, drop-out and repetition rates were low compared to the other two countries. This is mainly due to the policies of compulsory schooling and automatic promotion in Tanzania, rather than to better quality and internal efficiency. Whilst there are few gender differences in access to, and persistence in, school, gender disparities are nevertheless evident in examination performance (as in the other two countries).

Table 5.2 Educational indicators (percentage) in Ethiopia, Guinea and Tanzania, 1993-1994

	Ethiopia			Guinea			Tanzania		
	Total	M	F	Total	M	F	Total	M	F
GER	24	30	19	38	52	24	78	80	77
Proportion of repeaters	8.8	7.7	10.6	21.8	20.6	24.4	3.1	3.0	3.2
Drop-out rate in grade 1	25.2	23.6	27.6	3.2	1.7	5.9	6.2	6.4	6.0
Drop-out rate in grade 3	3.7	3.0	4.7	6.7	7.0	6.0	3.8	4.2	3.3

Source: Calculated from Ministry of Education, Ethiopia, (1996), MEPU-FP, (1996), MOEC (1995)

We have shown that, in Ethiopia and Guinea, primary school enrolment rates have remained low, and the gender gap has been widening in recent years. By contrast, in Tanzania, a narrow gender gap was maintained during periods of fluctuating enrolment rates. These differences are partly explained by variations in the policy environment between the countries. The next section examines the efforts that have been made to address gender differentials in schooling, in these countries, and their impact.

Policy Environment in Relation to Girls' Education

During the 1990s, the governments of each of the three countries committed themselves in various ways to improving education and, especially, gender equity within it. A specific objective of Ethiopian government policy (Transitional Government of Ethiopia, 1994) was to use education to change attitudes towards the role of women in development. This included giving attention to gender issues in curriculum design, placing special emphasis upon the recruitment, training and assignment of female teachers, and giving financial support to raising the participation of women in education.

The education of girls was also supported by a number of other government policies. The National Policy for Ethiopian Women (Transitional Government of Ethiopia, 1993a) specified strategies to ensure that women received vocational guidance at all institutions of education, had access to the same curricula as men, and were free to choose their field of study. Women were encouraged to take up jobs in the civil service and to perform public functions, including participation in decision-making – at both community and national levels. Communities were increasingly informed about the harm done by some traditional practices, such as circumcision and marriage of girls before they reach puberty. In support of this, the government's Population and Social Policy aims to increase the minimum age at marriage for girls from the current age of 15 to 18 years (equal to that of boys). It also emphasises the importance of giving special support to the education of women, and of ensuring equal employment opportunities. All of these measures should help to increase the demand for the schooling of girls.

The Government of Guinea has also strengthened its policies on gender and schooling. In the early 1990s, an 'Equity' Committee (Comité d'Équité) within the Ministry of National Education was established, charged with the responsibility of ensuring that as many girls went to school as possible. This committee organised gender-awareness campaigns, using programmes on rural radio, national radio and television, as well as the press. Policies discouraging girls – such as automatic expulsion of any who become pregnant – were changed. The committee ran pilot projects in those rural areas with very low female enrolments. Regular visits are made by committee members to these areas, to encourage parents to send their daughters to school. As incentives, prizes were awarded to girls who had performed well in school and, on special occasions, parents too, were awarded prizes.

Tanzania has had a long-standing commitment to the achievement of gender equality. Its 1984 'Bill of Rights' led to legislative reforms to remove discrimination against women. Women in Development (WID) sectoral focal-points were established so as to 'mainstream' WID issues, and a fund was created to improve women's access to credit. The government introduced a wide range of initiatives to increase women's participation in all sectors of the economy, to accord ownership and succession rights to women, and to tackle violence against them.

Donors have been important supporters of Tanzania's gender research and policy, particularly through their funding the education programmes of NGOs and of the Ministry of Education and Culture, as well as by their provision of gender training (Swainson *et al.*, 1998). A Gender Co-ordinating Committee (GCC) was established in 1995, comprising officers from various parts of the Ministry of Education and Culture, to co-ordinate and strengthen all of its gender-related activities. The committee successfully lobbied to keep boarding schools for girls at secondary level, arguing that they encourage the access and retention of girls, especially those from poor rural communities.

Thus, in all three countries, education policy-makers have paid more attention to gender issues in recent years. Tanzania's earlier policy changes benefited both boys and girls fairly equally, even as enrolments declined in the 1980s. Whilst each of the countries has been dependent on donor funding of education, the international agencies appear to have had more active on gender issues in Guinea and Tanzania, than in Ethiopia. Whilst the government in Ethiopia appears to have more control and ownership over policy, its resources have been relatively limited, and its ability to implement change has been less marked.

The above differences in policy design and implementation have had an important influence on the different education and gender outcomes in the three countries. We now turn to an examination of what can be learned about the underlying causes of low enrolment and high gender disparities from our survey work in the region.

Major Findings from School Surveys

Our survey work focused on two areas within Ethiopia, Guinea and Tanzania[1] using a combination of both quantitative and qualitative research tools. Individual questionnaire-based interviews were conducted with samples of teachers, pupils, drop-outs from school and those who had never enrolled. Focus-group discussions and interviews were held with education officials, teachers, pupils, school committees, parents and community elders. These provided a more detailed understanding of the processes and issues explored in the quantitative work. The surveys were designed on the basis of purposive, rather than random sampling methods, and were intended to provide case study information which could throw fresh light on the constraints affecting the participation and performance of girls and boys in school. The sampling procedure followed in each country involved the selection of two geographical regions, based on their differences in enrolment ratios and gender gaps in school enrolments, and in language, religion and economic conditions. Within each region, districts were selected which reflected the region's broader characteristics. Districts were stratified into rural and urban areas, where schools having sufficient pupils in the sixth grade were selected. Within the selected schools, random samples of Grade 6 pupils for the urban schools, and complete enumerations of such pupils in the rural schools, were undertaken. The selected schools and their catchment areas provided the basis for fieldwork, and formed natural clusters of pupils, drop-outs and non-enrolees (i.e. those who had never enrolled).[2]

The findings are presented according to the analytical framework that relates poverty, schooling and gender inequality, outlined earlier in Chapter 1. The results are discussed under the five main headings, suggested by Figure 1.1, namely direct costs, child labour, the supply of school places, the quality of physical provision, and the impact of gender relations. Evidence from the second-phase studies in Ghana, Malawi, Mali, Senegal, Uganda and Zambia is also referred to where appropriate.

---

[1]   The areas visited were East Gojjam and Jimma in Ethiopia, Forest and Middle regions in Guinea and Njombe and Bagamoyo districts in Tanzania. See, Peasgood *et al.* (1997) (Tanzania), Rose *et al.* (1997) (Ethiopia), Tembon *et al.* (1997) (Guinea), for further details.

[2]   Similar sampling methods were also used in the six second-phase studies. More details of the sampling and other methods used in all nine countries are given in the Technical Appendix and in each of the national reports.

Direct Costs

An inability to meet the direct costs of schooling was found to be one of the most important causes of non-attendance and early dropout from school in each of the SSA studies. Those who had dropped out of school cited a lack of money to pay for school expenses most frequently as an important reason for leaving school. Data for Ethiopia and Guinea are shown in Table 5.3.[3] A similar pattern of reasons for non-attendance was also given by those who had never enrolled in school.

Table 5.3 Reasons for dropping out of school

| | Ethiopia | | | | Guinea | | | |
| | Male | | Female | | Male | | Female | |
	No.	%	No.	%	No.	%	No.	%
Lack of money to pay for school expenses	25	40	16	30	10	38	2	6
Needed to work	24	39	15	28	3	12	9	26
Other[a]	13	19	22	41	13	50	23	68
Total	62	100	53	100	26	100	34	100

Note [a]:   'Other' includes distance from school, family problems, illness, lack of interest, marriage, and other reasons.

Results from the other country studies confirm this pattern. In Malawi, from over 1,000 drop-outs interviewed, half of the boys from rural areas and 44 per cent of the boys from urban areas cited the lack of money to pay for school expenses as the main reason for their having left school prematurely. It was most important for girls too, although a smaller proportion of girls than boys (about one-third in both rural and urban areas) indicated this (Kadzamira and Chibwana, 2000, p.61).

Many other children also indicated that the 'need to work' was dominant. This, again, is an economic cause – suggesting a need to earn income in a general sense rather than focussing only on school costs being too high. If these two sets of causes are combined, we usually find a majority of children citing economic circumstances as the main reasons for their having left school. They accounted for 57 per cent of the school drop-outs interviewed in Ghana, 75 per cent of those in Zambia, 70 per cent in Uganda and about 45 per cent in Malawi. Table 5.3

---

[3]   No data are available for drop-outs and non-enrolees in Tanzania in the tables. This is because very few children were out of school in the regions included in the study.

indicates that (taking males and females together) the proportions for Ethiopia and Guinea were 70 per cent and 40 per cent respectively.

In one of the Ethiopian regions surveyed, school fees had recently been abolished. In the other region, fees were still charged and, during focus group discussions, parents claimed to have difficulty in paying them, especially since they became due in September, when family income was at its lowest prior to the harvest. Parents also complained that, because they were unable to buy exercise books, pens and the necessary clothing for school, they were not able to enrol their children. Some parents mentioned that, even when their children did enrol in school, they often had to drop out during the first grade because they found it difficult to meet the direct costs involved.

The problem of meeting the direct costs of schooling was also found to be prevalent in Guinea. Even though tuition fees were not charged at the primary level, parents were expected to pay GF2000 ($US2) for registration, and to buy the necessary textbooks, exercise books, stationery, and the prescribed uniforms for their children. In Guinea, textbooks were the most expensive item of direct costs, followed by uniforms. In addition to making these payments, parents were obliged to produce certified true copies of a child's birth certificate as a requirement for school admission. Acquiring these documents was sometimes expensive, especially for parents in rural areas where administrative offices providing such services do not exist.

The costs of sending a child to school were not always predictable in Guinea. For example, in one of the schools visited, parents had been required to pay GF16,000 ($US16), to secure their child's entry to the first grade. A local contractor, who had recently finished building a government secondary school, had been informed that the government had insufficient resources to pay him. In response, the grade-one levy was introduced by the district education authorities, so as to raise enough money to allow the bill to be paid. Parents claimed that such levies (which had also included contributions towards the construction of classrooms, the purchase of furniture, and other school equipment) undermined their ability to send their children to school.

Although drop-out and non-enrolment is less frequent in Tanzania than in Ethiopia and Guinea, parents there also claimed they had difficulties in paying for uniforms, school equipment, UPE fees and a variety of other payments. Primary schooling is compulsory and the UPE fee is fixed across the country. There were, however, other, often more significant, fees levied by school committees such as test fees, building fees, desk fees, examination fees, and sports fees, depending on the needs of the schools. Some of these expenses were avoided by parents. For example, few, if any, sanctions were applied for non-payment of the UPE contribution. However, the fear of new contributions being required, and the uncertainty of these demands, sometimes resulted in non-enrolment. An investigation of the direct costs incurred by parents for a standard VII pupil in Tanzania ranged from T. Sh4,200 to T. Sh8,000. This was approximately equal to the price of one or two bags of maize respectively, (equivalent to at least one-fifth of an average family's annual harvest of maize). Uniforms were also found to be the most expensive cost item in Tanzania and girls' uniforms were perceived to be slightly more expensive than boys'.[4] Girls, in particular, were ashamed of having inappropriate clothes for school, which would sometimes result in them playing truant. Furthermore, children who lacked uniforms were sometimes punished, which also provoked drop-out. In some areas of Tanzania, payment systems were inflexible, requiring parents to pay fees at times of the year when money was scarce. In response, they delayed sending their children until they could afford the fees or, sometimes, enrolment of younger children had to await school completion by an older sibling. Since schooling is compulsory in Tanzania, problems of poverty were often reflected in absenteeism and in order to avoid potential prosecution, parents sometimes tried to disguise drop-out as a transfer between schools.

Table 5.4 Pupils working for cash to pay for their schooling

| | Ethiopia | | | | Guinea | | | | Tanzania | | | |
| | Male | | Female | | Male | | Female | | Male | | Female | |
	no.	%	no.	%	no.	%	no.	%	no.	%	no.	%
Yes	62	48	22	26	54	33	10	15	52	45	38	32
No	67	52	62	73	112	67	58	85	64	55	79	68
Total	129	100	84	100	166	100	68	100	116	100	117	100

To make up for parents' inability to pay for schooling, some children undertake paid work to finance their education. Our surveys revealed that a larger proportion of boys than girls earn money to help pay for their school expenses (Table 5.4). In the three countries, parents considered that the direct costs of schooling were similar for boys and girls.[5] However, boys were more able to attend school because, to some extent, they could support themselves. For example, a mother in Ethiopia reported that, when her husband died, her son did

---

[4] Earlier work in these countries suggested that clothes for school in Ethiopia and uniforms in Guinea and Tanzania were the highest direct cost items facing parents (USAID, 1994; Sow, 1994; Mason and Khandker, 1996).

[5] In Ethiopia, two earlier studies, in which economic constraints were found to be one of the main reasons for not sending children to school, suggest that the cost of sending girls and boys to school is similar (USAID, 1994; Yelfign *et al.*, 1995). In Guinea, however, Sow (1994) estimates that the cost of sending a boy to school is higher than sending a girl due to the higher cost of uniforms for boys. By contrast, Mason and Khandker (1996) calculate that, in Tanzania, direct costs of schooling are higher for girls at the primary level (although the opposite is the case at the secondary level, where expenditure on boys' uniforms and fees is found to be higher than girls', possibly because boys are sent to better schools).

not leave school because he could earn money through self-employment to pay his own registration fee. Her daughter dropped out of school, however, because girls are unable to find such jobs. A father also noted that, because boys were involved in trading activities, they could buy their own exercise books and pens. Girls, on the other hand, were involved in household chores and in some farm activities, which, he felt, did not help families so much in sharing the cost of their education. Even though girls' labour directly assists the family economy, it may not help them to stay in school, where it does not directly generate cash income.

Both boys and girls engage in petty trading. In Guinea, for example, it is common in the villages and towns to see young girls carrying large trays of groundnuts, fruits or other food items for sale. They also help their parents in food stalls in the market place. In all three countries girls are sometimes withdrawn from school and sent to work in urban areas as housemaids. However, rather than being able to use the money they earn as a contribution towards school expenses, it was reported that girls are usually obliged to give the income to their parents.

The ability to pay for children's schooling is obviously dependent upon the income of parents or households. Measuring this, in Africa, can be quite difficult, given that many rural households are hardly incorporated into the cash economy. However, parental education, occupation, and assets are often used, either singly or in combination, as an indication of the socio-economic status of a household. In our studies, socio-economic status was estimated by compiling a weighted index which included parents' education, occupation, ownership of household possessions (radio, car, bicycle and/or television), whether or not the house in which the child lived had a corrugated iron roof and used electricity for lighting, and whether or not the respondent was wearing shoes and/or socks at the time of interview.[6] The estimated mean wealth index of pupils in school, drop-outs and non-enrolees is presented in Table 5.5.

It can be seen that the mean wealth index of male and female pupils was in each case higher than that of respondents of the same gender who were not attending school (drop-outs and non-enrolees). Furthermore, amongst those out-of-school, the mean wealth index for school drop-outs was higher than for those who had never enrolled. Thus, children at school were, on average, from better-off households than those who had dropped out, who were, in turn, from wealthier backgrounds than school-age children who had never enrolled.[7]

---

[6] Each of these items was assigned a numeric value, and was totalled separately, for each of the individuals included in the surveys. The data in Table 5.5 are simple averages of these values for each of the respondent categories shown.

[7] Exactly the same results were found in the other country studies for Ghana (Avotri *et al.*, 2000, p.82), Malawi (Kadzamira and Chibwana, 2000, p.73), Mali (Sangaré *et al.,* 2000, p.64), Uganda (Tumushabe *et al.*, 2000, p.70) and Zambia (Kasonde-Ng'andu *et al.*, 2000, p.58). In Senegal the same monotonic relationship was found in the socio-economic ranking of male pupils, drop-outs and non-enrolled. But it was less clear for girls (Dioum Diokhané *et al.*, 2000, p.68).

Table 5.5 Average wealth index of pupils, drop outs and non-enrolees

	Pupils		Drop-outs		Non-enrolees	
	Male	Female	Male	Female	Male	Female
Ethiopia	5.7	6.6	4.1	4.4	3.1	3.2
	(2.9)	(3.0)	(2.1)	(2.1)	(1.7)	(1.9)
Guinea	8.0	11.8	7.4	8.2	5.6	6.3
	(4.1)	(4.6)	(3.1)	(4.1)	(2.9)	(2.6)
Tanzania	8.9	9.0	4.8	3.8	-	-
	(4.4)	(4.3)	(2.3)	(1.7)	-	-

Note: The figures in brackets represent the standard deviations.

Further multivariate analysis of these data, to examine the effects of the wealth index on the probability of a child attending and completing school revealed that for both boys and girls in Ethiopia, an increase in the wealth index improves the chances of going to school. For example by increasing the wealth index by one unit, a boy's chances of attending school were increased by 16 per cent whereas a girl's was increased by 41 per cent (Rose and Al-Samarrai, 2001). Although the impact is slightly less in Guinea, wealth still has a greater influence for girls than boys: whereas the effect is insignificant for boys the chances of a girl attending school is increased by nine per cent when her household wealth index is increased by one unit (Tembon and Al-Samarrai, 1999). These regression results broadly confirm those of bivariate analyses and show that the wealth of a household has a positive impact upon the probability of a child going to school. The results also suggest that poverty in a family will have a more detrimental effect upon the decision to enrol a girl in school than a boy. Thus, in these countries, boys are more likely to attend and complete primary school regardless of their socio-economic status, than girls.

Evidence for the negative impact of direct costs on schooling is revealed by the huge numbers of children who enrol in school when costs are sharply reduced. For example, following the implementation of fee-free primary education policies in Malawi and Uganda, primary enrolments increased, in the mid-1990s, by 52 per cent and 200 per cent, respectively.[8] By contrast, in Zambia, cost-sharing continues to exist and direct costs to parents have been found to be an important constraint on schooling such that some parents residing at the border between Zambia and Malawi send their children to school in Malawi where primary

---

[8]   It should be noted that other policies aimed at stimulating demand, such as the non-enforcement of uniform and a policy to allow pregnant girls back to school after delivery, accompanied the abolition of fees in Malawi.

schooling is free (Kadzamira and Chibwana, 2000; Kasonde-Ng'andu *et al.*, 2000; and Tumushabe *et al.*, 2000).

Financial constraints are even more severe for households affected by HIV/AIDS. Where family members are sick, their income will be reduced. In addition, the impact of HIV/AIDS is likely to have increased the number of orphans in recent years. Orphans cared for by extended families (including grandparents) already have inadequate resources for their own needs, and so are unlikely to have sufficient resources to care for children from other households. Furthermore, it is possible in countries such as Malawi and Zambia where the AIDS pandemic is spreading fast, that the next generation of children may have neither parents nor grandparents alive. Child-headed households are, therefore, likely to become increasingly prevalent with children lacking the financial resources to support their own education.

In Malawi, for example, of the 2204 children interviewed, a larger proportion of those not in school were orphans (35 percent of dropouts interviewed had at least one parent who had died, compared with 24 percent of children in school). Furthermore, the average socio-economic status of households in which orphans were residing was lower than for those whose parents were alive (almost one-half of orphans were in the poorest group, and three-quarters of orphans in the poorest group had dropped out of school). Thus, orphanhood affects the chances of school attendance, and orphans who attend school are likely to have fewer resources available for schooling (Rose, 2002; Kadzamira and Chibwana, 2000).

Although the abolition of school fees can strongly stimulate enrolment growth, acting alone it might not be a sufficient incentive for parents to enrol their children in school. Fees are no longer charged at the primary level in Guinea and Senegal, yet the enrolment rates in these countries remain low. This is partly because other direct costs of schooling, such as the cost of textbooks and uniforms, can be quite prohibitive. Furthermore, in Malawi and Uganda the increased enrolments were accompanied by high rates of subsequent drop-out, because parents were often unable to afford the other direct costs of schooling. Thus, strategies to reduce the costs of schooling need to recognise the abolition of fees as one (though not necessarily the most important) component of direct costs.

Child Labour

Where families use their children as a source of labour, sending them to school can be costly because the benefits of such labour are thereby lost, at least for the duration of the school day. The impact of these opportunity costs, combined with the direct costs of school attendance, can be very substantial for poor families and can be an important cause of children not being enrolled. Our field surveys revealed that opportunity costs were influential in explaining why children had not completed the primary cycle. As indicated earlier, amongst the most important reasons for dropping out of school given by survey respondents, the needs to earn money, or to work at home or on the farm were significant. They accounted for 39 per cent of the replies from Ethiopian male drop-outs and 28 per cent of those from girls (see Table 5.3). In Guinea, the relevant magnitudes were 12 per cent and 26 per cent, respectively. However, the types of activities which are the source of these opportunity costs differed sharply between the sexes. In both countries, the girls who dropped out for these reasons did so mainly in order to help the family in the home, whilst the boys who did so cited work on the family farm, or earning money as having been their main intent.

Discussions with those who had dropped out of school revealed that, whilst some boys are able to combine their income-earning activities with continued schooling, others find it difficult to do so, and eventually leave. Some of those interviewed in Guinea were disinclined to return to school because their current activities were more profitable in the short term. In Ethiopia, many children, of both sexes, who enrol in September, at the beginning of the school year, leave by November because demands on their labour during harvest time are great. In some cases, they re-enrol the following year in the same grade but, again, find themselves unable to complete the year.

An attempt was made in Tanzania to estimate the opportunity cost of a boy attending school by investigating the earnings forgone. It was found that a boy in standard seven could earn as much as T.Sh. 1000 ($US1.8) a day by engagement in petty trade, often selling small items along the highway. This opportunity cost far outweighs the direct cost of schooling, in Tanzania, suggesting that, for some children, it is a more important constraint. Since many of the activities performed by girls are unpaid, it is more difficult to estimate the opportunity cost of their time in financial terms.

An attempt in these countries to make accurate estimates of the duration of work undertaken by children for their families was not made owing to the unreliability of depending upon recall by the children themselves. However, it did prove possible for children to indicate both the range of their different tasks, and the frequency with which they undertook them. The responses to such questions allowed the construction of a weighted 'household help' index, based upon the frequency with which pupils, drop-outs and non-enrolees performed certain chores (including domestic work, work on the farm and income-earning activities for the household) – every day, every week, sometimes, or never. The results are presented in Table 5.6.

The major result which emerges from this exercise is that the household help index is, consistently, significantly higher for girls than for boys. This is true for each of the samples of pupils, drop-outs and non-enrolees, in the three countries. It is important to note that this index measures both the range of activities practised, and their frequency, but that it does not measure the duration of each activity. However, unless boys consistently spend longer working upon each activity than girls, these results strongly suggest that girls help their families more than boys, and that the opportunity costs of girls' schooling may, accordingly, be greater.[9]

---

[9]   Earlier work which has examined gender differences in schooling has also suggested that opportunity costs are higher for girls than boys. Furthermore, in Tanzania opportunity costs estimated in monetary terms have been found to be much higher than direct costs (Mason and Khandker, 1996). Girls have also been shown to be involved in a wider range of tasks than boys, many related to domestic work which

Table 5.6 Average index of household help

	Pupils		Drop-outs		Non-enrolees	
	Male	Female	Male	Female	Male	Female
Ethiopia	23.3	43.1	13.5	26.3	13.4	24.8
	(15.5)	(17.0)	(9.0)	(9.2)	(8.0)	(7.6)
Guinea	18.4	32.9	11.8	28.5	16.7	24.1
	(14.6)	(14.9)	(7.8)	(8.7)	(9.8)	(8.8)
Tanzania	25.4	28.3	13.6	28.0	-	-
	(14.4)	(13.1)	(9.3)	(14.4)	-	-

Note: The figures in brackets represent the standard deviations.

The surveys also revealed evidence of a strongly gendered division of labour. Female pupils, were generally more involved in household activities such as looking after siblings, preparing and cooking food, cleaning the house and fetching water and firewood. Boys, on the other hand, were mainly involved in working on the family farm, looking after livestock and fetching firewood and income-earning activities. Girls' labour-time for the household tends to be larger than boys' time because their household tasks are important to the well-being of the entire family and must be performed on a daily basis. The requirements on boys are less, and they tend to have greater control over their own time and resources. For example, in one area in Ethiopia, pupils and teachers noted that the work performed by boys is not necessarily incompatible with school work: they could study whilst in the fields looking after cattle, whereas girls were unable to do so while performing their household chores, which allowed little breathing space.

No evidence is apparent from Table 5.6 that drop-outs and non-enrolees helped their families at home more than pupils. Indeed, the task-loads carried by pupils in our surveys appear to have been greater than those of their peers who were not attending school. Of course, pupils are able to undertake their work for the household outside of school hours, particularly in situations where the school

---

have contributed to their absence or late arrival at school – see Sow (1994); USAID (1994), Yelfign *et al.* (1995), UNICEF (1995). In Tanzania, both boys and girls have been observed to be involved in income-earning activities which are perceived by parents in some cases to be more important than education, although this has been found to be a more important reason for boys dropping out of school than for girls (UNICEF, 1995).

day is short.[10] Nevertheless, if the opportunity costs of schooling are high, one would expect the school drop-outs and the non-enrolled to be undertaking more, rather than less, work than their pupil colleagues. However, we know that some of those who were out of school were conducting economic activity on their own account – and, therefore, contributing to household income. Thus, the average value of both household and income-earning tasks, taken together, could have been substantially greater for those not at school than for pupils. Furthermore, we know that the families of pupils and of those who are out of school differ in terms of socio-economic status, and other characteristics, which may be related to the incidence of opportunity costs. These inter-group comparisons could not, therefore, provide evidence for the relative levels of such costs unless such differences were taken into account in the analysis. Again, as was the case with pupils, a close examination of the data revealed that, for these groups, there was generally a distinctly gendered division of labour in the tasks performed.

Some of the second phase studies were able to construct 'time lines' whereby children not only indicated the type and frequency of activities performed on a typical school day, but also estimated their duration. This gave clearer evidence of the greater workloads undertaken by girls in comparison with boys. In Malawi, 1062 pupils interviewed spent seven to eight hours on school activities. In addition, however, the girls spent just over three hours on household work, whilst the boys spent about two and a quarter hours. This difference (of 33 per cent) was perceived, by all parties in the focus group discussions (pupils, drop-outs, teachers, parents and members of school committees), to be an important cause of female drop-out and under-performance relative to boys (Kadzamira and Chibwana, 2000, p.70).

The need for children, particularly girls, to substitute for the domestic work of adults in the household is becoming more severe in the context of HIV/AIDS which often means that girls are required to look after sick relatives, and take on roles of childcare and other domestic chores following the death of a parent (see, for example, Kadzamira and Chibwana, 2000; Kasonde-N'gandu, *et al.*, 2000).

Pupils in Uganda also spent about eight hours per day on schoolwork and a further two hours on domestic and income-earning activities. These latter were unevenly distributed, with girls spending approximately three-times as long on such chores as boys. The Ugandan evidence also shows that the work burden is greater for poorer children: the lower the socio-economic status of the household, the greater the amount of time pupils have to work when they are at home, with girls working significantly longer than boys (Tumushabe *et al.*, 2000, pp.69-71).

---

[10]   See the discussion about this under the section on school quality below. Drop-outs in both Uganda and Malawi were reported to spend at least twice as long on daily household tasks as pupils. Yet in Zambia, very few children mentioned domestic or other work as a reason for their dropping out of school. This appeared to be because the system of double/triple shifts in Zambia allows sufficient time for household/money earning tasks to be completed (Tumushabe *et al.*, 2000, p.72; Kadzamira and Chibwana, 2000, p.70; Kasonde-Ng'andu *et al.*, 2000, p.55).

These differences in household work responsibilities can affect girls' schooling chances not only directly, but also indirectly: in Zambia, amongst the 1189 pupils interviewed, 28 per cent of boys, and 17 per cent of the girls, contributed directly to meeting the costs of their own schooling. However, during focus group discussions, girls complained that boys had more time to earn money to pay school costs, because they were needed less for household chores. Thus the gender division of labour, from an early age, doubly penalises girls – both because they have to spend more time working than boys, and because both the type and duration of this work gives them fewer opportunities to earn cash to meet school expenses than boys (Kasonde-Ng'andu *et al.*, 2000, p.54).

The number of children in the household is also likely to affect the opportunity costs of schooling – although the direction of this impact is uncertain. On the one hand, the larger the number of children in the household, the more household work there is likely to be (especially for girls) and, therefore, the higher will be the opportunity costs of their time. Direct costs also increase with sending each additional child to school. On the other hand, a particular child from a larger household might have a higher probability of attending school because work is spread over a larger number of household members. Thus, the direct costs of schooling for all children taken together are greater in larger households, but the opportunity costs for at least some of them are likely to be lower than for children with fewer siblings. Some of the evidence from our surveys on these points, summarised in Table 5.7, is ambiguous. In Guinea, and Tanzania, there was no particular relationship between the number of siblings and schooling status.

Table 5.7 Number of children in the household

	Pupils		Drop-outs		Non-enrolees	
	Male	Female	Male	Female	Male	Female
Ethiopia	3.8	3.6	3.2	3.4	2.8	2.9
	(2.0)	(2.0)	(1.9)	(1.8)	(1.6)	(1.4)
Guinea	5.8	6.1	7.1	6.1	5.5	5.1
	(3.2)	(2.9)	(3.6)	(3.5)	(4.1)	(3.1)
Tanzania	5.6	4.6	4.9	9.2	-	-
	(3.6)	(2.7)	(2.2)	(10.4)	-	-

Note: The figures in brackets represent the standard deviations.

However the table shows that, in Ethiopia, both male and female pupils came from larger families than those who were not attending schools, and that, as the above analysis would suggest, the differences in numbers of siblings between pupils and non-pupils were greater for the girls than for the boys. This, then, is consistent with the view that children, and particularly girls, had a better chance of attending school if household work could be spread amongst a larger number of siblings (who themselves may or may not be in school), lowering the opportunity cost of each child's schooling. The studies in Malawi, Mali, and Zambia also found that children from families with larger numbers of children were more likely to be in school (Kadzamira and Chibwana, 2000, p.80; Sangaré *et al.*, 2000, p.51; Kasonde-Ng'andu *et al.*, 2000, p.61).

Other aspects of household structure can also influence opportunity costs. In Ethiopia, for example, a relatively large number of households are headed by females, by consequence either of the high divorce rate in the country or because many husbands died or migrated during the war. Girls in these households are often withdrawn from school to look after the household whilst their mother is engaged in income-generating activities to support the family. Boys in one school actually remarked that mothers do not usually work at home if they have a daughter, as she is expected to take over the household duties whilst the mother goes out to work. Further, if there are females at home, boys are not allowed to work at home. Boys in school recognise the constraint that household work places on their sisters.

One boy noted:

> When at home, boys don't help in the house. They refuse. Girls cannot refuse working in the house. Girls like to work in the house. Attendance depends on how many girls there are in the house – if many, they can have time to study. If not, others depend on her.

These results are consistent with, and add further substance to, the econometric analyses discussed in the last chapter: as indicated there, although the size of families does affect the likelihood of school attendance, a child's position relative to his/her siblings is separately important. Children in larger families are more likely to attend school. But, even in such cases, it is the girls – particularly those with older siblings, or with fewer sisters – who are least likely to attend.

School Places and Physical Provision

Problems of insufficient demand for primary schooling, due to high direct and opportunity costs, are compounded by an inadequate supply of schools, or of enough school places, in many countries. Ethiopia and Guinea are both cases where the distribution of primary schools is very uneven. In both countries, schools are concentrated in urban areas, whilst rural areas remain under-served. Here, as elsewhere, the greater is the distance from home to school, the less likely it is that a child will attend.[11] In our surveys, the distance between home and

---

[11]   In two earlier studies in Ethiopia (USAID, 1994; Anbesu and Junge, 1988) the majority of pupils lived within 30 minutes walk which, the authors argued, implied that enrolment was influenced by school accessibility. These studies gave no clear

school was estimated by drawing a map of the local village, showing key landmarks and the location of children's homes. In each of the countries, boys and girls who were in school lived relatively nearby (within two kilometres from the school, on average). In Ethiopia and Guinea, however, the rural schools visited were serving homes which were widely dispersed, suggesting that many more children, than those who actually attended, should have been in school. In Tanzania, the problem of distance to school has been reduced by the policy of ensuring that all villages have at least one primary school.

Although the length of the journey to school affects the attendance of both boys and girls, the effects of distance are more severe for girls. During focus group discussions in Ethiopia and Guinea, parents expressed their reluctance to send girls to schools which were far from home. This was partly because girls were considered by parents to be weaker than boys, and unable to expend the energy required to walk to and from school. However, their reluctance was also due to parental concern for girls' safety *en route* and to their fear that their daughters may be subject to sexual harassment.

Insufficient school places also leads to non-enrolment. In Guinea, more than two thirds of rural schools are incomplete, having only two or three grades. In such schools, admissions into the first grade are staggered – happening once every two or three years. This means that some children are forced to start school later than the official starting age, bringing negative implications for children's, and particularly for girls', chances of completing the primary cycle. In Tanzania, when there is a shortage of school places, older children are admitted first, whilst the younger ones wait until the next academic year. As a result children might effectively start school when they are aged nine or ten. Starting school late is likely to have more serious implications for the enrolment and persistence of girls than boys, since they are more likely to leave school when they reach puberty (see below).

Inadequate school facilities can also be a reason for non-enrolment and drop-out from school. The absence of latrines in schools, and particularly of separate latrines for girls, can cause girls to be absent from school, especially when they are menstruating. Fewer than half of the schools visited in Ethiopia had latrines, and, of these, only one was separated for boys and girls. Furthermore, in most cases, the latrines were not in a suitable condition for use. In Guinea, only one-third of the schools surveyed had latrines. Some girls in both countries expressed their need for private facilities, which were often absent in their schools. While there

---

indication that distance to school has a greater impact upon the enrolment of girls than boys, although in Guinea it is proposed that the lack of 'complete' schools (i.e. schools with all primary grades) particularly discourages the persistence of girls who are less likely to walk to a school with the grade they have reached (Anderson-Levitt *et al.*, 1994). In Tanzania, lack of school places due to overcrowded classrooms has been found to be a constraint on enrolment, even in rural areas where the population density is lower than in the towns. This has resulted in priority being given to older pupils. However, the studies in Tanzania have not reported any gender bias in the allocation of places (Sumra, 1993; Omari *et al.*, 1994).

were latrines in the schools visited in Tanzania, these were usually not private, with only three walls and no door. Some girls in the countries said they strongly felt the need for private facilities, which were often absent in their schools. The discomfort of not being able to clean themselves, or change clothing at school during menstruation, provided an additional cause of absence, and of subsequent poor performance or drop-out of girls. In Ethiopia, only one-fifth of the senior girls interviewed in school had started menstruating. This relatively small proportion reflects the tendency for girls to drop out of school before reaching puberty.

Classrooms in all the countries often lacked sufficient desks and chairs, especially in early grades where classrooms were over-crowded. In such situations, children would have to sit on the floor which could be particularly uncomfortable and inappropriate for girls given their need for modesty. In Ethiopia, it was suggested that sitting on the dusty earth floor was a reason for health problems, such as respiratory difficulties. In Tanzania, being squashed together at one desk or sitting on the floor was found to be a particular problem for girls during menstruation. Furthermore, the lack of facilities was reported to result in poor teaching and pupils' lack of interest.

In Guinea, the lack of secondary-school places in rural areas was also considered to be a problem for children, especially girls, because parents, fearing for their safety, are not comfortable sending them far from home. In Ethiopia, secondary schools are usually located only in towns, bringing added cost implications for children from rural areas. Money is needed to pay for accommodation and transport, and the urban way of life leads children to expect better quality clothes, further adding to the expense. During focus-group discussions, parents suggested that secondary schools should be built nearer the villages and/or that the local primary school should be expanded up to grade eight. In Tanzania, it was found that one of the main attractions of primary education was that it could lead to admission into secondary school. However, owing to limited places being available, many schools in rural areas would typically have no students selected for government secondary schools. This had a major demotivating influence on the parents, who became unwilling to enrol their children at primary level.

The lack of secondary school places was also found to be an important constraint on primary school expansion in the other countries. For example in providing a reason for low primary enrolment during focus group discussions in Mali a parent said:

Of what use is it to enrol a child in primary school when I am not sure that the child will continue his/her education? I am not able to bear the cost of sending my child to a secondary school in Menaka, 90 km from here, because I am a farmer. (Sangaré *et al.*, 2000, p.65)

School Quality

Poor school quality is associated with poor academic results, with higher levels of repetition and drop-out and with lower progression ratios to higher levels of the education system than is the case for better schools. Communities served by poor quality schools often recognise that they are likely to gain a more restricted range of benefits from schooling than people elsewhere. This therefore leads to lower demand, and to more children being out of school than in communities with high quality schools. Although it was not the intention in our surveys to measure and compare, in a strict quantitative sense, the differences between the quality of different schools, a number of aspects of school quality were shown to have an impact upon enrolment and performance outcomes.

One of these concerned the health environment of the schools. In the three countries, poor health, which is a consequence of either malnutrition or of common diseases, was found to be a constraint on schooling. The illnesses found most commonly amongst pupils included malaria, stomach problems, headaches, colds, flu, wounds and diarrhoea. In Ethiopia, not only was poor health an impediment to school attendance, it was also found to be a barrier to enrolment, because some parents were afraid of their children catching contagious diseases at school. The prevalence of these illnesses was further compounded by the fact that none of the schools visited, in either Ethiopia or Guinea, had their own water source, and in most cases pupils had to walk to the nearest stream to fetch it. The water source, for most of the schools, was a stream which could be as far as two kilometres from the school. By contrast, most schools visited in Tanzania had tap water, although there was usually no water in the toilets or any facilities to take water to the toilets. The conditions under which the water was stored and served were often unhygienic and could lead to diarrhoea. In Guinea, for example, one of the schools visited had a bucket of water for drinking at the front of each class. However, the buckets had no lids and all the children used the same cup.

The distribution of female teachers has an important impact on school quality for female pupils. They can act as role models and provide counselling, especially on issues relating to puberty. In fact, however, the proportion of female teachers varies widely between schools in the study countries. In Ethiopia fewer than one-third of the teachers in half of the schools visited were female while in the other schools over two-thirds were female. In Guinea, in the schools visited, only one-third of the teachers were female and in Tanzania, more than fifty per cent of the teachers were female in the primary schools visited. However, some of the rural schools in all three countries had no female teachers. The imbalance of female to male teachers in rural schools derives partly from working conditions. After graduating from teacher training colleges, female teachers tend to be posted to urban schools which are more accessible by public transport, have better access to markets and other social amenities, and bring fewer problems for those with partners working in towns.

In the school surveys, the people admired most by the boys and girls interviewed were usually of the same sex, and, for girls, were usually teachers or health workers. Female teachers can thus be influential role models for girls, particularly in rural areas, where there are often few women in authority, or involved in professional work. The importance of increasing the number of female teachers, as examples for girls, was raised by focus groups in most of the nine countries. Furthermore, in the surveys, between one-third and one-half of the girls indicated that they wanted to become teachers or nurses (corresponding with the occupation of the person they said they most admired), which further supported this view.[12]

Within schools, female teachers in Guinea were generally assigned to the lower classes (Grades 1-4) whereas male teachers were teaching in the top grades. This unequal distribution of teachers tends to have a negative effect on girls in the higher grades of primary school, who are approaching, or have already attained, puberty. The problem of a lack of female teachers was evident from one school in Ethiopia in which all the teachers were male. The teachers themselves were aware of the problems girls face when they reach puberty. They noted that they were unable to provide guidance concerning menstruation because girls were shy and they were afraid that girls might take it as sexual provocation. They were conscious, however, that girls stopped coming to school when they started menstruating. No school in any of the three countries had made provisions for guidance and counselling for girls. Each of these factors made it more likely that girls would drop out of their primary course before reaching the final grade.

An uneven distribution of teachers by gender within schools was also found in the other studies. In Malawi, female teachers were mainly concentrated in lower standards. The reason given for this by those interviewed was that the lower classes were easier to teach and pupils were less difficult to handle than those in senior classes. This overlooked the large number of pupils in the first few grades (often more than 100 per class), and perpetuated the notion that females' intellectual abilities were lower than males' (Kadzamira and Chibwana, 2000, p.101).

In situations where working conditions of teachers are poor, the effective execution of their duties can be constrained. For example in all three Phase I countries, teachers complained of low salaries, inadequate teaching materials and poor housing facilities especially in rural areas. Such poor working conditions often caused teacher absenteeism. In Ethiopia, teachers had to go to the district office, often on foot or mule, to collect their salaries. If (as was often the case) the salaries were not ready, they would stay there for a few days, missing lessons. In Guinea, teachers were sometimes involved in social activities such as naming, marriage or burial ceremonies and they could also be involved in other income generating activities. When there was no substitute teacher, pupils tended to play most of the time, or stay away from school when they knew that the teacher would be absent.

---

[12]   On these findings, see particularly Kasonde Ng'andu *et al.*, 2000, pp.67-69 (Zambia); Tumushabe *et al.*, 2000, pp.81-83 (Uganda); Kadzamira and Chibwana, 2000, pp.81-82 (Malawi); Rose *et al.*, 1997, pp.64-66 (Ethiopia) and Tembon *et al.*, 1997, pp.86-87 (Guinea).

The school curriculum, which establishes both what is taught and the duration of instruction, has an important influence on educational outcomes. In our studies, the content of the school curriculum was found to affect the demand for girls' schooling. For example in Guinea, discussions with teachers and parents revealed that some parents do not enrol their daughters in school or withdraw them from school prematurely, because the present primary curriculum was judged to be irrelevant to the livelihoods of girls. Subjects such as home economics, childcare and sewing, gardening and handicrafts, which were deemed by parents to be useful for girls, were absent from the curriculum. Parents tended to see the formal education of a girl as risking deviation from accepted societal norms and practices. Such attitudes are so entrenched that even some young girls of school-going age feel that they need only learn how to cook. For example, a girl in Ethiopia said:

> Girls are not allowed to go to school because of tradition ... girls are born for boys and it is enough for a girl if she knows how to cook sauce (*wat*) and how to keep house. Therefore no-one sends girls to school.

In Tanzania, the curriculum includes agriculture and self-reliance activities which help to earn income for the school. Most pupils mentioned that they disliked these activities. They were considered to be hard work, and provided a reason for them absenting themselves from school. Tanzanian parents also expressed their disappointment with primary schooling because the possibilities of gaining subsequent employment after primary education were remote. Sending a child to primary school wasted time and was expensive to the family. In Ethiopia, too, other studies have found that the perceived irrelevance of the school curriculum to rural life affects the enrolment of children in school (Tekeste, 1990).

Pupil-teacher interaction in class has an important impact on pupils' performance. Pupils perform better when the teacher identifies and attends to their individual needs. The level of attention that a child receives depends on the number of pupils in a classroom at any one time. During lessons teachers may pay attention mainly to those who sit in the front rows and to those who actively participate in class – asking or responding to questions. Children who sit in the back rows and those who are shy in class, such as the girls, are often neglected. The number of children per class varied between the countries. In Ethiopia, the average pupil/class ratio ranged from 25 to 87. In rural schools, the size of grade one classes ranged from 58 to 155. However, in the higher grades the number of pupils dropped considerably, often to fewer than fifteen pupils. Large class-size, in the early grades, was found to be a deterrent to children going to school. One teacher reported that children are put off learning in a classroom which is crowded 'like a jail'. In Guinea, the number of pupils per class varied from 27 to 90 with the larger classes being in the urban areas. For example, there were more than 100 children in an urban classroom, whereas in a rural school they were only 10 pupils in Grade six for one teacher. The number and range of pupils per class in Tanzania however – from 29 to 41 pupils – were comparatively low compared to Guinea and Ethiopia.

The problem of large pupil numbers in the lower classes was also present in Malawi and Uganda, where both their education systems had recently expanded, following the introduction of fee-free primary education. As one teacher noted in Uganda:

> Even if there was better pay, teachers will not manage the big numbers. No. To me, meaningful education goes with low numbers of pupils that a teacher can handle, mark their exercises and teacher-pupil contact must be there. Discipline can also be possible with few pupils. (Tumushabe *et al.*, 2000, p.98)

In Malawi, the problem of large class-size was found to be exacerbated by the unequal distribution of resources within schools. Over 20 per cent of Standard 1-4 classes were held outside, due to lack of classrooms, compared to less than 5 per cent of those in Standards 7 and 8. This was in spite of the facts that younger children would be more likely to be distracted by being out-of-doors and that untrained teachers were more frequently assigned to these classes (Kadzamira and Chibwana, 2000, p.99).

The length of the school day affects school attendance, especially of girls. The longer children have to stay in school, the less time they have to perform household duties. In Guinea, normal school hours were from 8.00 a.m. to 12.00 noon and from 2.30 p.m. to 5.30 p.m. In one of the surveyed regions, the children had to attend Koranic lessons before going to school which meant that the child's day began even earlier. Under these circumstances some parents refused to enrol their children because they were needed by the family. Similarly, in Ethiopia, parents claimed that rural children were often not enrolled because they were needed to help with work on the farm, especially during the harvest season. In one school, parents suggested that schooling for half the day would be preferable, so as to facilitate children's work for the family.

A related problem concerns obligations on children to undertake manual work at school during lesson time, which may negatively affect children's performance. Our surveys revealed that this occurred in most countries. A reinforcement of the household gender division of labour was found in schools. Girls were generally responsible for sweeping the classrooms and carrying water, whereas the boys cut the grass, cleared bushes, collected thatching grass, worked as hired labour on nearby farms and carried bricks. Discussion with pupils in Guinea revealed that children also worked for teachers, washing and ironing clothes, cleaning their homes and fetching water and firewood for them. Parents expressed concern at this, and some intended to withdraw their daughters if the practice continued. An index, compiled for Guinea, Ethiopia and Tanzania, showing the different tasks performed at school, revealed that, in general, girls were more involved with these work activities during school hours than boys.

Such circumstances are common elsewhere. In Malawi, it was found that girls in school were sometimes expected to substitute for male teachers' wives when they were away, performing tasks such as cleaning the house, fetching water and pounding maize. Almost one-quarter of the girls interviewed (in the Southern region of Malawi) reported that they cleaned teachers' houses, compared to 13 per cent of the boys (Kadzamira and Chibwana, 2000, p.93). In Zambia, where the school day was already short due to double, and sometimes triple, shifts, pupils and parents were resentful of the time spent by children working for teachers and on farms to make money for the school (Kasonde-Ng'andu *et al.*, 2000). Non-school work during lesson time was, however, found to be less of a problem in Ghana, Mali and Senegal (Avotri *et al.*, 2000; Dioum Diokhané *et al.*, 2000; Sangaré *et al.*, 2000).

Gender Relations and Attitudes

The above discussion of factors which lead to under-enrolment of school-age children – high direct costs, high opportunity costs, and the inadequate extent or quality of physical provision – has already alluded to aspects of gender relations which lead to differentiated outcomes in school enrolments and performance for girls and boys. The most important of these is the existence of a gendered division of labour within the household, which has led, in many of the countries studied, to higher opportunity costs being associated with the schooling of girls relative to boys. There are, however, other aspects of gender relations revealed by our work, which conspire systematically to reinforce such outcomes. These are discussed below, under the four headings – society, labour market, school and household – indicated by the framework set out in Chapter 1.

Society As mentioned, the gendered division of labour is a reflection of overall societal expectations of gender roles. The significant contributions made by girls to the household, by preparing food, cooking, fetching water, looking after siblings, etc. are vital for household production and reproduction. This contribution is unrecognised and unrewarded. By consequence, the financial constraints on school attendance are more binding for girls because, unlike boys, they are not even partially economically independent and because the resources of other family members are not pooled within the household. In some cases, the contrast is even more extreme. In one of the survey areas in Ethiopia, girls were involved in coffee trading. Their parents expected that any money they earned could be used for the common good of the household, and that their 'spare' time outside of trading activities was needed for household work. While girls were busy at home performing these household tasks, boys were free to play and study.

Factors related to cultural norms, traditional beliefs and practices can have a strong influence on girls' enrolment, persistence and performance in school. Some societies regard the pregnancy of unmarried daughters as culturally shameful. To avoid embarrassment, parents, in some rural areas, give their daughters in marriage as soon as they reach the age of puberty, and sometimes earlier. Once married, it is very unusual for girls to continue with their schooling. They are considered as adults and cannot participate in school activities, which are considered childish. Furthermore, other children in school tease them. It is not so uncommon, however, for boys to continue with their schooling after marriage. Early marriage was found to be common in Ethiopia and Guinea, and was frequently mentioned in the focus groups as a constraint on the schooling of girls.[13] In one of the regions visited in Ethiopia, girls are married as early as eight years of age. In this region, amongst those interviewed, almost half of the girls who had never enrolled in school, and one third of those who had dropped out, were either married or divorced. Their age of marriage varied between eight and fourteen years. In the area, it is often considered an embarrassment if girls are not married by the age of ten. One father reported that he had withdrawn his daughter from school because he had observed that if a girl stays in school beyond the age of ten she would not find a husband. As a father, he felt it was his responsibility to be concerned about her future and was afraid that the community suspected the purity of girls who stay in school much longer. An important reason for his concern was that he wanted to be respected by the community and believed that 'schools are less likely to guarantee us respect and fame'. In many parts of Ethiopia early marriage is hardly voluntary. It was reported in one of the regions that girls sometimes get 'kidnapped' on their way to school, or even from within the school compound itself, by the parents of boys, for marriage to their sons. As a result of this risk, some parents refuse to send their daughters to school.

One cause of girls marrying young is, again, the presence of economic constraints. As one farmer in Ethiopia noted, families with four children may arrange a marriage ceremony for all the children on the same day in order to save money, particularly where they are daughters. It follows that some of the daughters would be married at a young age. There are, however, choices to be made in the allocation of a family's scarce resources. For example, one Ethiopian community elder suggested that, if parents were wise, they would use the money spent on their daughter's wedding ceremony to cover the cost of their education at primary school instead. However, as found in Guinea, early marriage practices are further encouraged by rural parents believing that girls' education is costly, that its potential for returns, in terms of future family income is weak, and that whether it improves wifely and motherhood skills is doubtful. Thus, marrying daughters

---

[13] Some previous studies in the countries have acknowledged the impact of early marriage on girls' schooling. In Ethiopia, most of the studies mention that early marriage is an important reason for girls not enrolling in, or dropping out of, school (Anbesu and Junge, 1988; Asseffa, 1991). The extent of the problem differs across the country with one study proposing that early marriage was not a problem in the district surveyed (Yelfign *et al.*, 1996), and another suggesting that parents believed that early marriage is a less important constraint than economic factors, although it is seen as an important consideration in deciding between whether to send a boy or girl to school (USAID, 1994). Early marriage has also been highlighted as a constraint to girls schooling in Guinea (Kourouma, 1991; Sow, 1994). Sow (1994) reports that, in Guinea, where the lack of 'complete' schools results in higher grades being available at the expense of lower grades, the delay in opportunity of enrolling discourages parents from sending their daughters to school because they would already have reached marriageable age before completing schooling.

early reduced the economic burden for the girl's family, and increased the economic gains, in the form of dowries, from the family of the in-laws.[14]

Although early marriage was not found to be such an important issue in Tanzania, partly because primary schooling is compulsory and there is legislation to imprison parents who do not enrol their children, pregnancy was identified as an important reason for girls dropping out of school.[15] Pupils in all the group discussions mentioned this, and often believed the problem to be caused by girls being attracted to luxury gifts from older men. In addition, the inability of poorer girls to buy similar clothes and school materials to those afforded by their richer classmates encouraged them to seek sexual relationships. Thus, pregnancy is also an economic issue. Whereas girls dropped out of school on learning they were pregnant, the father of the child was not usually affected. Even where the identity of the father was revealed, there was little follow-up and in most cases the culprit was not called to account. In Guinea, although government policy allows pregnant girls to return to school after their delivery, teachers felt that very few girls, if any, do actually return.

In Malawi, pregnancy was also often mentioned as an important reason for girls leaving school early, although statistical evidence is sparse (Kadzamira and Chibwana, 2000, p.63). Again, this was partly attributed to some girls leaving school before they were discovered to be pregnant by the school. Also, one case of school-girl pregnancy could result in parents of other girls withdrawing them from school, to avoid the risk of it happening to them. As in Guinea, Malawi has recently changed policy, to allow pregnant girls back to school after giving birth. However, few girls have taken advantage of this, partly because their parents were afraid they would become pregnant again, and because the girls were afraid of being teased by fellow pupils. In Uganda, bridewealth was identified as an important factor influencing the decision to invest in girls' education. In one district, for example, parents reported that they were forced to 'persuade' daughters to get married during times of acute food shortages, in order to get some bridewealth to enable them to buy food. Pregnancy was also an important reason for drop-out in Uganda. Here, too, poverty was reported to affect its incidence, since schoolgirls lacking basic necessities could easily be lured into sexual

---

[14] In Ethiopia, an earlier study showed that parents believed that their returns to investment in a son's education was greater than for daughters, because the former remains at home after marriage whereas the latter moves away so that 'the investment in her education is lost to her family' (USAID, 1994). Similarly, in one district in Tanzania, parents felt that it was useless to send daughters to school, because their resources would be controlled by their husbands after marriage (UNICEF, 1995).

[15] Previous studies in Tanzania have suggested that (fear of) pregnancy is an important reason for girls dropping out of school. At the secondary level, it has been estimated that up to one-third of all girls enrolled are expelled due to pregnancy (World Bank, 1991). In one district in Tanzania, a significant proportion of girls get married immediately after primary school because of parental fear of them getting pregnant if they were to go to secondary school (UNICEF, 1995). Girls may themselves leave school when they become more physically developed than their fellow classmates because they feel ashamed (UNICEF, 1995).

relationships (Tumushabe *et al.*, 2000, pp.3-85). By contrast, in the studies in Ghana, Mali and Senegal, pregnancy did not appear to be an important reason for drop-out, although fear of pregnancy, often resulting in early marriage, was significant. In Senegal, for example, parents indicated that performance in school and academic qualifications were of secondary importance for women. More importantly, a woman achieves her status in society upon marriage. According to a *Wollof* saying: 'Marriage is the moral duty of a woman' (Dioum Diokhané *et al.*, 2000).

In some societies, initiation ceremonies are performed when children reach the age of puberty, which is considered to be the onset of adulthood. During the ceremony, knowledge and values concerning procreation, morals, sexual skills, birth control and pregnancy are passed on to the girls concerned. Boys undergo similar rituals preparing them for manhood. Where initiation ceremonies are socially obligatory, as in some areas of Guinea and Tanzania, they were found to be a constraint on primary schooling, but this was not the case in the areas visited in Ethiopia. In one of the survey areas in Guinea, these ceremonies were sometimes performed during term-time and they could cause absenteeism from school for periods ranging from one week to one month – sometimes with withdrawal from school being the end result. The impact was perceived to be greater for girls' schooling because it is often considered shameful for them to return to school after initiation, unlike the case of boys. In Tanzania, initiation ceremonies were considered to be a critical problem for girls' schooling. During discussions in Tanzania, teachers mentioned that girls' interest in schooling declines dramatically particularly after being initiated. They attributed this to the urge in girls to play adult roles effectively. They went on to stress that this often led to poor performance and eventual drop out from school.

In some cases, the way in which society moulds girls results in a lack of confidence and subservience, which sometimes prevents them going to school. One mother in Ethiopia noted, for example, that parents do not give girls the same freedom they give boys. Because of the strict control of parents, girls feel dependent, lacking confidence in themselves and in their education. In response to this, a father in the group said that their control of girls was for their own good – otherwise they might lose their purity and even get pregnant. Another Ethiopian father noted that parents, including himself, prefer to send boys to school. This was because boys out of school easily develop bad characteristics and may be engaged in crime, whereas girls stay at home without causing trouble, because parents find things for them to do in the house. This view was supported by a mother who reported that, since parents usually cannot send all children to school, they often prefer to send boys because they are difficult to control at home, whereas girls are easy to manage. The attitudes of boys and girls and the power of parents also influences school attendance. Some parents in Ethiopia noted that, unlike girls, boys refuse to accept their parents' wishes and so continue at school even if they disagree. Boys are in a stronger position to disobey their parents because of their financial independence. The opposite effect on attendance sometimes derives from lack of parental control, as observed in Tanzania. Ex-pupils in some areas were found to be a bad influence on boys, persuading them into truancy. Such behaviour was less common for girls, although where it occurred it was considered to be more damaging since it could lead to pregnancy.

Labour market As regards the labour market, in most countries, the tangible benefits of schooling are linked to the availability of employment opportunities in the formal sector.[16] In Ethiopia, the lack of opportunities for such employment, particularly so in the rural areas, and thus the absence of many school graduates who had succeeded in obtaining such employment, was a deterrent to parents sending their children to school. In focus group discussions, some parents reported that they had lost confidence in the education system and that the educated youth had become frustrated, sometimes leading school-leavers into crime. Some groups noted that high failure rates in the school certificate examination at Grade 12, amongst those who proceeded that far, added to the difficulties of finding a job. This was particularly important for girls since there were judged to be even fewer employment opportunities for them, and very few female role models. In one region, it was interesting to note that uneducated traders were often perceived to be more important role models than teachers or other educated people, because of the larger amounts of money they were able to earn.

In focus group discussions with parents in Senegal, it was revealed that parents were discouraged from enrolling their children due to high unemployment amongst the educated. Parents said that this shows that children do not need to be educated to earn money, mentioning many people who had succeeded socially and financially without any formal education (Dioum Diokhané *et al.*, 2000). In Zambia, it was noted that parents perceive a link between schooling and employment, rather than seeing education as an end in its own right. As a result, parents expressed disillusionment with education, especially at the primary level, because it does not provide opportunities to gain entry into the labour market. This would, therefore, be a reason for parents withdrawing their children from school (Kasonde-Ng'andu *et al.*, 2000). Similar views were found in Ghana, where lack of job opportunities for school leavers leads to a loss of interest in schooling and pupils becoming attracted to income-earning activities such as mineral mining, petty trading/street hawking, distilling of local gin, all of which are perceived to be more lucrative than schooling (Avotri *et al.*, 2000).

School As for the schools, the importance of achieving a better distribution of female teachers has already been mentioned as a means of securing higher quality

---

[16]   While the hope for improved access to waged employment is often a reason for sending children to school, where job opportunities are scarce and economic returns to education are perceived to be low this becomes an explanation for not sending children, especially girls, to school (Sow, 1994; USAID, 1994). In Tanzania, where declining quality of education partly as a result of economic decline has been seen to be a critical explanation for falling enrolments, it has been found that parents are dissatisfied with schooling because they feel they do not get 'value for money' and are disillusioned with the usefulness of education (TADREG, 1993; Sumra, 1993).

schooling for girls. However, teachers' attitudes, including those of both men and women, may merely reflect, rather than question, the gendered attitudes prevalent in the wider society. In some cultures, girls may be expected to be quiet, obedient, more submissive and less active in certain school activities than boys. This is also reflected in the tasks that teachers expect girls and boys to undertake during school time. As mentioned, both male and female pupils in the three countries revealed that, in general, girls spent more time performing non-school activities during school hours, such as cleaning the classroom and offices, cleaning the latrines (which in some cases in Ethiopia was proposed by boys to be 'girls' work'), fetching water for the school, and undertaking tasks for teachers. Such expectations result in girls being timid and less self confident of their abilities. This feeling perpetuates itself and manifests in their poor performance at school.[17]

Gender sensitivity of teachers can be inculcated via training. However, none of the teachers in Ethiopia and less than one-fifth in Guinea had attended gender-training courses. In the surveys, teachers were asked to give their views about pupils' performance in school. The results, shown in Table 5.8, reveal that teacher attitudes were biased against girls. In Guinea, male teachers had more positive views about boys' participation and interest, whereas the much smaller number of female teachers tended to have more positive views about girls than boys. However, in the Ethiopian surveys, the majority of both male and female teachers believed that boys were more intelligent, participated more in class, and were more interested in learning, than girls. Although teachers' attitudes in Tanzania appeared to be more balanced, a significant minority of both male and female teachers also believed that boys were better, on these three criteria, than girls. Even though a majority of teachers in all three countries, thought schooling to be of equal importance for boys and girls, it is not surprising that female pupils conform to the rather strong expectations of their teachers that they will be less successful than their male peers.[18]

---

[17]   The school environment itself has been shown by previous studies to be important in determining persistence and performance of girls in school relative to boys. In Tanzania, schools have been seen to perpetuate rather than challenge the perceived role of girls as domestic workers and carers. For example, teachers in some areas have been found to involve girls in activities such as fetching water for teachers and cleaning the office while boys are playing (UNICEF, 1995). In Guinea, it has been found that some female teachers use female pupils to run errands for their household needs while they teach, resulting in girls' absenteeism from school (Anderson-Levitt *et al.*, 1994).

[18]   Studies at the secondary level in Ethiopia and Tanzania have shown that the school environment reinforces girls' low self-esteem: girls stated that boys were better at studying than girls, were better able to think and used their time better. Furthermore, girls tended to be shy in asking questions and lacked self confidence, resulting in them giving up more easily than boys when they fail (Gennet, 1991; Sumra and Katunzi, 1991). In Guinea, both male and female teachers are reported to show gender bias in classroom interaction (for example, ignoring the shy pupils most of whom are girls, and undermining the confidence of older girls who have repeated) (World Bank, 1996b). Attitudes and behaviour of teachers have also been shown to affect girls'

Table 5.8 Teachers' attitudes

	Ethiopia				Guinea				Tanzania			
	Male		Female		Male		Female		Male		Female	
	no.	%	no.	%	no.	%	no.	%	no.	%	no.	%
Whom do you think is most intelligent?												
Boys	50	66	29	66	12	43	4	44	8	35	17	52
Girls	6	8	1	2	6	21	5	56	5	22	5	15
Both the same	19	25	14	32	10	36	0	0	10	43	11	33
Who participates most in class?												
Boys	70	93	39	89	16	57	3	33	9	39	13	39
Girls	3	4	0	0	4	14	6	67	5	22	7	22
Both the same	2	3	5	11	8	29	0	0	9	39	13	39
Who is more interested in learning?												
Boys	43	57	29	66	18	64	2	22	9	39	13	39
Girls	10	13	4	9	3	11	4	45	5	22	8	24
Both the same	22	30	11	25	7	25	3	33	10	43	12	36
For whom is schooling more important?												
Boys	4	5	1	2	2	7	1	1	5	22	6	18
Girls	7	9	7	16	4	14	5	56	1	4	8	24
Both the same	64	86	35	88	22	79	3	33	17	74	19	58

In Ghana, Malawi, Mali, Senegal, Uganda and Zambia it was found that teachers perceived non-school factors (by implication beyond their control) to be responsible for the poor performance of girls. They appeared to be unaware of the implications of their own actions on girls. In fact, however, their attitudes revealed distinct gender biases. As in the first-phase countries, the teachers believed that boys are more intelligent than girls. They also believed that girls are naturally better at arts subjects whereas boys are naturally better at sciences – although less so in Zambia than in the other countries (Avotri *et al.*, 2000, p.136; Dioum Diokhané *et al.*, 2000, p.126; Kadzamira and Chibwana, 2000, p.92; Kasonde-Ng'andu *et al.*, 2000; Sangaré *et al.*, 2000, p.131; Tumushabe *et al.*, 2000, p.104).

---

schooling. Anderson-Levitt *et al.*, (1994) report that in Guinea girls' rate of drop-out is directly related to what goes on in and around classrooms, and that the negative attitudes of teachers and boys towards girls are major constraints to the performance of girls.

The nature of power relations between the sexes in society is perpetuated by the way in which girls are treated by their teachers and male peers within schools.[19] In Guinea, for example, pupils revealed that it is not uncommon for girls to leave school because of sexual harassment. One girl told the story of another who had left the previous year following a teacher's sexual advances towards her, which she had rebutted. Subsequently, the teacher punished her in school, and reported to the girl's parents that she was impolite and did not respect teachers. The parents became angry and withdrew the girl from school. The study in Malawi found that sexual harassment occurred frequently in most of the schools visited. In several, boys used physical force if the girls rebuffed their sexual advances. Male teachers were reported to threaten to fail girls in their examinations, intimidate them in class or give them unjustified punishments for refusing their sexual advances (Kadzamira and Chibwana, 2000, p.95). Similar findings were reported in Uganda. Parents noted that, because teachers impregnate their daughters, they enrol them in school so that they can read and write, after which parents withdraw them to avoid the risk of sexual harassment by male teachers (Tumushabe *et al.*, 2000, p.85). In Mali, a focus group discussion with a Parent-Teacher Association mentioned that, although most parents appreciate the importance of school and are now enrolling their children, they fear the disruption of their daughter's education due to pregnancy resulting from sexual relations with teachers. Not only do these teachers not marry the girls, but the girls are expelled from school because of the pregnancy and, as a result, their future is destroyed (Sangaré, *et al.* 2000).

Household As regards households, expectations of gender roles associated with the traditional image of women as home-makers (wives and mothers) was also found to be an explanation for negative parental attitudes to girls' schooling. In Ethiopia, some parents mentioned that after 12 years of schooling, their daughters would be unable to perform housework and may not be able to find a husband, on account of being too old. Similar attitudes were expressed in Guinea, where some parents mentioned that primary schooling is irrelevant to girls' future roles. Girls are traditionally expected to know how to prepare meals, to clean the home, to do the laundry and care for young children, and to be obedient and submissive. To ensure that these skills are properly developed before the girls are given in marriage, some parents prefer to keep their daughters at home with their mothers. This is partly because parents believe that these skills are not properly taught in school and partly because they are ignorant of the overall benefits of girls' schooling. Some parents in Guinea also believed that daughters were not as intelligent as sons. Thus, sending them to school was considered more likely to be a waste of time and money, because, in the end, they were judged less likely to perform as well as boys.[20]

---

[19] In Tanzania, it has been suggested that parents are discouraged from sending daughters to school because of examples of male teachers seducing or impregnating girls (TADREG, 1993).

[20] Expectations of gender roles have been found by previous studies to result in negative parental attitudes towards sending girls to school (Long, 1990; Kourouma, 1991 in

Cultural practices leading to girls' low self-esteem have an impact on parents' perceptions of their daughters' abilities. For example in Ethiopia, a father proposed that enrolment is higher for boys because they have greater aspirations; girls are usually only interested in housework and marriage. He concluded that girls are therefore less interested in school and make less of an effort to stay on. As a result, parents send boys to school. In both study-areas in Ethiopia, schooling was sometimes considered to have negative consequences for girls. As one father noted, girls who go to school face problems because they cannot find a husband and do not have employment opportunities. They cannot stay with their family when they get older because they will bring shame on them. Thus, the only option he could see for educated girls was for them to migrate to bigger towns and to lead a miserable life (working as house-servants or even prostitutes).

The impact of cultural perceptions and practices on the decision to enrol children in school is related to socio-economic status and parents' own experience of schooling. In Ethiopia, a child was 19 per cent more likely to attend school if his/her father had formal education, and 16 per cent more likely if his/her mother was educated (Rose and Al-Samarrai, 2001). In Guinea, mothers' education had a positive and significant effect on girls' enrolment in school, increasing the probability of their attendance by 18 per cent. However, it did not have a significant influence on boys' enrolment. Furthermore, father's education was not significant for either boys or girls (Tembon and Al-Samarrai, 1999). In Tanzania the impact of the (male) head's primary education is much greater for male children, whereas the spouse's primary education has a greater influence on the enrolment of daughters (Al-Samarrai and Peasgood, 1998).[21] The greater influence of mothers' education on female children (as found in Guinea and Tanzania) may be due to mothers having a relatively stronger preference for daughters' education and to their having (via education) both increased household decision-making power and more control over resources within the household.[22] This influence of mothers on their daughters' education was confirmed by discussions with parents in Guinea. Fathers, for example, mentioned that, according to custom, they were in

---

Guinea; Asseffa, 1991, Yelfign *et al.*, 1996 in Ethiopia; UNICEF, 1995 in Tanzania). A study in one district in Tanzania found that there was a fear that girls who attend school are less submissive and obedient, and more resistant to patriarchal systems resulting in lowering of their bride wealth, or even that they might make their own decision about who to marry and lose their bride wealth altogether (Mbilinyi *et al.*, 1991). Furthermore, in Tanzania low expectations of the community have been suggested to result in girls lacking interest in their own schooling and making them more submissive and less competitive in school than boys (UNICEF 1995; Katunzi and Ladbury, 1992). Girls of marriageable age may weigh marrying against studying, and are likely to drop out of school if they are discouraged by teachers or bored by lessons (Katunzi and Ladbury, 1992).

[21] This relationship has also been found by other studies in Tanzania (Mason and Khandker, 1997).

[22] Other studies in Tanzania and Ethiopia also suggest that mothers' education is positively related to girls enrolment in school (Mason and Khandker, 1997; Yelfign *et al.*, 1996).

charge of sons, whereas mothers had control over their daughters. They often found themselves powerless to reverse the decisions of mothers concerning their daughters. By contrast, the withdrawal of daughters from school (where it occurred) appeared to reflect the high pressure of household and farm work on mothers. Discussions revealed that many such mothers were uneducated, and felt the immediate opportunity costs more strongly than the longer-term benefits of their daughters' schooling.

The importance of mothers' influence on girls' schooling was also highlighted during focus group discussions in Mali. A male member of a parent-teacher association said:

> It is always with mothers that we have problems. They do not want their daughters to go to school because girls provide an extra pair of hands to help with domestic work for free. Besides, in our society, if a woman is opposed to something, a man can do nothing about it because girls are seen as the responsibility of their mothers. (Sangaré *et al.*, 2000, p.58)

Table 5.9 Average age of pupils

	Male	**Female**
Ethiopia	14.4	13.4
	(2.7)	(1.9)
Guinea	14.4	13.9
	(1.6)	(1.6)
Tanzania	15.0	14.5
	(1.4)	(1.1)

Note: The figures in brackets represent the standard deviations.

Gender relations and the opportunity costs of schooling are closely linked to age. As children become older, the more likely they are to be withdrawn from school. The chances of girls being withdrawn to help with work at home, or to be given in marriage, increase with age, as does the probability of boys dropping out of school to work on the farm or earn income. Girls in the schools visited were, on average, younger than boys, especially in Ethiopia (Table 5.9).

Table 5.10 Average school starting age

	Pupils		Drop-outs	
	Male	Female	Male	Female
Ethiopia	7.7	7.2	8.9	8.9
	(1.8)	(1.3)	(2.1)	(1.9)
Guinea	7.7	7.2	8.2	7.3
	(1.6)	(1.3)	(1.5)	(1.3)
Tanzania	9.2	9.0	8.9	9.2
	(1.6)	(1.3)	(1.6)	(1.0)

Note: The figures in brackets represent the standard deviations.

The differences in age between males and females could be due to the fact that girls start school at an earlier age than boys, as shown in Table 5.10. In Ethiopia and Guinea, the average starting age of the samples of pupils was lower than that of drop-outs which supports the view that early enrolment has an effect on persistence in school, especially for girls.[23] Age differences between males and females could also indicate that the poorer performing boys tend to repeat grades, whereas the girls have a higher tendency to drop out. Nevertheless this, and other evidence, suggests that starting-age may be particularly important for the persistence of girls in school. Econometric results in Ethiopia support these findings. The younger the child starts school, the more likely (s)he is to complete: starting at the official age of seven years (i.e. one year earlier than the mean starting age of the population), increases the probability of completion by 14 per cent. Furthermore, girls are significantly less likely to complete schooling if they have repeated a grade (a girl repeating a grade is 12 per cent less likely to complete than a girl who does not repeat). Repetition, however, is not a significant predictor of completion for boys (Rose and Al-Samarrai, 2001). In Tanzania, contrasting results for girls and boys were found for the relationship between absenteeism and pupil age. Younger boys were found to be more likely to be absent, whereas the

---

23   An earlier study in one region in Ethiopia also found that girls who started school at an early age were likely to complete their schooling, whereas over-age children were more likely to drop-out which, the authors suggested, could be related to puberty (Anbesu and Junge, 1988). On the other hand, Sumra (1993) reports that in Tanzania, parents sometimes consider seven and eight year old children, particularly girls, to be too young to attend school and prefer their children to start school at a later age when they have achieved 'mental maturity'.

probability of girls being absent increases with age – probably, again, related to the onset of menstruation and the direct and indirect impact of initiation.

Over-age enrolment can also, of course, be caused by drop-out and subsequent re-entry. This pattern was observed in Ethiopia, particularly for boys in one of the areas surveyed, following the end of the war. Older boys, who had had to leave school during the war, were in a stronger position to return than girls, because they could finance themselves. Moreover, many of the girls would have already reached puberty, thereby reducing their chances of return.

Most girls in the schools visited in Ethiopia reported that they had not received any advice on menstruation. One of the girls commented that the community in her area considered that a menstruating girl is not a virgin so she hides the fact that she is menstruating from her parents. This ignorance reinforces the way in which cultural attitudes and practices can hinder girls' personal development. In Tanzania, when girls first start menstruating, parents often go to school to seek permission for them to remain at home. They stay at home for one week, during which they are taught how to take care of themselves in terms of cleanliness. Subsequently, girls would go to school whilst menstruating, but would return home during break or lunch-time to change. This sometimes results in them getting back to school late. Boys and girls admitted that a girl who is menstruating is often embarrassed in front of her classmates, who are often ignorant about menstruation issues and do not treat it as natural. It was, therefore, not unusual in Tanzania for such girls to be withdrawn from school.

Conclusions

The evidence from our surveys and focus-group discussions in nine SSA countries provides a rich seam of information. The results generated by these studies are, in almost all respects, complementary to the econometric evidence on the determinants of gender differences in African schooling which were analysed in Chapter 3. However, they add significantly to it, both by allowing greater confidence in attributing directions of causality, and in suggesting firmer answers to the questions as to why such persistent inequalities of access to schooling, and of performance once enrolled, exist.

The analytic framework set out in Chapter 1 appears to work reasonably well as an aid to understanding the most important influences on under-enrolment, and on its gendered characteristics. Supply-side problems – a lack of tolerably equipped schools, situated close to communities, and staffed by motivated teachers – have been shown to be critically important causes of under-enrolment in these African states. However, the evidence also shows that both the direct and indirect costs, to households, of school attendance are almost always present as additional 'demand-side' causes. In addition, gender relations in society – and, in particular, in the labour market, in households and families, and in schools themselves – have tended systematically to exacerbate inequalities in the patterns of enrolment and performance in school. Structural reforms which address each of these issues are needed. These are treated in the next chapter, which provides a comprehensive analysis of the prospects for equitably achieving schooling for all.

Chapter 6

Policies to Achieve Schooling for All

Introduction

We have seen that the education systems of many countries in Sub-Saharan Africa suffer from low capacity, wide gender gaps in school participation and poor school quality. Nevertheless, over the past two decades some countries have made considerable progress in increasing their primary enrolments amongst both boys and girls and, in some, the quality of provision has also improved, despite prevailing poor economic conditions. This chapter examines how such improvements can be made more widespread in SSA. Lessons drawn from international experience indicate that there are no standard recipes, nor solutions that fit all situations due to context specificity.[1] It is clear that success requires a selected mix of mutually reinforcing interventions. Policies to increase access to schooling often require additional resources. However, using resources in new ways, so as to promote higher quality, equity and efficiency of the system, is often of even greater importance.

Taking account of the constraints identified earlier in the book, this chapter outlines strategies that are both feasible and desirable to achieve primary schooling for all, over a 15-year period, in the nine countries covered by our work. In each of these countries detailed information was collected on all aspects of education financing for a base year.[2] This information is used in this chapter to analyse the cost implications of specific policy change. The chapter begins by examining the policy context for gender and educational reform in the nine countries. The next three sections discuss a range of potential strategies to increase access, equity and quality of schooling, many of which would require more resources.[3] Since each of the nine countries faced strong resource constraints, measures to improve access and quality needed to be combined with policies to reduce costs and improve the cost-effectiveness of the education system. These are discussed in the two

---

[1]   Examples of reform outcomes, from a wide range of countries, can be found in O'Gara *et al.* (1999), Odaga and Heneveld (1995), Tietjen (1991), King and Hill (1993), Herz *et al.* (1991).

[2]   The base year for each country was determined by the latest year for which data were available at the time of the study.

[3]   Evaluations of existing strategies in the nine countries are discussed where these are available. Some reforms, particularly those affecting gender relations, are relatively recent, and impact evaluations cannot yet be made (see O'Gara *et al.* 1999).

subsequent sections. The final section draws together the policy discussion, analysing the cost and resource implications of a package of reforms to achieve SFA in each of the nine countries.

The Local Context for Reform

The policy reforms which are appropriate for each country critically depend upon their initial enrolment levels, their gender gap in enrolments, and the existing policy environment. Ethiopia, Guinea, Mali and Senegal have lower enrolment ratios and wider gender gaps than Ghana, Malawi, Uganda and Tanzania. Thus, the appropriate set of reforms is likely to differ sharply between each of these country groups. It will be recalled, for example, that both Malawi and Uganda have shown recent commitment to achieving universal primary education. School fees were abolished and other supportive mechanisms were introduced. As indicated earlier, this resulted in massive increases in enrolment in both countries. However, although demand for schooling is high, its quality, in each country remains low and has, in fact, deteriorated. Both more resources, and their more efficient use, are required to attain an acceptable level of school quality. By contrast, in Ethiopia, the demand for education is very low (with a wide gender gap in enrolment) and, despite high schooling costs, quality is also poor. That country, therefore, faces a considerable challenge to increase demand whilst, at the same time, keeping costs under control, and even reducing them.

The achievement of gender equality in the context of moving towards schooling for all, is one of the key challenges facing the countries in our study. There is, however, considerable variation in the formulation and adoption of policies aimed at this objective. As summarised in Table 6.1, most of the countries have set targets for approaching or achieving UPE (defined as a GER of 100 per cent) and gender equality, over the next few years. The high enrolment countries have gone beyond this to set even more ambitious net enrolment targets. However, not all plans include specific strategies to address the causes of low enrolment, particularly amongst girls, without which the attainment of the proposed goals will probably not be feasible.

Although considerable progress has been made over the last decade, there have been some persistent shortcomings that have limited the results achieved. In some cases, gender-specific programmes of education have been initiated by international agencies, operating outside the mainstream planning process of the government. In Malawi, for example, the USAID-sponsored 'Girls' Attainment in Basic Literacy and Education' programme (GABLE), initiated in 1991, was extremely influential in increasing girls' enrolment (see Box 6.1). However, some observers argue that the absorption of GABLE strategies into government policy and plans was weak, and that local 'ownership' has been limited, raising doubts about the sustainability of the programme (Swainson, 2000). Zambia, too, has received support aimed at girls' schooling through the 'Programme for the Advancement of Girls' Education' (PAGE) initiated by UNICEF in conjunction with the Zambian Ministry of Education in 1995. A similar UNICEF programme,

'Complementary Opportunity to Primary Education' (COPE), with emphasis on girls, has also been underway in Uganda.

Table 6.1 Government targets for UPE and gender equality

	Education Plan	Enrolment Target	Gender Equality Target
Ethiopia*	Education Sector Development Programme (ESDP) 1997-2002 (1997)	GER of 100% by 2015	Girls' enrolment to 45% as proportion of total by 2005
Ghana	Free Compulsory and Universal Basic Education Program	GER 100% by 2005	Gender equality in enrolments by 2005
Guinea	Education Sector Investment Plan (ESIP) 1999/00-2011/12	GER 100% by 2011/12	Gender equality in enrolments by 2009/10
Malawi	Policy Investment Framework 2000-2015 (Jan. 2000)	NER of 95% by 2007	Gender equality in enrolment by 2002
Mali	Programme Décennal pour le Développement de l'Education (PRODEC) 1999/00 – 2009/10 (Ten-year Education Program)	GER of 95% by 2009/10	Gender equality in enrolments by 2009/10
Senegal	Programme Décennal de l'Education et de la Formation (PDEF), 1998–2008 (Ten-year Education and Training Program)	GER of 100% by 2008/09	Gender equality in enrolments by 2008
Tanzania	The Education Sector Reform and Development Programme (March 1999)	GER of 85% by 2002	Maintain parity in enrolments
Uganda	Education Sector Investment Programme (ESIP) 1998-2003 (1998)	NER of 100% by 2003	Gender equality in enrolments by 2003 (when NER of 100% reached)
Zambia	Basic Education Sub-Sector Investment Programme (BESSIP) 1999-2002 (1998) National Policy on Education (1996)	NER of 100% in primary (1-7) by 2005. NER of 100% in basic (1-9) by 2015	No specific target However, gender equality target is implied with attainment of NER of 100%

Note:
*   Each region in Ethiopia has developed its own education plan, and targets vary by region. The targets mentioned here are those set at the national level

An appetite for these kinds of focussed initiative has been encouraged by Ministries of Education segregating 'girls' education' activities from other educational endeavours. Gender units were established in most of the nine countries, which have been mainly occupied in providing support to projects funded by donors. As a result, achieving gender equity in the sector typically became the perceived responsibility of the gender unit, having little relevance for, or impact upon, the other activities in the Ministry, and the opportunity to 'mainstream' gender concerns throughout the sector was thereby lost. In Ghana, for example, the government created the girls' education unit in 1997, within the

Box 6.1 Gender and education policies in Malawi and Ghana

During the 1990s Malawi introduced a large number of reforms aimed at increasing the participation and performance of girls in school. At primary level, most of these were associated with the Girls' Attainment of Basic Literacy and Education (GABLE) programme, launched in 1991 with the assistance of USAID. This sector reform programme aimed to promote system-wide change, whilst also addressing gender disparities in primary schooling. Under the programme, disbursements of budgetary support were made conditional on policy reforms being implemented by the government.

Reforms to reduce the costs of schooling included school-fee waivers for non-repeating primary school girls, which benefited about one million girls over a two-year period, and abandonment of the requirement that pupils should wear school uniforms. In 1993 a new policy on schoolgirl pregnancies was adopted, allowing them to return to school after delivery. A social mobilisation campaign was used to counter negative attitudes towards girls' schooling, which had some success. The curriculum, and its supporting textbooks, were revised so as to remove gender bias. Gender training was offered to teacher trainers, primary school advisers, and schools personnel. The focus group discussions conducted as part of our schools surveys indicated some resentment amongst parents that only girls were initially targeted, given that household economic constraints also strongly affected the schooling of boys. Furthermore, the new pregnancy policy was not supported by all schools, some of which continued to exclude young mothers in the belief that this served as a deterrent to others having children.

Nevertheless, the reforms did appear to stimulate the enrolment and persistence of girls in school. Over the three years 1990/91–1993/94, girls' primary enrolments increased much more quickly than those of boys (13 per cent per year, as compared with 8 per cent), and by the later year girls' enrolments exceeded boys' in grades 1 and 2 for the first time. Villages where the social marketing campaign had been held witnessed unprecedented increases in enrolments one year later, particularly amongst girls. The key to success seems to have been the way in which the various factors constraining the participation of girls in school were tackled simultaneously, in the context of a broad sectoral approach, in which other constraints to the development of the school system were also targeted.

Ghana, too, introduced a series of reforms targeted at girls' education during the 1990s. These included a scholarship programme for girls, (with assistance, again, from USAID), school feeding programmes, a Science, Technology and Mathematics Education programme (STM) for girls which included one-week clinics at which girls' misconceptions about the difficulties of science were targeted, and various other initiatives in gender-sensitive curriculum reform. The STME programme is reported to have stimulated performance in science subjects, and the scholarship programme increased girls' enrolment in the targeted schools. However, these were small, pilot programmes, not linked into broader sectoral reforms. By consequence they proved unable to affect significantly the national trends in enrolment and performance of girls.

Sources: Kadzamira (2000a), Avotri (2000a).

basic education division of the Ghana Education Service. Subsequently, the unit undertook activities relevant to the improvement of girls' participation in schooling. These, however, were limited to donor-funded activities such as a scholarship programme for needy girls, advocacy and awareness initiatives, whereas a more general integration of gender concerns into the basic education reform programme was not achieved (Box 6.1).

The Ethiopian Education Sector Development Programme, developed in 1997, provides a more promising example of attempts to integrate gender strategies. However, their full implementation was constrained by a number of factors: political commitment to reform varied at different levels of the decentralised system; funding was insecure and the capacity of women's affairs officers was often low. In Uganda, too, the government initiated a National Strategy for Girls' Education in 1998, with the intention that this should be harmonised with its Education Sector Investment Programme. However, the strategy was developed in parallel with the ESIP, rather than being integrated within it. The ESIP documentation did not include any gender analysis, nor were specific strategies presented to achieve its stated objective of achieving gender equity by 2003 (see ODI/CEC, 2000). The practicality of incorporating a strong gender strategy, subsequent to the policies of ESIP being developed, and to funding being agreed, was questionable.

In Guinea and Mali, strategies to improve gender equity became an integral part of basic education reform programmes from the early 1990s. Their gender units were supposed to be responsible for analysing gender issues in education, providing advice to decision-makers and often supporting implementation. However, by the turn of the century, neither country had a gender-equity strategy document, and clearly stated objectives were lacking. Although the gender units were often expanded to regional levels and, in Mali, even to schools themselves, their abilities to influence policy decisions remained quite limited.

Thus, although progress has been made in addressing gender issues in education in a number of the countries, governments need to set clearer priorities for achieving SFA, with gender equity. However, we should recall that it is the economic, political and social environment which shapes the nature and extent of gender gaps in education, since gender inequalities in education reflect wider gender relations across society as a whole. Political commitment, effective leadership and the ability of governments to implement appropriate policies are each important if greater equality is to be achieved. Even where strategies are proposed, their successful implementation may be hindered by a variety of factors, including that the state itself is not gender-neutral (Stromquist, 1997). A determination to eliminate non-educational obstacles, including those relating to tradition, habit, legal systems and discrimination is necessary (Hyde and Miske, 2000). Thus, successful reform will, in most cases, require changes in attitudes that go well beyond the education sector. While the review of policies in this chapter focuses on those influenced mainly by Ministries of Education, an inter-sectoral approach to policy will be necessary to ensure effective reform.

Table 6.2 summarises the policy options which are discussed in this chapter, in the context of the nine countries. The table is divided into four main sections: strategies to increase access and move towards gender equity; strategies to enhance quality; efficiency reforms to save costs; and allocative reforms to shift costs between sub-sectors of the education system and from governments to the private sector. Some of these policies were already being implemented in some of the nine

Table 6.2   Recommended policy options for achieving primary schooling for all

	Et	Gu	Tz	Gh	Mw	Ma	Se	Ug	Za
A. INCREASE ACCESS AND GENDER EQUITY									
1. Reduce direct and indirect costs									
Abolish primary school fees	I/R	R		I	I	I	I	I	R
Abolish uniforms	I	R			I			I	I
Provide incentives/subsidies	R	R		I/R	I	R	R		R
Introduce flexible timetabling	I/R	R		R	R		R		
2. Reduce cultural impediments									
Strengthen school-community links	R	R	I/R		R	I/R	I	R	R
Increase female teachers	I/R	R	R	R	I/R	R	R	R	R
Reduce school starting age (official/actual)	R	R	I/R		R	R	R	R	R
Strengthen adult and non-formal education	R	I/R		I/R	R	R	R		R
Revise pregnancy policy		I			I		R	R	
B. ENHANCING QUALITY									
Improve infrastructure	R	I		I/R	R	R			
Provide more textbooks and learning materials	R	R	R	R	R	R	R	R	R
Reduce class size/increase teachers per class	R	R		R	R	R	R	R	
Improve gender sensitivity of learning environment	R	I	R	R	R		I	R	R
Improve teacher training	R	R			R	R	R		R
Improve working conditions of teachers	I	R	R		R	R	R	R	R
Improve supervision and support to teachers			R		R	R	R	R	R
Adapt language of instruction	I	R			I	I	I		
C. COST-SAVING									
Adopt automatic promotion	I	R			R			I	
Introduce/increase double-shifting and multi-grading	R	R	R	R	R	R	R	R	
Increase class size		R	R	R					R
Increase teacher workloads/reduce teachers per class	R		R	R		R			
Employ teaching assistants	R	I/R			R	R		R	
D. COST-SHIFTING									
Encourage private education provision		R	R	R	R	R	R	R	R
Reduce public financing of T & V	R	R						R	R
Reduce unit costs in teacher training	R	R	R			R			R

Notes: I = policy under implementation
R = policy recommended by the study

countries (indicated in the table as 'I'). Where they were not yet adopted by governments, but were recommended by our national studies, they are identified by 'R' in the table.[4] Both the final policy mix and the details of individual reforms within each category vary between countries, according to local conditions.[5]

Policies to Increase Access and Achieve Gender Equity

Reduce Direct and Indirect Costs of Primary Schooling

As discussed in Chapter 5, high direct costs of education – resulting from school fees, the purchase of textbooks, stationery and school clothing, and contributions towards the construction of school buildings – were found, in all the countries, to be a major constraint on enrolment and persistence of pupils in school. Furthermore, the loss of some benefits from children's work also influenced schooling decisions. This was particularly so for girls, who were often expected to spend more time on household activities than boys. Thus, achieving SFA depends significantly on mitigating the direct and indirect costs of schooling, especially for poor families.

Abolishing fees at primary level   Several African countries have abolished official primary school fees in recent years. This was often followed by substantial increases in enrolment of children in schools. In Malawi, the fee increases of the 1980s had had a disastrous effect upon enrolments, and following a change of government in 1994, the abolition of all compulsory school charges led to the immediate attainment of UPE (as earlier defined) with enrolment increasing by over 50 per cent (from 1.9 million to almost 3 million) in that year (see Box 6.2). Fees had represented only about seven per cent of total direct household costs of primary schooling by 1993/94. But other school contributions, for stationery and transport added to the burden, whilst school uniforms alone accounted for 43 per cent of household expenditures on schooling (Rose, 2002). Thus, a combination of positive factors, including widespread optimism about the changing political and economic environment and the impact of other reforms (Kadzamira and Rose, 2001) helped to strengthen the impact of fee abolition on the effective demand for schooling.

---

[4]   The recommendation of particular strategies by the national research teams does not imply that such reform proposals may not also have been made by other policy analysts. There is often considerable agreement between different studies about the type of change needed within a particular context.

[5]   The complete package of reforms includes policies aimed at all levels of the education system. Although the discussion below focuses mainly on those affecting primary education, complementary reforms throughout the system will also be necessary. Opportunities for secondary education will, for example, influence the demand for primary education. A fuller discussion of the complete set of national reforms can be found in each of the country reports.

Box 6.2 Cost-sharing and the enrolment response in Malawi and Zambia

Malawi and Zambia have had contrasting policies towards school fees over the last two decades. In Malawi, until the 1990s, primary school fees were charged as a cost-recovery measure to supplement the Government's budgetary resources. In addition, schools levied charges to cover sports and examination expenses, and parents also bore the costs of purchasing text and exercise books, writing materials and school uniforms. Fees were a small but significant part of the total private costs of sending children to school. During the early post-independence period, steady progress was made in increasing primary enrolments, but with a GER of 70, in 1981/82, their overall magnitude remained low.

In 1982, school fees were increased by 50 per cent in grades 1-5, and by 25 per cent in the higher grades. This was in response to advice from the World Bank (Thobani 1983) that the increased revenues from fees would enable expansion and improvement of the service, and thereby secure increased enrolments. In fact, the opposite happened. Absolute enrolments fell by 4 per cent over the following two years, and by 1984 the GER had declined to 63 – down 10 per cent from its earlier peak. Subsequently, enrolment growth resumed as inflation eroded the cost of the fees, but at a slower rate than had obtained prior to 1982.

From 1990, government policy began to change. A phased abolition of tuition fees began for all first grade pupils in 1991, followed, the next year, by fees being abolished for all those in second grade and all non-repeating girls at primary level (Box 6.1). The enrolment response was marked, and the GER increased from 75 to 93 over the three years 1990-93. Household costs remained significant, however, because parents were still required to provide books, and to make contributions to school construction and maintenance. In 1994, all school fees were abolished, and primary schooling became free (although in practice, monetary and in-kind contributions were still welcomed by the schools and were often made). The requirement to wear school uniforms was also abolished. The impact was dramatic. Enrolments increased by 50 per cent in 1995, and the GER rose to 134 – the highest in Africa. High enrolment ratios of around 120 were sustained throughout the remaining years of the century.

In Zambia, school fees were abolished in 1970-71, as part of the government's drive to create a welfare state in which services were universal and free. Enrolments expanded steadily, and UPE was reached by the early 1980s. This, however, was a period of deep recession – associated particularly with declining copper exports. The government reduced public spending, and school fees were re-introduced as a means of bolstering school revenues. The charges increased in scale and intensity through the 1990s, such that by 1996, between one-half and two-thirds of the unit costs of primary schooling were met by households. One consequence was enrolment decline and the primary GER fell back to around 90 by 1995. However, in 1999, it was decided that no child would be excluded from school because of their inability to pay school fees. This, together with increased attention to school quality, led to some recovery of enrolments, which seemed likely to be sustained.

Sources: Kadzamira (2000b), Kasonde-N'gandu (2000b)

Similarly, in Uganda, the introduction of the policy of Universal Primary Education in 1997 led to a sharp reduction in direct costs to households. Statutory primary school fees were abolished for up to a maximum of four children per family, with equal allocation of fee waivers for boys and girls in each household. As a result, primary enrolment more than doubled, from 2.8 million in 1996 to 5.3 million in 1997, and UPE was indeed achieved (Tumushabe *et al.* 2000). However, in both Malawi and Uganda, girls' enrolment remained lower than boys', mainly because more over-age boys than girls re-entered the education system. Moreover, although the new levels of enrolment were high in both countries, many children dropped out before completing the primary cycle. Repetition and drop-out rates in the late 1990s implied that only 18 per cent of those entering the first grade of primary would reach the final grade in Malawi, and only 28 per cent would do so in Uganda. In Malawi, our studies showed that after the abolition of fees inadequate clothing and lack of money to buy school supplies remained an important reason for non-enrolment (Kadzamira and Chibwana, 2000; see also Burchfield and Kadzamira, 1996). Although both governments increased the resources available to primary education following the abolition of fees,[6] schools continued to request contributions from households, to pay for sports equipment, water and other bills, and to meet the costs of labour and materials for school construction and maintenance.[7]

In the context of the decentralised system in Ethiopia, the setting of school fees became the responsibility of regions. At the time of our field-work, some regions were continuing to charge fees, whilst others had abolished them, with some positive results in terms of enrolment. In the Amhara region, for example, following the abolition of school fees in 1995/96, and a successful community-sensitisation programme which emphasised the importance to families of sending their children to school, enrolments increased significantly (Rose *et al.*, 1997). However, in the country as a whole, enrolment growth was slow, and gender gaps widened as enrolment increased. This indicated that complementary strategies were required to achieve both enrolment and gender-equity targets. Furthermore, contrary to the experience of Malawi and Uganda, additional government resources were not made available to compensate the schools for the loss of fee income. Given the low level of fees relative to total unit costs, this would have been well within the capacity of the government.[8]

---

[6]   In Uganda, the government committed itself to providing a capitation grant to schools equivalent to the previous level of school fees (Tumushabe *et al.*, 2000). In Malawi, although a direct financial transfer was not made to schools, primary recurrent expenditure increased by 11 per cent in real terms. This was not, however, sufficient to cover the massive increase in enrolment so that primary unit expenditures declined in real terms by 26 per cent (Kadzamira and Chibwana, 2000).

[7]   In Malawi, these additional costs varied substantially between schools and were often prohibitive for poorer households (Chimombo and Chonzi, 1999; Kadzamira and Chibwana, 2000; Rose, 2002).

[8]   For example, fees in Jimma zone were found to be approximately 5 Birr on average, compared with a primary recurrent unit cost of 200 Birr. However, given that the majority of primary recurrent expenditure is allocated to salaries, the additional

In 1992 the Tanzanian government reintroduced fees in primary schools to supplement constrained government finances. This 'Universal Primary Education (UPE) contribution' was set by central government and represented a very small proportion of the overall costs of primary education (see Mason and Khandker, 1996). In addition to this, however, school committees also set and managed a number of school-level contributions. These were supposed to be at rates appropriate for the local area, but they were sometimes set at a level higher than could be afforded by some parents. However, the reintroduction of fees, in 1992, was not accompanied by a sharp drop in enrolments, no doubt partly because fees remained a modest proportion of total household schooling costs. In 1998 the government doubled the UPE contribution, and further increases were proposed in the subsequent Education Sector Reform and Development Programme (United Republic of Tanzania, 1999). Appraisals suggested, however, that the increased costs to households were likely to prevent the government from achieving its enrolment goals (see Wangwe *et al.*, 1999). These considerations led to all primary school fees being abolished by the government early in 2002.

School fees were not officially charged in Ghana, Guinea, Mali and Senegal during the 1990s. However, other school levies were applied such as enrolment charges, and PTA levies. These varied locally because the amounts charged were set at the school level. Our research found their magnitude to be prohibitive for many rural people, and proposals were made for their abolition.

The government of Guinea attempted to reduce the financial burden of schooling on parents by adopting a policy of tax relief for families whose children enrolled in school. Although this move was positive, it had a number of shortcomings. Firstly, the savings were not sufficient to secure enhanced enrolment from families which were too poor to pay the cost of school supplies, or to forego the labour of their daughters at home. Secondly, the tax-relief system was not effectively monitored, so some parents would send their children to school during the tax season, only to withdraw them later in the year. Lessons from this experience however, led the government to consider other policies for reducing the cost of schooling to parents. With assistance from the World Bank, the government has developed a policy of procuring textbooks and distributing them to children in schools for a small rental fee (World Bank, 1995b).

Thus, the evidence suggests that, whilst the abolition of primary-school fees is necessary to improve access to schooling, it may not be sufficient to secure either gender equality or universal completion of schooling. However, in countries where primary-school fees are still charged, their abolition would provide more children with the opportunity to attend school. As indicated by Box 6.2, Zambia provides a case where the principle of cost-sharing remained explicit in national policy throughout the 1990s. Various types of fees were permitted, including Grade 1 registration fees, parent-teacher association fees, general purpose fund contributions, and examination fees. These fees were set at the school level and varied significantly between schools (Kasonde-N'gandu *et al.*, 2000). Based on

---

government contribution to learning materials would have had to rise considerably to compensate for the loss of fee income (from 0.61 Birr) (Rose *et al.*, 1997).

average fee levels in schools, government primary recurrent expenditures per pupil would have to have increased by approximately 10 per cent to meet the costs of the school fund and PTA contributions.[9] Given the extremely low level of government spending on primary schooling in Zambia (as shown in Chapter 4) a shift of these costs from households to the government was both desirable and feasible.

School uniforms   School uniforms represent another important direct cost to households. The national reports show that school uniforms often represent the most substantial direct cost of primary schooling, and that their cost can be greater for girls (see also Chapter 5). The reduction, or removal, of this cost would provide an important encouragement to participate in schooling. One possibility, implemented in some countries (including Ethiopia, Malawi, Uganda, Zambia and Tanzania) is to make the wearing of school uniform optional. While this enabled some children to attend school who might not otherwise have been able to afford it, evidence on the effects of this policy is mixed. In the Tanzania fieldwork, for example, pupils reported dropping out of school because they did not have a school uniform even though they had the right to attend school without it (see Peasgood *et al.*, 1977, p.133). Since all children have to wear clothes, school clothing is a non-discretionary expenditure. However, the question is whether special, more costly, clothes are bought when children attend school. This seems to happen. Children themselves – particularly older girls – have been found to feel shy if they do not have good clothes for school (Kadzamira and Chibwana, 2000). Even though school uniform was not compulsory for children in Malawi, only 10 per cent of households interviewed said that they did not buy clothes especially for school. In addition, older children cost more: the average cost of clothes bought for children in Standards 5-8 was almost double that for children in Standards 1-4 (Rose, 2002).

Guinea abandoned its policy of compulsory uniforms for pupils in the mod-1990s. However, implementation was patchy, because many schools continued to insist on pupils wearing uniforms. In Mali and Senegal uniforms were also not required in public schools. In Ghana however, they continued to be required, and our studies revealed that their high cost acted as a deterrent to girls' schooling. During the late 1990s the Ghanaian girls' education unit ran a pilot scheme in the Ahafo-Ano district, whereby needy girls were provided with school uniforms free of charge. An evaluation of its impact suggested that the programme was helping to increase girls' participation in schooling (Avotri *et al.*, 2000).

Incentives and subsidies for school attendance   Programmes providing financial incentives for improving gender equity in schooling have been implemented, with donor support, in some of the countries. These include the USAID-funded scholarship programme for girls in four pilot schools in Ghana, the GABLE fee-waiver programme for non-repeating secondary-school girls in Malawi (previously

---

9   The average school fund and PTA contribution was approximately 4,000-5,000 Kwacha per pupil (Lungwanga and Kelly, 1999; Kasonde-N'gandu *et al.*, 2000), compared with a primary recurrent unit cost of approximately 41,000 Kwacha in 1996/97.

targeted at the primary level before the abolition of primary school fees) and the World Bank-funded scholarship programme for secondary-school girls in Tanzania. The latter programme, begun in 1995, aimed to increase poor girls' participation in secondary education and to promote the effective participation of girls in secondary schools (Sumra, 1998), through selective bursaries, counselling, curriculum development and other gender-oriented improvements within secondary schools (Mbilinyi and Mduda, 1995). By 1998 1500 girls – representing approximately one per cent of total female lower-secondary enrolment – were recipients of support. The programme was successful in increasing female secondary-school participation, but not in improving female school-achievement. Whilst scholarship programmes have generally had some success in increasing the enrolment of girls, other lessons relating to their implementation are also evident. Evidence from Malawi indicates that many parents resent girls-only benefit programmes, because boys from poor households are also often unable to attend school (Kadzamira and Chibwana, 2000; Wolf, 1995; Swainson *et al.*, 1998). Furthermore, even with the fee-waiver, it appears that very few children, particularly girls, from lower income groups attended secondary school (Castro-Leal, 1996). Since the better-off children were more likely to obtain better primary-school grades than poorer children, more of them continued to secondary school. In these circumstances incentives would have been better targeted at needy, primary-level children. Careful identification of eligible groups – as in the Tanzanian case – would be an important criterion for success. Although targeting can be a difficult process, the community can usefully be involved in selection of the beneficiaries, and some of the target groups requiring financial assistance – for example orphans and street children – are relatively easy to identify, and an extremely important group to target, particularly in the context of HIV/AIDS (see UNESCO, 2002).

Table 6.3 shows the estimated impact on the base year primary unit cost of the introduction of an incentive programme in the six countries where this policy was proposed. The base-year costs are total government primary education expenditure per pupil for the year of data collection. The proposed incentive programmes were mainly for rural girls and they envisaged a cost-per-beneficiary in the range of $PPP30-100. A strategy of providing incentives for girls would be particularly important in Ethiopia, Ghana, Guinea, Mali and Senegal – countries with the lowest enrolments and the widest gender gaps. In Ethiopia where demand for girls' education is particularly low, for example, the proposed subsidies to cover the cost of stationery and exercise books, and of material for school clothes, would represent a substantial incentive for households to send their girls to school (Rose *et al.*, 1997). If the subsidy were targeted at rural areas in disadvantaged parts of the country where enrolment is lowest, approximately 20 per cent of school-aged children could benefit (Table 6.3). This would generate a nine per cent increase in the base-year unit cost for Ethiopia.[10] Although this is significant, the potential benefits are very substantial. Proposed subsidy programmes in other

---

[10]   The average primary unit cost does not increase by the total cost per beneficiary because not all enrolees would receive the subsidy.

countries where demand is low could be designed so as not to cause unit costs to rise significantly. For example in Ghana, Guinea, Mali and Senegal increases in unit costs as a consequence of the proposed subsidies for rural girls would range from 0.6 per cent in the case of Senegal to five per cent in Ghana.

Table 6.3 Effect on primary unit costs of incentive programmes

Country	Coverage	School children receiving incentive (%)	Cost per beneficiary ($PPP)	Increase in average primary unit cost (%)
(1)	(2)	(3)	(4)	(5)
Ethiopia	Rural girls in disadvantaged areas	20	100	10
Ghana	Rural girls from disadvantaged backgrounds	15	61	5
Guinea	Rural girls	13	31	2
Mali	Rural girls	2	35	1
Senegal	Rural children, particularly girls	2	44	0.6
Zambia	Children with special educational needs, orphans and street children	25	6	2
	Sanitary wear for girls in rural areas	8	32	4

Source: GAPS simulation models.
Notes: Column 2 describes the intended recipients of the subsidy while Column 3 reports the percentage of total enrolment, in the base year, represented by this group. Column 4 details the proposed size of the subsidy for each recipient. Column 5 shows the percentage increase in the base year average weighted unit cost of the proposed incentive programme assuming the reported level of coverage (column 3) and base year enrolment levels. Base year primary weighted unit costs and enrolment levels for each country are shown in Tables TA.1 and TA.2 of the Technical Appendix.

Even in countries where enrolments are high, there may be a need for subsidies, targeted at easily identifiable sub-groups of the population. For example, although overall enrolment in Zambia was high, children with special educational needs, orphans and street children continued to be excluded from school. Since the direct costs of schooling were an important cause of their non-enrolment, providing these children with a relatively modest subsidy of around $US6 could allow them the opportunity to attend, whilst increasing unit costs by only two per cent (Table 6.3). Furthermore, as indicated in Chapter 5, an important reason for female drop-out at puberty is a lack of sanitary wear. Thus, providing recyclable cloth for sanitary wear could help older girls to stay at school (Kasonde-Ng'andu *et al.*, 2000). Although the estimated annual cost of the cloth was relatively high, targeting primary-school girls who had started menstruating would increase unit costs by a relatively modest four per cent.

In food-insecure areas, one useful form of indirect subsidy can be provided by school-feeding programmes. These aim to ensure that children who do not receive sufficient food at home have an adequate nutritional intake which, in turn, provides them with energy to study more effectively. Many such schemes are funded by the World Food Programme (WFP), and by non-governmental organisations such as the Catholic Relief Services, in conjunction with Ministries of Education. The potential benefits of such programmes appear to be significant. For example, school-feeding programmes existed in areas of Ethiopia which had been affected by war and which suffered most from food insecurity. In Ghana, similar programmes existed in selected arid areas of the Upper West Region, where food rations were given to girls with good attendance records. It was reported that these schemes improved enrolment, dropout and performance, particularly for girls. However, costs have been high. In Ethiopia, for example, public expenditures per pupil would roughly have doubled if the government were to have fully financed the programme (Hodell, 1996). Given these costs, the wide extension of school-feeding programmes is unlikely to be feasible. However, continued targeting of vulnerable populations, in areas particularly affected by food insecurity, is likely to remain beneficial.

Flexible timetabling Results from our schools surveys, discussed in Chapter 5, indicated that the demands for both boys' and girls' labour fluctuate, depending on the time of year. In rural areas, the demand for children's labour is highest around harvest time. Schools reported that students are often absent for long periods at this time, and that subsequently, they do not always return to school. Peak demand for child labour varies according to the climatic conditions and location. Adjusting the timing of the school calendar to avoid such peaks could reduce absenteeism and dropout at little or no cost. In Ethiopia, for example, regional administrations already varied the school calendar: provided that schools opened for 205-210 days per year, patterns of attendance could be adapted to the agricultural demands of a region (Rose *et al.*, 1997).

In Malawi, the school calendar, which previously ran from October to July was changed, in 1997, to begin in January, with long holidays falling in November and December (the beginning of the 'hunger months'). Water shortages in boarding secondary schools and tertiary institutions, rather than an assessment of the household demands on pupils, led to them being closed from October to December (Kadzamira and Rose, 2000). By consequence, the new school year neither followed the agricultural calendar, nor avoided peak agricultural times, which aggravated the problem of children dropping out of school (Malawi MOE/UNICEF, 1998; Kaunda, 1999; Kadzamira and Chibwana, 2000). Altering the school calendar would provide a costless means of contributing towards improved school attendance.

In Mali, community schools have successfully implemented flexible schedules and school calendars whereby the school term begins at the end of harvest in November and continues until the beginning of May. Children are taught for two to three hours a day, six days a week for six and a half months. The impact of these changes has been positive in increasing girls' enrolments in these schools.

Recommendations in Ghana and Guinea regarding flexible time-tabling relate more to school schedules than to the school calendars. In both countries, the studies recommended that school schedules should be adjusted to accommodate seasonal changes and household demands on children's labour. For example classes could begin and end thirty minutes earlier than current schedules to permit children more time to undertake household chores that may keep them away from school.

Cultural Impediments to Attending School

We know from Chapter 5, that girls – more than boys – face a set of constraints affecting both their access to school, and their attitudes towards their roles and abilities once enrolled. While these constraints are often a reflection of broader societal attitudes, there are a range of strategies available within the education sector that can help reduce impediments to girls' participation and achievement within school. These strategies are often not costly in financial terms, yet, given the commitment of governments and schools personnel, their benefits can be very large. Examples of such strategies are discussed below.

Strengthening school-community relationships It is evident from our surveys that parental involvement in school governance is often minimal. In most of the countries, parental support was limited to involvement in self-help projects, and, particularly, to the provision of financial and material contributions for school construction, rehabilitation and maintenance, rather than more active participation in decision-making. Although school committees and/or parent-teacher associations existed in most schools, their effectiveness varied considerably between countries, and individual schools. In many cases, school committee members did not have the necessary experience to understand accounts or to handle their other responsibilities. Most needed training so as to provide more effective school management.

Responding to this need in Tanzania, the World Bank, UNICEF, DANIDA and Irish Aid, have been involved in strengthening the role of school committees. The aims of the World Bank-financed Community Education Fund Matching Grant project, for example, included the promotion of school-based management by giving parents greater control over expenditures (Peasgood *et al.*, 1997). In other countries, including Malawi, Mali and Uganda, innovative community-school programmes have been initiated, with the support of international agencies such as USAID, UNICEF and DFID. Their objectives included mobilising the community to contribute towards school construction providing labour and materials. In addition, they aimed to involve the community in decision-making at school level – for example by recruiting teachers from the local area – to give them a greater sense of ownership and control. In the Mali community schools programme, funded by Save the Children Fund, each village was required to have a committee which is responsible for school supervision, recruitment of pupils, management of teachers, and maintenance of school buildings. Committee members were trained to perform these functions. Reports indicate that community management in the schools has been strong, ensuring that schools remained responsive to the needs of local children, and that the curriculum remained consistent with that of the official system. The motivation of teachers in these schools was very high, even though their pay was much less than teachers in state schools.

Policy makers were aware of the success of such a locally responsive approach to schooling but its success on a wider scale remained to be proven (DFID, 2000). Whilst these schools performed favourably compared to their government counterparts, they often received a greater amount of technical and financial support. It may be better to promote greater community involvement in existing government schools than to allow a separate set of schools to develop based upon different principles. Two-tier education systems usually present equity dangers, which raise questions about their long-term viability. Questions also arise as to how students in these schools, which sometimes offer a reduced curriculum, can be integrated into the national education system at a later stage. Other, more conventional, models exist, such as the community schools of urban Zambia. These can be considered to be overflow 'state' schools, differing from government schools only because they are completely funded by local contributions and fees (Hyde, 1999). Thus, in most of the countries, there is potential for involving the community more in the running of schools and lessons from existing community-school programmes are instructive.

Community sensitisation campaigns have been shown to be a successful means of raising parental and societal awareness of the importance of schooling, particularly for girls. In Ethiopia, sensitisation campaigns succeeded partly because their integration with existing local government and traditional community structures, was effective in securing local support. The campaigns were carried out at little cost to the government, but had the greatest impact upon female enrolments where school fees were also abolished. Advocacy appears to work better when combined with other measures, such as reductions in the private costs of schooling. In a number of countries, FAWE national chapters have played an important role in sensitising rural communities about the importance of girls' education. In Zambia, for example, the Alliance for Community Action on Female Education and FAWE (Zambia) have successfully worked with community leaders to sensitise rural communities about the importance of girls' education (Kasonde-Ng'andu *et al.*, 2000).

In Malawi, the GABLE project used community sensitisation as a major means of encouraging enrolment. Some communication strategies, such as the use of participatory drama, focus group discussions, radio and other media provided effective ways to strengthen knowledge of the importance of girls' education. This helped to encourage the demand for schooling, despite its low quality, and led one USAID evaluation to conclude that education had been successfully marketed before being successfully produced (O'Gara *et al.*, 1999). Awareness campaigns, funded by donors, have also been common in the three Francophone countries. In Guinea and Mali, they have included informational broadcasts about girls' education on radio and television – often endorsed by entertainers, journalists and local dignitaries – and schools have had competitive award programmes. Their impact appears to have been positive for girls' participation in school and each of the national studies recommend that implementation of these strategies should continue (Tembon *et al.*, 1997; Sangaré *et al.*, 2000; Dioum Diokhané *et al.*, 2000).

Community sensitisation programmes have, therefore, taken a number of different forms, varying from community-led campaigns with government support, to more elaborate donor-driven programmes. The evidence suggests that such campaigns need not be costly, and can be particularly successful where the community is involved in their design and implementation. Countries with low demand for education, such as Ethiopia, Guinea, Mali and Senegal, would benefit from a continuation and reinforcement of their existing programmes, particularly in the more remote areas. Even in countries where enrolment is relatively high, such as Malawi, Uganda and Zambia, negative attitudes towards education in certain areas of the country can be positively influenced by continued advocacy.

Increasing the proportion of female teachers Earlier in this book, a range of macro and micro evidence was presented which suggested that female primary enrolments are responsive to the presence of women teachers. Correlation does not, of course, establish causality. However, our surveys provided more direct evidence for the importance of female role models in motivating parents to send their daughters to school. Female teachers are often the only women holding positions of authority in rural areas. Increasing their numbers demonstrates future career possibilities for girls, and improves their sense of security whilst at school. Furthermore our survey in Tanzania provided evidence that female teachers (and particularly female heads and education officers) were more sensitive to girls' problems, particularly those arising from menstruation, and were better placed than their male counterparts to increase the confidence of female students.

Nevertheless, in all nine countries, the teaching force remains predominantly male at both primary and secondary levels. The imbalance is particularly marked in rural areas. In Ethiopia, for example, 39 per cent of the urban primary teaching force was female, compared with only 21 per cent in rural areas (Ethiopia Ministry of Education, 1977). In Malawi, the comparable figures were 75 per cent and 27 per cent (Kadzamira and Chibwana, 2000), and in Guinea, 23 per cent and six per cent (World Bank, 1995b). In Senegal, in 1998, only 24 per cent of teachers at the primary level were females and most of them were teaching in urban schools. This unequal distribution of female teachers between urban and rural areas is often an inevitable outcome of government policy. In Ethiopia and Tanzania, for example, female teachers have been given preference when hiring, to jobs with close access to a main road or located near to a town. In many West African countries it is government policy for females to be given jobs close to where their spouses are working. Consequently, female teachers tend to be hired into urban schools. In Zambia, on the other hand, the PAGE programme has attempted to encourage female student teachers to work in rural areas by emphasising its importance for pupils and pointing to the greater opportunities for promotion to management positions that are available outside the towns (Kasonde Ng'andu *et al.*, 2000).

However, given the harsh conditions in some rural areas mere persuasion will be insufficient, and more direct incentives for female teachers to work in remote schools will be required. For example, the reports for the countries in East and Central Africa, propose better provision of teacher housing near to schools, of transportation to towns from time to time, and of financial inducements to encourage women to work in rural areas. Malawi has shown how increased provision of teachers' houses, with priority in allocation being given to female teachers, can be facilitated by community provision, with teachers paying a modest rent to contribute towards construction and maintenance costs (Kadzamira and Chibwana, 2000).

Table 6.4 Effect on primary unit costs of incentives for female teachers

(1)	Beneficiaries as % of total teachers (%) (2)	Increase in recipients' wages (%) (3)	Change in average primary unit costs (%) (4)
Malawi	33	10	3
Tanzania	35	43	12
Zambia	20	20	3

Source: GAPS simulation models.
Notes: Column 2 reports the proposed percentage of total teachers, in the base year, who will receive the salary increment. Column 3 details the proposed increase in the wage for each recipient. Column 4 shows the percentage increase in the base year average weighted unit cost of the proposed salary increment assuming the reported level of coverage (column 2) and base year female teacher levels. Base year primary weighted unit costs for each country are shown in Table TA.1 of the Technical Appendix.

Financial incentives for women to teach in rural areas were proposed in the reports for Malawi, Tanzania and Zambia, where teachers' salaries have been particularly low. Table 6.4 reports the impact on base year primary unit costs of the proposed salary increments for female teachers for these countries. The proportion of teachers who would receive the incentive would vary between 20 per cent in Zambia to approximately one-third in Malawi and Tanzania (see Column 2, Table 6.4). In Tanzania, where teachers' wages were the lowest of all nine countries, the proposed incentive would imply a relatively large increase in teachers' wages (43 per cent) for recipients, and a larger impact on unit costs (increasing by 12 per cent) than elsewhere. In general, however, the proposed increases would have strong incentive effects for female teachers, yet relatively modest implications for affordability.

An alternative means of increasing the number of female teachers working in rural areas would be to recruit and train women locally. As part of community school programmes in both Malawi and Mali, an increase in the number of females teaching in remote areas has been facilitated by the local recruitment and training of teachers, and their subsequent assignment to a school in their own village. Evidence from these community schools showed that the performance of pupils is not affected, even where the newly qualified trainees have lower qualifications than their more experienced colleagues (Hyde, 1999; Muskin, 1999).

In some countries, emphasis is placed upon increasing the number of female trainee teachers. In Ethiopia, for example, the Ministry of Education reserved at least 30 per cent of the places in Teacher Training Institutes for women. However, owing to difficulty in finding enough eligible female students, many with results below the normal requirements were allowed to enrol. In such cases, extra tuition, at the outset of their courses, was desirable, to help them compete equally with their male counterparts (Rose *et al.*, 1997). In Malawi, by contrast, two-thirds of the boarding places in Teacher Training Colleges were reserved for males, which inevitably prevented female teachers from representing more than one-third of the total. A clear need was identified to provide more boarding facilities for female trainees (Kadzamira and Chibwana, 2000).

In Guinea and Malawi, where male teachers predominated, the females tended to be assigned to lower classes. This can be counter-productive where sexual harassment by male teachers of the older school-girls is not uncommon. Female teachers can also play a particularly important role in the upper classes, by providing support to girls when they reach puberty. Thus, there was a clear need to change the present gender-hierarchy within the schools. Yet, our survey results revealed that in-service training opportunities enabling career advancement were more accessible to male than to female teachers. Furthermore, female teachers often have a heavier work-burden in the home, compared with their male counterparts, and may, therefore, be reluctant to take on further responsibilities at school. In order to encourage female teachers to accept additional responsibilities, the Uganda report proposed that each primary school should have at least one senior teacher trained to provide guidance and counselling, with preference in this role being given to female teachers. These teachers would receive a salary increment of five per cent in recognition of this additional responsibility (Tumushabe *et al.*, 2000). There remains a more general need to remove traditional barriers to the promotion of women in schools where, as in Uganda, unmarried females have not been eligible to become head teachers.

Reducing the official school starting age   The official age at which children start school in the case-study countries was either six or seven years. However, the results from the surveys revealed that late entry into school was common, with many children not starting until after the age of nine. Particularly those living in rural areas delayed entry, for reasons related to there being long distances and journey times between home and school. On the other hand, the results also suggested that children are more likely to complete primary schooling if they start school at a younger age. As indicated in Chapter 5, this is particularly true for girls, who are likely to drop out on reaching puberty, when household demands increase and when pressures to marry may begin in earnest. In Ethiopia, Guinea,

Mali and Senegal, for example, a reduction in the official entry-age from seven to six years, could help to encourage primary-cycle completion. In other countries, such as Malawi, and Uganda, where the official starting age is already six years, renewed efforts are required to encourage children to enrol at this age. School-mapping can be used to reduce the length of journeys from home to school, and the advantages of enrolling early need strong advocacy.

The differential impact of late enrolment for boys and girls was revealed particularly strongly in the Tanzanian surveys. Although boys' academic performance and their probability of dropping out appeared not to be affected by late enrolment, for girls it was associated with poorer attendance and performance, particularly around the onset of puberty. An earlier proposal to reduce the official starting age from seven to six years had met widespread opposition, particularly in rural areas. However, under the terms of the 1995 Education Act, it became compulsory for all seven-year-olds to attend primary school – leaving open the question as to whether they could or should also enrol before that age (Peasgood *et al.*, 1997).

Adult and non-formal education The results of our surveys, in common with those of many other studies, suggest that the education of parents, and particularly of mothers, has a significant effect on the likelihood of their children being in school. This is partly because parental education is associated with higher socio-economic status and, thus, with their being in a better financial position to send their children to school. However, it is also related to the existence of more positive parental attitudes towards education. Adult literacy programmes, particularly for mothers, have been judged to have a significant impact on girls' schooling and are being implemented in some of the countries. However, with the drive towards universal primary education, adult literacy programmes have, in some instances, become a forgotten priority. In Malawi, for example, adult education programmes were run by the Ministry of Community services. They were not integrated with the Ministry of Education's programmes and were often small-scale, suffering from insufficient funding (Kadzamira and Chibwana, 2000).

To the extent that a complementary relationship exists, it becomes important to increase the coverage of non-formal education courses for those who are beyond school age, both as an end in itself, and to help strengthen enrolment growth amongst the young. There are a great variety of such courses, many of which link skill-acquisition to people's daily activities. The incidence of study may be short, amounting, often, to no more than a few hours per week. Nevertheless, after following such courses, some pupils rejoin the conventional education system to continue their studies, and this can be an explicit aim of some programmes. Second-opportunity schools in Guinea provide an example of non-formal education centres, offering programmes based around school curricula (Tembon *et al.*, 1997).

Senegal has wide experience in the implementation of adult non-formal education programmes. Unusually, however, the government has adopted a strategy of contracting their provision to private providers. Between 1995 and 2000 the number of such providers quintupled from 80 to 400, their enrolments increased at more than five per cent per year, and more than 81 per cent of the students were female. The implementation of these non-formal and adult education programmes was a major factor in reducing the adult illiteracy rate by 22 percentage points in Senegal between 1988 and 1998.

In Mali, non-formal education programmes were managed mainly by the government. They included functional literacy programmes, for those aged 16 years or more, in 'Centres d'Alphabetisation Fonctionelle', and programmes for out-of-school youth, for those between the ages of nine and 15 years, at 'Centres d'Education pour le Développement'. Given that most illiterate adults in Mali are women, and some evidence that mothers who complete literacy training classes are more likely to send their children to school, the further extension of these programmes was recommended by the Mali study (Sangaré *et al.*, 2000).

Non-formal education is also provided in *medersas* or Koranic schools in Guinea, Mali and Senegal. In these schools, the Arabic language is used as a medium of communication, and is also taught as a separate subject. The curricula of *medersas* are generally of poor quality, and their leavers are seldom able to further their studies in the formal public system. The *medersas* appear to attract a higher proportion of girls – especially at the upper primary levels – than the formal French-medium schools. Thus, the harmonisation of curricula and standards between the *medersas* and the public system would probably be particularly beneficial to the presence and persistence of girls in school.

Pregnancy policy It has been common in Africa for pregnant girls to drop out of school with, in many cases, no subsequent opportunity to complete their studies. In some countries, girls are formally expelled from school if they are found to be pregnant. Malawi changed this practice, allowing girls back to school after they had given birth. However, problems with the implementation of this policy included an absence of guidelines as to how schools should deal with readmission, the presence of negative attitudes towards returning mothers, lack of publicity of the policy's provisions, an absence of counselling, and of monitoring of its implementation (Swainson *et al.*, 1998). By consequence, many girls, when pregnant, continued to dropout of school.

Both Tanzania and Guinea have adopted similarly non-punitive pregnancy policies which allow girls to return to school after delivery.[11] Little is yet known about their impact, although our interviews with teachers and female students in Guinea revealed that by no means all the young mothers returned to school. Nevertheless, the Senegal study recommended the implementation of non-punitive pregnancy policies along similar lines (Dioum Diokhané *et al.*, 2000).

---

[11] See United Republic of Tanzania, (1999) and Tembon *et al.*, (1997). In Guinea, the policy also provides that a teacher who has been shown to have been responsible for such a pregnancy will be sacked.

Policies to Enhance School Quality

Reforms to improve the quality of education are usually an important means of improving its internal efficiency. This is partly because low quality contributes to low demand for education. Children's learning potential is held back where there are insufficient or inappropriate inputs, such as trained teachers, textbooks, curriculum and teaching materials, or relevant teaching processes. In these circumstances rates of repetition and drop-out are, typically, high. Thus, securing quality improvement is an important means of improving the utilisation of resources, in education. However, to achieve this, in each of the countries covered by our studies, increased investment in schooling will be required.

Infrastructure Our case studies found that long distances between home and school, or the absence of some primary grades in a nearby school, prevented some children, especially girls, from attending school. Our studies also revealed that many school environments, in particular those in the poorer rural areas, lacked basic infrastructure such as adequate classrooms with desks and chairs, latrines and water. For example, in Malawi and Uganda, the massive expansion in enrolments led to many children having to study out-of-doors. Here, then, more classrooms were required to tackle the backlog. Elsewhere, the increase in enrolment necessary for SFA will also require a considerable expansion in classroom availability. International agencies are active in classroom construction in all the countries. However, the buildings they provide are often expensive, owing to their procurement practices using imported materials and contractors from outside the local area. Thus, reliance upon international agencies is unlikely to deliver sufficient classrooms over the short-to-medium term. Community involvement in construction and the use of local materials could help greatly. In countries such as Malawi and Zambia, World Bank-supported social funds, which aim to channel funds directly to projects prioritised by communities, have resulted in many classrooms being built, with support from the community and the use of local contractors (Parker and Serrano, 2000). In Guinea and Uganda, the reports suggested that, where building constraints persist, churches, mosques and other 'public' buildings could be used temporarily for teaching, as was already practised in Malawi (Tembon *et al.*, 1997; Tumushabe *et al.*, 2000).

Girls tend to be more affected by the lack of facilities in school than boys, especially after the start of menstruation. Where there are insufficient latrines, or where separate units for girls and boys do not already exist, their provision can reduce absenteeism and drop-out of girls. Guinea had already adopted a policy of building latrines with separate units for girls and boys as part of its Education Sector Investment Programme. The national reports proposed that schools in Ethiopia, Malawi and Mali would benefit from improved school facilities, and particularly from latrines, as a means of improving the quality of their education systems. Senegal, too, obtained credit from the World Bank to undertake re-fitting of primary schools with latrines and wells, and the rehabilitation and maintenance of classrooms (World Bank, 2000c). A similar initiative was undertaken in Guinea with IDA financing.

Textbooks and learning materials   In all nine countries, the surveys revealed shortages of teaching and learning materials in the classrooms, bringing great risks for educational quality and pupil performance. Table 6.5 shows that, on average, in these countries, about five pupils shared each textbook, although the range varied from two in Ghana to ten in Guinea. Strong variations also existed within countries, with fewer resources often being available to rural schools. The high cost of textbook provision was the main reason for their insufficient supply. In most of the countries, international agencies were heavily involved in financing textbook production, and, often, distribution, without which supply would have been even lower. As noted in Chapter 5, in some countries the costs of textbooks were still met by households, and accounted for a major part of the direct costs of schooling. In Guinea, for example, required textbook purchases amounted to the equivalent of 20 per cent of the total income of poor households (Tembon *et al.*, 1997). In these circumstances, the provision of free textbooks to primary school children, especially in rural areas, would be a significant incentive for enrolment.

Table 6.5   Effect on primary unit costs of an increase in expenditure on teaching and learning materials

	Base year pupil/textbook ratio	Unit costs of learning materials and school operating expenses ($PPP)		Increase in average primary unit cost (%)
		Base year	Target	
(1)	(2)	(3)	(4)	(5)
Ethiopia	5:1	3	20	9
Ghana	2:1	10	18	4
Guinea	10:1	14	31	7
Malawi	5:1	3	42	83
Mali	3:1	14	47	41
Senegal	6:1	1	5	3
Tanzania	4:1	6	7	2
Uganda	6:1	9	36	60
Zambia	5:1	2.5	16	21

Source: GAPS simulation models.
Notes: Column 3 reports government expenditure per primary school pupil in the base year for each country. Column 4 details the proposed level of expenditure per primary pupil on learning materials and school operating expenses. Column 5 shows the percentage increase in the base year average weighted unit cost of the proposed increase in spending on learning materials and school operating expenses. Base year primary weighted unit costs are shown in Table TA.1 of the Technical Appendix.

In Malawi, Uganda and Zambia, where textbooks were already provided free, their physical availability still needed to be sharply increased, as the data in Table 6.5 imply.

During the 1990s, very little was spent by the nine governments on educational supplies at the primary level. The unit costs of learning materials and school-level operating expenses ranged from just $PPP1 per pupil in Senegal to $PPP14 per pupil in Guinea and Mali (Column 3 Table 6.5). Even in those countries with relatively high expenditures, resources were still insufficient to cater for all school needs. The sustainability of such spending was also lower than it should have been, since international agencies provided substantial resources for textbook provision through the capital budget. Such commitments are short-term and can be affected by changing priorities of international agencies. In order to ensure continued and expanded supply, it is desirable for governments gradually to assume the responsibility for sustaining the financing of textbooks, including replacement costs, as part of the recurrent education budget. Thus, all national reports recommended an increase in public expenditure for textbooks and other learning materials. Based on national estimates of the cost of minimum learning requirements, and upon the feasibility of increasing resources for these purposes, expenditures per pupil on learning materials and school operating expenses were targeted to increase in all nine countries. Table 6.5 summarises these targets, and allows comparison with the actual amounts spent per pupil (Column 3). In Malawi and Uganda, which had achieved universal primary education but remained severely quality-constrained, the need to increase resources for teaching and learning materials was paramount. Given that both have had low per-pupil expenditures, the proposed increases would add substantially to their total unit costs (increasing them by up to 83 per cent in Malawi and 60 per cent in Uganda).

The increased expenditures on teaching and learning materials would need to be supported by the use of locally-available materials. The experience of the Village-Based Schools initiative in Malawi showed how teachers can be assisted to produce low cost teaching materials through local teacher-development centres (Hyde *et al.*, 1996). However, due to high initial costs, public resources alone may well be insufficient to sustain sufficient textbook supplies, particularly at higher levels of the school system. There is more potential for cost-sharing there, since existing public subsidies remain large, despite there being a higher ratio of private to social returns. Thus, to overcome the potential financial shortfall, it was proposed in Malawi that public financing at secondary level could be supplemented by households paying a book rental (Kadzamira and Chibwana, 2000). Similarly, the Zambia study proposed that a non-refundable textbook fee should be introduced in secondary schools (Kasonde-Ng'andu *et al.*, 2000). The book rental option was also recommended by the Senegal study and, as part of its ten-year education and training programme, the government intends to provide textbooks free of charge to pupils at the primary level and to put in place a textbook loan system at the secondary level.

Class-size and the number of teachers per class The average number of pupils per class needs to be reduced in many countries, whilst in others, as discussed below, there is scope for some increase. However, national averages mask variations between regions, zones, schools and even grades within the same school. In most countries, pupil/class ratios tend to be higher in urban areas compared with rural areas. Within schools, high enrolments tend to be concentrated in the first three primary grades, which, given the limited supply of teachers in the schools, translates into large class-sizes. For example in Malawi, the average pupil/class ratio at the primary level in 1997 was 68:1. However, it ranged from 119:1 in Grade 1 to 27:1 in Grade 8 (Kadzamira and Chibwana, 2000). Reductions in the pupil/class ratio would obviously require more teachers and classrooms, which would increase costs. The first four columns of Table 6.6 detail the proposed reductions in the primary pupil/class ratio in Malawi, Mali and Senegal (where it was initially very high). For example, in Mali the pupil/class ratio was targeted to fall from 56 to 45 pupils per class. From Table 6.6 these reductions would result in significantly increased unit costs (of 11 to 13 per cent) in the three countries, even though the average class-size in Malawi would remain relatively high (at 60 pupils per class). Given the massively increased enrolments, further reduction was not considered feasible within the medium term.

Table 6.6 Effect on primary unit costs of changes in the number of pupils per class and number of teachers per class

	Number of pupils per class			Number of teachers per class		
(1)	Base year (2)	Target (3)	Change in average primary unit cost (%) (4)	Base year (5)	Target (6)	Change in average primary unit cost (%) (7)
Ethiopia	43	-	-	1.4	-	-
Ghana	27	-	-	0.85	1	15
Guinea	41	-	-	0.88	-	-
Malawi	68	60	11	1.11	-	-
Mali	56	45	13	0.9	-	-
Senegal	51	45	12	1	-	-
Tanzania	36	-	-	0.99	-	-
Uganda	50	-	-	0.85	1	14
Zambia	35	-	-	0.91	-	-

Source: GAPS simulation models.
Notes: Columns 2 and 5 report the base year number of pupils and teachers per class for each country. Columns 3 and 6 detail the proposed level for the number of pupils and teachers per class. Columns 4 and 7 show the percentage increase in the base year average weighted unit cost of the proposed changes in the number of pupils and teachers per class. A '—' indicates that changes in these parameters were not proposed in that country case-study. Base year primary weighted unit costs are shown in Table TA.1 of the Technical Appendix.

In Ghana and Uganda it was found that the main problem was not so much the size of classes *per se*, as that the average teacher/class ratio was less than one. This shortage of teachers meant that in Uganda some classes had to be combined, resulting in a large class size. Alternatively, children were left to play or perform unsupervised manual work (Avotri *et al.*, 2000; Tumushabe *et al.*, 2000). The reports for both of these countries proposed that the number of teachers per class be increased to one, on average. This would have the effect of reducing the average number of pupils per teacher in both countries (from 32 to 27 in Ghana and from 59 to 50 in Uganda).[12] The last three columns of Table 6.6 show the impact on the average primary unit cost of increasing the teacher-per-class ratio in these countries. In both cases, it would have a relatively large impact (around 14–15 per cent) on unit. In Senegal, although the overall teacher-per-class ratio was just about right, our study revealed detailed evidence of enormous variation between urban and rural areas. A cost-effective strategy, recommended by the report, and already used in Guinea to address this problem, would be the redeployment of teachers from areas of high to low teacher-concentration, and from administrative posts to the classrooms.

Gender-sensitive learning environments   Classroom observation in all the countries revealed that boys and girls participated roughly equally in classroom activities in the lower grades, but that, in upper grades boys were generally more active than girls. Test results indicated that in Ghana, Senegal and Zambia, the achievement of boys and girls was roughly equal in the fourth grade of primary school.   However, by the sixth grade, in all nine countries, boys had an achievement advantage over girls, and they performed better in the primary school leaving examination.   National statistics also indicate that more boys than girls continue to higher levels of education.   This was partly attributed to low self-confidence on the part of girls, perpetuated by a school environment in which the presence of gender stereotypes in textbooks and intimidating or gender-insensitive attitudes amongst both peers and teachers were common.   Measures to eliminate gender stereotypes were underway in most of the countries, which should help to change the perceptions of both sexes regarding the ability of girls.   This is often a slow process.   For example, although Zambian textbooks had been revised, copies of the old textbooks were still in circulation, particularly in remote schools (Kasonde-Ng'andu *et al.*, 2000).

Each of the country studies proposed that, in order to sustain girls' enrolments throughout the primary cycle, teachers need to provide counselling to help girls at school.   This is needed to give girls more confidence in their own abilities, and to help them through academic or emotional difficulties, especially at puberty.   For it to be effective, teachers need training, and other support.   Tanzania has had a long-established intention of providing this: in 1988 the Counselling Unit of the Ministry of Education and Culture in Tanzania was established to encourage the provision of guidance and counselling services for all students regardless of gender.   Unfortunately, although objectives were set, activities planned, and programmes prepared, none were operationalised owing to financial constraints.

Specific strategies are required to encourage girls in mathematics and science, where their performance is often lowest.   Since 1996, the Female Education in

---

[12]   Given the relatively low class-size in Ghana, it was also proposed that this could be increased in order to reduce costs. The effect of this, along with reductions in class size proposed in other countries, is discussed below.

Mathematics and Science in Africa (FEMSA) project has been working in a number of the countries to promote girls' performance in these subjects by providing a supportive environment for girls (O'Connor, 2000). An important cause of girls' under-performance in these subjects is a lack of self-confidence. Attitude change, curriculum development, teacher education, and assessment methods are all targets for reform. In response, Zambia has successfully piloted single-sex classes in mathematics and science, with the support of the PAGE programmeme (Kasonde-Ng'andu *et al.*, 2000). Similarly, Malawi has secured an improvement in girls' performance by gender-streaming selected subjects in upper-primary classes, as part of the GABLE programme (Kadzamira and Chibwana, 2000). Where two streams exist in a school, they can be separated by gender at little or no extra cost.

Teacher training   In some countries, teachers without appropriate qualifications continue to be appointed. In Ethiopia and Zambia, for example, unqualified primary-school teachers are numerous. The high cost of conventional pre-service training programmes necessitates a search for more cost-effective alternatives particularly in countries where the education system has been expanding rapidly. In Malawi, for example, the massive recruitment of teachers required by the introduction of FPE resulted in one-half of the primary teaching force being untrained. Some of them received in-service training through the Malawi Integrated In-service Teacher Education Programme, although a substantial number remained untrained. These were often allocated to the lower school-grades where class size, and the challenge facing teachers were greatest.

After their initial training, most teachers in the study countries work for many years, without any form of further in-service training. Consequently, long-serving teachers may be unable to adapt their teaching methods according to changes in the curriculum. In Malawi, teachers were often not familiar with the teaching methods and materials stipulated in the new curriculum (Kadzamira and Chibwana, 2000). Similarly, in Ethiopia, teachers had not received any training following the change in language of instruction from Amharic to local languages (Rose *et al.*, 1997). There is, then, a need in most of the countries, for better provision of professional support and in-service training.

Both pre-service and in-service training programmes can also be influential in improving gender-sensitivity of teaching practices. In Ethiopia, efforts were being made to introduce gender-awareness training into pre-service teacher training, although it initially appeared to be in the form of an additional seminar rather than an integral part of the curriculum. In Guinea, gender-awareness training has formed part of a pre-service primary education programme, financed by the World Bank. In Zambia, the PAGE programme has provided gender-awareness training for teachers in the Eastern Province. However, results from our surveys indicated that teachers who had received this training continued to have attitudes biased against girls, suggesting the need for the stronger integration of training into conventional programmes (Kasonde-Ng'andu *et al.*, 2000).

In many countries, teacher availability is also affected by HIV/AIDS. In some cases, teachers have to take time off due to their own illness or to care for sick relatives. In addition, some teachers are dying from AIDS, as a result of which the attrition rate of teachers is likely to be increasing in some countries. While there is some debate about whether teachers are more likely to be affected by HIV/AIDS compared with other groups within a population, it is undeniable that HIV/AIDS is having some effect on the supply of teachers in many SSA countries.[13] As such, it has an influence over the number of teachers who need to be trained each year in order to replace teachers who are sick or have died. This is likely to increase the costs of teacher training. In addition, teacher training courses may need to be adapted to ensure that teachers are equipped to teach children about HIV/AIDS (UNESCO, 2002).

Working conditions of teachers There is much evidence to indicate that teachers' working conditions and remuneration strongly influence their morale and, consequently, the quality of services they provide. Furthermore, the quality of those joining the teaching profession is a function of the remuneration offered, relative to occupations competing for similar qualifications, skills and training. In many countries, teachers' salaries declined over the period 1980-2000 and they were often not paid on time. In countries such as Zambia, low and late remuneration forced teachers to take second jobs, reducing their time spent on teaching (see Box 4.1). A high turnover of teachers was evident where – as in Uganda – teachers became disillusioned with their poor conditions of service. Historically, Ugandan primary teachers received a salary supplement from parent-teacher association contributions. However, with the introduction of UPE, the amount they received declined in real terms (Tumushabe *et al.*, 2000). Even in Zambia, where there were large nominal increases in teachers' salaries in 1999-2000, their level was still not maintained in real terms (Kasonde-Ng'undu *et al.*, 2000).

As discussed in Chapter 4, teachers' salaries differ strongly across Africa. Those in the East and Central African countries studied (with the exception of Ethiopia) received low salaries, both in absolute terms and relative to those in West Africa. Poor teacher morale was a major issue, and the reports proposed that teachers' salaries in Malawi, Tanzania, Uganda and Zambia needed to be increased in real terms, taking account of resources available and of political feasibility. Table 6.7 details the proposed increases in teacher salaries in each country and shows the impact on the primary unit cost of these increases. Given that teachers' salaries comprise the largest proportion of primary unit costs, the cost-impact of these reforms in Malawi and Zambia, in particular, would be substantial, increasing the base year primary unit cost by 17 and 20 per cent respectively. However, they would bring important potential gains from improved staff retention and morale.

---

[13]　Bennell *et al.* (2002) suggest, for example, that estimates of teacher mortality rates calculated for some studies may be exaggerated. Their evidence suggests that teacher mortality may actually be lower than the general population in the same age group, because HIV/AIDS is related to poverty and, although teachers' salaries are low, they are not the poorest.

Table 6.7 Effect on primary unit costs of increases in teachers' wages

	Increase in teacher wage (%)	Average teacher wage ($PPP)		Change in average primary unit cost (%)
		Base year	Target	
(1)	(2)	(3)	(4)	(5)
Ethiopia	-	6592	6592	-
Ghana	-	6070	6070	-
Guinea	-	7264	7264	-
Malawi	20	2406	2887	17
Mali	-	3192	3192	-
Senegal	-	8248	8248	-
Tanzania	5	1666	1749	4
Uganda	10	2247	2472	8
Zambia	30	1786	2322	20

Source: GAPS simulation models.

Notes: Column 2 reports the proposed increase in the average teacher wage. Column 3 reports the average teacher wage in the base year for each country. Column 4 details the proposed average teacher wage. Column 5 shows the percentage increase in the base year average weighted unit cost of the wage increase shown in column 2. A '–' indicates that changes in teachers' wages were not proposed in that country study. Base year primary weighted unit costs are shown in Table TA.1 of the Technical Appendix.

Although the proposed increase appears to be more modest in Tanzania, this is not so after taking account of the targeted incentives to female teachers discussed earlier. An increase in teachers' salaries cannot always be introduced separately from those of other civil servants, yet in some countries teachers are clearly disadvantaged relative to their civil servant peers. In Malawi, for example, secretaries in the civil service could earn twice as much as primary school teachers (Miske, 1998 cited in Kadzamira and Chibwana, 2000).[14] Even if the proposed increases in average teachers' wages, in these countries were implemented, it can be seen that they would still remain, in $PPP terms, substantially lower than those in West Africa. However, further increases beyond those proposed would not be financially sustainable. Strategies to reduce the high levels of teacher costs in the West African countries are discussed in a later section.

Supervision of, and support to, teachers Administrative and supervisory support for teachers from school heads and inspectors can have an important influence on the quality of education. However, evidence showed that very few head teachers

---

[14] In countries where no real increase in teachers' salaries was proposed, they were assumed, in the modelling, to remain constant. Where real salary increases for primary teachers were proposed, the cost of appropriate increases for staff at other levels of the education system was also taken into account, in the calculation of the implications for total recurrent expenditure.

had had any specific training for their jobs, nor was promotion usually based on acquired leadership or management skills (Rose *et al.*, 1997). In addition, because teacher shortages in Ethiopia and Malawi led heads to combine both teaching and administrative responsibilities, little or no time was left for them to supervise the work of staff (Rose *et al.*, 1997; Kadzamira and Chibwana, 2000).

Table 6.8 Effect on primary unit costs of increases in the number of inspectors and operating expenses of inspection

	No. of teachers per inspector		Unit costs of inspector operating expenses ($PPP)		Change in average primary unit cost (%)
	Base year	Target	Base year	Target	
(1)	(2)	(3)	(4)	(5)	(6)
					-
Ethiopia	189	-	0.33	-	-
Ghana	100	-	0.03	-	-
Guinea	n.a.	-	0.36	-	-
Malawi	218	-	0.26	0.47	0.5
Mali	167	100	1.27	-	2.5
Senegal	100	70	0.56	-	0.7
Tanzania	208	160	0.30	0.39	0.4
Uganda	475	400	0.03	0.07	0.1
Zambia	592	296	0.06	0.41	0.9

Source: GAPS simulation models.
Notes: Columns 2 and 5 report the base year number of teachers per inspector and the unit cost of inspector operating expenses for each country. Columns 3 and 5 detail the proposed level for these parameters based on the country case-studies. Columns 6 shows the percentage increase in the base year average weighted unit cost of the proposed changes in both the number of teachers per inspector and the proposed increases in operating expenses. A '–' indicates that changes in these parameters were not proposed in that country case-study. n.a. – not available. Base year primary weighted unit costs are shown in Table TA.1 of the Technical Appendix.

Substantial differences are apparent in the number of teachers per inspector between different countries, with those in West Africa being typically about half the levels in the East and Central African countries. The number of budgeted inspection visits per school also varied between countries. In Uganda, inspectors were expected to visit each school under their control only once every two years (Tumushabe *et al.*, 2000). In Mali, Senegal, Tanzania, Uganda and Zambia it was found that there were insufficient inspectors to provide adequate supervision to schools, and increases in the number of inspectors were, in each case, proposed. Table 6.8 reports the number of teachers per inspector in the base year and details the proposed reductions in this ratio for each country. The Zambia report, for example, proposed that the number of schools which each inspector is expected to

visit should be halved from over 50, on average, to about 25 schools (Kasonde-Ng'andu *et al.*, 2000). The number of schools that can be adequately covered by one inspector partly depends on population density, which influences the distance travelled to each school. In the case of Malawi, where overall numbers were felt to be adequate, inspectors were nevertheless unable to perform their work satisfactorily, owing to insufficient travel funds being available. Four of the reports suggested an increase in the unit operating expenses of inspectors, for this purpose. Table 6.8 shows the base year operating expenditure per primary pupil for the inspectorate and the targeted increases. It can be seen that the overall impact of increasing the number of inspectors and their operating expenses has only a limited impact on primary unit costs due to the low initial costs of inspection.

Language of instruction In many African countries – notably the Francophone states – children who begin primary school are taught in a language with which they are not familiar. Our country case studies in Guinea, Senegal and Mali revealed that using French as the language of instruction poses a major problem: children in those countries find it difficult both to understand and to express themselves in French, even in the upper primary grades. In order to improve performance, each of the reports proposed that the curriculum should be taught, initially, in local languages, progressively moving to a second or foreign language in later classes, as appropriate. Opinions are divided as to the effectiveness of bilingual education for school performance. Resistance to the use of local languages is often linked to parental perceptions that its use might impair learning in English or French, which they consider to be critical in improving their children's future chances in the job market. There is also a belief that local languages are not equipped to deal with scientific and technical concepts. However, some countries have succeeded in overcoming these hurdles. Mali, for example, has effectively implemented a bilingual education programme known as 'Pédagogie Convergente'. This child-centred pedagogy uses national languages concomitantly with French as the medium of instruction. Between 1994 and 2000 the programme was operational in about 300 public schools. Gains from the programme include lower repetition and drop-out rates, higher attendance and promotion rates, and better performance in all subjects, including French, especially for girls and minority language children (World Education, 1998). In 2001 the government began taking the programme to scale, as part of its ten-year education programme.

  The studies in both Senegal and Guinea recommended bilingual education at the primary level as a quality-enhancing measure. In fact, based upon results of national and international research, the government of Senegal subsequently decided to introduce national languages, on an experimental basis, in the early grades of primary school, to facilitate general learning and to help the subsequent transition to French medium.

  In some East and Central African countries, primary schooling has historically been taught in the main national language (for example, Chichewa in

Malawi and Amharic in Ethiopia). These languages are as foreign to many nationals in these countries as is English. There have, therefore, been recent attempts to use local languages in the early grades. For example, from the mid-1990s, in Ethiopia, each of the regions could choose their own language of instruction, and local languages were also used in Malawi. However, problems were apparent. The costs of providing textbooks written in local languages is very high in Ethiopia (McNab and Stoye, 1999), whilst in Malawi, where textbooks remained available only in Chichewa, the implementation of the local language policy has, in practice, been limited (Chimombo, 1999).

Cost-Saving Reforms

The reforms to improve access, gender equality and school quality, discussed above, would provide a practical means of achieving progress towards SFA. Some of the equity and quality improvements could be achieved at little or no cost to the national governments. Other changes, however, would be costly to introduce. This is particularly so for the reforms which reduce direct and indirect costs to households, and those which improve school resources and teachers' salaries. Increased expenditures are, therefore, necessary in most countries, if the demand for schooling is to rise and if the benefits of primary education are to be properly secured. Table TA.2 of the Technical Appendix shows that, in the absence of other reforms, the proportionate increase in public spending which would be required to reach SFA over 15 years varies from more than a doubling in Malawi and Uganda to a five-fold increase in Mali and almost a ten-fold increase in Ethiopia.[15] These real expenditure increases could not be afforded, in any of the countries, on the basis of present economic trends. Accordingly, a critically important part of national strategies to achieve SFA will be the introduction of new efficiency reforms to reduce publicly financed costs of schooling, and to raise new resources to finance the expansion and qualitative changes required. A discussion of practical ways of achieving these objectives now follows.

Automatic promotion The qualitative improvements to the school systems in the study countries, discussed above, would help to improve their internal efficiency via reductions in rates of dropout and repetition. Their overall impact on enrolment would depend on the extent to which these inefficiencies currently prevail. Research evidence on the relationship between repetition and pupils' learning capacity is mixed. Some hold that repetition does not improve pupils' performance because children who repeat tend to have low self-esteem and are de-motivated to learn. They also argue that, where children's difficulties are a result of unfavourable teaching and learning conditions, repetition would be unlikely to help. Others suggest that repetition does improve learning outcomes and the

---

[15]   This is based on a comparison between primary recurrent expenditures shown in Columns 1 and 4 of Table TA.2 of the Technical Appendix.

probability of academic success (Eisemon, 1997). These latter views are often widely held, and are reflected in high repetition rates, particularly in Francophone countries: the studies revealed that more than 20 per cent of primary school pupils in Guinea, Senegal and Mali are repeaters, compared with less than 10 per cent in Ghana, Uganda and Zambia.

Reducing repetition increases the flow of pupils through the system, thus creating space for new pupils, and reducing the costs of producing a graduate at any level. Various strategies to achieve this have been used. First, they may be aimed at improving the material conditions in which learning takes place, via the better provision of textbooks, training of teachers and provision of facilities. Second, they may be aimed at improving the teaching-learning process via curriculum reform, improving teaching methods and encouraging greater awareness of cultural and linguistic differences. As discussed earlier, there is broad agreement on the positive impacts of using national and local languages as media of instruction – particularly in the early grades of primary school (UNESCO, 1996b).

One response to the problem of high levels of repetition, particularly in the lower grades, has been the implementation of an automatic promotion policy. Such a policy will only work effectively, however, after improvements to school quality have been made (see Box 6.3). In their absence, many children who would otherwise have repeated will move up to the next grade without having adequate skills. Some of the study countries have nominally adopted a policy of automatic promotion, although there is variation in the extent of its implementation. In Ethiopia, for example, the government introduced automatic promotion in the first three grades together with strategies aimed to improve the quality of education. These included reducing the number of subjects taught and introducing local languages as the medium of instruction (Rose *et al.*, 1997). The national reports propose similar strategies for the lower grades in Guinea and Malawi.

Teacher costs   Teacher costs, typically account for more than 90 per cent of the primary-school budget, and are determined by the interaction of average teacher salaries and the number of teachers employed. Although it is generally not politically feasible to reduce teacher salaries, other cost-reduction options are available. Strategies to use teachers more intensively in the classroom provide one approach, since the greater the number of pupils per teacher, the lower are teachers' wage costs per student. Since teachers' wages are a substantial proportion of unit costs, an increase in the pupil/teacher ratio can facilitate significant savings.

Box 6.3   Higher school quality lowers repetition rates, but not vice versa: lessons from Mali and Ghana

Historically, rates of repetition in Mali have been very high. Average rates for the 6 grades of primary schooling exceeded 30 per cent for both boys and girls until 1993/94, since when they began to fall. This was associated with a project to improve the quality of primary schooling, begun in 1991, and initially covering only part of the country. It included a re-training programme for teachers, focussing upon interactive teaching methods, and the designation of teaching targets for each primary grade. School heads were also re-trained. Supportive learning materials were widely distributed, and the book/pupil ratio was doubled within two years. School environments were improved by the provision of new facilities. By 1993/94 the repetition rate in schools covered by the project had fallen 10 percentage points below those in the rest of the country.

This success led to the project expanding to cover all primary schools. The quality enhancement measures were associated with an increase of the GER from around 30 per cent to 40 per cent between 1990/91 and 1995/96, whilst rates of repetition throughout the primary system fell to 18 per cent for both boys and girls. This powerfully demonstrated the linkage between the quality and the internal efficiency of schooling. In 1996, the government encouraged further efficiency gains by establishing clear criteria for repetition, and by setting a maximum acceptable rate of 15 per cent throughout primary schooling.

Nevertheless, the costs of repetition in Mali remained very high: about one-sixth of primary expenditures were for repeaters, which made little sense when well over half of all school-aged children remained out of school. The benefits to the children concerned were hardly compelling: our own schools surveys, for example, revealed no significant differences between test-scores in French and maths amongst samples of fourth and sixth-grade repeaters and non-repeaters in 1998. Furthermore, pupils' self-confidence was, if anything, undermined by the experience. The evidence suggested that further falls in repetition were possible, provided school quality improvements continued to be made.

By contrast, repetition rates in Ghana have been low for many years. From 1987, pupils were promoted to the next grade automatically, provided they had attended school during the year for at least 60 per cent of the time. This criterion produced repetition rates for both boys and girls of around three to four per cent, in each grade of primary school, during the 1990s. However, the separation of attendance from performance as the determinant of repetition, together with a somewhat lax attention to assessment standards, had negative effects upon school quality. Teacher absenteeism was high (up to 20 per cent in the mid-1990s), and the progression of pupils from primary to higher levels of schooling was not conditional upon particular learning targets having been achieved. By the turn of the century, it was widely believed in Ghana that the system of automatic promotion was not working, because it gave neither students nor teachers incentives to improve their performance. This led to knowledge assessment of pupils being reintroduced, alongside attendance, as joint criteria for grade promotion.

Sources: Sangare (2000), Avotri (2000b).

This can be achieved in a number of different ways, as indicated below.

Double-shift and multi-grade teaching The most widely used system of double-shifting is where one group of pupils attends school for the morning and a second group is taught in the afternoon (Bray, 1989). This reduces capital costs since the same classroom can be used for two classes in one day, thereby reducing total classroom requirements. However, the effect of this on unit costs depends on the type of system used. For example, if the two sets of pupils were taught by two teachers there would be savings in capital costs but not in salary costs. However, if the same teacher taught both sets of pupils, significant recurrent costs could also be saved, even if a salary supplement were paid for the heavier workload incurred. Teacher-training costs would also be reduced, owing to lower demand for teachers.

Double-shift teaching usually reduces the length of the school day for pupils, but not for teachers. Thus, individual pupils spend less time with teachers, but each teacher has more pupils than before. This might imply difficulties in covering the syllabus, and a negative impact on school quality. However, the number of instructional hours allocated for double shift sessions in some countries is longer than the time allocated for single shift systems elsewhere (Lockheed and Verspoor, 1991). In addition, comparisons of achievement in double-shift and single-shift classes in Senegal suggested that students performed as well in double-shift as in single-shift classes (Box 6.4. See also Colclough with Lewin, 1993, pp.128-133).

In most of our study countries, some form of double shifting is already in operation. Double-shift schooling was introduced in Tanzania in 1960, allowing a major increase in enrolment. By the mid-1990s Standards I and II shared classroom facilities throughout most of the system resulting in about one-fifth of primary classrooms, and a similar proportion of teachers, being occupied in double-shift work (Peasgood *et al.*, 1997, pp.186 and 218). Zambia practised double-shift and sometimes triple or even quadruple-shift schooling extensively in the 1980s and 1990s. An early estimate suggested that about 46 per cent of capital costs were saved as a result (Bray, 1989). However, experience in Zambia shows that the use of triple shifts in some schools, which further reduces the time spent by pupils in school, may well have adverse effects on learning (Kasonde-Ng'andu *et al.*, 2000). Malawi, too, has a system of overlapping double-shifts, where savings arise from the more intensive use of classrooms rather than from reducing the demand for teachers.

In some countries, double-shift schooling has the potential to reduce not only direct costs, but also the opportunity costs of schooling. In Ethiopia, for example, parents actually expressed preference for a double-shift system, because it implied that more working hours were available for children to help with household chores. This is particularly beneficial for girls who may otherwise leave school owing to household demands on their time. However, elsewhere parents' reactions were negative where their schedules were disrupted by having to look after their children during the time they were not attending school.

Not all countries practice double-shift teaching, partly because resistance from the teachers. However, Senegal's experience is instructive (see Box 6.4). Its double-shift system was modified in 1986/87, such that one teacher taught two sets of pupils and earned a 25 per cent increase to his/her basic salary. The increase in the teacher-pupil ratio brought dramatic reductions in unit costs. Similarly, to cope

Box 6.4 Double-shifting in Senegal and Uganda

Senegal suffered from low enrolment ratios, high class-sizes and a shortage of teachers for many years. In 1986/87 a new form of double-shift teaching was introduced, whereby a single class was split into two groups of pupils, taught by the same teacher alternately in the mornings and the afternoons. Each group, comprising between 40 and, at most, 55 primary students was taught for 20 hours per week (compared with 27 hours under single shifts) and each teacher was thus in charge of 80 to 110 pupils, over a 40-hour teaching week. By the late 1990s enrolments had expanded, and about one-third of pupils in primary schools were in double-shift classes. This allowed savings of about 15 per cent in the numbers of teachers and classrooms required, and of about 12 per cent of the total teachers' salary bill, after allowing for a 25 per cent additional salary allowance given to double-shift teachers, in recognition of their extra teaching load. The compounding of these savings over a number of years amounted to a highly significant sum.

Evaluations indicate that the impact of double-shifting in Senegal was not detrimental to school quality. Grade results in the principal disciplines were slightly better in double-shift classes than in control classes and rates of repetition and drop-out were no less favourable. Notwithstanding shorter teaching hours, the reduction of maximum class size from around 80 to 55 pupils appears to have been influential in improving the learning environment. This suggests the existence of increasing returns to reductions in the size of classes, with respect to school outcomes – at least over this range in Senegal.

These positive results should not be taken to imply that the system has been popular – either with parents or teachers. Our schools surveys and focus group discussions revealed that parents felt that the reduced teaching time disadvantaged their children relative to those in single-shift classes. Teachers lacked requisite training for their new tasks, they felt overworked and resented the fact that the salary supplement did not fully compensate for their increased teaching load. Nevertheless, the savings made, together with the apparent absence of significant associated costs, imply that the double shift system has provided an important instrument for the expansion of schooling in Senegal.

In Uganda, following the abolition of tuition and other fees, and the near doubling of primary enrolments over 1996-1999, massive over-crowding emerged in the lower grades, together with an acute shortage of trained teachers. Education's share of public spending doubled from 16 to 30 per cent over 1993/94-1997/78. As one means of reducing class-size and economising on teachers, a pilot double-shift scheme was introduced in November 1998. Morning and afternoon shifts lasted 4.5 hours, thereby increasing the work-load for shift-teachers by up to three hours per day. The first three or four primary grades were covered, although implementation differed between regions. As in Senegal, it was found that the scheme was not popular with either parents or teachers. The latter complained that the 25 per cent salary supplement agreed for extra work was often not paid, whilst the former feared negative consequences for their children's learning. This caused implementation to be patchy, notwithstanding the potential benefits to be gained.

Sources: Dioum Diokhané (2000b), Tumushabe (2000).

with the resource implications of the increased enrolments following its introduction of the universal primary education programme, Uganda introduced double-shift schooling in primary schools (see Box 6.4 and Tumushabe *et al.*, 2000).

Table 6.9 shows the effect on primary unit costs of expanding the double shift system in the study countries. Substantial increases in the proportion of primary classrooms using double-shift methods were proposed in some cases. For example, the Ethiopia report proposed an increase in double shifting from 20 per cent to 75 per cent of classrooms. With the exception of Tanzania, it was envisaged that teachers in schools operating a double-shift system would teach both shifts. The proposed salary increment for such teachers was generally 25 per cent (Column 4). The major impact of this reform is to increase the number of pupils per teacher. For example, in Guinea the pupil-teacher ratio would increase from 46 to 67 pupils per teacher with the expansion of double-shifting (Columns 5 and 6). Accordingly, these changes would generally result in fairly substantial reductions in the average primary unit cost, particularly in Ethiopia, where the cost of teachers was very high.

Table 6.9 Effects on primary unit costs of expanding the double-shift system

	Classrooms double-shifting (%)		Increment to teachers' wages for those teaching two shifts (%)	Pupil/teacher ratio		Overall change in average primary unit cost (%)
	Base year	Target		Base year	Target	
(1)	(2)	(3)	(4)	(5)	(6)	(7)
Ethiopia	20	75	25	31	54	-26
Ghana	21	-	-	-	-	-
Guinea	21	75	25	46	67	-13
Malawi	23	30	25	61	71	-5
Mali	28	-	-	-	-	-
Senegal	14	30	25			-8
Tanzania*	21	40	-	-	-	-
Uganda	0	5	10	58	62	-3
Zambia	35	-	-	-	-	-

Source: GAPS simulation models.

Notes: Columns 2 and 3 show the percentage of classrooms double shifting before and after the proposed increases. Column 4 reports the proposed salary increment for teachers teaching two shifts. Column 5 reports the pupil-teacher ratio in the base year. Increasing the number of double-shift teachers increases the pupil-teacher ratio (see text). Column 6 reports the pupil-teacher ratio implied by the levels of double shifting of classrooms and teachers shown in column 3. Column 7 shows the percentage increase in the base year average weighted unit cost of the proposed changes associated with increasing the double-shift system. A '–' indicates that changes in these parameters were not proposed in that country case-study. The proposed extension of double-shifting in Tanzania only affects classrooms, so there is no change in unit costs. Base year primary weighted unit costs are shown in Table TA.1 of the Technical Appendix.

Pupil-teacher ratios can also be increased in areas of low population density by establishing multi-grade classes, where pupils of different ages, grades and abilities are taught together by the same teacher (Little, 1995). For example, our study in Guinea revealed the prevalence of incomplete schools in rural areas, where population density is low. Most of these schools offered only some grades of the primary cycle and class sizes tended to be small (around ten pupils). By consequence, pupil-teacher ratios were extremely low, unit costs were very high and classrooms were operating well below capacity (Tembon *et al.*, 1997). In such cases, multi-grade classes, by saving on both teachers and classrooms, can assist in reducing both the recurrent and capital costs of schooling. In the island and mountainous areas of Uganda, where population density is also low, some schools were forced to reduce the number of classes offered or, sometimes, to close completely as a result of new government regulations for minimum acceptable pupil-teacher ratios (Tumushabe *et al.*, 2000). Thus, multi-grading in these areas would help to allow schooling to continue. However, the simultaneous management of more than one grade requires specific training for this type of teaching, and the development of instructional materials for self-study is also necessary.

Class size and the number of teachers per class Evidence from both developed and developing countries does not support the commonly held view that larger classes necessarily have negative effects on student achievement, at least within a range from 25 to 40 pupils. Although the limits for the upper bound have not been fully established, classes of up to 45 children are judged tolerable, where costs and resources dictate this (Colclough with Lewin, 1993, p.147).

It has been suggested that, in countries with particularly high pupil-class ratios, the quality of education would benefit from a reduction in these ratios. Equally, in countries where pupil-class ratios are lower than 45:1, there are opportunities to reduce costs by allowing class size to rise. In Ghana, Guinea, Tanzania and Zambia the number of pupils per class could feasibly be increased up to 45, although the diversity in class size between different areas of the country and, within schools, by grade needs to be recognised. In Zambia, an increase in class size might be achieved by expanding multi-grade teaching in areas where class size is small, although the size of classes in Lusaka schools generally need to be reduced (Kasonde-Ng'gandu *et al.*, 2000). The savings which would result from these changes are substantial. This is particularly so in Ghana, where, as shown in Table 6.10, increases in average class size could reduce unit costs by over one-quarter.

In Ethiopia, although average class size was already high enough, there was an opportunity to reduce the number of teachers at primary level, from approximately 1.4 to 1.2 teachers per class. The relatively high teacher-class ratio resulted from the introduction of local languages as the instruction medium in mid-1990s. An increase in staffing was required because not all teachers spoke the local language in the area of their school. A reduction in the number of teachers per class would, therefore, require some re-consideration of the allocation of teachers within the country, in the light of the adjustments to the language policy during the 1990s (Rose *et al.*, 1997).

Table 6.10   Effect on primary unit costs of a reduction in the number of pupils per class and teachers per class

	Number of pupils per class			Number of teachers per class		
	Base year	Target	Change in primary unit cost (%)	Base year	Target	Change in primary unit cost (%)
(1)	(2)	(3)	(4)	(5)	(6)	(7)
Ethiopia	43	-	-	1.4	1.2	-14
Ghana	27	40	-26	0.85	-	-
Guinea	41	45	-7	0.88	-	-
Malawi	68	-	-	1.11	-	-
Mali	56	-	-	0.9	-	-
Senegal	51	-	-	1.0	-	-
Tanzania	36	45	-16	0.9	-	-
Uganda	50	-	-	0.85	-	-
Zambia	35	45	-14	0.91	-	-

Source: GAPS simulation models.
Notes: Columns 2 and 5 report the base year number of pupils and teachers per class for each country. Columns 3 and 6 detail the proposed level for the number of pupils and teachers per class. Columns 4 and 7 show the percentage decrease in the base year average weighted unit cost of the proposed changes in the number of pupils and teachers per class. A '–' indicates that changes in these parameters were not proposed in that country case-study. Base year primary weighted unit costs are shown in Table TA.1 of the Technical Appendix.

In Ghana, Mali, Tanzania and Uganda there was scope to increase the average size of secondary classes. Furthermore, in almost all the countries, the average number of teachers per class was very high at secondary level. There were as many as two teachers per class in Ghana, Malawi, Mali, Senegal, Tanzania and Zambia, which implies that teachers were only spending half of the working day in the classroom. While more teachers are required at secondary than at primary level, owing to the requirements for subject specialisation, it was feasible in most cases to reduce the ratio below existing levels. In Malawi, for example, secondary-school teachers specialised in only one subject. Thus, increasing their areas of specialisation during training would enable them to teach more classes and, reduce the teacher-class ratio (Kadzamira and Chibwana, 2000).

Assistant and volunteer teachers   In 1995 Senegal introduced an experimental programme of recruiting *volontaires* (voluntary teachers), on low-cost terms at primary level. The starting salary of a volunteer was about CFA80,000 and the ratio of the salary costs of a voluntary teacher to that of a certified teacher in the civil service was about 1:5.4. This has enabled the government to reduce the unit salary costs per teacher in real terms and it has increased the number of teachers available. The experiment proved beneficial and was expanded. Legislation in 2000/01 stipulated that all teachers hired at divisional (Inspection Departmentale de l'Education Nationale) level would be *volontaires*, undergoing initial teacher-training for six months. After four years of service, they would convert to contract teachers, eventually gaining access to the civil service through competitive examinations for job-quotas to be determined annually at the decentralised levels (Ministère de l'Education Nationale, Senegal, 1996). The savings were potentially substantial during the first four years – although as more of the contract teachers transfer into the civil service, the wage bill will start to rise again, but not to previous levels.

Although the option to hire contract teachers significantly reduces the unit costs of teachers, concerns have been raised about the sustainability of the programme, owing to pressures for equal status from unions, and the teachers themselves (Traoré, 1996). Nevertheless, such programmes have been gaining prominence elsewhere. Voluntary teacher experiments have been introduced in Guinea and Mali, with recruitment and wages policies for primary teachers similar to those in Senegal.

The teacher-cost problem has also been tackled, in a number of countries, by recruiting secondary-school leavers, from the locality of the schools needing teachers, providing them with a short training programme, and supervising them regularly whilst they are in service. Although experience varies, such teachers often perform well, and provide significant cost savings. Additional benefits include the potential of reducing the migration to the towns of young qualified people, and of promoting favourable attitudes to education in the community. Furthermore, locally-recruited female teachers can serve as positive role models for the younger girls, as well as for their parents. Experience from such schemes shows that teachers recruited in this way are usually dedicated and interested in their work. The Save the Children Fund community school project in Mali, (based on the same principle as BRAC schools in Bangladesh) provides a good example of how low-cost teachers can be acquired. The teachers have been paid modest salaries and the project has been very successful in training teachers in a much shorter time and at less cost than the formal system (Muskin, 1999). In Malawi, the village-based schools, centred in Mangochi, have also shown that it is possible to increase the number of female teachers by local recruitment (Hyde *et al.*, 1996).

The use of assistant teachers, particularly females, is also reported to have had a positive effect on girls' enrolment in Tanzania. The number of teachers in isolated areas was increased by recruiting and training local female primary-school graduates who worked under the supervision of certified teachers. Partly as a result of this, and of a general increase in the number of teachers, girls' enrolment increased from 74 per cent of boys in 1974 to 95 per cent in 1981 (Chamie, 1983, cited in Tietjen, 1991).

The strategy of hiring teacher assistants is particularly relevant to Malawi and Uganda, where the recent surge in enrolments, particularly in the lower grades, has resulted in severe overcrowding. In Malawi, for example, our study suggested that community helpers could alleviate some of the pressure on teachers, particularly in lower standards, where classes are large. They could assist by helping with classroom management, supervision of group work, and organising sports activities (Kadzamira and Chibwana, 2000). In Ethiopia, where teacher costs have been particularly high, a similar scheme of community helpers was also believed to be beneficial.

Cost-Shifting Reforms

Between Levels

Throughout Africa, primary education includes larger numbers of children, and a higher proportion of the eligible age-group, than other levels of the system. In spite of this, in most countries secondary and tertiary levels receive by far the greatest allocation of educational resources. The main reasons for this are that teacher-pupil ratios and teachers' salaries are considerably more generous at the higher levels of the system. In addition student subsidies for living and boarding costs are often high – particularly for university and other tertiary students.

Across the nine countries, secondary unit costs were, on average, 4.4 times those at primary level. But the difference between primary and university costs was far greater than this. For the six countries for which data are available the mean university/primary cost ratio was 85:1 (Table 6.11). However, the variation between countries was large.

In Malawi, for example, the annual publicly financed cost of one secondary school student was equal to that of four primary pupils in 1997, whilst the annual public costs per university student were equivalent to the costs of 124 primary pupils (Table 6.11). Similarly, in Tanzania, cost ratios are 5 to 1 at secondary level, and as much as 252 to 1 for university students compared to primary pupils. University education in Guinea, Mali and Ethiopia is fee-free, and students receive an allowance to cover living expenses. By contrast, at the primary level, although school fees are not charged, parents have to pay for books, uniforms and other school charges, including some financial contributions towards the building of schools and classrooms. This pattern is common amongst all the countries.

In view of the high private returns to tertiary studies, the pattern of resource allocation described above is neither equitable nor efficient. There would be social gains from reducing publicly-provided tertiary subsidies, and reallocating the savings to the primary level. Our national reports recommended this strategy for Guinea and Mali, where significant proportions of the education budgets have been allocated for scholarships and subsidies to students at the secondary and tertiary levels. Senegal and Ghana, on the other hand, have already redistributed budgets in this way, so as to increase resources for primary education.

Similarly, there is scope for shifting some of the costs of technical and vocational education from the government to beneficiaries. The costs of such programmes, which typically require specialised equipment and small class-size, can be substantial. In the five countries with available data, the annual cost per

Table 6.11 Weighted unit cost-ratios, by level of education

	Eth 1993/94	Guin 1993/94	Tanz 1993/94	Gha 1996/97	Malw 1997	Mali 1997/98	Sen 1997/98	Ug 1997	Zam 1996	Av
Primary	100	100	100	100	100	100	100	100	100	100
Upper Basic/Junior Secondary	n.a.	n.a.	n.a.	142	n.a.	258	159	n.a.	95	164
Secondary	111	189	530	420	386	953	500	473	364	436
Technical & Vocational	1595	1105	n.a.	608	n.a.	1005	n.a.	1580	n.a.	1179
Teacher Training	897	968	1780	1430	1666	2501	2059	2058	1812	1685
University	3817	4793	25205	2074	12381	3077	n.a.	n.a.	n.a.	8558

Source: GAPS simulation models and reports
Notes: Ghana entry data for University education is based on 1998 data. Mali entry for University education is unweighted. The last column shows the simple unweighted average of each of the row entries.

student in technical and vocational training schools was, on average, equal to the costs of 12 primary pupils (Table 6.11). Since the skills learned in vocational schools benefit both the students in terms of future returns, and also the employers, who use the people trained by the government, it would be feasible for the government to recover some of their costs from employers via a payroll tax, or a similar mechanism. In Guinea, for example, there is great potential to introduce such a tax. Recent economic reforms are beginning to yield fruit by creating an enabling environment for trade and investment, and many overseas investors are being attracted by the country's mineral and agricultural potential. The enhanced growth of the private sector and the increasing demand for skilled workers are circumstances which may be propitious for selective cost-recovery measures in the vocational education sector.

As regards the teachers themselves, the level of general education and professional training they receive varies significantly between countries. The content of training courses depends on national priorities, and the proportion of time spent on supervised practice-teaching also differs strongly. There are no agreed standards on what constitutes an appropriate length of pre-service training. Evidence from research in a number of Francophone countries demonstrates that the pedagogic efficiency of an assistant teacher (*instituteur adjoint*) who had attained 10 years of general secondary education plus one year of teacher training, was not significantly different from that of a teacher (*instituteur*) who had attained 10 years of general education plus four years of teacher training or 12 years of general education plus one year of teacher training. But the salary premium for the teacher, in comparison with the assistant teacher, ranged from 20 to 30 per cent (ADEA, 1995). The studies concluded that, after a certain minimum level of general education, the recruitment of primary teachers with higher levels of general education, or longer formal training, would have no significant impact on children's level of knowledge acquisition. It is therefore more cost-effective to attract good students for shorter courses in which supervised practice-teaching is an important element (Traoré, 1996).

In the nine countries, the average unit cost of teacher training was almost four times as high as that of general secondary education (Table 6.11). Such high unit-costs arise from many factors including the small capacity of training institutions, low pupil-teacher ratios, relatively high teachers' salaries, and in some cases, boarding costs. By contrast, more school-based training can reduce the costs of training teachers both because trainees thereby contribute to teaching tasks in schools at low cost, and because their school-based monitors are cheaper per unit of tutoring than other teacher-training staff. A further professional advantage, so proponents of this model argue (Craig *et al.*, 1998), is that trainee teachers acquire better teaching skills and competencies when their training is influenced by practitioners from the primary schools than by those in teacher-training colleges. Some revision in the duration of initial teacher education, and in the time trainee teachers spend in schools as part of their training, was judged appropriate in Guinea and Mali, where pre-service teacher-training courses lasted up to four years. A policy of increasing school-based training had already been proposed by the government of Zambia (Kasonde-Ng'andu *et al.*, 2000). In Malawi, teacher-training courses have been adapted to a system of in-service training, to cope with the large numbers of untrained teachers presently in the system. Experience suggests, however, that this has been expensive, particularly because of a high donor involvement, making it unlikely that the government could take on full responsibility for the programme (Kunje and Lewin, 1999).

The cost of training teachers could also be reduced by careful use of distance education methods. Such approaches have been used successfully in the training of teachers in many countries in Sub-Saharan Africa. These typically involve some combination of correspondence, face-to-face and radio tuition. Distance education has been shown in a number of environments to be cost-effective (Lockheed and Verspoor, 1991). It is able to reach those who find it difficult to attend training courses away from home, such as married female teachers, and those teaching in isolated rural areas. During the 1970s Tanzania, faced with a huge shortage of teachers, introduced a distance teacher-education programme to good effect. Within eight years, more than 45,000 teachers had been trained, significantly reducing the shortage.

Private Provision

To the extent that parents choose to educate their children privately, per capita allocations of educational resources provided by the state are increased. Since the public sector is relieved of meeting the educational costs of privately educated pupils, more children can be educated in total, or the quality of schooling provided in public schools can be improved. Private schooling at primary level in Africa is not widespread. In Guinea, Mali, Senegal and Ghana, the proportion of students in private schools was less than ten per cent. In Malawi and Tanzania, where private schools were not allowed during the 1970s and 1980s, private schooling at the primary level was even lower. Nevertheless, private provision has recently been expanding in Malawi and in Uganda where the state system was unable to cope with the massive increases in primary enrolments. These schools are often unregistered, and do not conform to standards set by the government. Although there are significant equity dangers associated with uncontrolled expansion of private schooling, the impact upon costs in the public sector is significant, as shown in Table 6.12. In seven of the nine countries, the national reports envisaged at least doubling the proportion of privately educated primary pupils over a 15-year period, which implied significant reductions in the primary unit cost. For example, Table 6.12 shows that in Senegal, it would lead to a reduction in the primary unit cost of 20 per cent. Appropriate incentives to secure such expansion, including tax concessions, were suggested. But more extensive direct subsidies need to be minimised. Here, again, there are opportunities for savings. In Ethiopia, for example, the government paid the salaries of some of the teachers in private schools. If redirected to the state primary system, this would have provided a small but useful supplement for a badly under-funded system (Rose *et al.*, 1997).

The studies in Mali and Senegal envisaged significant increases in the provision of private education (see Table 6.12). If SFA were to be achieved within the 15-year period, many more school places would be needed. Given present budgets the ability of the public sector to provide all the required places is limited. However, more rapid expansion would be facilitated by governments encouraging the development of private education, in part by providing limited financial support to private schools. In Mali, results from earlier studies revealed that parents, particularly those from the better-off groups in urban areas, preferred to send their children to private schools. Such trends allow some decongestion of public schools, creating room for those from less well-off homes to be in school.

Table 6.12 Effect on primary unit costs of expansion in private primary school provision

(1)	Private enrolment as a percentage of total enrolment		Change in primary unit cost (%)
	Base year (2)	Target (3)	(4)
Ethiopia	10	-	-
Ghana	13	-	-
Guinea	4	10	-6
Malawi	0	5	-5
Mali	13	25	-10
Senegal	12	30	-20
Tanzania	0	3	-3
Uganda	8	15	-8
Zambia	1	5	-4

Source: GAPS simulation models.
Notes: Column 2 reports private enrolment as a percentage of total enrolment in the base year, whilst Column 3 reports its target proportion. Column 4 indicates the concomitant decrease in publicly funded costs per pupil, arising from the increased share of private spending in the total. Base year primary weighted unit costs are shown in Table TA.1 of the Technical Appendix.

Overall Cost and Resource Implications of Achieving SFA in the Nine Countries

Earlier sections of this chapter discussed sets of policy reforms for each country which would be instrumental in achieving schooling for all over a 15-year period. We now explore the overall cost and resource implications of these strategies. This is facilitated by the use of a simulation model of the education system, developed in general form and adapted for each country, which estimates the flows of students through each part of the system (Al-Samarrai, 1997). Enrolments are linked to unit-cost data, so as to generate estimates of total education costs over time. These can be compared, within the model, with projections of resources available, based upon assumptions about how these would grow over future years. The national models for each country reflect the particular characteristics of each education system. Further details of these simulation models are given in the Technical Appendix, at the end of the book.

The analysis in this section groups policy reforms into those which increase access, those which improve quality and those which reduce costs (the latter including both cost-saving and cost-shifting reforms). The specific reforms within each group differ in each of the countries and are detailed in Table 6.2. This section explores the impact, at the end of a 15-year projection period, of their sequential introduction, drawing upon the data shown in Table TA.2 of the Technical Appendix and the notes to that table provide a more detailed discussion of the results of each country simulation exercise.

We have defined schooling for all as the achievement of net enrolment ratios in the high 90s, in school systems which are of nationally acceptable quality. The operational definition adopted for the nine countries is the achievement of GERs of at least 100, in the context of sharply reduced rates of repetition and drop-out, compared to those which currently exist. The qualitative requirements have been proxied in our models by increasing the levels of resourcing in the schools, so as to improve productivity, access, and gender equity sharply. How do the cost and resource implications of these strategies compare?

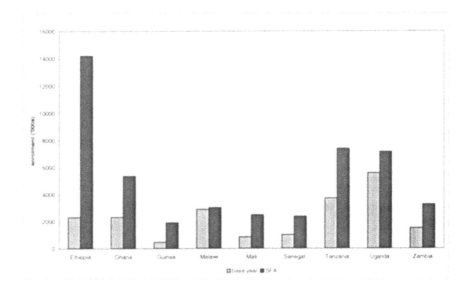

Figure 6.1 Change in primary enrolment over 15 years to achieve SFA

One of the key determinants of the overall costs of achieving SFA is, obviously, the initial level of enrolments. For some countries, the scale of the enrolment challenge is very large. Figure 6.1 shows the base year level of enrolments for each country and the enrolments that would be necessary after 15 years to achieve schooling for all. As can be seen from Figure 6.1, the SFA challenge is greatest in Ethiopia, where the equivalent of only one-quarter of the age-group were enrolled in the mid-1990s, and where enrolments need to increase five-fold to achieve SFA. The gap is least in Malawi and Uganda, where little further enrolment growth is needed following the recent UPE programmes in both these countries.

Not only does the required enrolment growth differ strongly between countries, but so also do the improvements sought in school quality. The unit costs (in PPP dollars) for the primary school systems in the nine countries are shown in Figure 6.2. The four high-cost cases of Ethiopia, Ghana, Guinea and Senegal – where unit costs are in the $PPP140-$PPP200 range – contrast strongly with the rest, where unit costs are around half these levels, in the range $PPP50-$PPP80. It can also be seen that the proposed reforms to improve quality, access and gender equity increase the unit costs of provision – in some cases (Uganda, Zambia, Malawi, Mali) substantially so. By contrast, the addition of efficiency reforms (the final bar in Figure 6.2), reduces costs consistently, in the ways intended.

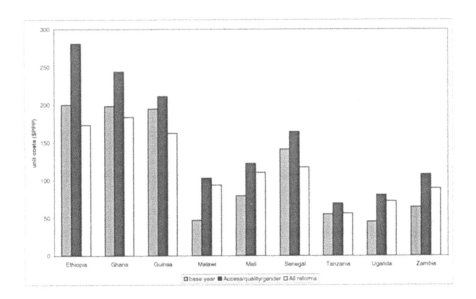

Figure 6.2 Effect of a package of reforms on unit costs ($PPP)

However, the net impact of these reforms differs importantly between countries. In the four high-cost cases, notwithstanding the proposed inputs to sharply improve gender equity and school quality, the efficiency reforms are capable of reducing unit costs to well below their pre-reform levels. In the other five countries, where both unit costs and school quality are particularly low, the net effects, post-reform, are higher levels of unit costs, so as to ensure that the desired levels of school quality can be achieved.

The implications for public recurrent expenditures follow fairly directly from the enrolment targets and unit costs (pre- and post-reform). How, then, do the required expenditures compare with the resources which are likely to be available? Are these strategies for SFA affordable in the nine countries, or are they likely to remain beyond reach?

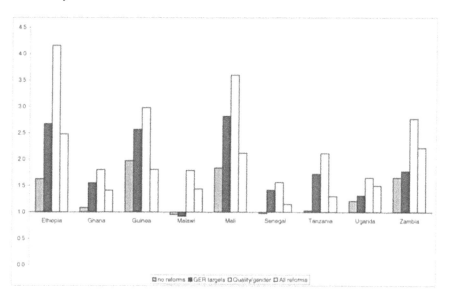

Figure 6.3   Effect of a package of SFA reforms on the balance between expenditure and resources after 15 years

Figure 6.3 provides such a comparison, on the assumption that real resources available for education spending by each government will grow at the same rate as its national population, over the 15-year period. In the initial period, there is a balance between expenditure and resources (i.e. expenditure relative to resources equals one). After 15 years, however, the first column in the bar charts for each country shows that a projection based upon recent enrolment trends, even without any change in targets for enrolment rates or implementation of any reforms, produces an imbalance between expenditure and resources. The extent of the imbalance would vary between countries. In Guinea, Mali and Zambia, for example, recent increases in the admission rate into the first grade would translate, at existing transition rates, into proportionately higher primary and secondary enrolments, and lead to a growing imbalance between expenditure and resources.

In Malawi, on the other hand, where the GER is already substantially higher than 100 per cent, recent reductions in the admission rate into Standard 1, imply that a balance between expenditure and resources would be maintained in the absence of any other reforms. A continuation of recent enrolment trends in Senegal and Tanzania would also be accommodated by the budget.

The second column in the bar charts for each country shows the impact of enrolment expansion to UPE levels, in the absence of any changes to levels of unit costs. In most countries, a large imbalance between expenditure and resources available now appears. In Ethiopia, Guinea and Mali, for example, expenditure would be two and a half to three times higher than resources available, in the absence of any other reforms.[16] These enrolment targets, however, also presuppose the implementation of the reforms to improve gender equity and quality, since demand would otherwise remain low. Once the costs of these are added (in the third column) it can be seen that the imbalance becomes very large, with expenditure rising to between two and four times higher than resources available in five of the nine countries. Even in Malawi, where the GER is already high, expenditure would exceed resources available by 80 per cent once reforms to achieve levels of acceptable quality were in place. Finally, Figure 6.3 shows the impact of introducing the efficiency reforms aimed at reducing unit costs. Although the imbalance between expenditure and resources declines in all of the countries, there remains a shortfall, of modest amounts in Senegal, Tanzania and Ghana, and more substantial gaps of 50-150 per cent in the other countries.

It follows that all the countries would need to increase past levels of real per capita public spending in the education sector in order to achieve primary schooling for all. Table 6.13 shows a comparison of base year actual expenditures on education with those we expect to be required to achieve SFA over 15 years. It can be seen that the implied annual rates of expenditure growth vary from about four per cent in Senegal to more than nine per cent in Ethiopia. In principle, these resources could be domestically generated partly by expenditure restructuring and partly by economic growth. In most of the countries, there is some scope to increase the proportion of government recurrent expenditure allocated to education. As Chapter 5 showed, many of them have been spending a lower proportion of GNP on the primary sector than other countries in SSA, and there is a need for public commitment to these spending goals to increase. For illustrative purposes, the table shows the impact of increasing education spending to 25 per cent of the recurrent budget (except in the case of Senegal, where this proportion was already exceeded). It can be seen that even with this notional restructuring of base-year expenditures – to a level which is high by the standards of other countries in SSA –

---

[16] Recall that, in all the countries, the target is to achieve a GER of at least 100 per cent within 15 years. Given the extremely low starting position in Ethiopia (where the GER is initially only 24 per cent), the achievement of UPE is limited to the first four grades of primary, with an overall GER at the primary level of 75 per cent. Allowances are also made for increases in the GER at the secondary level, as appropriate, and the cost of this is also included in the calculation of total recurrent expenditure.

Table 6.13 Resource implications of reforms

	Base year recurrent education spending as % of total	Required average annual expenditure growth to achieve SFA	
		Unchanged allocation	25% Allocation
(1)	(2)	(3)	(4)
Ethiopia	20	9.4	7.8
Ghana	22	5.4	4.5
Guinea	22	7.2	6.3
Malawi	21	5.1	3.9
Mali	19	8.1	6.1
Senegal	33	4.1	4.1
Tanzania	22	4.5	3.6
Uganda	22	5.3	4.4
Zambia	17	8.3	5.6

Source: GAPS simulation models.

Notes: Column (2) reports government expenditure on education as a percentage of total discretionary government expenditure for the base year. Column (3) indicates the extent to which real public spending on education would need to increase, annually (after all other reforms and spending changes had been made) to reach SFA in 15 years, with no change in the base-year allocation shown in Column (2). Column (4): as for Column (3), but with the base-year allocation increased to 25 per cent (except Senegal).

further substantial increments to real expenditures would still be required. These vary from growth of four to five per cent per year in Senegal, Tanzania, Malawi, Uganda and Ghana, to much higher rates of six to eight per cent in the other countries.   Thus, if all of these additional resources were to be delivered by economic growth, the implications of the projections remain demanding, given the stagnant or declining per capita incomes that have characterised most of these economies over the past two decades. It is clear that supplementation of domestic resources by international aid will be required, in ways investigated in the next chapter.

Chapter 7

Can Aid to African Schooling be Expected to Close the Financial and Policy Gaps?

Introduction

Earlier chapters have shown how schooling for all can be reached within 15 years in each of the nine countries. We have demonstrated that a strong mix of policy reforms, affecting the quality, availability and financing of schooling would need to be introduced, and sustained, by each of the governments, over the intervening years. However, even though much can be gained by the careful introduction of reforms to improve the efficiency of resource use, the achievement of SFA will, in each country, also require significantly more real *per capita* spending on education than has characterised the recent past. Yet, it is by no means clear that future economic growth in these countries will be strong enough to facilitate such spending increases. In that event, difficult choices about spending priorities would be required, and SFA may, once again, prove elusive.

The question arises as to whether the likely resource gaps could be met from overseas aid. This is the topic for the present chapter, which does three things. Firstly, we examine the aid record, and ask why resource transfers during the 1990s were lower than expected, and than had occurred during the previous decade. Secondly, the likely domestic funding gaps associated with reaching SFA in the nine countries are estimated. Finally, the chapter asks what levels of aid are likely to be available, and whether recent changes to the structure and modalities of aid transfers will help to promote the policy reforms necessary on the demand side, if all African girls and boys are to be enrolled in schools.

The Aid Record

Total aid to developing countries amounted to about $US56 bn. from 21 main OECD providers in 1999. About 70 per cent of it was provided bilaterally, on a government-to-government basis. The remainder came through multilateral channels – about half from the World Bank and the Regional Development Banks, with the remainder split roughly equally between the European Union and UN agencies. The following discussion focuses mainly upon bilateral flows and those from the World Bank, owing to their relative importance, particularly for Africa.

Bilateral Aid

During no other decade in recent times was the gap between words and actions on the matter of international aid as great as it became during the 1990s. The advocacy of the need for aid became stronger and more sophisticated, on the part of both the aid agencies and NGOs, whilst drought and natural disasters continued to provide dramatic copy for the world's press. A series of high-profile UN conferences – on education, the environment, women, AIDS, and other major topics – provided regular, and well defended, calls for international action. Additional resources were promised by the richer nations to address most of these themes. In mid-decade a major commitment was made by the international community to reduce by half those living in poverty by 2015. A series of other international development targets (IDTs), for health, nutrition, education, literacy, and women's empowerment was agreed in 1996, which indicated, in concrete terms, the means by which the problem of poverty would be alleviated. After further endorsement at a range of international meetings the IDTs became enshrined as the Millennium Development Goals (OECD, 1996; IMF, OECD, UN, World Bank, 2000). The main education targets were to achieve universal enrolment at primary level by 2015, gender parity in primary and secondary enrolments by 2005, and gender equality at all levels of education by 2015. These education targets had also been endorsed by the World Education Forum, held in Dakar in April 2000, when the industrialised countries pledged to ensure that no country would be prevented by a lack of resources from achieving them (UNESCO, 2000c, p.36). By implication then, when aid was genuinely needed to secure SFA, it would be forthcoming.

Notwithstanding these apparent commitments, and the continued buoyant economic climate in the north, total bilateral aid from OECD countries fell by almost one-third, in real terms, over the years 1990-98 (Table 7.1). This result was heavily influenced by the USA, where aid fell by almost two-thirds over those years. However, aid was also significantly reduced from Canada (by 15 per cent), Finland (49 per cent), Germany (20 per cent), Italy (60 per cent), and Switzerland (35 per cent). France and Japan dominated the group with rising aid flows, whilst the value of aid from UK and Netherlands remained roughly unchanged over the decade.

Aid to education followed this general falling trend. By 1998 it was some 30 per cent lower than in 1990, having maintained its share of around 13 per cent of total bilateral aid flows. It can be seen from Table 7.1 that France alone accounted for about one-third of all bilateral support for education, much of which was in the form of support to French language teaching in its former colonies. Germany and Japan were also major suppliers of educational aid, followed – at some distance – by Netherlands and UK. Amongst these major providers, only Japan significantly

Table 7.1 Bilateral aid 1990-1998 (constant 1998 $US millions)

	Total			Education			Education as % total		Basic education as % total	
	1990	1994	1998	1990	1994	1998	1990	1998	1994	1998
Australia	450	875	565	163	124	122	36	22	14	22
Austria	238	572	435	70	n.a.	75	30	17	n.a.	3
Belgium	570	421	546	106	53	58	19	11	2	4
Canada	1,471	1,196	1,266	177	125	92	12	7	n.a.	0
Denmark	653	767	674	8	23	23	1	3	36	15
Finland	504	179	254	8	7	18	2	7	38	62
France	3,419	5,294	4,362	2,448	1,578	1,520	72	35	n.a.	n.a.
Germany	4,284	3,928	3,475	911	982	821	21	24	12	11
Ireland	26	62	124	n.a.	n.a.	n.a.	n.a.	n.a.	n.a.	0
Italy	1,377	577	550	140	40	25	10	4	2	5
Japan	3,439	4,502	4,750	628	763	712	18	15	n.a.	n.a.
Luxembourg	n.a.	40	73	n.a.	n.a.	n.a.	n.a.	n.a.	n.a.	n.a.
Netherlands	2,113	2,259	2,078	271	141	187	13	9	24	48
New Zealand	49	79	99	n.a.	27	n.a.	n.a.	n.a.	0	n.a.
Norway	582	720	694	27	18	37	5	5	n.a.	34
Portugal	25	155	32	n.a.	n.a.	16	n.a.	50	n.a.	1
Spain	n.a.	261	666	n.a.	36	90	n.a.	14	23	10
Sweden	1,231	1,290	1,440	68	95	60	6	4	54	62
Switzerland	681	901	454	63	37	24	9	5	3	42
United Kingdom	2,328	2,197	2,328	271	217	176	12	8	n.a.	20
United States	23,590	8,942	6,875	538	400	119	2	2	n.a.	31
	47,032	35,219	31,740	5,899	4,666	4,176	13	13	5	10

Notes: Data are for Official Development Assistance in the form of Grants. DAC deflator for each donor country is used to produce constant 1998 series.

Source: OECD DAC on-line database, Tables 1 and 5.

increased its support over the 1990s. Elsewhere, the reductions in real educational aid were widely spread across the donor community, with particularly sharp reductions being made by Canada, Italy, USA, France and UK. In the latter two countries, aid to education halved as a proportion of the total – from 70 to 35 per cent in the case of France and from 16 to 8 per cent in UK, between the early and later parts of the decade.[1] Accordingly, there was no overall increase in the relative commitment by donors to educational spending, and a majority of bilateral agencies (10 out of 16 having the data) actually decreased the proportion of aid they allocated to education between 1990 and 1998.

The available OECD data are not sufficiently comprehensive to provide a clear indication of trends in the composition of educational aid. However, the data suggest that the real value of aid to basic education rose from 1994 until 1996 (by which date it accounted for around 12 per cent of educational aid), but declined thereafter, with particularly heavy reductions being made by Germany, Japan and USA. The Netherlands and UK, on the other hand, continued to increase their aid to basic education throughout the period. However, it is likely that some of these apparent trends were affected by increases in the quality of reporting to the DAC Secretariat over time, and too much confidence cannot be placed in them.

Table 7.2 Bilateral aid to SSA 1990-1998 (constant 1998 $US millions)

Year	Developing country total	Africa – south of the Sahara	SSA as % of total
1990	47,032	9,616	20
1991	37,646	10,308	27
1992	34,808	8,808	25
1993	34,207	8,821	26
1994	35,219	10,189	29
1995	33,042	7,105	22
1996	33,313	7,344	22
1997	30,131	7,548	25
1998	31,740	8,598	27

Note: DAC deflator for each donor country is used to produce constant 1998 series.
Source: OECD DAC on-line database Table 3a: Destination of Official Development Assistance and Official Aid – Commitments

As regards the direction of aid flows, SSA – having had the greatest levels of debt and most generalised levels of extreme poverty of any developing region –

---

[1]   Although Table 7.1 indicates that in 1990 British bilateral aid to education accounted for 12 per cent of its total aid, by 1992 this had risen to 16 per cent, before falling back later in the decade.

initially appeared to benefit. Bilateral aid to the region increased marginally over the first half of the 1990s, even though total aid had fallen by around one-quarter at this time. However, as shown in Table 7.2, the value of bilateral grants to SSA fell sharply over the years 1994-98, and, even after some recovery towards the end of the decade, aid to the region remained about 15 per cent lower than its value at the outset.

The surprising consequence of these trends is that the real value of total bilateral aid per person in OECD countries fell by 36 per cent, and that the *per capita* value of educational aid fell by one-third, over the period 1990-98. By contrast, during this period, real *per capita* incomes in OECD countries increased by more than 10 per cent.[2] The commitments to provide more resources for human development, particularly for Africa, that were declared and reaffirmed at the international conferences of the 1990s, appear to have been ignored. There is some evidence of increased targeting towards human development priorities, since aid to basic education and to SSA were slightly less strongly affected than other aid, but this was not sufficient to prevent sharp overall reductions in their value. It seems, then, that as northern populations became richer, they also became more reluctant to provide assistance to those who are less well off in the South.

World Bank Assistance

During the 1990s, total new lending commitments made by the World Bank increased by 15 per cent in real terms (Table 7.3), from $US24.7 billions to $US28.6 billions (1998 prices). Most of this increase was in the IBRD component of lending, which is provided on close to commercial terms. By contrast, the real value of IDA lending – the concessional side of the World Bank's operations – remained roughly unchanged. Accordingly, as a proportion of new commitments, it fell from about 30 to 25 per cent of total Bank lending by the end of the decade. Furthermore, although the value of IDA lending to eligible countries was maintained, not all countries and regions benefited similarly. In particular, the value of Bank lending to Sub-Saharan Africa was almost halved over the 1990s, mainly because of a slowdown in IDA lending to the region (Table 7.3).[3]

The World Bank's role in providing concessional finance for education in the poorer countries has been highly significant. For example, World Bank loans, over the 1990s, accounted for about 30 per cent of total external funding of education in developing countries, about 40 per cent of which – as can be seen from Table 7.4 – was on IDA terms. These IDA loans accounted for 12 per cent of all grants and loans for education, and for some 15 per cent of all concessional aid, if IBRD loans are excluded. With the exception of a small amount of IBRD lending in the early

---

2   These calculations are based upon population and GDP growth rates for OECD countries reported in World Bank (2000).

3   IDA lending comprised over 95 per cent of total Bank lending to SSA from 1993 through 1999. New commitments from the World Bank to SSA fell from an average annual level of $US4,288 millions to $US2,224 millions (in 1998 $US) between 1990-92 and 1997-99 (calculated from Table 7.3).

1990s to Côte d'Ivoire and Mauritius, all of the education lending to SSA has been on IDA terms. Thus, changes in the availability of concessional resources from the Bank could well have an important impact upon Africa's ability to reach SFA.

Table 7.3 World Bank development assistance 1990-1999 (constant 1998 $US millions)

	Total				Sub-Saharan Africa	
Year	IBRD	IDA	% IDA	Total	IBRD + IDA	% Total
1990	18,112	6,589	27	24,701	4,522	18.3
1991	18,872	7,245	28	26,117	3,895	14.9
1992	17,035	7,362	30	24,397	4,448	18.2
1993	18,598	7,410	28	26,008	3,092	11.9
1994	15,314	7,088	32	22,402	3,019	13.5
1995	17,734	5,966	26	23,700	2,404	10.1
1996	14,956	7,086	32	22,042	2,829	12.8
1997	14,707	4,680	24	19,387	1,759	9.1
1998	21,086	7,508	26	28,594	2,874	10.1
1999	21,855	6,711	23	28,566	2,038	7.1

Notes: 1998 figures are calculated by summing the individual project expenditures from the World Bank Annual Report, (1998). They differ from the totals shown in Appendices 14 and 15 of that report, which appear to be inconsistent with the text detail. The 1999 figures are also slightly different. DAC deflator for the United States used to produce constant price series.
Sources: World Bank Annual Reports (1990-1999).

Unlike the Bank's lending programme as a whole, however, it can be seen from Table 7.4 that its commitments for education declined by 15.5 per cent, in constant prices, over the 1990s. Furthermore, in SSA the fall in support for education was much worse. It can be seen that there, lending commitments for education fell by a massive 44 per cent between 1990-99,[4] broadly in line with the trend for total lending to SSA. By consequence, the World Bank's education lending commitments to SSA declined from 21 per cent to only 14 per cent of total education lending commitments over the decade.

During the 1980s, the World Bank had clearly identified primary schooling as a major priority for education lending, and, over the following decade, the lending programme gave primary education greater prominence. Data from the Bank's Annual Reports indicate that the real value of loan commitments aimed exclusively

---

[4]   This is the fall in the three year moving average of education commitments to SSA over the years 1990-92 ($US380 millions) and 1997-99 ($US213 millions), calculated from Table 7.4.

**Table 7.4 World Bank development assistance to education 1990-1999
(constant 1998 $US millions)**

| Year | Total | | | | Sub-Saharan Africa | | |
	IBRD	IDA	% IDA	Total	IBRD + IDA	% total ed.	% total asst. to SSA
1990	633	1,141	64	1,774	380	21	8
1991	1,745	848	33	2,592	306	12	8
1992	1,461	657	31	2,117	453	21	10
1993	1,062	1,140	52	2,202	458	21	15
1994	1,516	708	32	2,223	350	16	12
1995	1,348	859	64	2,206	212	10	9
1996	951	810	46	1,761	136	8	5
1997	772	258	25	1,030	76	7	4
1998	1,928	1,202	38	3,129	372	12	13
1999	793	532	40	1,324	191	14	9

Note: DAC deflator for USA has been used to produce the constant price series.
Sources: World Bank Annual Reports (1990-1999).

at basic education increased by 23 per cent between 1990-2 and 1997-9, and they rose from 20 per cent to 26 per cent of the value of all education loan commitments over the same period (Table 7.5).   On the other hand, if all loans with some element of support for basic education are included, their average real value was virtually unchanged over the decade, and they rose from 43 to only 47 per cent of all education commitments over the decade.

Girls' education projects also increased in both number and value. Gender had scarcely been mentioned in education projects at the beginning of the 1990s. Although there are some difficulties in interpreting the published information, those with a gender component appear to have risen to about 12 per cent of all education projects towards the end of the decade.[5] Furthermore, by the late 1990s, approximately 25 per cent of IDA education commitments (by value) were for projects which were stated as having an explicit gender dimension (Table 7.5).

Whether World Bank resources were targeted to the right countries, however, is a different matter. Within SSA, there was large international variation in the *per capita* value of education commitments. During 1990-94, for example, it varied from $US25-$US32 per person in Mauritius and Côte d'Ivoire, to less than $US2 in Tanzania and Zaire. For 1995-99, the range was from $US45 in Cape Verde to

---

[5]   The difficulties of interpretation are real. The importance assigned to gender issues by aid agencies during the 1990s increased the incentives for project managers to claim a gender impact. It seems, however, that project-design has changed much less than has the frequency of mention, in project documentation, of gender issues.

Table 7.5 World Bank assistance to basic education and gender

Year	Loans exclusively basic				Loans to basic and some basic				Loans to projects including gender component			
	IBRD	IDA	% total ed. IDA	% total	IBRD	IDA	% total ed. IDA	% total	IBRD	IDA	% total ed. IDA	% total
1990	0	134	12	8	108	461	40	32	0	0	0	0
1991	414	204	24	24	697	293	35	38	0	0	0	0
1992	557	34	5	28	797	479	73	60	0	129	20	6
1993	233	543	48	35	432	826	73	57	0	278	24	13
1994	972	238	34	54	1122	514	73	74	0	64	9	3
1995	158	675	79	38	401	726	85	51	0	187	22	8
1996	137	111	14	14	172	719	89	51	0	501	62	28
1997	115	14	6	13	220	184	71	39	33	102	40	13
1998	529	636	53	37	702	1143	95	59	0	119	10	4
1999	220	141	26	27	297	300	56	45	0	120	23	9

Notes: The first column of percentages for each loan group indicates the proportion of total IDA assistance for education in any year which was assigned to that loan group. The second column of percentages indicates the proportion of total assistance (IBRD+IDA) in any year which was assigned to that loan group.

Sources: Author's calculations from World Bank Annual Reports (1990-1999)

less than $US1 in Tanzania and Cameroon.[6] Moreover, in both periods, the richer countries tended to receive larger education loans.   This was particularly pronounced in the first half of the decade, when richer countries in SSA were receiving more than twice the *per capita* value of IDA education loans as countries at half their income level.[7] Similarly, although gender was subsequently targeted in education projects, more resources continued to be received by the countries with lower gender gaps.   For example, those countries with no gender gaps received, on average, twice the *per capita* value of education loans as countries where only half as many girls as boys were enrolled in school.   This tendency became slightly more marked during the decade. Thus, just as World Bank lending to SSA declined with the intensification of the region's economic problems, so, within SSA, it was biased towards the richer countries, where the need for external resources was less acute.

Other Multilateral Assistance

Judged according to the magnitude of financial assistance provided, easily the most significant multilateral agency after the World Bank, is the European Commission. Financial aid from the European Commission to developing countries grew rapidly during the 1990s. It increased by over 140 per cent in real terms, from $US2.9 billion to almost $US7 billion between 1990 and 1998. Nevertheless, the real value of commitments to SSA moved in the opposite direction.   There was considerable year-on-year variation.   However, taking a three-year average, commitments fell by three per cent, from $US1.9 billion to $US1.84 billion, between 1990-2 and 1996-8.[8] Accordingly, the proportion of EC aid going to SSA fell from one-half to about one-third of the total between those two three-year periods.   Recent data on the extent of education support are not available. However, finance for education was reported to comprise approximately 6 per cent of the total in the late 1990s, with only a small part of this being allocated to basic education.[9] In aggregate, the volume of concessional resources provided by the European Commission to SSA has been significant, amounting to the equivalent of around four-fifths of annual IDA funding to the region, over 1996-8. In principle the support provided by EC could be said to be more important than that from the World Bank since the former is provided as grants rather than as concessional loans. Nevertheless, a comparatively small portion of EC aid was allocated to education, and its declining trend indicates that the EC experienced similar problems to those of the World Bank, and some bilateral agencies, in providing support to education in Sub-Saharan Africa during the 1990s.

---

[6]   All data are in constant 1998 $US.

[7]   The relationship between real *per capita* income and the real *per capita* value of education loans from the World Bank is positive for both periods ($R^2 = 0.4$ and 0.14, respectively).

[8]   All data are in constant 1998 $US. Nominal data in source (OECD DAC on-line data base, Table 3a) have been deflated using the EC DAC deflator.

[9]   van Riesen (1998, p.85).

Aid and the Education Financing Gap in the Nine Countries

It is clear from the foregoing that aid to African education did not fare well during the last decade of the twentieth century. What implications might this have for the achievement of SFA in Africa? Can the resource requirements of a major expansion and qualitative improvement of primary schooling throughout the region be expected to be met from domestic sources? Or are there, perhaps, contradictions between the advocacy, by northern institutions, of the importance of achieving schooling for all – indicated by their adoption of the IDTs for education – and their apparent reluctance to increase the scale and scope of educational aid to the most needy states? These questions are tackled in the remainder of this chapter. We begin by focussing upon the aid record in our nine study countries, and upon their likely future financing requirements to achieve SFA. Implications for desirable levels of external finance are derived. This is followed by a broader assessment of future prospects for educational aid to the region.

Table 7.6 Average annual bilateral aid to education 1995/1996 and 1998/1999 (commitments)

	1995 and 1996			1998 and 1999		
	Ed. Aid ($USm)	Ed. Aid per person ($US)	Ed. as % of total bilateral	Ed. Aid ($USm)	Ed. Aid per person ($US)	Ed. as % of total bilateral
Ethiopia	39.3	0.68	7.0	38.4	0.62	8.9
Ghana	31.1	1.20	7.5	67.0	3.58	14.5
Guinea	9.0	1.35	4.4	26.3	3.67	18.5
Malawi	25.2	2.55	9.4	20.8	1.95	9.1
Mali	35.9	3.63	10.9	27.0	2.51	12.3
Senegal	29.7	3.49	7.4	34.0	3.71	9.6
Tanzania	26.6	0.88	4.8	43.3	1.33	5.8
Uganda	39.5	2.03	9.4	89.9	4.24	23.7
Zambia	26.2	2.88	6.0	45.0	4.60	9.6
Total	262.5	-	-	391.7	-	-
Average	29.2	2.08	7.4	43.5	2.91	12.4

Notes: All financial data are in 1998 constant prices.
          Data are simple annual averages for each pair of calendar years.
Source: Calculated from data in OECD (2001).

The quality and coverage of country-level data on aid receipts remain unsatisfactory. However, Table 7.6 compares aid commitments to education in the nine countries, from all bilateral sources, for the two pairs of years 1995/96 and 1998/99. It can be seen that, in contrast to the international trends summarised earlier, these nine countries received a 50 per cent overall increase in aid commitments for education between the middle and later years of the decade. The increase was not, of course, evenly spread. In fact, in three of the countries – Ethiopia, Malawi and Mali – the absolute value of aid commitments for education actually fell over the period. But elsewhere, commitments increased substantially. Their value more than doubled in Ghana, Guinea and Uganda, and they increased by around two-thirds in Tanzania and Zambia. By consequence, these nine countries were, by 1998, receiving more than one-tenth of total bilateral aid to education.[10]

We should note, however, that this increase in the value of educational aid was more a consequence of changed sectoral priorities than of increases in total aid volume. It can be seen from Table 7.6 that, in all cases except Malawi, the proportion of total bilateral aid commitments allocated to education rose over the period – and, in most cases, sharply so. On average, across all the countries, it increased from 7.4 per cent for the years 1995 and 1996 to 12.4 per cent by 1998 and 1999. By consequence of these changing sectoral priorities, whilst total bilateral aid commitments per person actually fell in all of these recipient countries except for Tanzania, educational aid per person increased in six of them over the second half of the decade.[11]

So, these countries did not, on average, fare as badly as many, in terms of the recent trends in aid for education. On the other hand, the distribution of aid resources between them gives less cause for comfort. Those countries where aid to education fell over the period – Ethiopia, Malawi and Tanzania – were, together with Mali, also the poorest of the group. These four countries, by 1998/99, received less aid for education from bilateral sources, per head of population, than the five richer countries (Table 7.6). The differences were strong, with Senegal, Guinea, Uganda and Zambia, receiving six times as much educational aid *per capita* as Ethiopia and two to three times as much as Malawi and Tanzania. Thus, just as was the case at the regional level, poverty targeting of educational aid within this group of nine SSA countries was weak. Furthermore, it will be shown that, even in the richer countries where educational aid was greater, the levels of external financing still generally fell far short of what would be required, if the international development targets were to be achieved.

The evidence for this is set out in Table 7.7. It will be recalled that our national simulation models, discussed in Chapter 6, provide estimates of minimum required expenditures to achieve SFA, over a 15-year period. These are 'minimum' expenditures in the sense that they presuppose an extended reform process being implemented in each country. Measures to improve the quality and internal efficiency of schooling would be needed, together with sets of cost-saving and cost-shifting reforms, intended both to reduce costs and increase resources available to finance the expansion and improvement of schooling.

The first two rows of Table 7.7 show the actual recurrent expenditures on education incurred in each country in the base year, together with the 'required'

---

[10]   Total bilateral aid to education amounted to $US4176 millions in 1998, of which some $US449 millions were committed for these nine countries in the same year (see Table 7.1 and OECD, 2001).

[11]   The exceptions, again, were Ethiopia, Malawi and Mali. See Table 7.6.

Table 7.7 Domestic resources, financing gaps and aid requirements to achieve schooling for all within 15 years

	Eth. 1993/4	Gha. 1996/7	Guin. 1993/4	Malw. 1997/8	Mali 1997/8	Sen. 1997/8	Tanz. 1993/4	Ug. 1997/8	Zam. 1996/7
1. Base Year Expenditure	144.9	244.1	57.6	92.0	57.9	128.4	140.5	150.7	79.3
2. Required Expenditure for SFA, year 15	559.6	537.7	162.6	194.5	185.4	233.5	270.2	327.5	262.1
3. Resources available: assumption (i)	225.7	380.4	89.8	135.2	87.7	200.1	212.6	218.2	118.2
4. Resources available: assumption (ii)	242.7	398.5	141.7	135.2	131.5	237.9	212.6	276.6	139.7
5. Resources available: assumption (iii)	280.2	460.6	163.8	156.4	152.1	275.1	245.8	320.4	161.5
6. Financing gap: assumption (i)	333.9	157.3	72.9	59.3	97.7	33.4	57.7	109.2	143.9
7. % of required expenditure	59.7	29.2	44.8	30.5	52.7	14.3	21.3	33.4	54.9
8. Financing gap: assumption (ii)	316.9	139.2	20.8	59.3	53.8	-	57.7	50.9	122.4
9. % of required expenditure	56.6	25.9	12.8	30.5	29.0	-	21.3	15.5	46.7
10. Financing gap: assumption (iii)	279.4	77.1	-	38.1	33.3	-	24.4	7.0	100.6
11. % of required expenditure	49.9	14.3	-	19.6	18.0	-	9.0	2.2	38.4
12. Memo items: av. Bilateral aid 95-99	37.0	45.3	14.8	23.4	31.1	29.7	37.5	55.9	31.4
13. Average World Bank aid 1994-99	15.2	15.0	8.5	11.7	11.0	6.6	3.2	13.2	6.4
14. Bilateral aid as % of gap (ii)	11.7	32.5	71.0	39.5	57.8	-	65.0	109.9	25.7
15. World Bank aid as % of gap (ii)	4.8	10.8	40.8	19.7	20.4	-	5.5	26.0	5.2
16. Bilateral aid as % of gap (iii)	13.2	58.8	-	61.4	93.4	-	153.4	793.9	31.2
17. World Bank aid as % of gap (iii)	5.4	19.5	-	30.7	33.0	-	13.1	187.5	6.4

Notes: All financial data are in US$ millions. Numbers in brackets below refer to rows in table.

(1) Public recurrent expenditure on education; (2) Public recurrent expenditure for SFA in year 15, in constant base year prices; (3) Assumption (i): real public recurrent expenditure per capita on education remains constant; (4) Assumption (ii): as for (i) except public spending on primary schooling is raised to a minimum of 2% of GNP; (5) Assumption (iii): real public recurrent expenditure per capita on education increases at 1 per cent per year over the 15 years. Otherwise as for (ii); (6) Row (2) minus Row (3); (7) Row (6) as % of Row (2); (8) Row (2) minus Row (4); (9) Row (8) as % of Row (2); (10) Row (2) minus Row (5); (11) Row (10) as % of Row (2); (12) Average bilateral commitments for education 1995-99 (base year prices); (13) Average World Bank commitments for education 1994-1999 (base year prices); (14) Row (12) as % of Row (8); (15) Row (13) as % of Row (8); (16) Row (12) as % of Row (10); (17) Row (13) as % of Row (10).

Sources: National Simulation Models, OECD, 2001, authors' calculations.

expenditures to meet SFA 15 years later. It can be seen that the increased expenditure required, notwithstanding the impact of policy reforms, would, in all cases, be substantial. Real recurrent spending would almost need to quadruple in Ethiopia, to roughly triple in Guinea, Mali and Zambia, and to double in Ghana, Malawi, Senegal, Tanzania and Uganda. Could such increases in spending really be financed from domestic sources? In order to answer this question, the table sets out the resource impact of three sets of assumptions. The first, reported in the third row of the table, is that the real resources available for recurrent education spending will grow at the same rate as the population, which, depending on the country, is likely to be between 2.5 and 3 per cent per year. Obviously, this condition would deliver constant real *per capita* recurrent public spending on education throughout the 15-year period. The second assumption (shown in the fourth row) adds an additional condition to the first – that public spending on primary schooling should rise to a minimum of two per cent of GNP (and that GNP itself grows at the same rate as the population). The third assumption retains the two per cent minimum, and adds the condition that *per capita* public spending on education should rise at one per cent per annum throughout the whole period.

How likely is it that any of these conditions will be met? It should be noted that even the first – *per capita* education spending being maintained in real terms – was achieved only in Uganda and Malawi over the decade prior to our studies being conducted. There, real *per capita* recurrent public spending on education increased by 14 and 11 per cent per year, respectively, between the early and late 1990s, in connection with the introduction of free primary schooling (Tumushabe, *et al.* 2000, Table 2.5; Kadzamira and Chibwana, 2000, Table 2.9). In the other countries, earlier levels of real *per capita* public spending on education had not been maintained over the previous decade. Nevertheless, it can be seen from Row 7 that, even were the first condition to be achieved in all nine countries, the financing gap (between resources available and those required for SFA) would in most cases be large: only in Senegal would it be less than 20 per cent of required expenditure, and in Ethiopia, Mali and Zambia more than half the annually required resources would still need to be found.

As regards the second condition, only the governments of Malawi and Tanzania were allocating, during the late 1990s, the equivalent of at least 2 per cent of GNP to expenditures on primary schooling. We argued earlier that since this was roughly equal to the average amount spent by SSA governments in the mid-1990s, it should be achievable by all states where enrolments remained low. Adding this condition to the first one would remove the projected financing gap in Senegal, and sharply reduce it in Guinea (from 45 per cent to 13 per cent of required expenditures), Mali (from 53 per cent to 29 per cent) and in Uganda (from 33 per cent to 16 cent), where erstwhile public spending levels had been low. Elsewhere the impact would be smaller, and funding gaps, in general, would remain large.

The third condition – a growth in *per capita* spending on education of one per cent per year over the 15-year period (whilst maintaining a minimum of two per cent of GNP as public spending on education) – is demanding. Whether it could be secured in these countries would depend strongly upon their return to sustained economic growth. Uganda, Ethiopia and Ghana appeared to have achieved this by the turn of the century (World Bank, 2001a, Table 1). But the economic outlook for the other countries was uncertain. In the absence of a return to growth, the prospect for annually increasing real public spending on education would become slight. In any event, Rows 10 and 11 of Table 7.7 show that even with this reform, financing gaps for SFA would still remain substantial in most countries. Although Senegal and Guinea could now meet their financing requirements, and Uganda would be close to doing so, in the other six countries, financing gaps of between 14 and 50 per cent of required spending on education would remain to be filled.

This analysis now provides a framework for evaluating the contribution that might be played by overseas aid. Actual bilateral and World Bank aid flows to education in the nine countries are shown in Rows 12 and 13 of Table 7.7.[12] The data are annual average commitments for the period 1994/95-1999, converted to prices pertaining in the base year for each of the countries. They can, therefore, be compared directly with the other financial information in the table, including the likely financing gaps projected for each country, in connection with the achievement of SFA.

Rows 14 and 15 of Table 7.7 indicate that aid contributions for education in these countries have usually been substantially less than what is likely to be required. If the second set of conditions, discussed above, were to be achieved (which, as a general case for all the countries, may be optimistic), past levels of aid to education would, in the main, fall significantly short of the financing required. The exceptions are Senegal, where domestic financing of SFA would be possible, if all of the efficiency and financing reforms were implemented, and Guinea and Uganda, where the combination of multilateral and bilateral aid flows would be sufficient to meet their resource gaps. In the other countries, it can be seen from Rows 14 and 15 that if its value were to be maintained in real terms, bilateral aid would be sufficient to cover between 12 per cent (Ethiopia) and 65 per cent (Tanzania) of the likely financing gaps, whilst World Bank support would cover a rather paltry five per cent (Ethiopia) to 20 per cent (Mali).

The situation would improve significantly if the third set of conditions were to hold. As indicated above, Guinea and Senegal would now be self-financing, and past levels of aid would be sufficient to meet the recurrent financing gap in Mali, Tanzania and Uganda. However, Rows 16 and 17 of Table 7.7 show that aid would still only cover around three-quarters of the gap in Ghana, about 40 per cent of it in Zambia, and less than 20 per cent in Ethiopia. In fact, the picture is dominated by Ethiopia, where total aid requirements of almost $US300 millions per year would account for approximately three-quarters of educational aid supplied annually to all nine of these countries in recent years. In aggregate, this analysis shows that educational aid to these countries will need to more than double in real terms, even if a return to sustained economic growth is achieved and if domestic policy reforms are implemented. Clearly, then, the amount of

---

[12]   No data are available for other multilateral aid to education. However, as indicated above, its volume would have been small relative to total bilateral and World Bank flows.

additional aid required to achieve SFA will be substantial, but its precise dimensions are very sensitive both to the particular countries included in the calculation, and to the extent of policy reform each of them can be expected to achieve.

In the past, most aid to education (and other sectors) has been for capital, rather than recurrent items. During the 1990s, there was a growing acceptance, on the part of aid agencies, that programme funding and sector support were increasingly needed, and that such funds should not be limited to supporting only the development budget. However, in the mid-1990s, the use of these modalities remained limited, and most of the aid flows summarised in Table 7.7 were provided for capital rather than recurrent spending (see below). The present analysis indicates how important is the need for change. All of the resources detailed above would be required in order to balance the recurrent budgets of the countries concerned, by consequence of the move to SFA. It is possible that recurrent resource gaps would turn out to be less than these estimates suggest, but only if a very healthy growth in *per capita* income were maintained in these countries, over the 15 years, and if some of the fruits of that growth were translated into public spending on education. However, as indicated earlier, the extent of reform already built into these projections is substantial. In the light of the economic history of Sub-Saharan Africa since 1980, it would be unwise to expect both that all the required policy changes will occur, and that a strong growth path will be able to be maintained in these economies, over many years. Thus, it follows that, if the international development targets are to be attained, most of the aid that is to be provided will be needed for recurrent rather than capital support. Capital aid will still be needed – although, as argued elsewhere, not usually at the primary level.[13] But it will be in addition to the sums discussed above, rather than being subsumed within them. We now turn to a consideration of whether aid resources for education are likely to be made available by the international community to the magnitude and in the forms required.

Aid Prospects: Flows and Modalities

Why has Aid to Education in Africa had Such a Dismal Record?

Earlier in this chapter we showed that, at the turn of the millennium, World Bank loans to education in Africa were running at a level of about half of their real value over the early 1990s. This was not simply a reflection of a decline in overall education lending by the Bank, since its real value fell by only 15 per cent between the beginning and the end of the decade. Lending for education was much more severely reduced in Africa than elsewhere. Similar trends were apparent in the case of the EC aid programme, and the prominence of SSA in bilateral aid programmes was less marked than intended, and promised, by most aid agencies.

---

[13]   Discussion of the case for recurrent versus capital support in the primary sector is given in Colclough with Lewin (1993, pp.249-254).

Why has there been such a general decline in support from both bilateral and multilateral institutions?

A paper initially prepared for the EFA 2000 Assessment, held in Dakar, suggested a number of reasons for the slowdown. These comprised political turmoil in some of the larger countries, the weak absorptive capacity of key institutions throughout the region, and the reluctance of some governments to introduce (education) policy reforms (World Bank, 2001b, p.62). Although advanced in the context of a paper on Bank lending for education in Africa, these explanations have more general importance. It is worth recalling that total lending to Africa fell by 48 per cent during the 1990s – a similar proportionate amount to the fall in education lending. By contrast, the Bank's global lending commitments increased by almost two per cent over the decade. Some of the problems which led to a slow-down in education lending to Africa were probably also reflected in the under-performance of the African lending programme as a whole. These may also have been factors which encouraged the decline in bilateral aid to SSA over the decade.

The paper also suggested – somewhat surprisingly – that the reduction in Bank support for Africa may have been influenced by the shift in lending priorities that occurred during the 1990s. In particular, 'the Bank might have focused limited staff resources too narrowly on basic education, at the expense of other sub-sectors and portfolio diversity' (loc. cit.). No further explanation is offered for how this might have slowed down lending. However, it is presumably implied that the primary sector needs more preparatory work, or is less able to absorb funds rapidly, than programmes focussed upon higher levels of the education system. If so, there is a danger that it could act to slow down future lending for primary schooling in SSA, as it has in the past.

Starting in the fiscal year 2000, a doubling of the World Bank's annual lending programme for education in SSA (to around $US350 millions) was planned to be achieved within two years. The Bank believed the climate for policy reform to be better than during the 1990s, with governments being more willing to respond positively to a policy dialogue than was earlier the case.[14] However, the main ways in which the Bank intended to achieve these goals were linked to two changes in the modalities of the aid relationship. On the one hand, opportunities for future expansion were seen in the use of new lending instruments: three of the seven new loans approved in 1999-2000 were adjustable programme loans, designed to support long-term sector-wide education development, with future loan tranches being activated by pre-determined policy triggers (and thus not needing the amount of preparation and negotiation required for new loans, nor, indeed, presentation to the Board). On the other hand, expanded debt relief under the HIPC initiative 'presents opportunities to free funds to strengthen the national resource base to sustain accelerated education development' (World Bank, 2001b, p.63). It is important, therefore, to ask whether these innovations do in fact hold

---

[14] Birger Fredriksen (Senior Adviser on Human Resources, Africa Region, World Bank) – personal communication.

out the prospect of facilitating major changes in the aid relationship with SSA, so as to provide a means whereby increased resource transfers could be made.

Debt Relief as Saviour? – the HIPC Initiative

During the 1990s there were increasing opportunities for the poorest countries to reschedule their debts, to have them reduced or, in the case of some creditors, fully removed. Nevertheless, the total debt burden of the most indebted countries continued to increase. It became clear that for many of these countries the burden of debt would undermine their growth prospects over the medium-term and, thus, would be unsustainable. One of the reasons for this circumstance was that multilateral debt had been excluded from the provisions of debt relief arrangements. Thus, the only means whereby the World Bank and the IMF could provide assistance in meeting debt repayment responsibilities was by increasing their own lending, so as to provide new finance for their clients to service earlier credits. This caused multilateral debt to assume even greater importance. By consequence, between 1990 and 1998, it rose from 45 to 56 per cent of long-term debt in 44 of the 48 least developed countries having the data for both those years (UNCTAD, 2000, Table 17).

In response to these circumstances, a new debt relief initiative for the heavily indebted poor countries (HIPC) was introduced in 1996. This widened the coverage of eligible debt to include that due to the multilateral institutions. Its central contribution was to provide a commitment of additional assistance to the 41 most indebted poor countries, in circumstances where debt repayments could not be reduced to 'sustainable' levels via existing instruments. Sustainability was defined in terms of the ratio between the present value of future debt-service obligations and the country's exports (or government revenue). Initially, the maximum ratios considered sustainable were 250 per cent for exports and 280 per cent for revenue. However, the conditions were enhanced in 1999, when they were lowered to 150 per cent and 250 per cent, respectively.

Nevertheless, a wide range of other conditions had to be satisfied prior to resources for debt relief being made available to creditors. A three-year record of good performance under World Bank/IMF-supported adjustment programmes was needed before a country could be judged eligible for HIPC support – the so-called 'decision point'. Moreover, two or three further years would normally be required to introduce 'sound' macroeconomic policies, agreed and monitorable structural reforms and policies for social development. Depending upon progress, additional resources could then be committed – the so-called 'completion point' – over a phased period into the future. Poverty-reduction objectives were added to the list of conditionalities, and these, consequently, became more demanding than those required by the Enhanced Structural Adjustment Facility, under which earlier adjustment lending had taken place. Countries were required to prepare Poverty Reduction Strategy Papers every three years, setting out the detailed basis for economic and social policies to secure growth and poverty reduction. These documents, supported by Bank/Fund Staff Assessments, and having had endorsement by the Boards of both the Bank and Fund, were to be a necessary condition for HIPC initiative arrangements to proceed. Additional conditions were attached to the use of the funds released by the HIPC initiative. Governments had to channel them into increased expenditures on health and education, and into poverty action funds. This was partly a response to the criticism that earlier debt-service obligations had directly undermined the ability of governments to educate and improve the health status of their populations. Amongst our group of case-study countries, for example, debt service payments due, as a proportion of public spending on health and education, amounted to 111 per cent in Mali and 225 per cent in Tanzania, over the years 1995/96 to 1997/98 (UNCTAD, 2000, Table 38).

As a result of these requirements both the time and the technical effort needed to trigger HIPC funding became substantial.[15] Although all of the nine case-study countries had debt levels which were considered unsustainable – making all of them eligible for HIPC funds – by the end of 2001 only Uganda and Tanzania had reached their completion points. Even they, however, had not yet received actual cash draw-down under the revised HIPC framework. All of the other countries, except Ghana, had reached their decisions points, although they confronted several years of further preparation, policy change and uncertainty, before being able to benefit.[16]

What, then, is the scale of benefits that countries which opted for HIPC assistance could expect? For the 21 countries that had reached their decision points by December 2001, the average reduction of the present value of outstanding debt was estimated by the IMF to be 45 per cent, with reductions of two-thirds or more in some cases (e.g. Rwanda, Guinea-Bissau and Zambia). By any standards this is substantial. However, what particularly matters, from the point of view of resources saved, is the impact that these debt-reductions may have upon the flow of payments to service it. We should recall that many countries had been unable to meet all their debt-service obligations in the past. Thus, a critical comparison is the difference between the debt-service payments that had actually been made, and those required under the HIPC provisions.

Unfortunately, the results of such a comparison, for many HIPC countries, are less than impressive. In Uganda, approximately $US70 millions per year would be saved, in comparison with pre-HIPC payments – an amount equivalent to about 8 per cent of ODA received by Uganda in 1997 and roughly equal to the annual aid it received for education over 1995-1999 (see Table 7.7). Although this is significant, the portion of these resources available for education (of around one-third) would amount to only about five per cent of Uganda's public recurrent expenditure on education in 1997/98, and to only about two per cent of the annual expenditures which, we estimate, will be needed for SFA (Table 7.7). Furthermore, in Tanzania, the debt-service reduction was estimated by UNCTAD

---

[15]   The 'overload' of conditionalities and the delays which were thereby imposed upon the HIPC process were two of the main criticisms made by Commonwealth Finance Ministers, at their annual meeting in September 2000 (see Commonwealth Secretariat 2000 and, for more technical detail, Killick, 2000).

[16]   A summary of the objectives of the HIPC initiative, and of progress with its implementation is given in IMF (2001).

to be a mere $US13.6 millions – which, in total, would represent only about two per cent of required SFA annual expenditures – whilst in Mali, required debt service payments post-HIPC were estimated to increase to some $US15 millions more than actual annual payments made by that country in the late 1990s. More generally, estimates for all HIPC countries showed that the annual savings on debt servicing would probably be equivalent to only about one tenth of total net resource flows to those countries in recent years (UNCTAD, 2000, Tables 36 and 38; Martin, 2000: Table 1). If these resources were allocated equally to health, education and poverty-action funds, the average increase in education spending thus facilitated would amount to the equivalent of about three per cent of total aid receipts.

Thus, resources released as a direct consequence of the HIPC initiative are likely to be fairly small. We should recall, however, that the PRSP instrument is concerned also to restructure public spending towards a greater focus on health, education and poverty-reduction goals. Thus, some shift of public expenditures towards those ends may well be sought by the process, irrespective of the size of net savings actually forthcoming under the HIPC provisions. Whether such restructuring will actually occur, in the absence of the governments concerned making fully compensatory savings, remains to be seen: the political economy of this process leaves scope for considerable scepticism on this point. Furthermore, from the perspective of the nine SSA countries studied here, it is doubtful that further expenditure reallocation – beyond that already envisaged in the national reforms – could be a viable part of a long term solution. Ultimately additional resources will be needed either from aid, from economic growth, or both, to sustain educational spending at the higher levels required for SFA.

Will Sector-wide Approaches Facilitate Increased Aid?

During the past two decades, project aid to education had disappointing results. The reasons are many and complex. Often, however, project effectiveness was undermined not only by poor design or implementation, but also by deficiencies in the broader context within which project initiatives were taken. For example, newly trained teachers cannot be effective if texts are not available to help them deliver the curriculum. New teaching materials cannot bring benefits to pupils if teachers are not trained in their use.[17] Providing better teachers' housing will not improve teacher morale if real reductions in their salaries continue unchecked. Thus, in order to secure higher quality outcomes from the use of aid, it may be necessary to improve other aspects of the education system which lie beyond the immediate influence of project support.

One response to this circumstance has been a greater willingness, on the part of the aid community, to provide support to the entire sector, rather than only for individual projects within it. The World Bank introduced sector investment programmes (SIPs) from the mid-1990s. These covered investment commitments

---

[17]   Heneveld and Craig (1996) document the ways in which these obvious linkages were ignored, and led to failure in a range of World Bank education projects.

for the sector as a whole over a given period, in the context of pre-determined activities and objectives for the sector, and a strengthened financing and accounting framework. In 1996, the European Community introduced sectoral development programmes (SDPs), with similar objectives to those of the Bank.[18] Other bilateral and multilateral agencies also introduced new financing instruments which provided longer-term assurances of support to the sector, and include provision for selective recurrent budget financing. Many of these initiatives were broader than the SIP approach, being concerned less with the instruments for lending, than with the overall framework for sectoral policy and its results. They were characterised by donor involvement being more flexible, facilitated by regular reviews of policy and performance, and by the host government being expected to take the lead in both policy design and implementation.

Although some details of these 'sector-wide approaches' (SWAs) have differed between agencies, those described by DFID (1999, p.38) are typical of most.[19] First, recipient governments were expected to define medium-term expenditure frameworks, which indicated the resources available for the sectors concerned. A consultative process with investing partners, also initiated by the government, would then establish the overall sectoral policy, priorities and performance indicators, required expenditures, management and accounting arrangements. Donors would agree jointly to help finance the resulting programme, being ready to provide technical support only if requested by the recipient government. DFID believed that this approach, which was set to expand rapidly,[20] offered the potential of prioritising scarce resources around a spending framework with commonly shared objectives. DFID welcomed the implication that the aid programme would thereby move away from project funding towards the provision of direct budgetary support (loc. cit.).

These recent and intended shifts in the composition and modalities of aid brought the potential of some undoubted benefits for recipients as compared with earlier project-centred approaches. Obvious benefits include the reduction in the extent to which aid is tied to particular uses (thereby saving costs to the recipient),

---

[18]   The SDP is defined – somewhat laboriously – as 'a process of negotiation leading to a transparent agreement in the form of a coherent operational programme in the context of a sectoral strategy, with financial commitment by all parties over an agreed period, in a co-ordinated manner' (European Commission, Horizon 2000 meeting, quoted in van Riesen,1998, p.85).

[19]   See Cassels (1997) and Ratcliffe and Macrae (1999) for further discussion and evidence.

[20]   At the turn of the century, SWAs were supported by DFID in 12 countries, mostly in Africa, including in six of our nine study-countries. In total, it was estimated that some 25-30 African and Asian countries had SWAs wholly or partly financed by international agencies at that time (Ratcliffe and Macrae, 1999, p.47). However, not all of these SWAs fit easily with the 'ideal-type' description given above. Nor were many of them the result of a planning and negotiating process which had been led by the recipient government in the way sought by DFID. Generally, in these cases, the aid agencies had retained a stronger role in designing and drafting the details of the programmes than had been envisaged.

the reduction of control and interference by donors in the sectoral work of the recipient, and the increased ownership of the development process which this should bring for recipients. Since project detail is no longer the focus of donor efforts, the amount of work needed to run large programmes of support is not significantly different from that needed for small programmes. Thus the new modality should allow large amounts of aid resources to be disbursed speedily and efficiently.

With this increased flexibility, however, came greater attendant risk. Donors participating in SWAs no longer know the precise purposes for which their funds are being used, and therefore have to accept collective accountability for their combined programmes. The reduced authority and control of agencies over the micro-use of funds places much greater importance upon the integrity of local monitoring, accounting and auditing mechanisms. In much of SSA, these systems are less transparent and dependable than their northern counterparts. In these circumstances, agencies may find their relative loss of budgetary control difficult to justify (and their own parliaments, ultimately, may not be prepared to accept it).

Changes, too, are implied for the nature of the policy dialogue, by consequence of these new modalities for aid. Project assistance was dependent upon agreement being reached between donor and recipient, as to the aims and objectives of funded projects, and as to the technical feasibility of these outcomes being delivered by the project inputs. Although funding agencies were interested in the overall policy framework for the sector – if only because of the fungibility of resources provided for project support – this was seldom a negotiated item. By contrast, the policy framework assumes paramount importance as part of the preconditions for sectoral support. Clearly, if an aid agency did not agree with the aims and objectives of a government's educational policy, it would be irrational for that agency to participate in a SWA. The notion of 'partnership', which, by 2000, had become the main term used to allude to the relationship between donors and recipients, implies a meeting of like-minded equals. However, the idea that the policy agenda will not be a major terrain for negotiation is, in most cases, illusion. Both the initial conditions required by donors for sectoral support, and the performance criteria used to secure their continued involvement, are now framed at a more macro level than had been required by earlier project support. Just as the aid input is 'sector-wide', so are the terms and conditions attached to its use.

By the start of the new century, the World Bank, as with many of the bilateral agencies, saw SWAs as an important means of increasing its support to education in SSA. But there were unresolved paradoxes in its thinking. The Bank recognised that more of the project/programme preparation work would need to be undertaken by national staff, so as to secure greater ownership, and that 'processes and timetables will need to be designed so that national staff can carry out quality work' (World Bank, 2001b, p.71). The ways in which this could be made compatible with an increased volume of lending being secured were not, however, explored. SWAs bring increased demands on national planning and implementation capacity, and on donors to harmonise their procurement, accounting and programming priorities and procedures. The more numerous the actors involved in financing such programmes, the more time is needed for completing programme development, preparation and agreement. Scale economies should be secured, by significantly reducing the extent of bilateral negotiations on the elements of an education programme (which, when put together, may still fall short of a coherent strategy). However, it remains an open question as to whether these benefits will more than compensate for the increased transaction costs involved in establishing SWAs.

These approaches also need a new flexibility in applying earlier procedures. The Bank recognises that 'in the context of sector-wide investment programmes, where all external resources are channelled through the government budget, and so are fungible, the Bank's reluctance to fund operating costs has no clear justification.' (op. cit, p.73). The composition of World Bank lending for education changed from about 75 per cent being for capital expenditure in the early 1980s to less than half by the early 1990s. Over the interim, there was a large increase in expenditures on textbooks and teaching materials, training, technical assistance and the beginnings of recurrent cost support (Mundy, 2001, Table 2). However, the proportion of recurrent funding required in future will need to be increased substantially beyond the tiny shares so far achieved.

Progress with a 'low enrolment strategy' for 16 SSA countries having GERs of less than 60, encouraged optimism in the Bank that a new understanding of the need for education and fiscal reform was dawning in Africa. The aim of this initiative was to encourage an education dialogue at the highest political level in these countries, to help promote understanding of the need for reform. This led to an education conference for heads of state and ministers of education and finance of the six Sahelian countries,[21] held in Bamako in November 2000. This facilitated the completion of sector programmes in Senegal and Mali, and others were to follow during 2001/02. Such optimism, however, does not, in fact, fit easily with the stated conditions which would have to be satisfied before SWAs could be financed by the Bank. 'Sound macroeconomic and fiscal policies, a demonstrated commitment to good governance, a clearly specified sector policy framework, and readiness and capacity to implement the often difficult policy decisions associated with education and financial policy reforms must be prerequisites for large-scale Bank investments in education (World Bank, 2001b, p.75). Notwithstanding recent progress, the literal interpretation of these macro conditions would still appear to exclude much of Africa from SWAs. Thus, whether this new modality for educational aid will represent a major means of increasing resource transfers in the future remains, for the present, unclear.

The Gender Impact of Sector-wide Approaches

It is important to consider whether the changed nature of the policy dialogue, which is a central characteristic of SWAs, will facilitate a more consistent policy framework for education, even if the resources available from the international community remained constrained. It is, of course, more than possible that the net effects of policy dialogue will prove to be negative. Many analysts have argued

---

21   These countries comprise Burkina Faso, Chad, Guinea, Mali, Niger and Senegal.

that this has been one consequence of the policy conditionalities attached to structural adjustment lending, in SSA and elsewhere, over recent years. The constraints on budgetary and other policies imposed by SALs appear, often, not to have facilitated a return to economic growth, and, sometimes, to have actually aggravated poverty in adjusting countries. Similar outcomes have not been entirely absent in the case of education. For example, during the 1980s, the cost-recovery policies advocated for education, including primary schooling, were as likely to have aggravated, as to have improved economic welfare in some of the poorest African and Asian countries (Tilak, 1997). The mere fact of increased debate about what constitutes 'good' policy in the South cannot, then, be taken necessarily to assure better policy choice by the governments concerned. On the other hand, in cases where government policies presently overlook – or act against – the best interests of important sections of the population (such as the poor, minority population groups, or women), further debate about the aims and instruments of policy may well bring net benefits. Important to our theme, therefore, is whether gender equity in schooling is likely to be helped or hindered by the shift towards SWAs.

Past experience can provide some pointers. Most aid in support of this objective has been in project form. Targeted interventions have been focussed upon initiatives in 'girls' education', often aimed rather narrowly at increasing their participation, by reducing constraints on attendance.[22] Scholarship schemes, and other subsidy programmes targeted at girls have been common strategies. As mentioned in Chapter 6, one of the more successful of these has been the GABLE[23] project in Malawi. Its major elements comprised the waiving of primary school fees for non-repeating girls – and for secondary-school girls following the implementation of free primary education – redesign of the curriculum to make it more gender-sensitive, provision of teacher training in gender awareness, and community sensitisation on the importance of sending girls to school. This was rather an exception to the rule, being more complex, and integrated than most project-based initiatives. In general, however, such projects have seldom tried to diagnose and tackle the broader range of constraints which conspire to keep girls out of school, or to under-perform when enrolled.

Nevertheless, it has been increasingly recognised that successful action to promote gender equity – in education and in other sectors – requires far more than single project-based interventions. In the case of the UK Department for International Development, for example, policy statements during the 1990s became increasingly strong on gender commitments – arguing that there is a structural link between gender inequality and poverty. Policy papers began to place central emphasis upon it, although, as with other agencies which have reconfirmed the international development targets, both strategic and wishful thinking too often sit uncomfortably together. For example, consider the following quotation:

---

[22]   Many such initiatives are documented by King and Hill (1993).
[23]   This is the Girls' Attainment in Basic Literacy and Education project.

> Reform to remove gender disparities in primary and secondary schooling by 2005 will receive strong support from DFID. It is an essential component of the poverty-elimination agenda. It is a strategic objective for people-centred development. This will be the second major benchmark against which DFID will assess its contribution to education for poverty elimination. (DFID, 1999, p.30)

By the year in which the paper was published, there was already no chance of achieving gender equality in educational access and attainment by 2005. Nevertheless, the central place assigned to promoting gender equality in educational strategy is required, if a rapid transition to SFA is to be achieved.

Experience varies amongst other agencies. In the case of SIDA, for example, gender guidelines for planning, taking account of the needs of women and men, and recognising women's greater workloads, were adopted in 1985. Ten years later, gender equality was formally adopted as a central goal for Sweden's development cooperation. However, although SIDA's education policy has been strongly focussed upon basic education for many years, unlike the rest of its aid policy, the articulation of gender issues in education appears to have been less highly developed (Schalkwyk, 1995, Swainson, 1997). Amongst the multilaterals, UNICEF, being a specialist agency whose primary mandate is children, has always recognised that the gender issue is central to its work, and it has stressed equality and the empowerment of girls and women as major objectives (Swainson, 1997, p.9). Moreover, as one of the four sponsors of the World Conference on Education for All in 1990, its impact upon EFA has been profound, and its spending upon basic education (primary and non-formal education [NFE]) increased markedly over the 1990s. By contrast, an internal evaluation of World Bank support (Winter and Macina, 2000) suggests that, at least in Africa, Bank lending tended not to tackle girls' education via a package of interventions addressing the full range of barriers faced by girls. It reports a focus on improving education quality and gender-sensitivity, enhancing access to school facilities and providing non-formal educational opportunities. However, unlike countries in South Asia, efforts to address the effects of poverty on girls' enrolment and retention rates were reported by the authors to be rare and, where they existed, were small-scale pilot operations. They conclude that 'it is not clear why projects in Africa do not generally include initiatives to address poverty. It can only be surmised that institutional capacity to implement such programmes may be limited' (op. cit, p.9).

Notwithstanding this varied experience, there is evidence of growing agreement between representatives of international agencies that gender 'mainstreaming', which presupposes a more comprehensive approach,[24] is needed.

---

[24]   Gender mainstreaming was proposed as a central strategy for reducing the inequalities between women and men at the Fourth World Conference on Women (Beijing, September 1995). It was defined as 'the process of assessing the implications for women and men of any planned action, including legislation, policies or programmes, in any area and at all levels. It is a strategy for making women's and men's concerns and experiences an integral dimension in the design, implementation, monitoring and evaluation of policies and programmes in all political, economic and societal spheres so that women and men benefit equally, and inequality is not perpetuated' (UN

DAC guidelines suggest two criteria for success in this regard: first, that a concern for gender equality should be integrated into the analysis and formulation of all policies, programmes and projects; second, that initiatives to enable women as well as men to formulate and express their views, and to participate in decision-making across all development issues, should be made (OECD, 1999, p.15). It follows that the task of securing reforms which allow the whole education system to work equally well for girls and boys, cannot be adequately addressed via the direct influence of one or more individual projects. Thus, a shift towards sector-wide approaches, and towards the broader policy conditionality associated with them should, in principle, enable agencies to influence gender mainstreaming in education – defined as above – more strongly than was the case with project aid.

One way to investigate the likelihood and practicality of such outcomes is to consider the experience of USAID, which has experimented with an education sectoral strategy (ESS) for educational aid for many years. It suggests what can be expected from adopting an integrated approach to the sector if SWAs were to become as widespread as many agencies presently wish and intend. The ESS approach emerged in response to several factors: first, a general consensus that a systemic approach was required for achieving lasting educational change; second, a recognition that both governments and donors must plan and act within existing resource constraints; third, a renewed acknowledgement of the fundamental role played by basic education in development; and fourth, a willingness to commit relatively large sums of money to basic education in Africa. The main form of support has been non-project assistance, disbursed to governments in tranches when mutually established conditions are met. These conditions have reflected the implementation of key policy, institutional and expenditure reforms.

During the 1990s, USAID had ESS programmes in 12 countries in SSA. Their goal was to increase the number of children entering and completing primary school, and to improve the quality of their learning in ways that were efficient and sustainable. Tietjen (1997, p.3) reports that these four dimensions – access, quality, efficiency and sustainability – were emphasised according to the needs of the individual country. However, almost all of these ESS programmes included a fifth dimension – equity – stressing the needs of poor children and girls in particular. The equity aims were generally subsidiary to those of restructuring and stabilisation. Nonetheless, eight of the ESS programmes contained notable components aimed at alleviating gender differences in educational outcomes. Of these the Malawi ESS was the only one in which girls constituted the prime focus of the programme – both as targeted primary beneficiaries, and in terms of programme content and policy reform.[25] In most other countries, girls were

---

ECOSOC, 1997). These principles were adopted by UNICEF, the Commonwealth Secretariat, UNESCO, ILO and many other international agencies, to guide programming objectives in their own sectors. A useful and full discussion of concepts and definitions can be found in UNESCO (2000d). The definitions given by OECD DAC, in the text, are further examples of these.

[25] It is interesting to note that the Malawi case – in which gender equity was stated as the sole purpose of the programme – appears to have been informed as much by a wish on

targeted beneficiaries, with programme components designed to improve their participation in primary schooling. Conditionalities attached to these programmes required progress with such participation to have been achieved, in order to gain access to further funding.

The approach was innovative and important in several respects. Evaluations, based upon an assessment of results in the 12 SSA countries, indicated that ESS worked well where the government commitment to reform was strong, where the sectoral strategy was well-defined and where the reform agenda did not greatly exceed existing or attainable institutional capacity within the country.[26]

A later assessment of the progress with girls' education in these countries (O'Gara *et al.*, 1999) concludes that in most, there were significant improvements in the enrolment, persistence, or performance of girls since the start of USAID support. Furthermore, the improvements were stronger where USAID had made girls a primary client of the ESS programme, where it helped the government define the policy reform framework, and where performance conditions to provided leverage for policy change were put in place.

> Such improvements are most often brought about through a series of actions that includes policies and programmes to carry them out, and that takes place simultaneously in several areas and at several levels in an education system. (op. cit, p.10)

In principle, then, this experience seems encouraging for the potential positive impact of SWAs, which share a number of common features with the ESS approach.

Whether similar success has occurred in practice, however, is difficult to tell. One evaluation of SWAs in Uganda and Ghana found that policy coherence in education, including the importance given to gender equity in policies and budgets, had improved in Uganda as a consequence of its SWA, but that there was no significant improvement in the case of Ghana.[27] There were signs of gendered benefits being gained from sector-wide analysis, from longer-term planning perspectives, and from cross-sectoral linkages. But in neither country were these potential benefits of the SWA approach properly exploited. In addition, donor

---

the part of USAID to secure fertility decline (via increasing the educational level of women) as to secure gender equity in education *per se* (Tietjen, 1997, p.4). Hitherto USAID believed that high levels of fertility in Malawi represented a development constraint which could and should be tackled. They claimed that the evidence on the relationship between female education and fertility decline was sufficiently strong to justify the agency's education strategy in those terms. On the other hand, since education had not been included in USAID's country plan, whereas population control had been included, the emphasis given to the link between education and fertility, could be interpreted more cynically – as being merely necessary to gain headquarters' approval for an education programme in Malawi.

[26] See USAID (1995b). For a detailed description of each of the national programmes in SSA see USAID (1995a).

[27] ODI/CEC (2000, Annex 4).

agencies' funding strategies for the sector were 'diverse and contradictory' in Ghana (though not in Uganda), and in both countries some ambiguity of commitment to gender equity goals in education remained. Whether the emphasis upon local leadership of the process would be conducive of greater gender equity was thus uncertain. Nevertheless, the review concludes that:

> not only in our three country studies, but also from … the literature review, it can be seen that as long as governments and donors are engaged in a constructive fashion, processes may be initiated which reinforce the potential strengths. (op. cit., p.31)

More generally this experience suggests that, in order to influence gender equity positively, SWAs need to be coherent, and agencies need to have a shared understanding of what constitutes an appropriate gender strategy in education. The latter often appears to have been absent, with poor communication between gender specialists and other professionals being frequent. Even where this is not so, however, it is unlikely that SWAs, acting alone, could drive policy change. A strong national policy is needed within and beyond the education sector, with a supporting institutional framework backed by the aid agencies. 'Mainstreaming' implies that the process should be reflected throughout the entire sector – not just packaged as a series of 'girls' education' projects. All those involved in planning need to take responsibility for the gender aspects of their sectoral responsibilities, rather than leaving these matters to gender specialists. This has seldom happened in practice. Careful diagnosis of the local constraints to achieving gender equity is needed. These differ from country to country, and imply that national policies need to be locally designed. Thus, the process of preparing and agreeing a SWA can provide an opportunity for the establishment of gender mainstreaming, provided that the appropriate local preconditions exist, and provided that the parties to the partnership have a shared vision of what can be achieved.

Conclusions

To return to the questions posed at the outset of this chapter, it is certain that aid to education would need to increase very substantially if SFA in Africa were to be achieved within 15 years. Even given the implementation of strong policy reform, a return to healthy economic growth and increased commitment of African governments to spending more of the resources generated by that growth on education, annual aid for education in the nine countries studied here would need to more than double, in real terms, over a 15-year period to achieve SFA. These resources would be needed as annual recurrent expenditure support.

Whether resources on this scale will be made available is, of course, highly uncertain. Over the 1990s northern aid representatives talked much about their commitment to provide increased resource transfers, whilst, at the same time, their political masters reduced their scale substantially. The cuts were very unequally felt, with those affecting Africa being more intense than elsewhere. Education, notwithstanding its direct impact upon poverty alleviation, caught out almost *pro rata* with other sectors. The reasons for the anti-Africa bias in aid allocations were not recognised, let alone tackled. There are, therefore, grounds to doubt that the next decade will see the transformation in aid relations with Africa that is required, if SFA is to be broadly achieved by 2015.

Debt rescheduling, and debt forgiveness, remain very important means of reducing future resource outflows from SSA. Further concessions, under the auspices of the Paris Club, will be needed to help reduce budgetary constraints in future years. As regards the HIPC provisions for reducing multilateral and bilateral debt, we have argued that the arrangements holding in 2000/01 will have only a limited impact upon net resource generation in the most indebted countries. Targeting HIPC resources towards the social sectors will help, but in some of the poorest countries in SSA, their impact will be more strongly felt in providing legitimacy for earlier levels of default on debt-service payments, than upon the total resources available for education or other purposes. We conclude that the expectations of the World Bank and others, concerning the extent to which expanded debt relief under the HIPC initiative can sustain accelerated education development, are likely, on present evidence, to prove over-optimistic.

The move to sector-wide approaches, whilst welcome, brings some uncomfortable attendant risks. It appears unlikely that this changed modality will, *per se,* stimulate an increased volume of aid over the medium term, although it may provide localised scale economies for individual countries. New kinds of transaction costs are likely to slow the process, in ways that are presently unpredictable. Not all aid agencies will, in any case, find it possible to switch away from their earlier modalities. Finally, although the policy dialogue, which is intrinsic to a sectoral approach, provides new opportunities for making creative progress on gender concerns, such an outcome would require strong concurrence between all parties to the partnership. There will be new challenges for knowledge-sharing, policy planning and co-ordination, which have not been notable characteristics of the aid dialogue in the past.

Chapter 8

Conclusions –
What Have We Learned?

Introduction

The analysis of problems of education, gender and development can be informed by at least three analytic perspectives. The first of these is a 'rights-based' approach. Notions of equality and social justice support the view that each individual has a right to be treated equally as regards access to publicly provided goods and services, and to the opportunities arising from such access. The second is a framework informed by notions of individual capacity and capability. If development success is measured in these terms, and if education can promote such capacities, increasing equitable access to education becomes a direct means of achieving development. The third derives from the role of education in helping men and women to achieve other desired development goals – such as economic prosperity, better health, lower mortality and fairer societies. These three notions – that education is a right, that increased participation in it directly constitutes development, and that it indirectly promotes other development goals – are not necessarily competitive with each other. They may all be true, and if they are, the case for trying to achieve both increased enrolments and greater equality in the enrolments of girls and boys is, *prima facie*, strong.

We have not chosen, in this book, to add to the large amount of evidence relevant to each of these notions. Rather, we have taken it as given that achieving schooling for all with gender equity – which comprise two of the eight universally adopted millennium development goals – are desirable aims for national and international policy. Our interest and intent has been to investigate why the achievement of these goals remains stubbornly elusive and, in doing so, to help identify the national and international strategies which could be instrumental in turning things around. This final chapter draws together the evidence and analysis of earlier chapters, and assesses what we have learned.

Explaining the Levels and Composition of Enrolments

Explaining the relative levels of school enrolments in different countries, together with their gendered characteristics, has been an important aim of this book. One way of tackling this question is summarised in Figure 8.1. This is a standard economic approach, whereby the supply of schooling is given by national expenditures, costs and population size, and where its demand is given by household incomes, direct and indirect costs, expected benefits and other influences on choice. These latter would include gender relations, household preferences and the extent to which schooling is wanted as an end-in-itself. Such a formulation informed our analysis, particularly, though not only, in Chapters 2 and 4. However, one problem with it is that gender is relegated to the 'other' category, and seems to be more of an afterthought than an important determinant of the process. This is unsatisfactory, since gender may strongly and directly affect other individual determinants, particularly costs and benefits, both of which are important ingredients in the demand picture.

Supply:

National expenditures on education

Average costs per pupil

Size of the school-age population

Demand:

Household income

Costs per pupil

Expected benefits

Other determinants of choice, e.g. gender roles

Figure 8.1 Determinants of school enrolments

Accordingly, in Chapter 1, we suggested a framework in which low incomes and high costs facing both states and households might lead to low enrolments, whilst gender relations in households, schools, the labour market and in society more broadly, were mainly responsible for their gender composition. This may be neat, but it is also too reductionist: gender does not influence outcomes sequentially – i.e. only after the aggregate enrolment decision has been made. Rather, it affects directly all aspects of the household choice to send children to school. However, the framework is useful in that it suggests a broader terrain than is present in many economic inquiries. Gender is often used as a dummy variable in empirical analyses, so as to examine its impact upon other variables of interest. Here, a more disaggregated approach is implied. Rather than treating gender as an ascribed characteristic – like being over six feet tall, or having blue eyes – our framework invites analysis of its social context. It suggests closer investigation of how, and in what ways, gender has an influence upon schooling outcomes, so as to reveal more about how the latter can best be improved. The main results arising from the use of these different, but complementary, analytic approaches will be discussed from the perspective of states and households (macro and micro issues) separately.

Macro Issues

Room for manoeuvre   Although poorer states tend to have lower primary enrolments than richer ones, the strength of this relationship is, in fact, surprisingly weak. The range of primary enrolment ratios in SSA, amongst countries at similar income levels – e.g. from around 30 in Ethiopia and Mali to over 100 in Malawi, and Uganda – itself suggests that variables other than income tend to have decisive influence. Chapter 2 demonstrated that the simple relationship between gross enrolment rates and per capita income is only weakly positive across countries, and Chapter 3 confirms that this remains so even when other relevant variables are controlled. Furthermore, across all countries, a 10 per cent increase in per capita income was associated with an increase in the primary enrolment ratio of only about one per cent, with little difference being apparent for the enrolment of girls and boys. The main point here is not that getting richer makes little difference. Rather it is that governments appear to have viable options to achieve high levels of primary enrolments, even if overall resources, at the macro level, are constrained. Thus, the policy space to achieve UPE, if not the more demanding SFA is larger than at first seems possible for the poorer countries of Africa.

Public expenditures   The supply of primary school places requires buildings, books, equipment, teachers and other staff. The costs of these items are mainly met by governments. Accordingly, public spending has a critical role in producing high levels of primary enrolment in good quality schools. However, because resources can be used either to provide more school places, or to improve the quality of schooling for those already enrolled, there is no simple relationship between public spending and enrolments. On the other hand, where both enrolments and school quality are low, as in much of SSA, it is almost certain that public spending – its magnitude, composition or both – is partly to blame.

It was shown in Chapter 2 that, uniquely amongst developing regions, enrolment ratios in SSA fell over 1980-90, recovering somewhat by the turn of the century. This was in spite of the fact that average public expenditure allocations to education (as a proportion of GNP) increased over those years, such that SSA's allocation was actually higher than any other developing region. But because national incomes were stagnant or falling this increased emphasis was compatible with many countries incurring sharp declines in real spending on a *per capita* or per pupil basis. Teachers' morale was badly hit, particularly by the falling value of their salaries, and the quality of schooling fell into widespread decline. By contrast, in most other developing regions the real value of public educational spending increased, and steady increases in primary enrolment ratios were achieved.   Thus, the enrolment gap between SSA and other regions rose considerably over these two decades, such that, by 2000 almost half of the world's out-of-school primary-level children lived in SSA.

To add to the difficulties caused by declining incomes, the pattern of relatively high commitment to public spending on primary schooling was not reflected throughout the region. Some countries were spending far less than others, and substantially less than they could have afforded. Our calculations in Chapter 2 showed that 10 countries, with GERs ranging between 48 and 90 in the early 1990s could have universalised provision (at existing levels of unit costs) by raising their primary spending to the regional average level of 2 per cent of GNP. Using data for later in the decade, Chapter 4 showed that public commitment to spending on primary schooling in our nine case-study countries varied greatly, but that, in a majority of them, it was too low. Moreover, four of the countries – Guinea, Senegal, Mali and Zambia – could have universalised provision if they had increased their public spending on the primary system to the average level for SSA.

Costs In many countries, too, the costs of primary schooling presented severe problems. In some, a major constraint was the total cost per school completer, which was high because of deeply embedded inefficiencies in the school systems. High levels of repetition and of drop-out from primary school resulted in only a minority of enrolled children ever completing it. In the cases of Guinea, Malawi and Uganda, the total years of study taken per completer amounted to between two and three times as long as the primary course. In these circumstances, achieving the educational gains from completing primary schooling cost more than twice as much as should have been required.

In most of the low-enrolment countries in SSA, notwithstanding the overall adequacy of their spending allocations, high unit costs of schooling constituted a particular constraint on the ability of governments to universalise primary schooling. By consequence, for a majority of the 12 countries in this category in the early 1990s, universal provision would have required their governments to make very large expenditure commitments for this purpose. Annual expenditure allocations (relative to GNP) of between 1.5 and 3 times the SSA average would have been needed.

Thus, both expenditures on primary schooling (as a proportion of GNP) and costs per pupil (relative to per capita income) vary widely across SSA, within a range of around 1:10 in each case. Most of the nine countries to which we gave particular attention were 'low commitment' cases, so the expenditure variation was smaller, with a range of less than 1:3 as between Guinea and Mali on the one hand and Malawi on the other. Of the nine governments, only that of Malawi spent more than the SSA mean value of two per cent of GNP on primary schooling. There was, however, greater variation in unit costs, with extreme values (relative to per capita income) in a ratio of 1:9 as between Uganda and Ethiopia and 1:5 in absolute $PPP terms for the same two countries.

Not surprisingly, then, being able to keep expenditures per pupil at relatively modest levels turns out to have had a major influence upon the ability of governments to secure high rates of enrolment. Across the nine countries, the simple relationship between unit costs and enrolment rates was strongly negative, with over 70 per cent of the variance in GERs being explained by unit cost differences. More generally, our multivariate analysis in Chapter 3 showed that, across all developing regions, a 10 per cent increase in unit costs (for values around the mean levels) was associated with a fall in primary gross enrolment rates of just over two per cent.

This negative association between unit costs and enrolment rates strongly suggests that a major priority for policy reform in Africa will be a search for effective measures to reduce the unit costs of primary schooling. However, although this is true, it does not necessarily imply that a policy of minimising unit costs must be sought under all circumstances. This becomes plain if we consider how unit costs are determined. In SSA, those countries with high unit costs also had high teacher salaries (relative to per capita incomes). Sometimes this had structural causes – as in Ethiopia, where formal employment was very low and teachers were in a skilled and particularly privileged minority of the labour force. Sometimes there were historical causes. In the Francophone countries, for example, teachers have been highly paid, relative to other groups, for many years. We have shown that their earnings fell substantially, relative both to per capita incomes, and to earnings in the Anglophone countries, over the last two decades of the twentieth century. But further adjustment would be needed in several of them, if SFA were to be achieved in the near future. There are however, limits to the desirability of this process. For example, whilst it is true that low teacher-earnings in Malawi and Uganda (the high enrollers, and the lowest-cost cases amongst the nine) facilitated rapid expansion of primary schooling, they were also partly caused by the expansion itself. Acute shortages of trained teachers, in the face of rapidly increasing demand, led to a large number of new, young, untrained teachers being taken on in both countries. They were paid much less than most of the existing staff, and average salary costs per teacher fell accordingly. Although this helped alleviate the government's financial constraint, the final mix of trained and untrained teachers was by no means optimal from the point of view of the quality of schooling available.

A second example is given by pupil-teacher ratios, which have a major influence upon unit costs – the higher the former the lower the latter. Accordingly, they can also be used to make high teacher-earnings more affordable. We found that this option was taken up particularly by Francophone states. In those countries, the cost-impact of teachers' salaries, which were, on average, almost three-times as large as those in Anglophone Africa (relative to per capita income), was substantially reduced by pupil-teacher ratios being 50 per cent greater than in the Anglophone countries. More generally, our cross-country analysis in Chapter 3 indicated that, keeping income and other factors constant, a ten percentage increase in the pupil-teacher ratio was associated with an increase in the GER of around three per cent.

This, then, provides an important additional instrument for securing increased enrolments. Again, however, it turns out to be feasible only within limits. In the nine countries, pupil-teacher ratios varied between 30:1 and 75:1, on average.

Those countries with high ratios, which included Mali, Malawi, and Uganda, often had intolerably large classes, particularly in the early years of schooling, by consequence of which pupils' learning clearly suffered. We demonstrate in Chapter 6 that it is possible to increase pupil-teacher ratios, by using double-shift and other arrangements, in ways which can help to protect class size whilst reducing costs. But such initiatives have often not been used carefully enough in SSA. More frequent have been circumstances where high pupil-teacher (and pupil-class) ratios have undermined school quality, whilst very low salaries have directly undermined teacher-morale. Accordingly, the particular combination of values for these items becomes critically important. Experience suggests that countries should aim at the middle-range in each case: pupil-class ratios of around 40-45 and salaries about four times as large as per capita incomes, seem about right in most SSA circumstances.[1]

The final important cost-item is learning materials. Expenditures on these items are less significant in the case of SSA countries than is desirable. In the nine countries, provision for learning materials was usually grossly inadequate. Textbooks were generally provided by aid agencies, and nationally-financed expenditures were very low. On average, in our case-study countries, they amounted to about 9 per cent of annual per-pupil expenditures, and less than $US8 per child (in PPP terms). Although these items are critical to the quality of schooling, they tend to be dispensed with first when public sectors experience economic adversity. This is because they can usually be cut back with lower attendant political (though not educational) costs than is entailed by salary decline or redundancy.

Gender Girls' enrolments and performance in school remain low, relative to those of boys, in much of SSA. Although the gaps narrowed somewhat during the 1990s, this was primarily because male enrolment ratios fell more quickly than those of females, rather than because of particularly strong progress being made on behalf of girls. In the absence of policy change, as enrolment growth begins to recover, there is more than a possibility that the process will be reversed, and that the gender gap will widen again.

Obviously there are natural limits to this process in that, even with strong discrimination being present, after the point where most boys were enrolled, further progress in enrolment growth would have to be delivered by a growth in female enrolments. Nevertheless, such change can be slow and patchy. We showed in Chapter 2 that, although the extent of gender bias does reduce as enrolments rise across countries, the relationship is loose, and there are many cases where GERs approach 100, yet where strong enrolment imbalances between the genders remain.

Furthermore, national income per head appears to have even less influence upon the inequality of enrolments between boys and girls than it does upon their absolute levels. It emerged as having neither statistical nor economic significance

---

[1]   This compares with salaries which were twice as large as per capita income in Uganda, where teacher earnings were much too low, and twelve times as large as per capita income in Ethiopia, where they were considerably higher than the average.

in explaining the gender gap in the multivariate analysis of Chapter 3. A more concrete example is provided by comparing Guinea, on the one hand, where less than half the number of girls are enrolled as boys, with Tanzania on the other, where rough gender equality in enrolments has been maintained. Such differences have nothing to do with their relative levels of per capita income. Tanzania, a poorer country than Guinea, has pursued a set of gender policies over many years, which has produced these enrolment outcomes. Its experience has demonstrated that policy reforms focussed upon achieving gender equality need not be particularly expensive – yet they can make a large difference to the absolute size and composition of enrolments.

The macro analysis clearly suggests that the achievement of gender equality in enrolments and performance will not be delivered as an automatic product either of the overall expansion of access to schooling, nor by awaiting the diffused benefits from economic growth. The main causes of enrolment imbalances between girls and boys appear to lie mainly elsewhere, and require a more targeted approach if they are to be addressed. The design of such policies requires a more micro, inter-disciplinary approach to the identification of constraints, particularly at the levels of the household and the school. It is to these aspects of our results that we now turn.

Micro Issues

Household incomes Perhaps surprisingly, in view of what has been said above, the evidence reviewed in Chapter 3, from household surveys in Africa, suggested that higher household income improves the chances of a child attending school, and that this positive impact tends to remain even when some of the factors correlated with income, such as location and school quality, are included. Further, where measures of income have been unavailable, many studies have found that household assets, such as land and livestock, have been positively associated with enrolment. As regards the gendered impact of income, one study in Guinea found significant income elasticities of demand for schooling, which were higher for girls than boys, although most other studies were incorclusive on this point, and firm conclusions could not be drawn.

In our own schools surveys, discussed in Chapter 5, however, low household assets and income were found to be strongly associated with low school attendance, and in this case, particularly for girls. Those attending school in all nine countries were from better-off households than school drop-outs, who, in turn, were from richer households than those who had never enrolled in school. Increased household incomes and assets were found to have a strong impact upon school attendance, and more so for girls than for boys.

How can these different results from macro and micro analyses be reconciled? There are probably two main factors. First, measures of *per capita* income are silent about the distribution of income amongst households. Countries where inequality has been high, such as Guinea, have had a larger proportion of poor households than a country like Tanzania, where inequality, historically, has been lower. This may be one cause of their different levels and composition of school enrolments, which cannot be detected in macro analyses, in the absence of good proxies for income distribution. Second, micro studies have a much better chance of measuring other factors relevant to household schooling decisions, such as family size and structure and the direct costs of school attendance, which allow income effects to be revealed. Our results imply, therefore, that it is *pro-poor* growth, rather than economic growth *per se* (or the structure of growth rather than its overall magnitude) which is helpful to achieving SFA.

Costs Direct costs to households were revealed by our surveys to be a critical constraint affecting school attendance. Private household expenditures in all nine countries were high. In the seven for which we have comparable data, they varied from $US40-60 per child (in PPP terms), which represented between 20 and 50 per cent of total primary unit costs. By consequence, these costs were a critical deterrent to parents sending their children to school. In all of the country studies, they were shown to be the most important single cause of early-leaving and of children not being enrolled in primary school. In each of the countries, their largest constituent elements were school fees and, in particular, the cost of purchasing school uniforms, or other clothing to wear at school. As the experiences of Malawi and Uganda have demonstrated, the reduction or removal of these costs represents one of the most potent instruments available to African governments wishing to affect the overall level of primary enrolments.

As regards the indirect costs incurred by households in sending their children to school, the surveys in all the countries indicated that children's need to work for money, or to help in the household or family farm, were important reasons for non-enrolment. But different gender relations and expectations concerning the roles of boys and girls lead to a complex pattern of opportunity costs. Whether they were attending school or not, girls performed more work in the household than boys. They were thus more likely to drop out of school, both because higher opportunity costs were associated with their attendance and because demands from home made them likely to perform worse than boys at school. Their work in the household also prevented girls earning money so easily as boys. This affected their schooling opportunities since boys' earnings were often used to help meet their own schooling costs. Rarely were these made available to support the education of siblings. The household work-burden was greater for children from poorer households, and it is, therefore, the girls from such households who lose out most in terms of schooling opportunities.

Complex interactions were revealed between household size and the incidence of child work. In large households with a high child/adult ratio, the opportunity costs of school attendance per child are lower, because household tasks can be shared amongst more children. So, the probability of school attendance was greater amongst children of such households. But, even in such cases, the evidence suggests that age-structure, birth order and gender are all separately important in determining schooling chances. In particular, it seems that girls from poor households, with few sisters and with older brothers were least likely to attend school. These results are largely supported by the household survey evidence reviewed in Chapter 3, where being early in the birth order within a larger family has been found, in a number of studies, to increase the probability of attending school.

Physical provision It is obvious that, if children are to enrol in primary education, there has to be a school close enough from them to attend. It is unsurprising therefore that our surveys confirmed that the greater the physical distance from home to school, the less likely it is that children will enrol. There was evidence from the focus group discussions that the negative effects of distance were stronger for girls owing mainly to greater parental fears for the safety of their daughters *en route* to school. Most of the African household surveys reviewed in Chapter 3 also found that distance to school had a negative and significant impact upon demand for schooling. On the other hand, although a number of these studies have hypothesised that the effects for girls would be greater, no empirical evidence for this was found.

Our surveys confirmed that an absence of latrines, and particularly of private facilities for girls have a negative impact on enrolment and attendance. Insufficient desks and chairs emerged as significant additional items in the focus group discussions with gender effects again being present. Finally, the lack of nearby access to a secondary school was also found to reduce the demand for primary schooling in a number of the study countries. Some of these characteristics have also been identified in earlier qualitative studies of constraints on school attendance in Africa, and our own work in the nine countries strengthens this evidence considerably.

School quality It is difficult, using cross-country macro evidence, to demonstrate connections between school quality and the level or structure of enrolments, although Chapter 3 did show that inefficient school systems, where levels of repetition were high, have lower female enrolments, relative to those of males, than more efficient systems. However, evidence from our school surveys and focus groups indicated that parents were influenced, in deciding to educate their children, by whether or not they thought that the school was effective. Class-size, whether teaching occurred out of doors and the length of the school day were all factors which influenced the parental views of school quality, and decisions about whether to enrol their children. In some cases, parents wanted 'relevant' education for their children – expressed as curricula which included some teaching in life-skills such as agriculture – but they did not support children having to undertake practical work activities which raised money for the school, or which provided unpaid domestic help to the teachers.

The econometric analysis in Chapter 3 showed that, across countries, a higher proportion of female teachers is strongly associated with greater equality between male and female primary enrolments, after controlling for income differences and other relevant variables. At a more micro level, the evidence from our school surveys and focus groups discussed in Chapter 5, also confirmed that a good balance of female teachers in schools had an important impact on the likelihood of girls enrolling and staying in school. This is because female teachers tend to improve the self-confidence of girl pupils, partly by providing them with role models, particularly in rural areas where few other women may be in positions of authority. They also provide an important source of advice and support during the transition to puberty, when many girls otherwise leave school. Parents were more likely to send their daughters to schools having women teachers. They felt that teaching would be more effective, and their fears for the physical and sexual safety of their daughters were more likely to be allayed.

Other aspects of gender relations The detailed results from our schools surveys and focus group discussions showed that many other aspects of gender relations also helped to produce the differential outcomes in school enrolments and performance for girls and boys. Cultural norms and traditional beliefs and practices concerning gender roles were found to have a strong influence. These results added rich texture to the implications that could be gleaned from the cross-country work and from the household demand studies. For example, using the average age of girls at first marriage as a proxy for the prevalence of traditional mores in society, our cross country results established that early marriage-age was associated with significantly lower enrolment ratios, particularly for girls, after controlling for income and other relevant variables. However, material from our schools surveys allows detailed description of the nature of some of the traditional practices, correlated with early marriage, which lead to the under-enrolment and under-performance of girls in school. This elucidation of the causal processes involved, goes well beyond what can be concluded from the results of the more aggregated empirical work.

A discussion of these results and conclusions is provided in Chapter 5 and will not be further undertaken here. They confirm, however, that it is necessary to examine the context and detail of gender-relations, if their impact upon the relative life-chances of girls and boys is to be understood. Thus, societal practices as regards the initiation of young people, pregnancy, and early marriage, which often lead to girls' early withdrawal from school, are strongly influenced by tradition and poverty. These interactions need to be documented in each country, if policy responses to them are to be introduced, let alone to stand much chance of success. Similarly, the gendered division of labour, both in the household and in the labour market, result in discriminatory outcomes which disadvantage girls, increasing the costs and reducing the benefits of schooling, to both themselves and their parents. Our studies confirmed the results found by many of the African household surveys, that the educational background of parents affects their children's schooling, and that the education of mothers was particularly influential in determining daughters' education. In this way, where girls receive less access to schooling than boys, the bias tends to be passed on inter-generationally. More generally, common attitudes and opinions held in society at large tend to be reinforced within the school environment. Thus, our surveys also showed that school-teachers' attitudes towards children's intelligence and competence in different subjects, and their opinions about the extent to which children are likely to find schooling useful, were systematically more favourable to boys than to girls. The perceived risk of sexual harassment, from teachers as well as peers, also provided further disincentives for parents to enrol their daughters. These and other characteristics provide a formidable array of constraints – in society, labour market, school and household – which add to the tendencies towards low school enrolments in poorer societies, but which work to the particular disadvantage of girls.

Implications for Theory

This has been primarily an empirical study. However, since we began the book with a review of theoretical approaches to problems of gender, education and development, it would be useful to indicate some of the implications of our work for this more abstract terrain. Many of our results have strong relevance for the ways in which gendered educational outcomes are explained. Firstly, there seems little evidence for the view, advocated by some liberal theorists, that under-enrolment at primary level, both in general and of girls in particular, are phenomena which are primarily caused by low national incomes. If it were true, paying attention to accelerating national income growth could be expected to alleviate the enrolment problem *pari passu*. Yet we have shown that achieving increased levels of *per capita* income is neither a necessary nor a sufficient condition for higher enrolments, and the statistical relationship between these variables is weak. On the other hand, our work suggests that household incomes, which are poorly proxied by measures of national income *per capita*, do have a major influence upon enrolments. Thus, it appears that at least pro-poor growth is required if the enrolment problem is to be alleviated. We have also shown that the gendered composition of enrolments is less strongly explained by income than by other variables. So, within poor states, the distribution of income is likely to matter greatly to enrolment outcomes, and the gendered pattern of enrolments, though influenced by household income, is importantly linked to other variables. We can conclude, therefore, that achieving schooling for all in SSA will require far more than merely a return to healthy economic growth over the medium term.

One branch of orthodox theory suggests that discriminatory behaviour in the labour market, which is one of the causes of girls being more frequently out of school than boys, is a form of market imperfection – where the tastes of employers, employees, or both, lead to the wages paid to women being a lower proportion of their marginal value products than those paid to men. This hypothesis, associated with the work of Becker and others, appears flawed in its own terms, in that competitive pressures from those employers prepared to use more of the cheaper (female) labour should, over time, lead to the removal of discrimination if its source were so simply founded. That this seems not to happen gives us cause to doubt its veracity. Our own work, however, suggests that it is in any case likely to have only partial relevance in the context of African states. This is mainly because wage discrimination is neither the only nor, probably, the most important manifestation of gender inequality in African labour markets. There are strong traditions of job reservation, of differences in promotion practices and in access to posts with more responsibility, which consistently favour males. A lack of role models leads women to be content with less than they deserve, and men to expect that this will be so. Thus, a theory of discrimination in African labour markets needs to go beyond accounting for the persistence of 'irrational' wage differentials between men and women. It needs also to focus upon the mechanisms of access to, and rationing of opportunities in the labour market. Such processes of discrimination are not easy to summarise by means of a single statistic, such as Becker's 'discrimination coefficient'. These mechanisms (which take the form of institutions or conventions) would still have a decisive impact upon the relative life chances of African women and men, even if, within occupations, the remuneration of all people with similar human capital characteristics were the same.

It follows that, in Africa, non-wage-related labour-market signals should form a more prominent part of the explanation for the existence of differential gendered incentives to attend school than in more industrialised settings. A second, and not unrelated implication of our work, is that the range of constraints faced by girls in gaining access to schooling – which, as indicated later, go well beyond labour market incentives – is also greater in Africa. Thus the presuppositions of standard theories of discrimination, in the tradition of Becker, do not adequately capture the complexity of African society, and their predictive value in these settings is, therefore, limited.

Those economic models which seem better in capturing the reality usually incorporate the notion of there being different social conventions which influence the returns to education differently for boys and girls. For example, some approaches integrate differences in the use of male and female child labour, or different societal roles for men and women, showing how these, in turn, lead to gendered differences in the economic returns to education. In such cases, standard economic theory can begin to flourish, positing, for example, the existence of principal-agent problems which lead to parental discrimination between the education of sons and daughters, or of lower market returns to women, leading them to expect fewer benefits from education than men, etc. In these circumstances economic theory can utilise its traditional methods of predicting outcomes, given particular sets of assumptions about how society works, to explain the persistence of gender gaps in the schooling process.

These approaches allow some progress to be made. Yet they are typically limited to demonstrating the sub-optimality of outcomes determined in the context of imperfect markets. They show that, if the social and economic constraints leading to gender inequalities were overcome, most people would be better off. What is missing, however – because these 'imperfections' are incorporated as part of the logic used to predict the outcomes – is some explanation of their causes. This is necessary if we are to understand how best they might be removed. It is as if the very act of pointing to the irrationality of gender inequalities will lead to their being rejected and reformed.

We showed in Chapter 1 that this mode of theorising also characterised WID theories during the early stages of analytic work on gender inequality. Writers in this tradition certainly added to our understanding, by providing detailed descriptions of the dynamics of inequality in its stereotypical terrains – wages, education, access to services and to other opportunities. But these approaches retained a rather simplified economic cloak. They tended still to emphasise the social irrationality of inequality, and to suggest how much better off developing countries would be if they recognised the hidden, and presently wasted, human resource represented by their women. They argued that policy change was needed, so that these resources could be utilised. The policy process however, remained unanalysed in most of these writings. It was as if things would change fundamentally if those at the top of the policy pyramid realised the errors of their ways, and simply changed their approach to what they did.

Our work has shown that this is a most misguided set of assumptions to use. The nature of gender relations in society is capable of affecting substantially the logic of rationality. For example, although conventionally estimated rates-of-return may suggest parental irrationality in favouring boys' over girls' schooling, the prices used in such calculations often do not reflect household realities. Higher opportunity costs of attendance for girls are not reflected in estimations which use wages foregone as a proxy. Further, female unemployment is usually underestimated and the impact of uncertainty (and tradition) on household behaviour is ignored. So, it is safer to assume that revealed behaviour is a rational response to the opportunities and constraints faced by households, some of which are ignored by traditional analysis. Simple advocacy of change, in response to revealed inequality, is unlikely to affect the basis for such behaviour in any serious way. This can only be done by changing the nature or intensity of the constraints themselves.

We have shown that these are indeed profound. Although at the household level there tends to be a hierarchy of constraints – with both direct and indirect costs of schooling usually being the most important – both their range and intensity differ sharply between countries. We have found it helpful to consider the domains of household, school, labour market and society separately – in spite of obvious areas of overlap between these categories. Some factors appeared frequently across different countries. For example, in addition to household costs, we found that the gendered division of labour at home and in the labour market, the lack of female role models, the prevalence of sexist attitudes and behaviour in schools, inadequate school facilities for girls, the age of marriage, initiation practices and customary beliefs were amongst the most commonly recurring constraints affecting female enrolment and performance. It is important to note that few of these are specific to the education sector. Most are society-wide phenomena which have an important influence upon gender equity more generally. Moreover, their particular characteristics, and the degree to which they affect household behaviour, differ sharply between countries. Accordingly, there is no single package of policies that can be applied to address gender inequality in schooling. Local analysis and diagnosis of the problem is crucial, and the relevance of particular policy changes depends entirely upon local circumstances.

Our analysis does however, strongly suggest the need to go beyond the kind of economic methodology summarised by Figure 8.1. Although its concentration upon costs and expenditures by the State, and upon incomes and costs at household level, are well reflected in our own approach, the range and importance of the additional constraints to achieving gender equality in schooling, which our work has demonstrated, tends to be totally overlooked. The framework suggested in

Chapter 1 (Figure 1.1), where economic factors and gender relations interact with each other, appears to give them better weight. It indicates more clearly that achieving SFA will require simultaneous actions to increase State expenditures on primary schooling, to reduce household costs and – equally importantly – to reduce the intensity of constraints to achieving gender equality in schools and throughout society.

The Political Economy of Reform

The education and economic reforms required of developing country governments, if the millenium development goals are to be met, are considerable. Chapter 2 showed that around half of the low enrolment countries in SSA could, in principle, expand enrolments to UPE levels by increasing public spending to the regional average amount (relative to GNP).[2] However, the other half would need much higher spending levels, and cost reductions would also need to be an important part of their reform strategy. Chapter 4 showed that amongst our nine country cases, four of the seven low enrollers could meet the costs of UPE with an allocation of public spending equal to the regional average. Resource requirements in two of the others were higher, but could probably be met, but in Ethiopia the resource gap appeared very difficult to bridge.

The demands of SFA, however, are considerably greater than this. Enrolments would be higher than UPE levels, to the extent that any repetition or over-age enrolment remained in the system. Quality-focussed reforms to teacher costs, class size and learning materials all require more resources than UPE – sometimes substantially so. Nevertheless, Chapter 6 showed how the nine countries could achieve SFA, whilst indicating that the extent of additional spending required would be, in some cases, very large indeed. Chapter 7 analysed the resource gaps in more detail, and showed that a very substantial increase in external aid to education would be needed if all the gaps were to be closed. It concluded that achieving SFA over 15 years in these nine countries, which in the mid-1990s were recipients of about 10 per cent of total educational

---

[2]   It is important to recall the distinction we have drawn in this book between UPE and SFA. The former, universal primary education, has traditionally been taken to be achieved when primary GERs reach 100 or more. Here, there would be no need for further primary expansion (beyond that needed to accommodate population growth) provided that the proportion of repeaters, amongst those enrolled, were small. This condition, however, is frequently not met. Further, the quality of primary schooling is often unsatisfactorily low. Accordingly, we have used a rather different target as a criterion for success. Schooling for All (SFA) we have defined as requiring the enrolment of all eligible children within the primary school age group (i.e. a net enrolment ratio of close to 100) in schools of minimally acceptable quality. These criteria are proxied in our modelling by achieving GERs higher than 100, repetition rates being reduced to acceptable levels, and by the introduction of qualitative reforms requiring more resources per pupil.

aid, would require more than a doubling of annual aid, depending upon the amount of domestic reform each country achieved. The reform requirements of achieving SFA, for both donors and recipient governments alike, therefore, are substantial.

Whether serious reform programmes will be designed and implemented is likely to depend as much upon the politics as the economics of the process. Existing policies, in many countries, are not capable of delivering SFA within a reasonable time period. Yet it would be a mistake to assume that securing the necessary policy shifts will be an easy process. On the one hand there may be disagreement at a technical level about how best to achieve SFA. On the other hand even if there is agreement about methods, the trade-offs which are always present in policy change may prove unpopular, and hamper implementation.

As regards the first of these possibilities, what is remarkable about the current state of debate about strategies for education in developing countries, is the extent to which there is widespread agreement on major policy priorities. There is a consensus that first priority should be given to achieving the quantitative, qualitative and equity dimensions of primary schooling for all. Most economists and education specialists are united in the importance of this major aim, as a means of delivering growth, poverty alleviation and equitable development. As regards the means of achieving this goal, it is also fairly widely agreed that subsidies to the higher levels of education have generally been too great in comparison with those made available to the base, that the costs of primary schooling to households should be minimised, that class-size should be brought down to around 40-45 pupils, that expenditures on learning materials have been too low, and that teacher earnings should be set at a level which is affordable, yet which gives proper incentives to staff. These aspects can be thought of as elements in a macro-education strategy, about which there is broad agreement as to the desirable directions for policy change.

There is however much greater debate about the more detailed means of achieving these objectives. For example, as indicated in Chapter 6, although the evidence about the power of shift-systems to reduce both class-size and unit costs is strong, the implementation of double shifts, particularly in urban schools, remains a contested solution amongst both education officials and the wider public. Equally there remains debate about the most appropriate means of improving school efficiency, about the role of automatic promotion, about the benefits of assistant teachers for improved quality or reduced costs, and about the implications of alternative forms of devolution for the autonomy and performance of schools. These, and many other technical issues – which form the necessary detail of more micro-education strategy – can delay implementation in cases where opinion is divided as to how they can best be resolved.

There are other lacunae, however, which give greater cause for concern. One of the most important of these concerns the issue of gender equality. Although there is no disagreement, internationally, about its having a centrally important place in the macro-strategy for education, there is often far too little articulation, in both national and international policy documents, about how the objective is to be achieved. This appears to arise partly from a lack of appreciation of the complexity of the constraints preventing girls' equal access to schooling, and of the extent of policy change required if gender equality is to be achieved. One example is provided by the millennium goal of achieving gender parity in school enrolments by 2005. Its establishment, with an extremely tight deadline of five years, in many ways represents a clear articulation of the WID approach, discussed in Chapter 1. It indicates that some of its elements remained influential through the 1990s, and continued to affect important parts of the more popular end of international policy discourse. The architects of the target either misunderstood, or chose to ignore, the complexities and difficulties its implementation would involve. The notion that gender parity in enrolments could be attained ten years prior to the universal enrolment of both boys and girls in many societies suggests a misunderstanding of its causes. Moreover, its universal achievement, within five years, would have required such profound reform, and at such a pace, that its feasibility was remote.

Turning to the second set of reasons why reform will not be an easy process, it may seem surprising to suggest that the popularity of policy reform in education may be in question. After all, if the reforms are aimed at improving the educational standards of a large majority of the population, how could they not be popular? It should certainly be true that education policies which work could be expected to be supported by their beneficiaries. But if their implementation requires sacrifices from articulate groups – even if they are minorities – there may be ample time for effective opposition to be expressed before the benefits of the new policies have been fully revealed.[3]

The countries of SSA are by no means strangers to policy reform. Indeed a number of countries in the region – including Kenya, Madagascar, Nigeria, Tanzania and Zambia – had earlier enrolment drives which led to student numbers being sustained at or close to UPE levels for a number of years. All of them, however, fell back during the 1980s and 1990s, for reasons discussed in Chapter 2, and elsewhere, in this book. This experience suggests, however, that it is generally easier to achieve reforms which secure increased access to schooling than it is to emplace robust improvements in school quality, even though there are some fairly obvious and straightforward ways in which the quality of African schooling could be improved. Indeed, one of the reasons why enrolments were not maintained in a number of these countries was precisely that parents and pupils became dissatisfied with the quality of education that was available in the schools.

Are there explanations for this apparent paradox? One possibility is that improvements in the coverage of the school system are simply more visible than those affecting schooling quality. Some analysts have argued that access reforms are associated with a defined group of beneficiaries (those newly enrolled), whereas those who benefit from improved quality are more diffuse, and what they receive is less tangible (Corrales, 1999). The former category of reform is thus more likely to be politically popular than the latter. If either of these sets of reforms is financed from general taxation, those who bear the costs are diffuse, and

---

[3] For an assessment of similar arguments for the more general case of economic reform, see Rodrik (1996).

may in any case be unaware of any change. On the other hand, where the reforms are financed from specific taxes falling on particular groups – as with, for example, the introduction of cost-recovery at tertiary level for the purposes of subsidising primary expansion – it can be expected that the cost-bearers will resist the introduction of the proposed reforms.

This kind of argument leads to the conclusion that access reforms may indeed be easier to introduce than quality reforms, particularly if they are financed from either general taxation or from aid sources. In this case a highly tangible outcome brings clear beneficiaries. The politics of reform are thus likely to be supportive, with popular benefits clearly perceived and with few people aware that they are directly or indirectly meeting the costs. If, on the other hand, access reforms were financed by shifts of expenditure from other sectors, by the reduction of subsidies or the introduction of cost-recovery measures to other branches of the education system, the cost-bearers could be expected to object, and reforms may be delayed or defeated.

We argued earlier that the notions of reducing relative subsidies at tertiary levels, promoting cross-subsidy for lower levels from other sectors, and setting targets for affordable teacher-earnings over the long term, are all increasingly important constituents of the macro-education policy orthodoxy. However, they are also policies where those who bear the costs are clearly defined. Such reforms are likely to be the locus for domestic political contest and their implementation will require strong government. It may be that they prove easier to introduce in democratic systems, as some research seems to suggest (Stasavage, 2001). But success can by no means be taken for granted, and the path to reform will remain difficult in a number of the African countries that are farthest from SFA.

This process can be assisted by the aid community. The widespread introduction of programmes of sectoral assistance, complemented by the World-Bank-initiated poverty reduction strategy papers (PRSPs), have helped to place emphasis upon redesigning educational policy, with the primary sector being given first importance. Nevertheless, this book has shown that very significant increases in educational aid to Africa will be required if schooling for all is to be achieved, with increases of two-to-three fold – depending upon the amount of domestic policy reform achieved – being needed in the nine countries focussed upon here. Although the commitments made by the aid community during 2001/02 looked capable of providing the financial resources required, past promises, as shown in Chapter 7, have not proved to be a reliable guide to action. Notwithstanding earlier pledges to the contrary, aid fell in real terms throughout the 1990s, and aid to education provided no exception to this trend. The particularly disappointing aid record in Africa appeared to be further aggravated by spending difficulties within the region. Strong determination will therefore be required by all parties, if all this is to change. The international community has accepted a major responsibility to promote and assist genuine programmes of primary school expansion and improvement. However, the limitations of international agencies in supporting the process of political reform need to be acknowledged. For example, previous chapters have noted that many of the programmes targeting girls' education have been implemented by international agencies, which invites questions as to their financial sustainability, should international priorities change. Their role has also resulted in limited acceptance of the programmes by national governments, which do not always appear convinced of the importance of such targeted reforms.

The key priority, therefore, will be the espousal of a genuine national reform process, within Africa, if SFA is to be achieved. There are many desirable attributes of such initiatives. However, this book has argued that national commitment to sustained and effective spending on primary schooling (often at higher levels than in the past), and to efficient containment of its unit costs will be required. The introduction of gender reforms – embracing changes going well beyond the education system, yet having a critical influence upon the achievement of equality within it – will represent a further crucial component. We have shown that schooling for all can be achieved in Africa, within the period envisaged by the millennium goals. However, in addition to much higher levels of aid for education, the strong presence of the above three components in national programmes of educational reform will, almost certainly, prove to be a necessary condition for their success.

Tables Appendix

Table 3A.1 Cross-country correlations

	GER	Male GER	Female GER	Gender Gap	Urban	GNP per capita	Religion	Age at marriage	Female teachers	Repetition	School age population	Pupil teacher ratio	Unit cost	Population density	Agricultural value added
GER	1.00														
Male GER	0.96	1.00													
Female GER	0.98	0.88	1.00												
Gender Gap	0.71	0.51	0.84	1.00											
Urban	0.49	0.43	0.52	0.46	1.00										
GNP per capita	0.49	0.41	0.53	0.47	0.68	1.00									
Religion	-0.13	-0.03	-0.20	-0.36	-0.04	-0.06	1.00								
Age at marriage	0.61	0.51	0.66	0.61	0.34	0.48	-0.19	1.00							
Female teachers	0.61	0.43	0.72	0.81	0.58	0.55	-0.44	0.67	1.00						
Repetition	-0.34	-0.21	-0.43	-0.56	-0.22	-0.33	0.02	-0.41	-0.45	1.00					
School age population	-0.20	-0.26	-0.15	0.07	-0.05	-0.15	-0.06	-0.06	-0.01	0.10	1.00				
Pupil teacher ratio	-0.39	-0.29	-0.44	-0.46	-0.53	-0.61	-0.02	-0.48	-0.52	0.65	0.22	1.00			
Unit cost	-0.58	-0.60	-0.52	-0.33	-0.34	-0.19	0.17	-0.23	-0.31	0.06	0.01	-0.03	1.00		
Population density	0.04	0.02	0.05	0.12	-0.21	-0.03	0.18	0.00	-0.07	-0.20	-0.18	0.13	-0.17	1.00	
Agricult. value added	-0.59	-0.48	-0.66	-0.62	-0.66	-0.75	0.12	-0.59	-0.63	0.37	-0.02	0.53	0.25	0.05	1.00

Table 3A.2　Characteristics of studies included in review

Study (1)	Country and year (2)	Age range (3)	Sample Size (4)	Dependent Variable (5)	Only primary? (6)
Al-Samarrai and Reilly (2000)	Tanzania, 1993/94	7-15	Urban -2289 Rural – 2378	Currently enrolled in primary	Yes
Al-Samarrai and Peasgood (1998)	Rural Tanzania, 1992	7-55	2617	Ever attended primary school	Yes
Appleton *et al.* (1990)	Côte d'Ivoire, 1986	11-18	Total – 2433 Boys – 1265 Girls – 1168	Ever received any primary schooling	Yes
Birdsall and Orivel (1996)	Rural Mali, 1981-82	6-14	123	Number of people enrolled divided by people in h/h aged 6-14	Yes
Chao and Alper (1998)	Ghana, 1991/92	10-14	2222	Ever attended primary or jss school	No
Chernichovsky (1985)	Rural Botswana, 1974	6-18	2253	Whether child is currently in school	No
Glick and Sahn (2000)	Conakry, Guinea, 1990	10-18	Boys – 899 Girls – 766	Whether child is currently in school	No

Table 3A.2 (Cont'd) Characteristics of studies included in review

Study (1)	Country and year (2)	Age range (3)	Sample Size (4)	Dependent Variable (5)	Only primary? (6)
Grootaert (1999)	Côte d'Ivoire	7-17	Urban – 1177 Rural – 1650	Whether child is in school and not working	No
Lavy (1996)	Rural Ghana, 1987	5-12	1733	Ever attended primary school	Yes
Mason and Khandker (1996)	Tanzania	7-15	Total – 4689 Boys – 2385 Girls – 2304	Whether child is currently enrolled in primary school	Yes
Mingat and Tan (1986)	Malawi, 1983	All siblings	1455	Proportion of eligible siblings enrolled in primary or secondary	No
Montgomery *et al.* (1995)	Côte d'Ivoire, 1985-87	5 upwards	Total –8175 Rural –5067 Urban –3108	Currently enrolled in school	No
	Ghana, 1987-89	5 upwards	Total – 7880 Urban –5384 Rural - 2496	Currently enrolled in school	No
Rose and Al-Samarrai (2001)	Ethiopia, 1995	9-25	275	Currently enrolled in primary school	Yes

Table 3A.2 (Cont'd) Characteristics of studies included in review

Study (1)	Country and year (2)	Age range (3)	Sample Size (4)	Dependent Variable (5)	Only primary? (6)
Tansel (1997)	Côte d'Ivoire, 1985-1987	16-36	Male - 2983 Female - 3628	Ever attended primary school	Yes
	Ghana, 1987-89	16-36	Male - 3366 Female - 4015	Ever attended primary school	Yes
Tembon and Al-Samarrai (1999)	Guinea, 1995	10-19	380	Currently enrolled in primary school	Yes
Weir (2000)	Ethiopia, 1995	Primary school age	387	Currently enrolled in primary school	Yes
Weir and Knight (1996)	Ethiopia, 1994	7-23	n.a.	Currently enrolled in school	No
World Bank (1996)	Ethiopia	7-12	n.a.	Currently enrolled in primary school	Yes

Notes:

a) The table details all the studies reviewed for this chapter. The information included in the table also indicates the specific regressions looked at in each study.

b) Column 6 reports whether the study looks solely at primary school enrolment.

c) n.a. – not available.

Technical Appendix

This appendix indicates the main sources of data used in the book and details the survey methodology employed in the country case-studies. The simulation model, used in Chapter 6 to assess the feasibility of achieving primary schooling for all in the nine countries, is also briefly outlined.

A Note on Data Sources

The main sources of international statistical data for Chapters 1–3 are the following:

1. UNESCO Statistical Yearbooks, various years.
2. UNESCO World Education Reports, various years.
3. World Development Reports, various years.
4. World Development Indicators CD ROM, 2000 and World Bank STARS database.
5. Human Development Reports, various years.

Some inconsistencies between these sources are evident. For example, public expenditure figures often differ between World Education Reports and UNESCO Statistical Yearbooks. Chapters 4–6 supplement data from these sources with national data collected for the nine country case-studies. Where these differ from the data in international sources, they are preferred, owing to the extensive work undertaken by the study authors to collect reliable and accurate education data. A full description of national data sources is given in each of the country reports.

Chapter 4 analyses government recurrent education expenditure using national data. One aim of that chapter is to compare absolute levels of education spending across countries, which is not straightforward. Nominal exchange rates do not generally reflect relative prices across countries, and therefore do not allow dependable comparisons of absolute spending levels. Partly to eliminate this problem, purchasing power parity (PPP) exchange rates were used to convert local currencies to US dollars. PPP exchange rates for the countries covered in Chapter 4 were taken from the World Bank's 'World Development Indicators 2000'. The PPP exchange rate reflects the purchasing power of a unit of the local currency, (for example, the cedi/dollar cost of a given basket of goods in Ghana and the USA respectively), rather than the number of dollars it can buy on the foreign exchange market. By using the PPP exchange rate, comparisons of absolute levels of education expenditure across countries can be more meaningfully made.

Chapter 7 analyses trends in bilateral and multilateral aid during the 1990s. Information on World Bank financing was compiled from the World Bank Annual reports over the period. Aid from bilateral and other multilateral agencies was obtained from the OECD DAC On-line Database.

Sampling Methodology

In order to examine the causes of non-enrolment, drop-out and poor performance of girls relative to boys, the survey work in the nine countries used a combination of both quantitative and qualitative research tools. Qualitative methods were used to facilitate a more detailed understanding of the processes and issues focussed on in the quantitative work. This allowed a fairly comprehensive study of access to, and performance in school, gaining insights from the views of different members of the community (including education officials, teachers, pupils, parents and community elders).

Table TA.1 details the sample characteristics for the school-based surveys conducted in each country. The surveys conducted in 1998 were larger in scale than the earlier rounds, owing to greater resources becoming available for the conduct of the surveys. In general, two large and contrasting geographical regions were selected in each country. While selection criteria were country-specific, they included the overall primary gross enrolment ratio, females as a proportion of total primary enrolments, and variations in socio-economic conditions such as economic activity, ethnicity and religion. The objective was to select areas that contrasted with each other. For example, in Malawi the Southern region, with low primary enrolments relative to the national average, and the Northern region, with higher than average enrolments were selected.

Within these broad geographical units, smaller administrative areas (e.g. districts) were selected which were typical of the larger area as a whole. A representative sample of schools within each area was then chosen ensuring that both rural and urban schools were represented. The detailed ways in which schools were selected differed across countries and are described in the country reports. The selected schools and their catchment areas provided the basis for the fieldwork, and formed natural clusters of primary-school pupils and teachers, primary-school drop-outs and non-enrolees. Pupils in the highest primary grade, together with, in some cases, a lower primary grade were selected for interview. Where the number of pupils in any grade exceeded the required sample size, a random sample of pupils was taken. In the later (1998) surveys, this random selection was carried out on male and female sub-samples separately, which ensured the selection of equal numbers of boys and girls.

The sampling of children who were not enrolled in school was less structured than that of the school-based survey. Attempts were made in each country to identify out-of-school children who were similar in age to the pupils surveyed. In each school-catchment area the survey teams used a variety of tools to identify and locate school drop-outs and those who had never been enrolled. For example, community maps, drawn by children currently attending school, provided useful information on the location of children who were out-of-school.

Table TA.1 Sample characteristics for the country surveys

Country	Year of survey	No. regions	No. districts	No. schools	No. teachers	No. pupils	Grades sampled	No. drop-outs	No. non-enrolees
Ethiopia	1995	2	4	11	110	213	6	115	160
Guinea	1995	2	2	6	37	234	6	60	86
Tanzania	1995	2	2	7	57	241	7	25	-
Ghana	1998	2	4	24	126	1132	3 and 6	230	161
Malawi	1998	2	4	20	349	1140	3 and 7	1064	-
Mali	1998	3	-	25	141	1234	4 and 6	190	194
Senegal	1998	2	4	24	200	1200	Cm2 and Ce2	200	100
Uganda	1998	2	4	25	285	1200	4 and 6	384	-
Zambia	1998	2	4	20	230	1189	4 and 6	301	-

Source: GAPS country reports.

Table TA.1 shows the number of out-of-school children surveyed in each country. In some of the countries – Tanzania, Malawi, Uganda and Zambia – it proved impossible to identify and locate a meaningful number of children who had never enrolled in school and who were of similar age to the pupils surveyed. In general, this was due to most children having, at some time, attended school, thereby properly being classified as school drop-outs, rather than 'never enrolled'.

DATA COLLECTION AT DISTRICT EDUCATION OFFICES

INTERVIEWS WITH EDUCATION OFFICIALS
DATA COLLECTION ON SCHOOL ENROLMENT

ONE-TO-ONE INTERVIEWS IN SCHOOLS WITH

HEAD TEACHERS
TEACHERS
PRIMARY SCHOOL PUPILS
PRIMARY SCHOOL DROPOUTS
NON-ENROLEES

OTHER SOURCES OF INFORMATION AT THE SCHOOL LEVEL

SCHOOL RECORDS
MAPS SHOWING DISTANCE OF HOME TO SCHOOL AND OUT OF SCHOOL CHILDREN
WEIGHT AND HEIGHT OF CHILDREN

FOCUS GROUP DISCUSSIONS IN EACH COMMUNITY

TEACHERS
SCHOOL MANAGEMENT COMMITTEE
PARENTS OF CHILDREN IN AND OUT OF SCHOOL
KEY MEMBERS OF THE COMMUNITY
PUPILS (SEPARATE GROUPS BY GENDER)

Figure TA.1 Fieldwork instruments

A range of different instruments was used to collect information on educational participation in the catchment area of schools. Figure TA.1 details the fieldwork instruments used. In each school catchment-area, focus-group discussions were undertaken with teachers, school management committees, pupils, parents and other key members of the community. The mix of instruments used in the fieldwork was tailored to local circumstances.

The survey work was not intended to be representative, in a statistical sense, of the countries as a whole. The survey method was purposive, and was designed to complement the results of earlier household surveys. It aimed to achieve a fuller understanding of the different causes of school participation and performance across areas with very different social and economic characteristics, than would have been possible using a purely quantitative approach. Each country report provides a full description of the sampling methodology and fieldwork instruments used, and detailed analysis of the information gathered.

Simulation Model

Chapter 6 uses simulation models of the education system, designed for each country, to estimate the cost and resource implications of achieving primary schooling for all over a fifteen-year period. This section briefly describes the structure of these models and explains how they have been used in our work. Further technical descriptions can be found in Al-Samarrai (1997) and the country reports.

There are five main parts of the simulation model:

1. *Enrolment module* This part of the model establishes the structure of the education system in terms of the length, in years, of different levels of education and how they are linked (e.g. how many years of secondary are needed before entry into technical or vocational school etc.). It also includes information on levels of enrolment, and rates of repetition and drop-out, at each level, by grade and by sex.
2. *Unit cost module* This sets out the cost per pupil of providing education at each level of the system.
3. *Teacher module* This provides information on the number of teachers in each part of the education system.
4. *Classroom module* This provides information on the number of classrooms in each part of the education system.
5. *Expenditure and resources module* This section of the model summarises the different resources available for education and compares these with the cost of the education system.

The starting point for using the model is the collection of information on the current parameters of the education system. Data on all its quantitative aspects, for a base year, are needed in order to project enrolment and costs forward for up to 15 years ahead. In Guinea, Ethiopia and Tanzania the base year was 1993/94, in

Ghana and Zambia 1996/97, in Uganda 1997, in Senegal 1997/98 and in Mali 1998. Although the major focus for the national studies was primary schooling, data for all levels of the education system were collected for the simulation model.

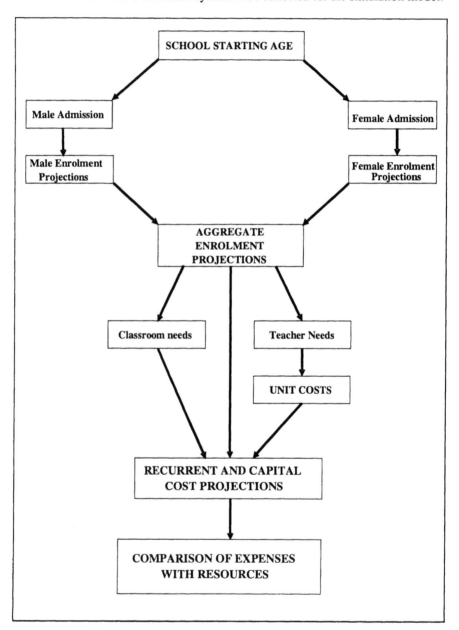

Figure TA.2 Structure of the simulation model

This allowed resource reallocation decisions to be analysed at the macro-level, and the system-wide impact of the expansion and improvement of primary schooling to be explored.

Figure TA.2 outlines the general structure of the simulation models for each country. In order to analyse enrolment changes for male and female students separately, the simulation model has separate sections for male and female enrolment. The model uses target rates for admission (from the school starting-age population), repetition, promotion and drop-out in order to project enrolment forward from the base year. In each case, for example, increases in admission rates over the fifteen-year projection period are modelled, to assess the overall capacity of the primary education system necessary for the achievement of primary schooling for all. Based on these targets, levels of enrolment for each year of the fifteen-year projection period are derived. The separate projections for male and female enrolment are then combined to produce the aggregate enrolment projections, as indicated in Figure TA.2.

Turning to teacher needs, information on the number of teachers in the education system, pupil-teacher ratios at each level, and teacher-attrition rates are included in this part of the model. Combined with the enrolment projections already calculated, the model can estimate the number of teachers required, and, thus the annual required output of trained teachers for each level of the system. Classroom needs are calculated in a similar way. Annual teacher and classroom requirements are based on projected pupil enrolment and on targets for the pupil-teacher and pupil-classroom ratios at each level.

The unit cost of schooling is split into its principal components (salary costs, teaching and learning materials etc.) and projected forward on the basis of targets for each of them. Most of the national reports envisage improvements being secured in the availability of teaching and learning materials over the fifteen-year period, with concomitant increases in expected unit costs.

The enrolment and unit-cost projections are translated by the simulation model into projected year-by-year recurrent costs for each level of the system. The costs of constructing the required classrooms are also calculated. The final section of the model allows comparison of projected expenditures with projected resources available for education, for each year of the period.

Using the model, the impact of school expansion in each country can be examined by changing the targets for admission rates into primary school so as to obtain the required GERs. The simulation of SFA is also fairly straightforward. In each of the national studies sets of quality-enhancing, cost-saving, cost-shifting and resource-shifting reforms are proposed, so as to be able to achieve the targeted levels of primary-school enrolment (see next section). Their cost implications are included in the relevant part of the simulation model. Quality-enhancing reforms recommended in the country case studies often required increased expenditure on teaching and learning materials. Increases in the per-pupil cost of teaching and learning materials are entered into the unit cost section of the model (see Figure TA.2). One commonly proposed cost-saving reform was to increase the pupil-teacher ratio at the primary level. Such changes are entered into the 'teacher needs' component of the simulation model, and affect both the per-pupil cost of

Table TA.2 Primary enrolments, publicly financed costs and expenditures: base year actuals and estimated impact of selected reforms to achieve SFA over 15 years

	Base year data	No reforms: past trend only	No reforms: enrolment expansion to GER target	Quality/gender reforms	Cost-saving reforms	Cost-shifting reforms	Resource increasing reforms
	(1)	(2)	(3)	(4)	(5)	(6)	(7)
Ethiopia (1993/94)							
Primary GER	24%	36%	70%	79%	75%	75%	75%
Primary Enrolments (000s)	2328	6751	13290	14981	14185	14185	14185
Primary Unit Costs ($PPP)	200	200	200	281	176	174	174
Primary Unit Costs (as a % of GDP per capita)	39%	39%	39%	54%	34%	34%	34%
Primary Recurrent Education Expenditure ($PPP)	466	1367	2685	4211	2497	2462	2462
Total Recurrent Expenditure ($PPP millions)	738	1874	3076	4782	2920	2854	2854
Total Required Expenditure/Total Available Resources	1	1.63	2.67	4.16	2.54	2.48	0.98
Ghana (1996/97)							
Primary GER	77%	78%	105%	105%	105%	105%	105%
Primary Enrolments (000s)	2334	3974	5372	5372	5372	5372	5372
Primary Unit Costs ($PPP)	198	198	198	244	184	184	184
Primary Unit Costs (as a % of GDP per capita)	14%	14%	14%	17%	13%	13%	13%
Primary Recurrent Education Expenditure ($PPP)	463	789	1066	1312	988	988	988
Total Recurrent Expenditure ($PPP millions)	1091	1848	2638	3072	2512	2403	2403
Total Required Expenditure/Total Available Resources	1	1.09	1.55	1.81	1.48	1.41	0.99
Guinea (1993/94)							
Primary GER	38%	48%	118%	124%	101%	101%	101%
Primary Enrolments (000s)	472	916	2232	2358	1914	1914	1914
Primary Unit Costs ($PPP)	195	195	195	211	173	163	163
Primary Unit Costs (as a % of GDP per capita)	12%	12%	0.12	13%	10%	10%	10%
Primary Recurrent Education Expenditure ($PPP)	92	179	435	498	330	310	310
Total Recurrent Expenditure ($PPP millions)	179	549	715	830	589	504	504
Total Required Expenditure/Total Available Resources	1	1.97	2.57	2.98	2.12	1.81	1.02

Table TA.2 (Cont'd) Primary enrolments, publicly financed costs and expenditures: base year actuals and estimated impact of selected reforms to achieve SFA over 15 years

	Base year data	No reforms: past trend only	No reforms: enrolment expansion to GER target	Quality/gender reforms	Cost-saving reforms	Cost-shifting reforms	Resource increasing reforms
	(1)	(2)	(3)	(4)	(5)	(6)	(7)
Malawi (1997)							
Primary GER	139%	134%	116%	116%	110%	110%	110%
Primary Enrolments (000s)	2906	3687	3196	3196	3036	3036	3036
Primary Unit Costs ($PPP)	47	47	47	103	99	94	94
Primary Unit Costs (as a % of GDP per capita)	8%	8%	8%	18%	18%	17%	17%
Primary Recurrent Education Expenditure ($PPP)	138	175	151	329	300	285	285
Total Recurrent Expenditure ($PPP millions)	213	298	287	559	512	449	449
Total Required Expenditure/Total Available Resources	1	0.96	0.92	1.79	1.64	1.44	0.96
Mali (1997/98)							
Primary GER	50%	63%	116%	116%	101%	101%	101%
Primary Enrolments (000s)	866	1556	2869	2869	2498	2498	2498
Primary Unit Costs ($PPP)	80	80	80	122	122	110	110
Primary Unit Costs (as a % of GDP per capita)	14%	14%	14%	21%	21%	19%	19%
Primary Recurrent Education Expenditure ($PPP)	62	112	207	318	277	250	250
Total Recurrent Expenditure ($PPP millions)	160	444	683	871	570	513	513
Total Required Expenditure/Total Available Resources	1	1.84	2.82	3.6	2.36	2.12	1
Senegal (1997/98)							
Primary GER	69%	80%	120%	120%	109%	109%	109%
Primary Enrolments (000s)	1027	1753	2624	2624	2387	2387	2387
Primary Unit Costs ($PPP)	141	141	141	164	146	117	117
Primary Unit Costs (as a % of GDP per capita)	11%	11%	11%	13%	11%	9%	9%
Primary Recurrent Education Expenditure ($PPP)	144	249	372	433	349	280	280
Total Recurrent Expenditure ($PPP millions)	385	586	852	940	759	690	690
Total Required Expenditure/Total Available Resources	1	0.98	1.42	1.56	1.26	1.15	1

Table TA.2 (Cont'd)   Primary enrolments, publicly financed costs and expenditures: base year actuals and estimated impact of selected reforms to achieve SFA over 15 years

	Base year data	No reforms: past trend only	No reforms: enrolment expansion to GER target	Quality/gender reforms	Cost-saving reforms	Cost-shifting reforms	Resource increasing reforms
	(1)	(2)	(3)	(4)	(5)	(6)	(7)
Tanzania (1993/94)							
Primary GER	78%	82%	108%	108%	108%	108%	108%
Primary Enrolments ('000s)	3737	5640	7400	7400	7400	7400	7400
Primary Unit Costs ($PPP)	55	55	55	70	58	56	56
Primary Unit Costs (as a % of GDP per capita)	14%	14%	14%	17%	14%	14%	14%
Primary Recurrent Education Expenditure ($PPP)	207	320	409	515	430	417	417
Total Recurrent Expenditure ($PPP millions)	266	420	704	863	728	530	530
Total Required Expenditure/Total Available Resources	1	1.03	1.72	2.11	1.78	1.3	1
Uganda (1997/98)							
Primary GER	135%	144%	115%	115%	115%	115%	115%
Primary Enrolments ('000s)	5604	8939	7168	7168	7168	7168	7168
Primary Unit Costs ($PPP)	46	46	46	81	79	73	73
Primary Unit Costs (as a % of GDP per capita)	4%	4%	4%	8%	8%	7%	7%
Primary Recurrent Education Expenditure ($PPP)	254	407	328	579	563	520	520
Total Recurrent Expenditure ($PPP millions)	508	894	967	1222	1151	1108	1108
Total Required Expenditure/Total Available Resources	1	1.21	1.31	1.66	1.56	1.5	1
Zambia (1996/97)							
Primary GER	96%	124%	110%	110%	110%	110%	110%
Primary Enrolments ('000s)	1514	3697	3280	3280	3280	3280	3280
Primary Unit Costs ($PPP)	65	65	65	108	93	90	90
Primary Unit Costs (as a % of GDP per capita)	9%	9%	9%	14%	12%	12%	12%
Primary Recurrent Education Expenditure ($PPP)	98	240	213	354	305	294	294
Total Recurrent Expenditure ($PPP millions)	158	391	420	655	558	524	524
Total Required Expenditure/Total Available Resources	1	1.65	1.78	2.77	2.36	2.22	0.98

Notes: See notes accompanying table for description of indicators and column definitions and explanations.

Source: GAPS Simulation Models

teachers and the annual number of teachers required. Resource-shifting reforms such as increasing the share of the central government education budget allocated to the primary sub-sector, are modelled in the final section of the model.

Simulation Model Results for the Case Study Countries

Table TA.2 summarises the results of the simulation exercises carried out in the country case studies. Each of them projects the cost and resource implications of reaching SFA within 15 years. Table TA.2 reports the following parameters for each country:

1. Primary gross enrolment ratio.
2. Primary weighted unit cost in $PPP and as a percentage of GDP per capita.
3. Primary recurrent education expenditure in $PPP.
4. Total recurrent education expenditure in $PPP millions.
5. The ratio between required recurrent expenditures and resources available to finance this expenditure.

The first column gives the value of these parameters in the base year, the date of which differs, for each country, as reported in the table. For all countries, the ratio of recurrent expenditures to available resources, shown in Column 1, is equal to one, implying that recurrent expenditures were then equal to the resources allocated to meet them. Subsequent columns of Table TA.2 show the impact of introducing each of the sets of reforms discussed in Chapter 6, for each country, over 15 years. The impact shown in each column is cumulative, in the sense that the changes shown in preceding columns are held in place. It should also be noted that resources for education are assumed to grow at the same rate as the population for Columns 2 to 7, over the 15-year period.

The second column of Table TA.2 shows the situation at the end of 15 years, if the main parameters of the education system were to remain unchanged (i.e. if the base year grade one admission rate were to be maintained and if no changes were made to repetition and drop-out rates, nor to unit costs), and if no other reforms were introduced. For example, in Malawi the primary gross enrolment rate is shown to fall slightly from 139 per cent to 134 per cent over the 15-year period if the parameters of the education system remained the same as in the recent past. Further, the modelling exercise shows that, under these circumstances, the required expenditure would easily be covered by the available resources at the end of the 15-year period (i.e. the ratio between recurrent expenditures and resources, for Malawi, is less than unity).

The third column of the table shows the evolution of the parameters when admissions to primary are adjusted so as to achieve the SFA enrolment target for each country by the end of the 15-year projection period – again, without introducing other reforms. With the exception of Malawi, Zambia and Uganda this would imply a considerable increase in the primary gross enrolment ratio above its base-year level. In most cases the enrolment expansion would lead to the emergence of significant gaps between resources available and required expenditures.

We have identified the poor quality of primary schooling as a particular constraint, in all the countries, leading to low pupil-performance and low demand for schooling. Chapter 6 outlined, for each country, a set of reforms aimed at improving the quality of primary education and improving gender equality. The projected impact of these reforms on the education system is shown in the fourth column of Table TA.2. The improvements in quality are expected to lead to reductions in repetition rates which imply that children move more quickly through the system and hence reduce the total costs of primary education. However, drop-out, too, will be reduced which, by increasing enrolments, will move costs in the opposite direction. On balance, the combined quality and gender reforms generally increase the costs of SFA dramatically. For example, in Ethiopia the primary cost increases by 40 per cent to $PPP 281, with the introduction of the quality enhancing reforms, resulting in a large increase in the expected gap between required and available resources. Nevertheless, a range of opportunities to introduce cost-saving reforms, such as increases in class-size and measures to utilise teachers more effectively, were identified. Their impact is shown in Column 5 of the table.

The more detailed impact on unit costs of the proposed quality improvements and of the measures to save costs for each country are indicated in Table TA.3. It shows, for example, that the sources of cost increases in Ethiopia would be fairly evenly distributed between increased pupil subsidies, improved learning materials, enhanced teacher qualifications and better working conditions. However, equivalent cost-reductions would arise from measures to increase the pupil-teacher ratio and the incidence of double-shift teaching. In addition to these measures to reduce costs, sets of cost-shifting reforms - including limiting the growth of higher levels of the education system, and encouraging the growth of the private sector - were also modelled for each of the countries. Their impact is shown in Column 6 of Table TA.2.

Although, in general, the cost-saving and cost-shifting reforms modelled would dramatically reduce the costs of SFA, it can be seen, from Column 6, that a gap between expenditure and resources remains. For example, in Ghana the total expenditure required to introduce all the enrolment expansion, quality, gender, cost-saving and cost-shifting reforms exceeds the available resources by over 40 per cent. In all of the case study countries it follows that resources allocated to education, and particularly primary education, would need to be further increased in order to achieve SFA. Ways of doing so are investigated by our simulations, and Column 7 shows their impact on the affordability of SFA. Although it suggests that the financing gap can be closed by domestic policy change, it requires, in several countries, a strong (and optimistic) set of assumptions as regards the potential for economic growth and increased domestic spending on education. The realism of these assumptions is assessed in Chapter 7.

Table TA.3 Effect on primary unit costs of individual reforms

	Primary subsidy (%)	Learning materials (%)	Pupil/teacher ratio reductions (%)	Qualified teachers (%)	Teacher conditions (%)	Teacher incentives (%)	Supervision (%)	Double shift (%)	Pupil/teacher ratio increases (%)	Increasing private primary school enrolment (%)
Ethiopia	9	9	-	14	8	-	-	-26	-14	-
Ghana	4	4	15	-	-	-	-	-	-26	-
Guinea	2	7	-	-	-	-	1	-13	-7	-6
Malawi	-	83	11	-	17	3	1	-5	-	-5
Mali	1	41	13	-	-	-	3	-	-	-10
Senegal	1	3	12	-	-	-	1	-8	-	-20
Tanzania	-	2	-	-	4	12	0	-	-16	-3
Uganda	-	60	14	-	8	-	0	-3	-	-8
Zambia	6	22	-	1	20	3	1	-	-14	-4

Note: Each column represents proposed reforms outlined in Table 6.1 that impact on the primary unit cost. The percentages for each country represent the percentage change in the primary unit cost from its base year level arising out of introducing the specific reform. If a country has no entry for a specific reform this means the reform was not proposed for the country. See Chapter 6 for further explanation.

Source: GAPS Simulation Models

Bibliography

Abraham, Kinfe (1994), *Ethiopia. From Bullets to the Ballot Box*, Red Sea Press Inc., Lawrenceville.

Adams, J. (1986), 'Peasant Rationality: Individuals, Groups, Cultures', *World Development*, Vol. 14(2), pp. 273-282.

Agarwal, B. (1986), 'Women, Poverty and Agricultural Growth in India', *Journal of Peasant Studies*, Vol. 13(4), pp. 165-220.

Aigner, D.J. and Cain, G.G. (1977), 'Statistical Theories of Discrimination in the Labour Market', *Industrial and Labour Relations Review*, pp. 175-187.

Akerloff, G.A. (1983), 'Loyalty Filters', *American Economic Review*, No. 73, pp. 54-63.

Alderman, H., Behrman, J. R., Lavy, V. and Rekha, M. (1997), 'Child Nutrition, Child Health, and School Enrollment. A longitudinal analysis', *Policy Research Working Paper*, No. 1700, Poverty and Human Resources Division, Policy Research Department, World Bank, Washington, DC.

Alderman, H., Haddad, L. and Hoddinott, J. (1997), 'Policy Issues and Intrahousehold Resource Allocation: Conclusions', Chapter 17 in L. Haddad *et al.*, *Intrahousehold Resource Allocation in Developing Countries: Models, Methods and Policy*, Johns Hopkins University Press, Baltimore, pp. 275-291.

Al-Samarrai, S. (1997), *Simulation Model for Educational Development*, IDS, Brighton.

Al-Samarrai, S. and Peasgood, T. (1998), 'Educational Attainments and Household Characteristics in Tanzania', *Economics of Education Review*, Vol. 17(4), pp. 395-417.

Al-Samarrai, S. and Reilly, B. (2000), 'Urban and Rural Differences in Primary School Attendance: an empirical study of Tanzania', *Journal of African Economies*, Vol. 9(4), pp. 430-474.

Anbesu, Biazen and Junge, B. (1988), *Problems in Primary School Participation and Performance in Bahir Dar Awraja*, Ministry of Education and UNICEF, Addis Ababa.

Anderson-Levitt, K., Bloch, M. and Soumaré, A. (1994), *Inside Classrooms in Guinea: Girls' Experiences*, World Bank, Washington DC.

Appleton, S., Collier, P. and Horsnell, P. (1990), 'Gender, Education and Employment in Côte d'Ivoire', *Social Dimensions of Adjustment in Sub-Saharan Africa. Working Paper No. 8*, World Bank, Washington DC.

Arrow, K.J. (1972), 'Models of Job Discrimination', in A.H. Pascal (ed.) *Racial Discrimination in Economic Life*, DC. Heath, Lexington, pp. 83-102.

Asseffa Beyene (1991), *Female Participation and Performance in Rural Schools in Ethiopia*, ICDR, MOE Addis Ababa.

Association for the Development of Education in Africa (ADEA) (1995), Gestion et Mobilisation des Personnels Enseignants dans les Pays d'Afrique Sub-Saharienne. Groupe de Travail sur la Profession Enseignante (GTPE) Section Francophone.

Avotri, R. (2000a), 'Gender Reforms in Ghana', IDS, Brighton (mimeo).

Avotri, R. (2000b), 'Repetition and its impact on performance in Ghanaian schools', IDS, Brighton (mimeo).

Avotri, R, Owusu-Darko, L., Eghan, H. and Ocansey, S. (2000), *Gender and Primary Schooling in Ghana*, Research Report 37, IDS, Brighton.

Baden, S. and Goetz, A.M. (1998), 'Who Needs (Sex) When You Can Have (Gender)?' in C. Jackson and R. Pearson (eds), *Feminist Visions of Development: Gender Analysis and Policy*, Routledge, London. pp. 19-38.

Becker, G. (1957), *The Economics of Discrimination*, University of Chicago Press, Chicago.

Becker, G. (1965), 'A Theory of the Allocation of Time', *Economic Journal*, No. 5, pp. 493-517.

Behrman, J.R. and J.C. Knowles (1999), 'Household Income and Child Schooling in Vietnam', *World Bank Economic Review*, Vol. 13(2), pp. 211-256.

Bennell, P., Hyde, K. and Swainson, N. (2002), *The Impact of the HIV/AIDS Epidemic on the Education Sector in Sub-Saharan Africa*, Centre for International Education, University of Sussex, Brighton.

Bergmann, H. (1996), 'Quality of Education and the Demand for Education – evidence from developing countries', *International Review of Education*, Vol. 42(6), pp. 581-604.

Birdsall, N. and Orivel, F. (1996), 'Demand for Primary Schooling in Rural Mali: should user fees be increased?', *Education Economics*, Vol. 4(3), pp. 279-296.

Blaug, M. (1976), 'The Empirical Status of Human Capital Theory – A Slightly Jaundiced Survey', *Journal of Economic Literature*, Vol. 14(3), pp. 827-855.

Bliss, C.J. and Stern, N.H. (1982), *Palanpur: the Economy of an Indian Village*, Clarendon Press, Oxford.

Boserup, E. (1970), (1989 2nd edition), *Women's Role in Economic Development*, St. Martin's Press, New York.

Boserup, E. (1975), *Integration of Women in Development: Why, When, How?*, UNDP, New York.

Bowles, S. and Gintis, H. (1976), *Schooling in Capitalist America: Educational Reform and the Contradictions of Economic Life*, Routledge, London.

Bray, M. (1989), *Multi-Shift Schooling: Design and Operation for Cost Effectiveness*, Commonwealth Secretariat, London.

Bray, M. (1996), *Counting the Full Cost. Parental and Community Financing of Education in East Asia*, World Bank, Washington DC.

Brock, C. and Cammish, N (1991), 'Factors Affecting Female Participation in Education in Six Developing Countries', *Overseas Development Administration Occasional Papers on Education*, No. 9, Overseas Development Administration, London.

Brock-Utne, B. (1993), 'Education in Africa. Education for self-reliance or recolonization?', Vol. I(3), Institute for Educational Research, University of Oslo, Oslo.

Buchert, L. (1994), 'Education and Development: a study of donor agency policies on education in Sweden, Holland and Denmark', *International Journal of Educational Development*, Vol. 14(2), pp. 143-157.

Burchfield, S.A. and Kadzamira, E.C. (1996), Malawi GABLE social mobilization campaign activities: A review of research and report on findings of KAP follow-up study, Washington, DC: Creative Associates International, Inc./USAID.

Cameron, J. and Dodd, W.H. (1970), *Schools, Society, and Progress in Tanzania*, Pergamon Press, Oxford.

Caplan, P. (1981), 'Development Policies for Tanzania: Some Implications for Women', in N. Nelson (ed.) 'African Women in the Development Process', Special Issue, *Journal of Development Studies*, Vol. 17, No. 3, pp. 98-108.

Carline, D., Pissarides, C., Siebert, W. and Sloane, P. (1985), *Surveys in Economics: Labour Economics*, Longman, London and New York.

Cassels, A. (1997), 'A Guide to Sector-Wide Approaches for Health Development: Concepts, Issues and Working Arrangements', World Health Organisation, Geneva.

Castro-Leal, F. (1996), 'Who benefits from public education spending in Malawi? Results from the recent education reform', *Discussion Paper*, No.3 50, World Bank, Washington DC.

Chao, S. and Alper, O. (1998), 'Accessing Basic Education in Ghana' *Studies in Human Development No. 1*, Africa Region, World Bank, Washington DC.

Chernichovsky, D. (1985), 'Socioeconomic and Demographic Aspects of School Enrolment and Attendance in Rural Botswana', *Economic Development and Cultural Change*, Vol. 33(2), pp. 319-332.

Chimombo J.P.G. (1999), 'Implementing Educational Innovations: A Study of Free Primary Education in Malawi', unpublished PhD Thesis: University of Sussex.

Chimombo, J.P.G. and Chonzi, R. (1999), 'School drop-out and teenage pregnancy: its causes and magnitude', draft report, Centre for Educational Research and Training, University of Malawi, Zomba.

Colclough, C. (ed.) (1997a), *Marketizing Education and Health in Developing Countries: Miracle or Mirage?*, Clarendon Press, Oxford.

Colclough, C. (1997b), 'Economic Stagnation and Earnings Decline in Zambia, 1975-91', in Colclough, C. (ed.), *Public-Sector Pay and Adjustment: Lessons from Five Countries*, Routledge, London, pp. 68-112.

Colclough, C. and Al-Samarrai, S. (2000), 'Achieving Schooling for All: Budgetary Expenditures on Education in Sub-Saharan Africa and South Asia', *World Development*, Vol. 28(11), pp. 1927-1944.

Colclough, C. with Lewin, K. (1993), *Educating All the Children: Strategies for Primary Schooling in the South*, Clarendon Press, Oxford.

Colclough, C., Rose, P. and Tembon, M. (2000), 'Gender Inequalities in Primary Schooling: The Roles of Poverty and Adverse Cultural Practice', *International Journal for Educational Development*, Vol. 20(1), pp. 5-27.

Commonwealth Secretariat (2000), 'Overcoming Barriers to HIPC Debt Relief: Need for Reappraisal', paper prepared for the Commonwealth Finance Ministers' Meeting, Malta, 19-21 September 2000, Commonwealth Secretariat, London.

Connell, R.W. (1987), *Gender and Power*, Polity Press, Cambridge.

Corrales, J. (1999), 'The Politics of Education Reform: Bolstering the Supply and Demand; Overcoming Institutional Blocks', *Education Reform and Management Series, Vol. II(1)*, World Bank, Washington DC.

Cox Edwards, A. (1993), 'Teacher Compensation in Developing Countries' in Farrell and Oliveira, *Teachers in Developing Countries: Improving Effectiveness and Managing Costs*, Washington DC.

Craig, H., Kraft, R. and du Plessis, J. (1998), *Teacher Development: Making An Impact*, USAID, Advanced Basic Education and Literacy Program/World Bank Human Development Network Effective Schools and Teachers.

Department for International Development (DFID) (2000), *Towards Responsive Schools: Case Studies from Save the Children*, DFID Education Papers, Serial No. 38.

Dey, J. (1981), 'Gambian Women: Unequal Partners in Rice Development Projects?', in N. Nelson (ed.), 'African Women in the Development Process', Special Issue, *Journal of Development Studies*, Vol. 17, No. 3, pp. 109-122.

DFID (1999), *Learning Opportunities for All: A policy framework for education*, Department for International Development, London.

DFID (2001), *The Challenge of Universal Primary Education: Strategies for achieving the international development targets*, Department for International Development, London.

Dioum Diokané, M. (2000a), 'The cost of education in Senegal', IDS, Brighton, (mimeo).

Dioum Diokané, M. (2000b), 'The system of double-shifting in Senegal', IDS, Brighton, (mimeo).

Dioum Diokhané, M., Khairy Diallo, O., Sy, A. and Touré, M. (2000), *Genre et fréquentation scolaire dans l'enseignement élémentaire au Sénégal*, Research Report 38, IDS, Brighton.

Economist (1990), *The Economist Book of Vital World Statistics*, Hutchinson Business, London.

Eicher, J.C. (1984), 'Educational Costing and Financing in Developing Countries: Focus on Sub-Saharan Africa', *World Bank Staff Working Paper No. 655*, World Bank, Washington DC.

Eisemon, J. (1997), 'Reducing Repetition: Issues and Strategies. Fundamentals of Educational Planning No. 55', UNESCO/IIEP, Paris.

Eisenstein, Z. (1981), *The Radical Future of Liberal Feminism*, Longman, New York.

Elson, D. (1995), 'Introduction', *World Development*, Vol. 23(11), Special Issue.

Fallon, P. and Verry, D. (1988), *The Economics of Labour Markets*, Philip Allan, Oxford and New Jersey.

Fassil Kiros (1990), 'Implementing Educational Policies in Ethiopia', World Bank Discussion Paper, No. 84, World Bank, Washington DC.

Gennet Zewide (1991), 'Women in Primary and Secondary Education', in T. Berhane-Selassie (ed.) *Gender Issues in Ethiopia*, Institute of Ethiopian Studies, Addis Ababa University, Addis Ababa.

Gertler, P. and Glewwe, P. (1992), 'The Willingness to Pay for Education for Daughters in Contrast to Sons: evidence from rural Peru', *World Bank Economic Review*, Vol. 6(1), pp. 171-188.

Glewwe, P. and Jacoby, H. (1993), 'Student Achievement and Schooling Choice in Low-income Countries: evidence from Ghana', *Journal of Human Resources*, Vol. 14(3), pp. 843-864.

Glick, P. and Sahn, D. E. (2000), 'Schooling of Girls and Boys in a West African country: the effects of parental education, income, and household structure', *Economics of Education Review*, Vol. 19(1), pp. 63-87.

Gordon, E. (1981), 'An Analysis of the Impact of Labour Migration on the Lives of Women in Lesotho', in N. Nelson (ed.), 'African Women in the Development Process', Special Issue, *Journal of Development Studies*, Vol. 17, No. 3, pp. 59-76.

Grootaert, C. (1999), 'Child Labor in Côte d'Ivoire', in C. Grootaert and H.A. Patrinos (eds), *The Policy Analysis of Child Labor*, St. Martins Press, New York, pp. 23-62.

Haddad, L., Hoddinott, J. and Alderman, H. (1994), 'Intrahousehold Resource Allocation: an overview', *Policy Research Working Paper*, No. 1255, World Bank, Washington DC.

Haddad, L., Hoddinott, J. and Alderman, H. (eds) (1997a), *Intrahousehold Resource Allocation in Developing Countries: Models, Methods and Policy*, Johns Hopkins University Press, Baltimore.

Haddad, L., Hoddinott, J., Alderman, H. (1997b), 'Introduction: The Scope of Intrahousehold Resource Allocation Issues', Chapter 1, in L. Haddad *et al.*, *Intrahousehold Resource Allocation in Developing Countries: Models, Methods and Policy*, Johns Hopkins University Press, Baltimore, pp. 1-16.

Haddad, L. and Kanbur, R. (1990), 'Are Better-off Households More Unequal or Less Unequal?', Research Administrator's Office, World Bank, Washington DC.

Hailey, Lord (1957), *An African Survey*, Oxford University Press, London.

Halliday, F. and Molyneux, M. (1981), *The Ethiopian Revolution*. London, Verso Editions.

Handa, S. (1996), 'Maternal Education and Child Attainment in Jamaica: testing the bargaining power hypothesis', *Oxford Bulletin of Economics and Statistics*, Vol. 58(1), pp. 119-137.

Hanushek, E.A. (1986), 'The Economics of Schooling: Production and Efficiency in Public Schools', *Journal of Economic Literature*, Vol. 24, pp. 1141-1177.

Hartmann, H. (1979), 'Capitalism, Patriarchy and Job Segregation by Sex', in Z. Eisenstein (ed.), *Capitalism, Patriarchy and the Case for Socialist Feminism*, Monthly Review Press, New York.

Heneveld, W. and Craig, H. (1996), 'Schools Count: World Bank Project Designs and the Quality of Primary Education in Sub-Saharan Africa', *Technical Paper No. 303*, Africa Technical Department Series, World Bank, Washington DC.

Herz, B., K. Subbarao *et al.* (1991), 'Letting girls learn: Promising approaches in primary and secondary education', *World Bank Discussion Papers*, No. 133, World Bank, Washington DC.

Heyneman, S. (1999), 'Education in Sub-Saharan Africa: Serious Problems, Significant Opportunities', paper presented at Africa Summit Conference, Houston, Texas, April (mimeo).

Hirsch, W.Z. (1970), *The Economics of State and Local Government*, McGraw Hill, New York.

Hobcraft, J. (1993), 'Women's Education, Child Welfare and Child Survival: A Review of the Evidence', *Health Transition Review*, Vol. 3(2), pp. 159-175.

Hoddinott, J., Alderman, H. and Haddad, L. (1997), 'Testing Competing Models and Intrahousehold Allocation', Chapter 8 in L. Haddad *et al.*, *Intrahousehold Resource Allocation in Developing Countries: Models, Methods and Policy*, Johns Hopkins University Press, Baltimore, pp. 129-141.

Hodell, E. (1996), Management Review Cum Pre-appraisal of Project 4929 'Improving Education through Feeding', World Food Programme, Addis Ababa.

Hunter, G. (1962), *The New Societies of Tropical Africa: A Selective Study*, Oxford University Press, London.

Hyde, K. (1999), 'Expanding educational opportunities at primary level: Are community schools the answer?', Oxford Conference on Educational Development, Oxford.

Hyde, K.A. (2000), 'Education for all 2000 assessment. Thematic study: Girl's education', draft, International Consultative Forum on Education for All, World Education Forum, Dakar, Senegal, 26-28 April 2000.

Hyde, K.A.L., Kadzamira, E.C., Sichinga, J.S., Chibwana, M.P. and Ridker, R.G. (1996), 'Village Based Schools in Mangochi evaluation report', Centre for Educational Research and Training, University of Malawi, Zomba.

Hyde, K. and Miske, S. (2000), 'Thematic Studies: Girls' Education', UNESCO, Paris.

ILO/UNCTAD (2001), *The Minimum Income for School Attendance (MISA) Initiative*, Geneva, May.

IMF (2001), 'Debt Relief under the Heavily Indebted Poor Countries (HIPC) Initiative: a Factsheet', http://www.imf.org/external/np/hipc/hipc.htm, International Monetary Fund, Washington DC, November.

IMF, OECD, UN and World Bank (2000), *A Better World for All: Progress Towards the International Development Goals*, Washington DC.

International Labour Office (ILO) (1973), *Employment, Incomes and Equality: A Strategy for Increasing Productive Employment in Kenya*, Geneva.

International Labour Office (ILO) (1977), *Narrowing the Gaps: Planning for Basic Needs and Productive Employment in Zambia*, Jobs and Skills Programme for Africa, Addis Ababa.

Jackson, C. (1998), 'Rescuing Gender from the Poverty Trap', in C. Jackson and R. Pearson, (eds), *Feminist Visions of Development: Gender Analysis and Policy*, Routledge, London, pp. 39-64.

Jackson, C., and Pearson, R. (eds) (1998), *Feminist Visions of Development: Gender Analysis and Policy*, Routledge, London.

Jeffery, P. and Jeffery, R. (1998), 'Silver Bullet or Passing Fancy? Girls' Schooling and Population Policy', in C. Jackson and R. Pearson (eds), *Feminist Visions of Development: Gender Analysis and Policy*, Routledge, London, pp. 239-258.

Kabeer, N. (1994), *Reversed Realities: Gender Hierarchies in Development Thought*, Verso, London.

Kadzamira, E. (2000a), 'The experience of gender reforms in Malawi', IDS, Brighton (mimeo).

Kadzamira, E. (2000b), 'Cost-Sharing and the Enrolment Response in Malawi', IDS, Brighton (mimeo).

Kadzamira, E. and Chibwana, M.P. (2000), *Gender and Primary Schooling in Malawi*, Research Report 40, IDS, Brighton.

Kasonde-Ng'andu, S., Namiloli Chilala, W. and Imutowana-Katukula, N. (2000), *Gender and Primary Schooling in Zambia*, Research Report 39, IDS, Brighton.

Kasonde-Ng'andu, S. (2000a), 'Teacher costs in Zambia', IDS, Brighton (mimeo).

Kasonde-Ng'andu, S. (2000b), 'Cost-Sharing and the Enrolment Response in Zambia', IDS, Brighton (mimeo).

Kadzamira, E. and Rose, P. (2001), 'Educational Policy Choice and Policy Practice in Malawi: Dilemmas and disjunctures', *IDS Working Paper*, No. 124, IDS, Brighton.

Kaunda, Z. (1999), SMC-EQ research findings. Paper Presented at a Policy Makers' Briefing Meeting Mangochi, July 1999.

Killick, T. (2000), 'HIPC II and Conditionality: Business as Before or a New Beginning?', Commonwealth Secretariat Poverty Workshop on Debt, HIPC and Poverty Reduction, 17/18 July, London.

King, E. M. and Hill, M. A. (eds) (1993), *Women's Education in Developing Countries. Barriers, Benefits and Policies*, Johns Hopkins University Press, Baltimore.

Knodel, J. (1997), 'The Closing of the Gender Gap in Schooling: The Case of Thailand', *Comparative Education*, Vol. 33(1), pp. 61-86.

Knodel, J. and Jones, G. (1996), 'Post-Cairo Population Policy: Does Promoting Girls' Schooling Miss the Mark?', *Population and Development Review*, Vol. 22, No. 4, pp. 683-702.

Komba, D. (1995), 'Declining Enrolment and Quality of Primary Education in Tanzania Mainland: An analysis of key data and documentation and review of explanatory factors', a report of a study initiated by MOEC and sponsored by UNICEF, Faculty of Education, University of Dar-es-Salaam, Dar-es-Salaam (mimeo).

Kourouma, P. (1991), *Étude portant sur les aspects socio-culturels et socio-économiques de la la scolarisation des filles au niveau du primaire: cas de la Guinée*, Ministère de l'Education Nationale, Secrétariat d'Etat à l'Enseignement Pré-Universitaire, Conakry.

Kunje and Lewin, K. (1999), 'The Costs and Financing of Teacher Education in Malawi', *Discussion Paper 2*, Brighton, University of Sussex.

Lavy, V. (1996), 'School Supply Constraints and Children's Educational Outcomes in Rural Ghana', *Journal of Development Economics*, Vol. 51(2), pp. 291-314.

Lloyd, C. B. and Blanc, A. K. (1996), 'Children's Schooling in Sub-Saharan Africa: the role of fathers, mothers, and others', *Population and Development Review*, Vol. 22(2), pp. 265-298.

Lockheed, M. and Verspoor, A. (1991), *Improving Primary Education in Developing Countries*, Oxford University Press, Oxford.

Lockwood, M. (1992), 'Engendering Adjustment, or Adjusting Gender: Some New Approaches to Women and Development in Africa', *IDS Discussion Paper No. 315*, Brighton.

Long, L. (1990), *Study of Girls' Access to Primary Schooling in Guinea*, USAID, Conakry.

Lungwangwa, G., and Kelly, M. (1999), 'Basic education for some: Factors affecting primary school attendance in Zambia', Ministry of Finance and Economic Development, Lusaka.

Malawi Ministry of Education and UNICEF (1998), *Free Primary Education. The Malawi Experience*, Ministry of Education, Lilongwe.

Markakis, J. (1974), *Ethiopia. Anatomy of a Traditional Polity*, Clarendon Press, Oxford.

Martin, M. (2000), 'Financing Poverty Reduction in the Heavily Indebted Poor Countries: Beyond HIPC II', Commonwealth Secretariat Poverty Workshop on Debt, HIPC and Poverty Reduction, 17/18 July, London.

Mason, A.D. and Khandker, S. R. (1996), 'Measuring the Opportunity Costs of Children's Time in a Developing Country: Implications for Education Sector Analysis and Interventions', *Human Capital Development Working Papers*, No. 72, World Bank, Washington DC.

Mason, A. D. and Khandker, S. R. (1997), 'Household schooling decisions in Tanzania', Poverty and Social Development Department, World Bank, Washington DC.

Mbilinyi, D.A.S. and Mduda, A.G. (1995), 'Girls Secondary Education Support Pilot'. Dar-es-Salaam: Ministry of Education and Culture, United Republic of Tanzania.

Mbilinyi, M., Mbughuni, P., Meena, R. and Olekambaine, P. (1991), 'Education in Tanzania with a Gender Perspective', *Education Division Documents*, No. 53, SIDA, Sweden.

McMahon, W. W. (1970), 'An Economic Analysis of Major Determinants of Expenditures on Public Education', *Review of Economics and Statistics*, Vol. 52(3), pp. 242-252.

McMahon, W.W. (1999), *Education and Development: Measuring the Social Benefits*, Oxford University Press, Oxford.

McNab, C. (1989), *Language Policy and Language Practice. Implementation Dilemmas in Ethiopian Education*, Institute of International Education, University of Stockholm, Stockholm.

McNab, C. and Stoye, P. (1999), 'Language Policy in Ethiopian Education: Implications for the Costs of Textbook Production', in F. Leach and A. Little (eds), *Education, Cultures and Economics: Dilemmas for Development*, Chapter 8, pp. 143-158, Falmer Press, New York.

Mehrotra, S. and Buckland, P. (1998), 'Managing Teacher Costs for Access and Quality', *UNICEF Staff Working Paper* No. EPP-EVL-98-004, UNICEF, New York.

Meier, G. (1964), *Leading Issues in Development Economics*, Oxford University Press, Oxford. Subsequent editions issued as *Leading Issues in Economic Development*, in 1970, 1976, 1984, 1989, 1995, and (with James E. Rauch), 2000.

MEPU-FP (1996) 'Situation de l'Education de Base', Ministry of Education, Republic of Guinea (mimeo).

Mingat, A. (1998), 'Assessing Priorities for Education Policy in the Sahel from a Comparative Perspective,' IREDU, Dijon, September (mimeo).

Mingat, A. and Tan, J.-P. (1986), 'Expanding Education Through User Charges: What Can be Achieved in Malawi and Other LDCs?', *Economics of Education Review*, Vol. 5(3), pp. 273-286.

Mingat, A. and Tan, J.-P. (1988), *Analytical Tools for Sector Work in Education*, Johns Hopkins University Press, Baltimore.

Mingat, A. and Tan, J.-P. (1998), 'The Mechanics of Progress in Education. Evidence from Cross-country Data', *Policy Research Working Paper* No. 2015, Education Group, Human Development Department, World Bank, Washington, DC.

Ministère de l'Education de Base, Mali (2000), Programme Décennal pour le Développement de l'Education.

Ministère de l'Education Nationale, Senegal (1996), Programme Décennal de l'Education et la Formation (PDEF).

Ministry of Education, Ethiopia (1989), *Gender Analysis of Primary School Textbooks*, Curriculum Evaluation and Educational Research Division, Ministry of Education, Addis Ababa.

Ministry of Education, Ethiopia (1994), *Basic Education Statistics, 1992/93*, Education Management Information Systems, Ministry of Education, Addis Ababa.

Ministry of Education, Ethiopia (1995), *Education Statistics, Annual Abstract, 1986 E.C. (1993/94)*, Ministry of Education, Addis Ababa.

Ministry of Education, Ethiopia (1996), *Education Statistics, Annual Abstract, 1987 E.C. (1994/95)*, Ministry of Education, Addis Ababa.

Ministry of Education, Ethiopia (1997), *Education Statistics Annual Abstract, 1995/96*, Education Management Information Systems, Ministry of Education, Addis Ababa.

Mitchell, J. (1975), *Psychoanalysis and Feminism*, Penguin, Harmondsworth.

MOEC (1995), Tanzania Integrated Education and Training Policy, Analysis of Gender Issues and Recommendations for Improvement, Dar-es-Salaam.

Montgomery, M., Oliver R. and Kouame, A. (1995), 'The Trade-off Between Number of Children and Child Schooling: Evidence from Côte d'Ivoire and Ghana', *LSMS Working Paper*, No. 112, World Bank, Washington DC.

Mundy, K. (2002), 'Retrospect and Prospect: Education in a Reforming World Bank', *International Journal of Educational Development*.

Muskin, J. A. (1999), 'Including local priorities to assess school quality: The case of Save the Children community schools in Mali', *Comparative Education Review*, Vol. 43, No. 1, pp. 36-63.

Nelson, N. (1981), 'Mobilising Village Women: Some Organisational and Management Considerations', in N. Nelson (ed.), 'African Women in the Development Process', Special Issue, *Journal of Development Studies*, Vol. 17, No. 3, pp. 47-58.

Nelson, N. (ed.) (1981), 'African Women in the Development Process', Special Issue, *Journal of Development Studies*, Vol. 17, No. 3.

O'Connor, J. (2000), 'The Way Forward for FEMSA in Phase II', FEMSA, FAWE, Nairobi, October (mimeo).

O'Gara, C., Benoliel, S., Sutton, M, and Tietjen, K. (1999), *More But Not Yet Better: an evaluation of USAID's programmes and policies to improve girls' education*, USAID Programme and Operations Assessment Report No. 25, USAID, Washington DC.

Oakley, A. (1972), *Sex, Gender and Society*, Maurice Temple Smith, London.

Odaga, A. and Heneveld, W. (1995), 'Girls and Schools in sub-Saharan Africa: From analysis to action', *Africa Technical Department Series. World Bank Technical Paper*, No. 298, World Bank, Washington DC.

ODI/CEC (2000), *Mainstreaming Gender through Sector-Wide Approaches in Education – Synthesis Report*, DFID, London, October.

OECD DAC (1999), 'DAC Guidelines for Gender Equality and Women's Empowerment in Development Co-operation', Development Assistance Committee, Paris.

OECD (1996), *Shaping the 21st Century: the Contribution of Development Cooperation*, Development Assistance Committee, Paris.

OECD (2001), *Geographical Distribution of Financial Flows to Aid Recipients, 1995-1999*, Paris.

Omari, I.M. (1994), 'Review of Critical Issues in Tanzanian Education', unpublished paper prepared for the Investing in Human Capital Workshop, Arusha, Tanzania.

Omari, I.M., Sumra, S.A. and Levine, R. (1994), 'Availability, Quality and Utilization of Social Services: preliminary results from focused area studies techniques', Paper for the World Bank Workshop on Investing in Human Capital, Arusha, Tanzania.

Opolot, J. (1994), 'Study on Costs and Cost-effective Approaches to Primary Education in Uganda', UNICEF, Kampala (mimeo).

Parker, A. and Serrano, S. (2000), 'Promoting good local governance through social funds and decentralization', Social Protection Discussion Paper 0022, World Bank, Washington DC.

Peasgood, T., Bendera, S., Abrahams, N. and Kisanga, M. (1997), *Gender and Primary Schooling in Tanzania*, Research Report 33, IDS, Brighton.

Penrose, P. (1998), 'Cost Sharing in Education. Public Finance, School and Household Perspectives', *DFID Education Research Report* No. 27, DFID, London.

Ratcliffe, M. and Macrae, M. (1999), 'Sector Wide Approaches to Education: A Strategic Analysis', *Education Research Serial No. 32*, Department for International Development, London.

Republic of Zambia (1996), *Educating Our Future: National Policy on Education*, Ministry of Education, Lusaka.

Rodrik, D. (1996), 'Understanding Economic Policy Reform', *Journal of Economic Literature*, Vol. XXXIV, March, pp. 9-41.

Rogers, B., 1980, *The Domestication of Women: Discrimination in Developing Societies*, Kogan Page, London.

Rose, P. (1995), 'Female Education and Adjustment Programmes: A Cross-Country Statistical Analysis', *World Development*, Vol. 23(1), pp. 1931-1949.

Rose, P. (2002), 'Cost-sharing in Malawian Primary Schooling: from the Washington to the post-Washington consensus', PhD thesis, University of Sussex.

Rose, P. and Al-Samarrai, S. (2001), 'Household Constraints on Schooling by Gender: empirical evidence from Ethiopia', *Comparative Education Review*, Vol. 45(1).

Rose, P., Yoseph, G., Berihun, A. and Nuresu, T. (1997), *Gender and Primary Schooling in Ethiopia*, Research Report 31, IDS, Brighton.

Russell, B. (1961), *History of Western Philosophy*, (New edition), Allen and Unwin, London.

Saffioti, H. (1977), 'Women, Mode of Production, and Social Formations', *Latin American Perspectives*, Vol. IV(1 and 2), pp. 27-37.

Sangaré, S. (2000), 'The reduction of the repetition rate in Mali', IDS, Brighton (mimeo).

Sangaré, S., Tounkara, A., Tangara, D. and Assétou Kéïta, N. (2000), *Genre et fréquentation scolaire au premier cycle de l'enseignement fondamental au Mali*, Research Report 41, IDS, Brighton.

Sapsford, D. and Tzannatos, Z. (1993), *The Economics of the Labour Market*, Macmillan, London.

Schalkwyk, J. (1995), 'Review of documents related to SIDA's strategy on gender and development', SIDA Policy Department, Stockholm.

Schultz, T. P. (1985), 'School Expenditures and Enrolments, 1960-1980: the effects of income, prices and population growth', in D. G. Johnson and R. Lee (eds), *Population Growth and Economic Development*, University of Wisconsin Press, Madison.

Schultz, T.P. (ed.) (1995a), *Investment in Women's Human Capital*, University of Chicago Press, Chicago and London.

Schultz, T.P. (1995b), 'Investments in the Schooling and Health of Women and Men: quantities and returns', in T.P. Schultz (ed.), *Investment in Women's Human Capital*, University of Chicago, Chicago.

Schultz, T.P. (1995c), 'Accounting for Public Expenditures on Education: An International Panel Study', *Center Discussion Paper*, No. 61, Economic Growth Center, Yale University.

Schultz, T.W. (1964), *Transforming Traditional Agriculture*, University of Chicago Press, Chicago.

Scott, J.C. (1976), *The Moral Economy of the Peasant Rebellion and Subsistence in South-East Asia*, Yale University Press, New Haven.

Seged Abraha *et al.* (1991), 'What Factors Shape Girls' School Performance? Evidence from Ethiopia', *International Journal of Educational Development*, Vol. 11(2), pp. 107-118.

Sen, A. (1990), 'Gender and Cooperative Conflicts', in I. Tinker (ed.), *Persistent Inequalities*, Oxford University Press, Oxford, pp. 195-223.

Seyoum, Teffera (1986), 'The Education of Women in Ethiopia: a missing piece in the development puzzle', *Ethiopian Journal of Education*, Vol. 1(10).

Siebert, W.S. (1985), 'Developments in the Economics of Human Capital', in D. Carline *et al.*, *Surveys in Economics: Labour Economics*, Longman, London and New York, pp. 5-77.

Sloane, P.J. (1985), 'Discrimination in the Labour Market', in D. Carline *et al.*, *Surveys in Economics: Labour Economics*, Longman, London and New York, pp. 78-158.

Sow, A. (1994), *Enquête sur la Scolarisation des Filles en Milieu Rural: Rapport de synthèse*, Ministère de l'Enseignement Pré-Universitaire et de la Formation Professionnelle, Conakry, République de Guinée.

Stasavage, D. (2001), 'Electoral Competition and Public Spending on Education: Evidence from African Countries', *Working Paper WPS/2001, 17*, Centre for the Study of African Economies, University of Oxford.

Stromquist, N. (1989), 'Determinants of Educational Participation and Achievement of Women in the Third World: A Review of the Evidence and a Theoretical Critique', *Review of Educational Research*, Vol. 59(2), pp. 143-183.

Stromquist, N. (1994), 'Gender and Basic Education in International Development Cooperation', *UNICEF Staff Working Papers*, No.13, UNICEF, New York.

Stromquist, N. (1995), 'Romancing the State: Gender and Power in Education', *Comparative Education Review*, Vol. 39(4), pp. 423-454.

Stromquist, N. (1997), 'Gender sensitive educational strategies and their implementation', *International Journal of Educational Development*, Vol. 17(2), pp. 205-214.

Stromquist, N. (1998), 'The Institutionalisation of Gender and its Impact on Educational Policy', *Comparative Education*, Vol. 34(1), pp. 85-100.

Summers, L. (1994), 'Investing in all the People: Educating Women in Developing Countries', *EDI Seminar Paper* No. 45, World Bank, Washington DC.

Sumra, S. (1993), 'Primary Education and the Urban Poor; a study of parental attitudes towards schooling in the Burguruni and Vingungutti wards in Dar-es-Salaam', a study prepared for PLAN International, Dar-es-Salaam.

Sumra, S. (1998), '*Interim review and evaluation of the girls' secondary Education Support (GSES) Programme*', Faculty of Education, University of Dar-es-Salaam.

Sumra, S. and Katunzi, N. (1991), 'The Struggle for Education: school fees and girls' education in Tanzania', Women, Education, and Development, *WED Report*, No. 5, Dar-es-Salaam.

Swainson, N. (1995), 'Redressing gender inequalities in education: A review of constraints and priorities in Malawi, Zambia and Zimbabwe', ODA, London.

Swainson, N. (1997), *Promoting Girls' Education in Africa: The design and implementation of policy interventionsm*, Report to the Economic and Social Committee on Overseas Research, London.

Swainson, N. (2000), 'Knowledge and power: the design and implementation of gender policies in education in Malawi, Tanzania and Zimbabwe', *International Journal of Educational Development*, Vol. 20(1), pp. 49-64.

Swainson, N., Bendera, S., Gordon, R.; Kadzamira, E. (1998), 'Promoting Girls' Education in Africa: The design and implementation of policy interventions', *Education Research Serial*, No. 25, Department for International Development, London.

Tan, J.-P., Lee, K. H. and Mingat, A. (1984), 'User Charges for Education: The ability and willingness to pay in Malawi', World Bank Staff Working Papers No. 661, World Bank, Washington DC.

Tan, J.-P. and Mingat, A. (1992), *Education in Asia: A Comparative Study of Cost and Financing*, World Bank, Washington DC.

Tansel, A. (1997), 'School Attainment, Parental Education and Gender in Côte d'Ivoire and Ghana', *Economic Development and Cultural Change*, Vol. 45(4), pp. 825-856.

Tanzania Development Research Group TADREG (1993), 'Parents Attitudes towards Education in Rural Tanzania, *Research Report No. 5*, November, Dar-es-Salaam: TADREG.

Tekeste Negash (1990), *The Crisis of Ethiopian Education: Some Implications for Nation-Building*, Uppsala Reports on Education, No. 29, Department of Education, Uppsala University, Uppsala, Sweden.

Tembon, M. and Al-Samarrai, S. (1999), 'Who Gets Primary Schooling and Why? Evidence of Gender Inequalities Within Families in Guinea', *Working Paper*, No. 85, IDS, Brighton.

Tembon, M., Diallo, I.S., Barry, D. and Barry, A.A. (1997), *Gender and Primary Schooling in Guinea*, Research Report 32, IDS, Brighton.

Temu, E. (1995), *Successful Schools in Tanzania, A Case Study of Academic and Production Programs in Primary and Secondary Schools*, Institute of International Education, Stockholm University, Stockholm.

Teshome Wagaw (1979), *Education in Ethiopia: Prospect and Retrospect*, Ann Arbor, The University of Michigan Press, Michigan.

Thobani, M. (1983), 'Charging User Fees for Social Services: the Case of Education in Malawi', *World Bank Staff Working Paper No. 572*, World Bank, Washington DC.

Thobani, M. (1984), 'Charging User Fees for Social Service: Education in Malawi', *Comparative Education Review*, Vol. 28(3), pp. 402-23.

Tibi, C. (1983), 'Les Determinants des Côuts de l'éducation', IIEP, Paris.

Tietjen, K. (1991), *Educating Girls: Strategies to increase access, persistence and achievement*, USAID, Washington DC.

Tietjen, K. (1997), 'Educating Girls in Sub-Saharan Africa: USAID's Approach and Lessons for Donors', *Technical Paper No. 54*, Bureau for Africa, USAID, Washington DC.

Tilak, J.B.G. (1997), 'Lessons from Cost-Recovery in Education' in C. Colclough (ed.), *Marketizing Education and Health in Developing Countries: Miracle or Mirage?*, Clarendon Press, Oxford, pp. 63-89.

Transitional Government of Ethiopia (1993a), *National Policy on Ethiopian Women*, TGE, Addis Ababa.

Transitional Government of Ethiopia (1993b), *Population Policy*, TGE, Addis Ababa.

Transitional Government of Ethiopia (1993c), *Social Policy*, TGE, Addis Ababa.

Transitional Government of Ethiopia (1994), *Education and Training Policy*, TGE, Addis Ababa.

Traoré Antoine (1996), *La Gestion du Personnel Enseignant en Afrique Francophone*, UNESCO/IIEP, Paris.

Tumushabe, J. (2000), 'Primary School double-shifting in Uganda', IDS, Brighton, (mimeo).

Tumushabe, J., Barasa, C.A., Muhanguzi, F.K. and Otim-Nape, J.F. (2000), *Gender and Primary Schooling in Uganda*, Research Report 42, IDS, Brighton.

UN (1995a), *World Summit for Social Development: Programme of Action*, UN, New York.

UN (1995b), *Beijing Declaration and Platform for Action*, Fourth World Conference on Women, UN, New York.

UN ECOSOC (1997), 'Agreed Conclusions on Gender Mainstreaming', E/1997/100.

UNCTAD (2000), *The Least Developed Countries 2000 Report*, United Nations, New York and Geneva.

UNDP (1992), *Human Development Report*, UNDP, Oxford University Press.

UNDP (1994), *Human Development Report*, UNDP, Oxford University Press.

UNDP (1995), *Human Development Report*, UNDP, Oxford University Press.

UNDP (1999), *Human Development Report*, UNDP, Oxford University Press.

UNESCO (1989), *Statistical Yearbook*, 1989, UNESCO, Paris.

UNESCO (1993), *Statistical Yearbook*, 1993, UNESCO, Paris

UNESCO (1994), *Statistical Yearbook*, 1994, UNESCO, Paris.

UNESCO (1995a), *Statistical Yearbook*, 1995, UNESCO, Paris.

UNESCO (1995b), *World Education Report*, UNESCO, Paris.

UNESCO (1996a), *Statistical Yearbook*, 1996, UNESCO, Paris.

UNESCO (1996b), Primary School Repetition: A Global Perspective.   UNESCO International Bureau of Education.

UNESCO (1997), *Statistical Yearbook*, 1997, UNESCO, Paris.

UNESCO (1998a), *Statistical Yearbook*, 1998, UNESCO, Paris.

UNESCO (1998b), *World Education Report 1998*, UNESCO, Paris.

UNESCO (1999), *Human Development Report*, UNESCO, Paris.

UNESCO (2000a), *Education for All 2000 Assessment: Statistical Document*, Institute for Statistics, UNESCO, Paris.

UNESCO (2000b), *World Education Report*, UNESCO, Paris.

UNESCO (2000c), *Final Report*, World Education Forum, Paris.

UNESCO (2000d), 'The UNESCO Agenda for Gender Equality and Equity, Five Years after Beijing', Unit for the Promotion of the Status of Women and Gender Equality, Paris (mimeo).

UNESCO (2002), *Education for All: Is the World on Track*, Education For All Global Monitoring Report, UNESCO, Paris.

UNICEF (1995), 'No Home is My Home: the girl child in Tanzania', unpublished National Research Report, Dar-es-Salaam.

UNICEF (1999), *The State of the World's Children 1999: Education*, UNICEF, New York.

United Nations (1987), 'Education and Fertility', in *Fertility Behaviour in the Context of Development: Evidence From the World Fertility Survey*, New York.

United Republic of Tanzania (1999), *The Education Sector Reform and Development Programme: Main document for the appraisal mission*, March, 1999.

USAID (1994), 'The Demand for Primary Schooling in Rural Ethiopia. A research study' (mimeo), USAID, Addis Ababa.

USAID (1995a), 'Overview of USAID Basic Education Programmes in Sub-Saharan Africa', *Technical Paper No. 13*, SD Publication Series, USAID, Washington DC.

USAID (1995b), 'Basic Education in Africa: USAID's Approach to Sustainable Reform in the 1990's', (by J. DeStefano, A. Hartwell and K. Tietjen), *Technical Paper No. 14*, SD Publication Series, USAID, Washington DC.

van Riesen, M. (1998), 'The European Community Programme', in J. Randel and T. German (eds), *The Reality of Aid 1998/99*, Earthscan, London, pp. 80-89.

Walby, S. (1989), 'Theorising Patriarchy' *Sociology*, Vol. 23(2), pp. 213-234.

Wangwe, S., Fine, J.C., Chijoriga, M., Foster, M., Hooper, R. and Kaduma, I. (1999), 'Tanzania Education Sector Development Programme Appraisal: Financial Planning and Management Review Team Final Report', Dar-es-Salaam.

WCEFA (1990), *World Declaration on Education for All and Framework for Action to Meet Basic Learning Needs*, World Conference on Education for All, Jomtien, Thailand.

Weekes, R.V. (1978) (ed.), *Muslim Peoples – A World Ethnography Survey*, Greenwood Press, Westport, Conn.

Weir, S. (2000), 'Concealed Preferences: Parental Attitudes to Education and Enrolment Choice in Rural Ethiopia', *Working Paper Series*, No. 2000-1, Centre for the Study of African Economies, Oxford.

Weir, S. and Knight, J. (1996), 'Demand for Schooling in Rural Ethiopia', PHRD Study, No. 1a, World Bank, Washington DC.

Whitehead, A. (1979), 'Some Preliminary Notes on the Subordination of Women', *IDS Bulletin*, Vol. 10(3), pp. 10-13, Brighton.

Winter, C., and Macina, R. (2000), 'Girls' Education: World Bank Support through IDA' Human Development Network, World Bank, Washington DC.

Wolf, J. (1995), 'An analysis of USAID programs to improve equity in Malawi and Ghana's education systems', *Sustainable Development Publication Series. Technical Paper* No. 10, USAID, Washington, DC.

World Bank (1970), *Lending in Education*, Washington DC.

World Bank (1988), *Education in Sub-Saharan Africa: Policies for Adjustment, Revitalization and Expansion*, World Bank Policy Study, Washington DC.

World Bank (1990-99), *World Bank Annual Report*, (for each year shown), World Bank, Washington DC.

World Bank (1991), *United Republic of Tanzania, Teachers and the Financing of Education*, Population and Human Resources Division, Southern African Department, World Bank, Washington, DC.

World Bank (1993), *World Development Report 1993, Investing in Health*, Oxford University Press, New York.

World Bank (1994a), *World Tables*, World Bank, Washington DC.

World Bank (1994b), *Ethiopia: Public Expenditure Policy for Transition*, World Bank, Washington DC.

World Bank (1995a), *Priorities and Strategies for Education: a World Bank Review*, World Bank, Washington DC.

World Bank (1995b), *Developing Girls' Education in Guinea. Issues and Policies*, World Bank Population and Human Resources Division, World Bank, Washington DC.

World Bank (1995c), Project Appraisal Document – Guinea No. 13472-Gui Equity and School Improvement Project, World Bank, Washington DC.

World Bank (1995d), *Ethiopia. Public Expenditure Review: Issues in Public Expenditure*, World Bank, Washington DC.

World Bank (1996a), 'Household Demand for Schooling' Report No. 1 (final draft), World Bank, Addis Ababa.

World Bank (1996b), 'Beyond Poverty: how supply factors influence girls' education in Guinea: Issues and strategies', *Report No. 14488-GUI*, World Bank, Washington DC.

World Bank (1996c), *Republic of Zambia Education and Training Sector Expenditure Review*, World Bank, Washington DC.

World Bank (1998), World Development Indicators 1998, World Bank, Washington DC.

World Bank (1999), World Development Report, World Bank, Washington DC.

World Bank (2000a), World Development Indicators 2000, World Bank, Washington DC.

World Bank (2000b), World Development Report, World Bank, Washington DC.

World Bank (2000c), Project Appraisal Document – Senegal No. 19610-SE Ten-year Education and Training Program, World Bank, Washington DC.

World Bank (2001a), *World Development Report, 2000/20001 – Attacking Poverty*, Washington DC.

World Bank (2001b), *A Chance to Learn: Knowledge and Finance for Education in Sub-Saharan Africa*, Africa Region Human Development Series, Washington DC.

World Education (1998), Evaluation de la Pédagogie Convergente et des Performances dans les Ecoles Communautaires, Septembre.

Yelfign Worku, Zewdu Desta, Alemnesh H/Mariam, Abbesu Biazen (1995), *Primary School Female Participation and Performance in Cheha District*, Ministry of Education, Addis Ababa.

Young, K. (1979), 'Editorial' in *Special Issue on the Continuing Subordination of Women in the Development Process*, IDS Bulletin Vol. 10(3), pp. 1-4, Brighton.

Young, K., Wolkowitz, C. and McCullagh, C. (eds) (1981), *Of Marriage and Market. Women's Subordination in International Perspective*, CSE Books, London.

Index

www.ingramcontent.com/pod-product-compliance
Ingram Content Group UK Ltd.
Pitfield, Milton Keynes, MK11 3LW, UK
UKHW020359010325
455677UK00021B/539